QUEEN of the

MIDNIGHT SKIES
The Story of America's Air Force Night Fighters

Garry R. Pape & Ronald C. Harrison

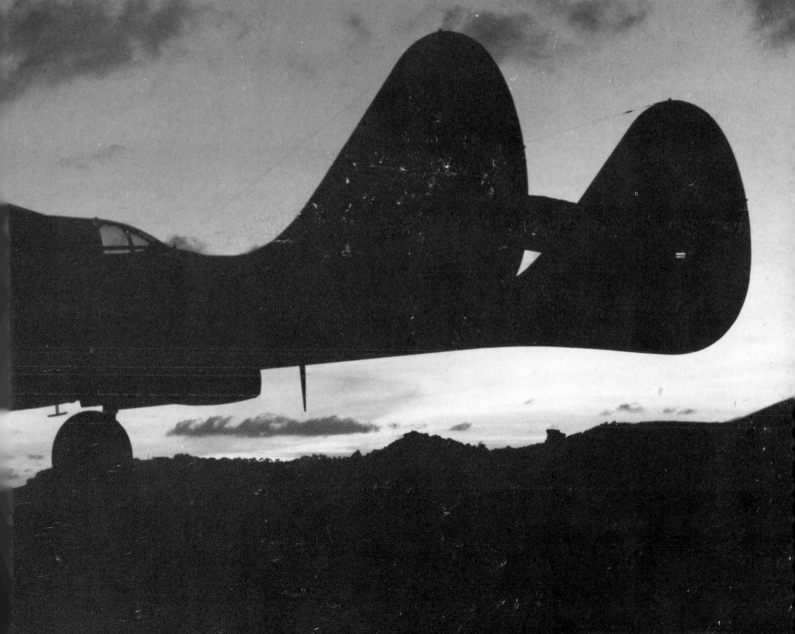

Schiffer Military History
West Chester, PA

Dust Jacket Artwork by Steve Ferguson, Colorado Springs, CO

WOLF OF ORMOC BAY - December 28, 1944

On the evening of November 28, 1944, P-61A commander Lt. Owen Wolf, radar officer 2nd Lt. Byron Allain and gunner S/Sgt. Don Trabing of the 421st Night Fighter Squadron overtook a pair of ZEROs just west of the U.S. Navy fleet anchored in Ormoc Bay. Unseen by the enemy wingmen, Wolf took his heavily armed Black Widow through one lethal firing pass from dead astern and both targets fell into the sea.

This same deadly trio had scored the unit's first kill back in July. Wolf and Allain, with another noncom gunner, had shot and damaged their second victim on November 16. After the original trio rejoined for the last double-kill over Ormoc Bay, they scored again for the last time on January 24, 1945.

The squadron claimed thirteen victories overall with their final victory in March near Lingayen Air Field on Luzon Island. As was the misfortune of all night fighter units, the lone interceptions of 421 NFS were summarily listed as unconfirmed by the USAAF.

Photo Credits

Every photo used in this book has its source identified in brackets at the end of the caption. Normally the identification is the last name of the person supplying the photo. Listed below are the names of all those persons and organizations who have supplied the illustrating photos.

Carl Absmeier
Julius Alford
Louis Alford
Oakley Allen
American Aviation Historical Society
Bud Anderson
John W. Anderson
George Arthur
Roy Atwell
Norm Avery
Jerry Balzer
Bell Aerospace
Henry Bockstege
Mel Bode
Bob Bolinder
Bob Boucher
Peter M. Bowers
James Bradford
Bill Bradley
Jack Bradner
Harold Burdue
John and Donna Campbell
Castle Graphics
Bill Charlesworth
Ira Chart
John Chew
John Conway
Bunyan Crain
N. A. Cypert
Chrles M. Daniels, Jr.
Larry Davis
Harold Dawson
Jean Desclos
Earl Dickey
Paul DiLabbio
Edward Donnelly
John Dowd
Joseph Downey
Dick Ehlert
George Ellings
Craig Elrod

Toras Eretzian
Herman Ernst
Bob Esposito
Jim Farmer
Harry Gann
George Garrett
Ray Gaudette
Gerhart
Drago Golemac
Goodyear Aerospace
Robert F. Graham
Robert G. Graham
Robert Boucher
Robert Gray
Joe Greenbaum
Bill Greenhalgh
Charles Greggs
Tony Grotzinger
Dale Haberman
Robert Hagen
Jack Hahn
Carl Hale
Leonard Hall
Jerome Hansen
Mrs. Jerome Hansen
Dave Hatfield
Bill Hellriegel
Bob Hernandez
Hickam Air Force Base
Doug Hinkson
Glenn Holcomb
Dave Hopwood
Horton Collection
Bob Hughes
Bill Humenick
George Irwin
Tom Ivie
Steve Izenour
Joe Jenkins
Fred Johnson
M. Scott Johnson

Oris B. Johnson
Geoffrey Jones
Lee Kendall
Winston W. Kratz
Fred Lefever
Harvey Lippincott
A.T. Lloyd
Lockheed Corporation
Russ Lortz
Al Lukas
Joe Maita
Birch Matthews
Mc Donnell Douglas
William McKeon
John McPartland
Avery Miller
Raoul Morales
Frank Moran
George Mulholland
National Air and Space Museum
National Archives (US)
North American Aviation
Northrop Corporation
Northrop University
Ed Noyes
Bill Odell
Merle Olmsted
Jack Pabst
Hugo Pink
George Porter
Jim Postlewaite
Pratt & Whitney/United Technologies
Jim Reed
Roy Reed
Duke Reynolds
Thomas Roberts
James Rogers
William Ross
Kenn Rust
Kenneth Schrieber
Fred Secord

Bill Smelzer
Carroll Smith
Smithsonian Institution
Karl Soukikian
Stegner Collection
Victoria Stegner
Mel Stevick
Ken Sumney
The MIT Museum
Robert Tierney
Tinker Air Force Base
Ernest Thomas
Ernie Thompson
Warren Thompson
Robert Tierney
Earl Tigner
Tinker Air Force Base
Umbarger
United States Air Force
United States Air Force Historical
   Research Center
United States Air Force Museum
United States Army
United States Army Air Forces
United States Navy
Dave Vincent
Dave Weisman
Walt Wernsing
Western Electric
Joe Wheeler
Donald White
John Wilfong
Newell Witte
Roy Wolford
Stan Woolley
423th Night Fighter Squadron
   Association
425th Night Fighter Squadron
   Association

Book Design by Robert Biondi

First Edition
Copyright © 1992 by Garry R. Pape & Ronald C. Harrison.
Library of Congress Catalog Number: 92-60359

Printed in the United States of America.
ISBN: 0-88740-415-4

We are interested in hearing from authors with book ideas on related topics.

Published by Schiffer Publishing Ltd.
1469 Morstein Rd.
West Chester, PA 19380
Please write for a free catalog.
This book may be purchased from the publisher.
Please include $2.95 postage.
Try your bookstore first.

Contents

Color section follows page 160

Foreword

QUEEN OF THE MIDNIGHT SKIES is the story of American Night Fighters during World War II. Garry Pape has meticulously chronicled the many, and I do mean many, trials and tribulations that World War II night fighters had to endure to succeed.

At the start of the war in 1941, the Army Air Corps was basically a day flying force. The British had learned they had to fight at night, both offensively and defensively. Our military leaders made the decision that the Unites States needed to develop a capability for night fighting. Having no experience in the area, they turned to the British for guidance. Garry Pape spent countless hours of research in searching out the decisions made, revised and amended so many times. This indecision led to considerable loss of time in developing a true operational capability. As late as June 1944, some individuals were convinced the P-61 should be scrapped and replaced by some other aircraft. Fortunately, their view did not prevail. We went into combat with the P-61 and proved our capability. Regardless of almost daily setbacks, young men who believed in what they were doing found ways to get the job done.

Details of encounters by all squadrons, as well as a number of personal experiences are presented in a superior manner. It was my privilege to command the 348th Night Fighter Training Squadron before I activated the 422nd Night Fighter Squadron. As a result I knew and was friends with all the squadron commanders and many of the crew members in the night fighter squadrons.

As I read this manuscript, I was filled with great pride that I was part of this small band of pioneers who did much with so little. Our night fighter squadrons were few in number compared to the day fighters and bombers. Our intelligence was questioned because we enjoyed flying at night and took pride in instrument flying. Our radar and weapons were primitive by today's standards, but tactics and techniques were developed in this untried area of air combat.

Our efforts laid the foundation and provided the basis for today's all-weather Air Force that performed so effectively twenty-four hours a day during Desert Storm. Every man, officers and airmen, can take great pride in their accomplishments as members of night fighter squadrons in World War II.

Garry Pape is to be commended for so accurately presenting these courageous endeavors.

Oris B. Johnson
Major General USAF (Ret.)

Acknowledgements

If it wasn't for the support of the Night Fighters, the story told in this book could not have been accomplished. In the mid-1960s the authors, both in the infant stages of independently researching the history of the Northrop P-61 Black Widow night fighter, joined forces in this endeavor. As little was then available on the aircraft, it was suggested by the ex-Army Air Forces night fighters then contacted that we widen our scope and delve into the entire U.S. Army Air Corps/Army Air Forces night fighter program of World War II. It was through the generosity and patience of a number of the Night Fighters, who are no longer with us, that enabled us to initiate this task. Brig.Gen. Winston W. "Winkie" Kratz had guided the fledgling night fighter program from shortly after its inception throughout the war. His early guidance, many interviews, and material provided immense help; but his friendship, encouragement, and support is what kept us going.

In the late 1960s we met Lt.Col. Roy Atwell for the first time; this was shortly after his retirement from the Air Force and he was just settling in the San Jose, California area. He flew both the Beaufighter and Mosquito in the Mediterranean theater (the Mosquito was the plane he loved). He enlightened us of the mostly untold story of the four American Beaufighter squadrons that flew under Twelfth Air Force.

A fire was lit under us by Lt.Col. C.R. "Dick" Ehlert, USAF (Ret), as far as the Douglas P-70 operations goes. There was quite a story behind those early days in the Pacific where the Air Force's night fighters had to struggle with an aircraft of limited ability, a command structure that had no idea what a night fighter was or how to employ it (this continued throughout the war in most areas of operations), and an elusive enemy that was like finding a needle in a hay stack. Our gratitude to these men is immeasurable. We are sorry that this effort couldn't have come to fruition prior to their passing.

There have been many ex-Night Fighters that have contributed to the telling of this story. Direct assistance with information and/or photos, which often brought to light previously unrecorded facts, came from the following: Col. Julius E. Alford (6th NFS), Alvin E. Anderson (425th NFS), George Arthur (547th NFS), Lt.Col. Roy M. Atwell (416th NFS), Paul H. Baldwin (547th NFS), Mack Ballard (421st NFS), Donald J. Boatman (416th NFS), Col. Henry F. Bockstege (415th NFS), Carroll H. Bolender (414th NFS), Lt.Col. Frank L. Bosch (547th NFS), William T. Bradley (421st NFS), Lt.Col. Jack F. Bradner (6th NFS), George C. Brainard (NF Training), Allen S. Clark (415th NFS), Donald D. Coski (550th NFS), Col. Robert D. Curtis, (548th NFS), Newton A. Cypert (415th NFS), Col. Donald M. Dessert (419th NFS), Paul DiLabbio (6th NFS), John R. Dowd (417th NFS), Lt.Col. C.R. "Dick" Ehlert (6th NFS), Herman E. Ernst (422nd NFS), Paul Evans (414th NFS), Lt.Col. Romeo R. Ferretti (415th NFS), John E. Florence (6th NFS), Rolland L. Forrester (421st NFS), Russell Glasser (425th NFS), Robert F. Graham (422nd NFS), Robert J. Gray (415th NFS), Charles R. Greggs, Jr. (425th NFS), Dale F. Haberman (6th NFS), Robert P. Hagen (416th NFS), Lt.Col. Carl F. Hale, Jr. (6th NFS), Col. Leonard R. Hall (NF Training), Eugene H. Harris (419th NFS), Col. William C. Hellriege (426th NFS), David P Hopwood (P-38M/418th & 421st NFSs), Philip K. Horrigan (548th NFS), C.S. Izenour, Jr. (547th NFS), Jesse H. Jenkins (422nd NFS), Joe C. Jenkins (414th NFS), William Jennings (6th & 548th NFS), Maj.Gen. Oris B. Johnson (422nd NFS), Lt.Col. Frederic J. Kahn (419th NFS), Brig.Gen. Winston W. Kratz (NF Training), Frederick M. Kuykendall, Jr. (548th NFS), Lt.Col. Laurence W. Lackey (421st NFS), William M. Laird (422nd NFS), Col. William A. Larsen (417th NFS), Bruce K. Leford (548th NFS), Col. Leon G. Lewis (425th NFS), Albert W. Lockard (421st NFS), Efraim L. Lopez (421st NFS), Thomas R. Ludlow, Jr. (6th NFS), Alphonse Lukas (419th NFS), Victor M. Mahr (P-38M/418th & 421st NFSs), Richard L. Mathews (547th NFS), Charles K. McEwen, Jr. (422nd NFS), William G. McKeon (423rd NFS), John J. McPartland (415th NFS), Lt.Col. Avery J. Miller (548th NFS), Raoul M. Morales (6th NFS), Lt.Col. James A. Null (418th NFS), Col. William C. Odell (547th NFS), Lt.Col. John G. Pabst (6th NFS), Lt.Col. Austin G. Petry (415th NFS), Walter S. Pharr (421st NFS), Douglas C. Ponsford (421st NFS), James F. Postlewaite III (422nd NFS), Mathias Raab, Jr. (426th NFS), Col. Phillip A. Rand (419th NFS), Peter H. Raymen (6th NFS), James R. Reed (422nd NFS), L.C. "Duke" Reynolds, Jr. (426th NFS), William F. Ross (418th NFS), Prosper F. Rufer (418th NFS), Lt.Col. Francis V. Sartanowicz (425th NFS), W.R. Schrader (425th NFS), Lt.Col. Kenneth R. Schrieber (547th NFS), James F. Schroth (419th NFS), Fred Secord (6th NFS), Col. Carroll C. Smith (418th NFS), Paul A. Smith (422nd NFS), Karl E. Soukikian (425th NFS), Lt.Col. Philip R. Teske (6th NFS), Robert E. Tierney (422nd NFS), Earl M. Tigner (549th NFS), Col. Charles M. Townsend (421st NFS), Lt.Col. Churchill K. Wilcox (422nd NFS), and Porter B. Williamson (NF Training).

The World War II Night Fighters organization and the individual night fighter squadron associations have been quite generous in their support. We have had the pleasure of working with most of the present officers of the World War II Night Fighters: Don Flaherty, President; Frank L. Bosch, Executive Vice President; Al Lockard, VP-Treasurer; Al "Super Luke" Lukas, VP-Communications; A.E. "Bud" Anderson, VP-Community Relations; and Dave Weisman, VP-Merchandise/Promotions. These men have given much material assistance and encouragement over the many years of our research.

Many of the Night Fighters have submitted to interviews and reams of correspondence. Col. William C. Odell, who was a member of the Air Corps initial aborted attempt to form a night fighter squadron and later was a major player in forming the night fighter training program and even later to take a squadron into the Pacific, has provided invaluable assistance. From those who became "aces" – Herman Ernst (pilot, 422nd NFS), Bob Graham (R/O, 422nd NFS), Paul Smith (pilot, 422nd NFS), C.C. Smith (pilot, 418th NFS), and Bob Tierney (R/O, 422nd NFS), to those who spent their entire night fighter life flying dangerous interdiction missions, we thank you: this is your story.

A number of other organizations have also aided in this effort. The USAF Historical Research Center at Maxwell AFB, Alabama has been most helpful in researching the official USAF archives. In our first few years of research, Gerard E. Hasselwander was of much assistance. Dr. Maurer Maurer, Historical Studies Branch Chief, assisted in gaining access to the archives. Marguerite K. Kennedy was of great assistance in our visit to the archives. Lt.Col. William H. Greenhalgh, while working as a historian at the archives after his retirement from the Air Force, provided extensive research assistance for us over many years.

The Air Force Logistics Command headquartered at Wright-Patterson AFB, Ohio has also been quite helpful. From the Office of History, Paul M. Davis, Robert J. Smith, Vernon D. Burk, and John D. Weber have accomplished a good amount of research on our behalf and have come up with some very needed documents. Also, Carl Seiley and CMSgt Terry W. Morgan of AFLC's Directorate of Information Management have been quite helpful in obtaining historical studies performed by the Army Air Forces' Air Materiel Command. Also at Wright-Patterson, the Air Force Museum has been of much assistance. Royal D. Frey and Charles G. Worman have been quite generous over the years in taking time to answer our correspondence and give assistance during a research visit to that facility.

In Washington, D.C. the U.S. National Archives has provided well over 100 documents and many photographs. Most of this very appreciated assistance was rendered by Herman G. Goldbeck, Thomas E. Hohmann, and Edwin R. Flatequal. Also located in Washington is the National Air and Space Museum of the Smithsonian Institution. Here Robert B. Wood, Dominick A. Pisano, and Dan Hagedorn have ably assisted us. Debbie D. Griggs and Matthew Humphrey of NASM's Suitland, Maryland facility have helped in locating Individual Aircraft Record Cards. At nearby Andrews AFB, Air Force Systems Command historian Donald R. McVeigh was also kind enough to respond to our many letters.

Our research into the history of radar and the part that the Radiation Laboratory at the Massachusetts Institute of Technology played in the development of radar could not have been completed without the help of Sally Beddow of The MIT Museum. The documents and photographs obtained from the Museum's archives could be found no where else.

On the aircraft side, we have been assisted by the public relations departments and historians at Lockheed, Douglas, and Northrop. When we first started researching the Black Widow, Northrop's Charlie Barr and Tony Cantafio gave us a great push in getting started. Over the years Dr. Ira E. Chart, Northrop historian, has been of tremendous assistance and a good friend. Other past and present Northrop employees have assisted us – the late Jack Northrop, Irving Ashkenas, Fred Baum, Walt Cerny, Herb DeCenzo, Scott Johnson, Hugo Pink, Roy Wolford, John Myers, the late Vladimir Pavlecka, Dr. William Sears, Max Stanley, and many others. On the Douglas side, Harry Gann (company historian) has assisted in putting together the P-70 and XA-26A stories.

The American Aviation Historical Society and other fellow historical enthusiasts have been of great help and encouragement. Among the many that have befriended us over the years are Gerry Balzer, Dana Bell, the late Drs. James H. and William M. Belote, John and Donna Campbell, Bob Hernandez, Harvey Lippincott, Kenn Rust, and Warren Thompson. These, and many more, have generously shared their material with us.

Mr. Peter B. Schiffer, president, and Mr. Robert Biondi, our editor, of Schiffer Publishing Ltd., have been most understanding and patient. The authors would like to thank Ms. Carol K. Broede for her sage council and editorial expertise.

Finally, the authors owe much to their respective wives, Barbara J. Pape and Nancy Harrison, for constant encouragement and for performing many tasks connected with preparing the manuscript.

Garry R. Pape
Rowland Heights, California

Ronald C. Harrison
Roswell, Georgia

January 1992

Introduction

Development of radar in the world between the turn of the century and the beginning of the Second World War was carried out by a number of nations with very little sharing, or for that matter, very little knowledge, of each others effort. This was partly due to world communications not being what it is today and in part due to purposeful security. This condition was exaggerated in the United States where the Army and Navy kept much to themselves (history seems to indicate that inter-service rivalry has a very detrimental effect in many areas of endeavor, including aircraft design, electronics, and intelligence – including code breaking).

In the 1930s, with the thunder of hob-nailed boots beating a deadly tune in Europe, Britain, for its own survival, took the lead in radar development. It was due to their dire need of additional development and manufacturing capacity that the Tizard Commission was allowed to come to America with many of Britain's secrets, including its advanced stage in radar development. Under the direction of the recently formed Radiation Laboratory at the Massachusetts Institute of Technology in Cambridge, the Anglo-American radar development effort took to the air.

From the beginning of Adolf Hitler's reign of terror, American civilian and military personnel at the various diplomatic posts in Europe started taking note and sending their findings back to the States. More and more "observers" were trudging back and forth across the Atlantic to see what was happening. Both their numbers and length of stays increased as England was drawn into the fighting. From the darkened skies over London, night fighting came of age. The Americans initially observed; but as time went on, the Royal Air Force took their American allies into their confidence to some extent.

The task was soon clear. The Air Corps needed to develop a light airborne radar unit, develop aircraft to mount it in, develop the proper tactics and prepare a training program. But the United States was soon engulfed in the war themselves before much could be accomplished. While trying to develop a defensive system against aerial attack on American soil, the Air Corps decided to make an instantaneous jump into the realm of night fighting. The 15th Bomb Squadron stationed in Georgia was sent to England where it was to be trained in what the British felt was the end-all in night fighting – the Turbinlite night fighter. The only common link between the 15th Bomb

With the California coastline and a shimmering Pacific as a backdrop, a YP-61 flies a training mission in 1944. The lighting is just right to give a ghostly view of the SCR-720's antenna housed in the nose of the Widow. (USAF)

Squadron and the Royal Air Force units that were to train them was that they flew similar types of aircraft. The Turbinlite night fighter was a failure, and it turned out for the best that the 15th, which had been redesignated the 1st Pursuit Squadron (Night Fighter) just prior to going to England, reverted back to its initial role and made the history books as the first American air unit to enter combat against the German forces.

On the other side of the world, the Hawaiian Islands were reeling from the devastating attack that Admiral Chuichi Nagumo and his Imperial Japanese Naval forces had inflicted on the American installations in that area. Though minor in nature, the few Japanese night attacks that shortly followed had the military scurrying around to come up with a night defense system. Their initial effort was to send pilots with no night flying experience, also lacking in instrument flying ability, into the blackened sky in Curtiss P-40 Warhawks. The results should not have been unexpected!

Back at the ranch, actually Orlando, Florida, the Air Forces night fighter training program was being initiated. Initially under the tutelage of Col. Don Brummel and Capt. Leonard Hall, the first order of business was a fight to get facilities, airplanes, and personnel. Soon Lt.Col. Winston Katz and a number of American pilots who had flown night fighters in the Royal Air Force and Royal Canadian Air Force arrived from England.

The battle for men, equipment, and their place within the American fighting machine would continue throughout the war. As the night fighters developed their skills, so did American industry forge ahead in perfecting the radar and aircraft within which the night fighters would wage their lonely war. Though the main theme of this book is the story of the men who crewed and maintained these electronic flying machines, it would not be complete without the parallel story of those who developed and manufactured the radar and aircraft that would be melded together to produce the "night fighter."

Although the authors bear full responsibility for the conclusions drawn in this book, their debt to many others is considerable. This is their story. A story of struggle, of triumph, of misunderstanding of superiors, and largely of unsung heroes. All efforts have been made to present an accurate and complete picture.

Dedication

This book is dedicated
to those pioneers who flew through the ink black skies
in defense of the free world.

Chapter 1

Eyes of the Cat

Today such terms as Radar, detection, target, and interception are commonplace in military parlance and are generally understood by the public. With the "stealth" fighter and "stealth" bomber appearing in today's headlines, it can been seen that radar plays an important role in both offensive and defensive scenarios. As a military weapon, its potential was only faintly realized in the early 1930s; but it was catapulted to the forefront of technology by World War II.

Scottish physicist James C. Maxwell theorized, and demonstrated mathematically, that electromagnetic radiation travels through space in transverse waves, that these waves are formed by pulsating electrical and magnetic fields, and that light and electricity obey the same laws of physics. Maxwell's works were summed up in the 1873 publication entitled, "Treatise on Electricity and Magnetism." Soon after German physicist Heinrich R. Hertz set out to test Maxwell's theory. In the mid-1880s he had initial results, and in 1888 he proved that electrical waves can be reflected, refracted, and polarized in the same way as light and found that the electrical waves traveled at the speed of light. It would be for Nikola Tesla to first mention the possibility of distance measurement and detection of objects by electromagnetic waves at the turn of the century. Based on these principles, German engineer Christian Hulsmeyer demonstrated the use of radio waves in detecting obstacles and for ship navigation. The state of technology at that time limited the rang of such efforts to about a mile. Because of this limitation, the German navy showed very little interest. Undaunted, Hulsmeyer continued his work obtaining patents for his device in 1904.

Italian inventor and Nobel Prize recipient in physics, Guglielmo Marconi, spoke before a joint meeting of the American Institute of Electrical Engineers and The Institute of Radio Engineers in New York City on June 20, 1922. In his speech he spoke of Hertz's works on the reflection of electric waves by conducting bodies. Towards the end of his talk he related to his own experiences in this realm of investigation.

The Navy Leads Radar Development in US

On September 22nd of that year, Dr. Albert Hoyt Taylor and Leo C. Young were performing very high frequency (VHF) propagation experiments at the US Naval Aircraft Laboratory's Radio Division at Naval Air Station (NAS) Anacostia, DC. It is quite possible that Marconi's speech had some bearing on their experiments. In performing their experiments, they had positioned a receiver across the Potomac River from the Naval Air Station. They noted a reflection phenomena as a wooden steamship passed through the radio beam. Being quite elated, they wrote a memorandum to the US Navy's Bureau of Engineering which included the mention of aircraft detection by radio waves. The Bureau showed no interest!

The cathode-ray tube is the heart of the display unit which portrays the received electrical signals in a useable fashion for an operator. This device had been around since World War I. The transmitter, receiver, and antenna technologies were now being developed to a point that crude radar systems could be assembled.

Working along with Taylor and Young at NAS Anacostia, in what had become the Naval Research Laboratory, was Dr. Lawrence A. "Pat" Hyland. Dr. Hyland would be credited with the first detection of an aircraft by radar, though that was not the intent of the experiment. On June 24, 1930 Hyland was investigating the directional properties of an aircraft high frequency (HF) antenna system. The aircraft, which had the receiver, and Dr. Hyland were at the Army Air Corps' Bolling Field, also in Washington, D.C. Some two miles away at the Naval Research Laboratory was the beacon at 32.8-megacycles transmitting HF signals, along with Leo Young. Hyland noted that as an airplane flew through the path of the radio beam, the signal's intensity on his receiver increased. With great enthusiasm, Hyland reported his observations. The following day the experiment was repeated with numerous bystanders. Though the Laboratory supported further research, it progressed at a slow pace because of a lack of interest within the government.

Pulsed Radar Signals

These early radars were known as radio echo equipment in the US Navy or radio position finding in the US Army Signal Corps in the 1930s. They were a type of radar called "continuous-wave," or CW, because the signal was transmitted in a continuous fashion. These early systems were also referred to as "CW wave-interference" because it depended on the "target" going through (interfering with) the signal path between the receiver and transmitter. Later they were called "bistatic"; that is, the receiver and antenna were in different locations in fixed positions. These systems had limited range and determining the location of the target was quite difficult.

In 1921 a breakthrough came in meeting the power requirements for operating at centimetric wavelengths. Dr. Albert W. Hull of the General Electric Company in Schenectady, New York, developed a device called a magnetron. A pulsed radar signal was first used in experiments performed by Drs. Gregory Breit and Merle A. Tuve at the Carnegie Institution's Terrestrial Magnetism Laboratory in 1925. Their experiment concerned measuring the height of the ionosphere. In 1934 the Naval Research Laboratory took up investigation into pulsed radar signals. As with the CW radar work, this too was at a low priority. Taylor was able, however, to get some additional funding for this effort. Dr. Robert M. Page was in charge of the research team carrying out the experiments.

The initial tests in late 1934 and early 1935 were unquestionable failures, but lessons were learned. After additional experimentation and the redesigning of equipment, pulsed signals were successfully received on April 28, 1936. This was a low frequency radar of 28.3-megacycles and obtained a range of only 2.5 miles. This was a step in the right direction for by June they were getting ranges of about 25 miles. It was realized that higher frequency systems with smaller antennas were desireable. By late July 1936 they had a 200-megacycle system operational which was also the first system to incorporate a common antenna for both transmitter and receiver. By this time the Navy was interested and classified everything SECRET.

Interchange

In the 1920s and 1930s there was very little, if any, interchange of ideas or sharing of successes, or failures, between the military services much less with civilian entities. As stated earlier, the General Electric Company was active in the radar component field. The Radio Corporation of America (RCA) had carried on some radar experimentation beginning in the early 1930s. Bell Telephone Laboratories, the research arm of Bell Telephone System, had been active in this field for some time also. As a matter of fact, the Naval Research Laboratory was quite startled when three of Bell Telephone Laboratories' engineers reported at a meeting of the Institute of Radio Engineers in mid-January 1933 that they had detected aircraft with their radar equipment during the course of their experimentation. In January 1936, Army Signal Corps personnel visited the Naval Research Laboratory and were briefed on pulse radar development. In 1937 the Naval Research Laboratory let both RCA and Bell Telephone Laboratories in on the secret also. In 1940, thanks to the British, open cooperation between all would be in full operation – it only took a pending war!

US Army Development

Most of the US Army's radar development was accomplished at the Signal Corps Laboratories at Fort Monmouth, near Red Bank, New Jersey. Under its original name of Camp Alfred Vail, the Signal Corps established their Radio Laboratories in March 1918. In June 1930 Major William R. Blair became Director of the Laboratories.

Major Blair held a PhD. degree and had a deep interest in what would become known as radar. Upon his arrival, the laboratories main thrust was in sound detection and location devices. Major Blair felt, and pursued with some vigor, the use of alternative devices – heat and radio wave devices. The visit to the Naval Research Laboratory in 1936 was all he needed. The new information from the Navy, coupled with their research to date, enabled them to have a functioning pulsed radar by the end of the year.

Development continued including an emphasis on improved antenna design. In May 1937, a 240-megacycle system was demonstrated on two occasions. The second, on the 26th, was for the Secretary of War, Henry A. Woodring, and the Chief of the Air Corps, Major Gen. Oscar Westover. So elated were the observers of the demonstration that enthusiastic reports went to the President. The outcome was Army support and additional funds for the project. From this came the SCR-268 Searchlight Controller which was used in conjunction with searchlights in the first operational radar enhanced antiaircraft fire control system.

The story of making the SCR-268 the first American airborne radar is well documented in a book published by the US Government Printing Office entitled UNITED STATES ARMY IN WORLD WAR II, The Technical Services, THE SIGNAL CORPS: THE EMERGENCY (To December 1941):

The first order of business after the opening talks with the Tizard Mission was to follow the British example and put pulse equipment, however cumbersome, in the air. The visiting scientists had acknowledged that their own airborne pulse radar had to be 'nursed along in order to keep in operation.'

The Signal Corps had the means to do as much as that. Arrangements promptly got under way for elements of an SCR-268 to be tried out in an airplane. There was no question of including its antennas. 'No one ever believed airborne antennas (Yagis) would be feasible at 2 or 3 meters [the SCR-268's antenna length]. Even when the British sets were first received at ARL there was much doubt as to whether anyone would take up a U.S. plane with them.' The engineers on the project temporarily rigged up a single horizontal dipole and mounted it on the nose of a B-18. Then, since an airplane could go to the radar set more easily than the radar set could go to the airplane, the engineers had the B-18 flown to Red Bank airport, where they attached the receiving antennas along the sides of the fuselage. There followed a hurriedly designed transmitter, the SCR-268 receiver, a commercial oscilloscope, a modulator to provide 4,000 pulses a second, and a gasoline-powered generator.

On October 2, 1940, a date coinciding with the departure of the mission, preparations at Red Bank were completed. Bad weather prevented test flights there, the B-18 went back to Wright Field for no better luck, and it was the beginning of November before airborne trials could commence. In advance of them, the crew kept the bomber on the ground and short pulses at a basic training plane five or six miles distant in the air. The results were distinct, for the basic trainer reflected pips upon the oscilloscope. Had the B-18 been flying, this application would have approximated AI. On November 4 it did fly, from Wright Field over Lake Erie. Now the equipment was being tested as an ASV. Up in the air, it surpassed the 6 miles of the ground test and attained 17 against an ore boat, 23 against shore lines and islands. This was only half the distance the British claimed for their ASV, but for a first try it was encouraging. That the patchwork of components worked well at all was proof of the soundness of the SCR-268 and of the engineering skill which had adapted it.

The Aircraft Radio Laboratory experiments were under no illusions about what they had.

For practical aircraft use the transmitter, keyer, receiver, indicator and power supply would all need to be completely redesigned mechanically . . . Until a pulse less than a micro-second is obtained with the [Signal Corps Laboratories] equipment or until equipment modeled after the 500 megacycle [Naval Research Laboratory] pulse altimeter . . . is completed, flight tests on aircraft detection will be

This 1948 photo shows, from left to right, Dr. Karl T. Compton, Secretary of Defense James V. Forrestal, Dr. Vannevar Bush, and Secretary of the Navy John L. Sullivan. In 1939 Dr. Bush, then chairman of the National Advisory Committee for Aeronautics and president of Carnegie Institution, initiated meetings with a small group to discuss upgrading America's technology for the war that it would surely be in. Included in that group were Drs. Compton, president of the Massachusetts Institute of Technology, James B. Conant, president of Harvard, Frank B. Jewett, president of the National Academy of Sciences, and Richard C. Tolman, dean of the graduate school at the California Institute of Technology. (The MIT Museum)

suspended. (Letter, Col. Gardner to Chief Signal Officer, 6 Nov. 1940, subj: Detection of water-borne target Project 61C-1.)

This was the view of the ARL director. The Air Corps view at Wright Field was more sanguine, with the chief of the Experimental Section declaring that, 'the results obtained from this equipment were very encouraging and show that a means of detection of surface vessels from airplanes is available. To be made practicable, this equipment needs only to be reduced in size and weight.' (Memo Lt.Col. Franklin O. Carroll, AC, Chief of Experimental Section Material Division, for Chief of Material Division, 20 Nov. 1940, sub: Location and tracking of water-borne target (part of BTO project).

Great Britain had first experimented with putting radar aboard aircraft in 1937. The Signal Corps had radar by then. What were the obstructions which had so long blocked the Americans? Lack of free communication must bear part of the responsibility. No doubt can remain that with a readier flow and exchange of knowledge, American Army radar would have had a much shorter infancy. 'The 268 projects were kept so secret that few at ARL knew of them. I did not,' was the remark of Col. William L. Bayer, one of the half dozen who first tested the SCR-268 components over Lake Erie. Lack of funds, absence of basic research, unflagging Air Corps attempts to absorb the Aircraft Radio Laboratory also contributed barriers. But the main reason why nobody up to this point had got pulse radar up into the air was doubtless that nobody had thought of it – a reason which directs admiration toward the British scientists. 'It is easy to say now that the weight and size limitation might have been overcome but it would not have been easy to visualize the 268 as flyable. How the British [imagined] it still baffles me.'

Bayer's tribute came from a man who knew the problems.

National Defense Research Committee

In 1939 Europe was embroiled in war. The survival of Britain was in question. America's entry into the hostilities was just a question of time. Much of America's scientific energies were being spent in an independent fashion within the various service laboratories, the commercial laboratories, and at various universities. There was no real coordination and very little exchange of information. The first step in integrating the scientific community was in mid-1939 when President Franklin D. Roosevelt made the National Advisory Committee for Aeronautics [NACA, the forerunner of the National Aeronautics and Space Administration (NASA)] as the focal point for aeronautical matters, both civilian and military.

Just the year prior, Dr. Vannevar Bush became a member of NACA. Dr. Bush was a distinguished electrical engineer, inventor and educator; he became president of the Carnegie Institution in Washington, DC that same year after a distinguished career at the Massachusetts Institute of Technology (MIT) where he was vice president and the first dean of the School of Engineering. It was from a suggestion of Dr. Bush's to President Roosevelt that the National Defense Research Committee (NDRC) was created by executive order on June 27, 1940, with Bush as its head. Four fields of activity were initially

envisioned for the NDRC: ordnance, chemistry, communications, and physics. Dr. Karl T. Compton, president of MIT, held cognizance over the physics activities which would soon include radar activities.

Scientists and engineers from the universities, industry, and the military services were all part of the Committee. The armed services representatives briefed the other committee members on the research and development work that was being carried out at the various military laboratories. To bring the NDRC into these efforts, the military research and development projects were divided into the four NDRC fields of activities mentioned above. NDRC Division D (physics) was thus broken up into sections. Section 1 became detection devices, also referred to as the Committee on Detection Devices. This committee soon found their emphasis to be in the direction of devices in the microwave frequencies; they would be soon renamed the Microwave Division/Microwave Committee.

Dr. Alfred L. Loomis, an attorney and physicist, was appointed to head the committee. Dr. Loomis had his own laboratory in Tuxedo Park, New York, from which he had carried out his own and cooperative research projects since the early 1920s. Some years prior to his appointment he had been carrying on his own research into microwave devices. The first meeting of the Microwave Committee was held at Dr. Loomis' Tuxedo Park facility on July 13, 1940. The object of the meeting – get organized.

Drs. Compton and Loomis soon were on the road. They visited the Naval Research Laboratory at NAS Anacostia, DC, and the Signal Corps laboratories at Fort Monmouth, New Jersey. As a result of these visits Dr. Loomis suggested that his committee concentrate on devices in the microwave arena so as not to duplicate the efforts being carried out by the service laboratories in the longer wavelengths. It was from this decision to limit their research that the committee changed its name to match their intended endeavors.

British Radar Development

Britain's entry into the field of aircraft detection by radio waves came about when Robert A. Watson Watt, then Superintendent of the Radio Department of the National Physical Laboratory, was asked if such waves could be used to destroy an aircraft. The man who would be eventually known as the father of British radar, and become Sir Watson-Watt, gave it careful thought. His answer was that the technology was not available to produce enough energy to accomplish destruction of an aircraft or injure the pilot. But, it was feasible to detect an aircraft! So in early 1935 Britain embarked into this new science.

So, in late January 1935, the Committee for Scientific Survey of Air Defence was established with Henry T. Tizard as its chairman, who was at the time chairman of the Aeronautical Research Committee. With Watson-Watt now part of the effort, they took up their research at the National Physical Laboratory at Slough. Their first test was on February 26, 1935. They had arranged for a Royal Air Force (RAF) Handley Page Heyford

As the British developed airborne radar, a suitable platform had to be found. Single engine, single place aircraft did not fit the bill. In development of the radar a number of different aircraft were used in flight testing. But it was the Bristol Blenheim that would first go operational with the Mark I AI radar. With lackluster results, the RAF would go to a newer Bristol product, the Beaufighter. Day fighter variants similar to the one shown above were modified into night fighters. (Campbell Collection)

The Bristol Beaufighter, as shown above, was quite successful as a night fighter during the Battle of Britain. When the US Army Air Forces night fighters started training in this aircraft some three years later, it was then "old technology" and its poor ground handling characteristics would be an eternal thorn in the night fighters' sides. (USAF)

bomber to repeatedly fly through the high power radio beam of a BBC radio station. Watson-Watt and his team were in a field in Northamptonshire where they followed the bomber on their experimental receiver. They moved their shop on May 13th to Orfordness Airfield in Suffolk. This move didn't seem to slow them down as they had an operating combined transmitter-receiver later that month.

Under the guiding hand of Watson-Watt, progress on what was now referred to as RDF (usually defined as Radio Direction Finding) accelerated. Their efforts were broken up into two major projects. The main thrust concerned RDF 1. This was a ground based early warning system which would eventually become Great Britain's famous Chain Home (abbreviated CH) and, for low flying aircraft, Chain Home Low (CHL) network which served that island nation so well in warning them of the swarms of German aircraft en route to their mission of destruction. RDF 2 was the development of a radar for installation in an aircraft. It would seem that the initial impetus behind this idea was Henry Tizard. The RDF 2 project got under way in the summer of 1936 shortly after Watson-Watt and his team moved again; this time to the Bawdsey Research Station in Essex.

Dr. Edward G. Bowen was a one-man team on the project for the first few months. His work was initially on a receiver design. He would have liked to design a system that worked on 1 to 2 meter wavelengths, but the technology was not yet available. As a start, he put together a system operating on 6.7-meters. To test the system, he located the transmitter in one tower of Bawdsey Manor and the receiver in another. To his delight the system worked. His next task now was to get it airborne. With the transmitter weighing several tons, the likelihood of getting it airborne was quite slim. The next best alternative was to set up the transmitter as a ground station and install the receiver in an airplane. In the autumn of 1936, Dr. Bowen and his team had installed the receiver in a Handley Page Heyford. A number of flights were made during which they were able to detect other aircraft at increasing ranges. There was some disagreement among the scientists as to the usefulness of additional work on this system. The death blow was Watson-Watts being against it.

By the spring of 1937, P.A. Hibberd had produced a transmitter that could be installed in an aircraft which was installed in the Heyford. Though other airborne aircraft were not detected during these test flights, they were able to obtain good indications from ground installations. By that summer they had the use of two full time Avro Anson aircraft for their experimentation. At this time their efforts were towards what would be called air to surface vessel (ASV) radar. During air-sea exercises in the North Sea in early September 1937, one of their Ansons found the fleet in very inclement weather. They were also able to pick up the radar echo of the Fairey Swordfish that rose from their aircraft carrier to find the Anson. With this success, continued support for radar development was assured in Great Britain.

As 1938 was concluding, so was Dr. Bowen and his group's priority work towards ASV radar. Now, as in the beginning of their efforts towards airborne radar, they could again devote most of their energies towards what would be called AI radar. AI, depending upon which authoritative source

Britain's Prime Minister Winston Churchill during an inspection tour of a RAF station. It was through Churchill's support that the Tizard mission came to America and it was through the amalgamation of the British and American science communities that radar development took off like a rocket. (Hernandez Collection)

one uses, means Aircraft Interception, Airborne Interception, Air Interception, or Aircraft Intercept. Whichever, it is radar installed in one aircraft whose mission is to locate another aircraft through the use of that equipment.

Based on their work on the ASV equipment, AI development forged on. Added to their fleet of two Ansons were three light bombers built by Fairey called Battles; they were thought to be the first night fighters that would enter service. At this time the detection of another aircraft was coming along smoothly, but the determination of location and altitude still had to be worked out. The team developed equipment and flight tested it through that winter and spring. By May 1939, they had developed what could be considered the first truly operational AI. It was installed in a Battle and test flown on the 21st. This equipment was designated AI Mk I. Further demonstrations were conducted for government and RAF officials, which brought nothing but support for the AI; but the Battle was soon determined not the most suitable aircraft for the night fighter mission.

An aircraft with enough capacity for the radar equipment and operator and of twin engine design was desired. The Bristol Blenheim was chosen, and two of these craft were provided to the radar engineers that July. By August 1939, additional Blenheims were being fitted with AI Mk I sets for operational use in the RAF. Because these sets were each basically handmade and installed, the equipment needed to be redesigned for production ability; the result was AI Mk II. When war broke out on September 3, 1939, 15 Blenheims with AI Mk I sets installed had been delivered to the RAF's 25 Squadron stationed at Northolt.

One of the engineers from Bawdsey assisting at Northolt was Hanbury Brown. Brown found that though the Home Chain\Home Chain Low early warning stations could adequately direct day fighters close enough for the pilots to visually locate the enemy formations, it was not accurate enough for a night fighter to locate a single aircraft in the black of the night. The answer was the rapid development of Ground Control(ed) Intercept (GCI) radar; as well as IFF (identification friendly or foe) equipment which would be carried by allied aircraft with interrogation equipment on ground stations.

Probably one of the most significant breakthroughs in radar development was through the work of Henry A.H. Boot and John T. Randall at Birmingham University in England in February 1940. The heart of a radar transmitter is the electrical device which will generate sufficient power. Such vacuum tube oscillators as the magnetron (which can be traced back to Dr. Albert Hull's work at GE during World War I) and the klystron (developed by Russell H. and Sigurd F. Varian, brothers, and W.W. Hansen while at Stanford University in California) in the late 1930s and other such devices had been around in some form for some time. Most performed in the meter wavelengths but only the magnetron, klystron, and crystal diode technologies worked in the centimeter range though with insufficient power output. With the resonant cavity magnetron produced by Boot and Randall at Professor M.L. Oliphant's laboratory at Birmingham University, there was finally a device with sufficient power made available to the radar engineers.

Three of the primary players in bringing together the British and American radar scientists. From right to left are Dr. Alfred L. Loomis, Sir Henry Tizard, and Dr. Lee A. DuBridge. Dr. Loomis was an attorney and physicist who had his own laboratory prior to the establishment of the National Defense Research Committee's Microwave Committee. Once established, Dr. Loomis became its chairman. DuBridge became director of the Radiation Laboratory at MIT under which the Microwave Committee functioned. (The MIT Museum)

The British Are Coming!
The British Are Coming!

In late 1939 Henry Tizard suggested that one of his colleagues, Professor Archibald V. Hill, go to the United States and establish contact with American scientists in preparation for closer working relationships between the scientific communities of the two nations. It would also seem to be somewhat of a spy mission as Hill was also to evaluate the US military's research programs in a very inconspicuous manner. He was given temporary assignment as Scientific Attache in Washington, DC, where he carried out his mission between February and June 1940. When Tizard originally made his suggestion that Britain share all of her secrets with the United States, he met with resistance, including Watson-Watt, who felt that the US had nothing to give in return. With the fall of France, and Britain feeling quite isolated, the thinking changed.

Permission was granted by the British Cabinet, Winston Churchill, and President Roosevelt. The "British Technical and Scientific Mission to the United States" headed by Sir Henry Tizard, and more often than not referred to as the "Tizard Mission," started assembling their documentation and equipment for one of the greatest "Show and Tell" shows in history. In late August 1940, Tizard arrived in Washington, D.C., ahead of the rest of the mission personnel for final arrangements. The rest of the team arrived in early September. Soon after the mission personnel were sharing with the Americans their secrets in the fields of jet engines, rockets, proximity fuses and radar.

By mid-month the mission had shared with the US armed services, as well as Dr. Vannevar Bush and the National

From the roof tops of MIT's many buildings sprung special facilities of the Radiation Laboratory. Within the domed structure shown in the above photograph is a radar antenna which could be used to detect either air or waterborne traffic. (The MIT Museum)

Defense Research Committee, their entire spectrum of radar development and operational lessons learned to date. To reciprocate, the mission personnel were taken to the Naval Research Laboratory at Anacostia Naval Air Station and the Army laboratories at Fort Monmouth. It was soon ascertained that the US and Britain were nearly on par as far as development of meter wavelength radar systems went, but there was no comparison when it came to centimeter wavelength (microwave) type radar. So it was decided that the US Army and Navy would continue their work on metric radar and, with the help of the British information, the National Defense Research Committee would work in the centimetric radar realm. The mission had brought over their latest versions of ASV and AI radars, Mk II and Mk IV, respectively. The Mk IV AI was taken to Wright Field in Ohio where it was installed in a Douglas A-20 Havoc in November. It was demonstrated for the US Army Air Corps, though the British, on the lookout for a better platform for their radar systems, were probably interested in how this combina-

tion worked also. Bell Telephone's production organization, Western Electric, was included in this effort as they would soon be manufacturing the British Mk IV AI as the Signal Corps' SCR-540.

The mission's radar expert, physicist and communications engineer Dr. Edward G. Bowen, met with the National Defense Research Committee's Microwave Committee at Dr. Alfred Loomis' Tuxedo Park laboratory on September 30th. With Dr. Bowen was drawings, data, and one of Britain's first production variants of their resonant cavity magnetrons. Two decisions were soon made. First, that the Microwave Committee would develop a 10-centimeter AI radar system. Second, that production of the British magnetron in the US should start as soon as possible.

For the production effort, Dr. Bowen and members of the Microwave Committee went to Bell Telephone in New York in early October during which time Bell personnel were briefed on the British developed cavity magnetron. A few days later the magnetron was operating at Bell's Whippany, New Jersey, Laboratory. With the drawings, technical data, and example brought across the Atlantic, Bell started the production process. A snag was found almost immediately; the drawings did not match the example they had in hand. Dr. Bowen was called in; and after some trans-Atlantic phone conversations, it was determined that the drawings were to the original six-hole design and the example was one of the new eight-hole designs. Using the drawings for the six-hole design and an x-ray photo of the eight-hole variant, Bell soon produced their first eight-hole US produced magnetron. Within a month, 30 had been produced.

For the development of microwave radar in the US, the Committee with British guidance decided that the work be carried out by a contractor. At first they thought of Carnegie Institution's Terrestrial Magnetism department. They probably were considered because of their earlier work which started with Breit and Merle's work in pulsed radar signals. Upon further investigation, they determined that due to other research work that the Institution's own facilities were already at capacity. Next they felt that Bolling Field, in Washington, D.C. also, would be a good location and Carnegie could oversee the effort. But the Army Air Corps had other plans so that idea was scratched also.

Drs. Bush and Loomis suggested Massachusetts Institute of Technology in Cambridge, Massachusetts. They also realized that Boston's harbour would give them access to waterways and, for aerial experimentation, the National Guard facility at the East Boston Airport would be perfect. Dr. Karl T. Compton made a call to MIT and within hours the project was ago. Initially, the new Radiation Laboratory would be under the supervision of MIT's Electrical Engineering Department. Because of the department's earlier work in microwave frequencies in conjunction with an Air Corps/Sperry Gyroscope Company project, they were as well qualified as any for overseeing the initial development of this new laboratory. To help in staffing the new organization, Professor Ernest O. Lawrence of the University of California was brought in. By November 10, 1940, the Laboratory, with 15 scientists, was organized, with Dr. Lee A. DuBridge as its Director.

The Radiation Laboratory staff along with the Microwave Committee, England's Dr. Bowen being attached to the committee, came up with their initial list of projects that the Laboratory would undertake, one being 10-centimeter AI radar. For the next couple of months they were busy staffing, ordering material, and setting up their laboratories. By year's end they had assembled their first 10-centimeter radar.

A peaceful London. Soon the Blitz and it, as well as the rest of the world, would never be the same. (Hernandez Collection)

Chapter 2

War Clouds

September 1940 was quite a month. It marked the first anniversary of the war that would become "World War II," and it would also see the start of the Blitz – a time not soon forgotten by Londoners. It was also a month in which the American military defensive posture would take its basic form for many years to come. The result of heavy traffic going across the Atlantic would do much towards forming the Army Air Corps air defense scenario. This month would also see the arrival of the Tizard Mission in the United States with many revelations. The disclosure of England's development of the resonant cavity magnetron and advancements in 10-centimeter AI radar by the Mission would greatly influence the shape of the Air Corps air defense efforts, including night fighter development. A similar impact would occur in the field of 3-centimeter radar which the US Navy and Marine Corps would use in their carrier based night fighters. All travelers were not from east to west. Since the beginning of hostilities in Europe, the US armed services were crossing the Atlantic to see for themselves how the war was being fought and to learn as much as possible about the equipment and strategies being utilized.

Developing an Air Defense

With the uneasiness in Europe in the mid-1930s, many nations felt it prudent to evaluate the condition of their military forces. As the 1930s progressed the rumblings grew louder and louder. In President Franklin Delano Roosevelt's speech of January 28, 1938 he spoke of rearming the United States in the interests of "national defense." By 1939 it was recognized that air power would be a major factor in the next war. In January of that year Roosevelt spoke in terms of expanding the Army's air strength as a defensive measure for the security of the hemisphere. Air defense included the entire spectrum of the air arms of the US military, especially long range bombers. It was felt that a good defensive operation included hitting an adversary's ground

installations and naval forces before they could violate US territories. Fighter aircraft to intercept the enemy, basically day fighters which would soon prove to be poor performers during night and inclement weather, as well as anti-aircraft artillery and aircraft locating equipment were the defensive mechanism for protecting the continental United States and strategic points over seas.

Until the Battle of Britain was observed, the Air Corps was mainly concerned with defense at a distance philosophy. Besides the push for the long range bomber, the War Department was struggling with the proper relationship of the Army's air arm in relation with the rest of the US Army. Between the mid-1930s and the early part of the 1940s there were many reorganizations. It was through one of these reorganizations that the Air Defense Command was established.

As related earlier, the Army's air arm seemed to be constantly struggling for its place within the US military. Upon the suggestion of Lt.Gen. Henry H. "Hap" Arnold (Chief of the Air Corps) to Gen. George C. Marshall (the US Army's Chief of Staff) and his subsequent approval, that the Air Corps take over the air defense duties of the Army's Coast Artillery, the Air Defense Command was established on February 26, 1940. The Command was set up at Mitchel Field on New York's Long Island with Brig.Gen. James E. Chaney commanding, who was known for his planning capabilities. Assisting Chaney, and complementing his executive qualities, was Capt. Gordon P. Saville, a superb engineering officer. Their charter was to lay out a defensive network for certain cities, industrial areas and military installations both in the US and over seas. With a small staff they had to encompass the entire gamut of air defense – antiaircraft artillery, aircraft location equipment, radio communications, pursuit aircraft, and barrage balloons. The interpretation of air defense for the Command was in the strictest sense, area defense, no interdiction missions or preemptive strikes against the enemy's bases.

The form the US Army's ground and air defense system would take was through lessons learned to date in Europe.

Northrop Aircraft of Hawthorne, California, was formed by noted aeronautical engineer John K. Northrop in 1939. "Jack" Northrop wanted a company that could delve into new technologies, especially his favorite project, a flying wing. But money was needed to accomplish this. First orders were obtained for Northrop Aircraft to build portions of other manufacturers aircraft. Then in March, 1940, a contract to design and build the N-3PB patrol planes for the Norwegian Government was obtained. (Northrop)

In September, 1940 Northrop received a contract to build the Vultee V-72 Vengeance for the British. The Vultee lines in Nashville, Tennessee, were at capacity and the British wanted more, and now! Jack Northrop didn't think much of the design, but the British did not have the time to wait – Europe was about to fall. This contract put more work in the shops and money ($17 million, half of which was paid up front) on the books. (Northrop)

Germany's aggression against Czechoslovakia in March and then their invasion of Poland in September 1939 dashed all hopes for a political settlement. On September 3rd England, France, Australia, and New Zealand declared war against Germany. But hostilities seemed to slacken immediately afterwards. Hitler was apparently awaiting for a peace initiative from England and France, and they in turn were waiting for Germany's next move. The RAF flew missions, but more leaflets than bombs were dropped; history would record this period as the "phoney war."

In the spring of 1940 it was not only the ice and snow that melted away, the calm that had set in also disappeared. In April German troops were on the move again, and this time it was Norway and Denmark that felt the thunder of the goose-stepping boots of the Wehrmacht. Then, in May, Adolf Hitler sent his forces into the Netherlands which marked the beginning of Hitler's Western Offensive. War had come, and a new government was installed in England. The new prime minister would soon become a principal player among the wartime governments – Winston Churchill.

Hap Arnold realized he needed to know more about the situation taking place in Europe. Intelligence was being gathered by US Military Attaches, which included Air Corps officers, assigned to the American embassies in Europe. This information was relayed back to the War Department, but Arnold and his staff were not privy to it. Arnold suggested to his boss, General Marshall, that Air Corps "observers" be sent to England and Europe. Marshall saw the validity of the proposal and gave the go-ahead. To put the plan into operation Arnold turned to his assistant, Brig.Gen. Barton K. Yount. The first group picked were four of the best choices the Air Corps could

have made. Capt. Benjamin S. Kelsey was to go to London. Captain Kelsey, had over 10 years in the Air Corps with a good bit of experience in test flying pursuit aircraft. He had served with Jimmy Doolittle in the late 1920s at the Full Flight Laboratory, broke a speed record in October 1938 while flying from Wright Field, Ohio, to Buffalo, New York, and was the project officer for Lockheed's new interceptor, the XP-38. Lt.Col. Frank O.D. "Monk" Hunter was initially assigned to Paris, but it was soon to fall and he too would go to England. Hunter had distinguished himself in World War I as a pursuit pilot and had become an expert in that field in the intervening years. Capt. Willard R. Wolfinbarger would go to the German capitol. Col. Carl A. "Tooey" Spaatz, Air Corps Chief of Plans, would also head for England. This group was headed into harms way as the Western Offensive was but a week old when they departed the US on May 17th. In ten days Calais, France would fall and the famed evacuation from Dunkirk would start.

As observers, their interest was in the political as well as the military. Though America was officially neutral, these men on temporary duty did more than just "observe." They made the cocktail circuit as well as holding discussions with military leaders and making numerous trips to RAF airdromes. While at 12 Group, Tooey Spaatz spent an evening in their operations room watching RAF night fighters being directed to targets. What he wasn't told was that they were equipped with AI radar. The next month the Tizard Mission would arrive in the US and the Air Corps would be told all.

Not only was American military posture being shaped, but Anglo-American joint war plans were in the making. There was a constant flow of observers, with their stay lasting from weeks to months. These observers really got an eye full as the Battle of Britain commenced in July. That saving grace for the RAF, but deadly for the civilian population, known as the London "Blitz" erupted on September 7th.

The observer ranks included "the brass" also. In early August the Assistant Chief of Naval Operations, Rear Admiral Robert L. Ghormley, along with the Army's Chief of the War Plans Division, Brig.Gen. George V. Strong, and Maj.Gen. Delos L. Emmons, Commander of GHQ Air Force, arrived. Emmons along with Tooey Spaatz, who had arrived earlier, left in September to brief the War Department and Air Corps command personnel on the war situation. A good bit of their report was to counter America's ambassador in London, Joseph P. Kennedy report that nothing could stop the Germans and that England was on the verge of eminent defeat.

New Tactics, New Equipment

From the reports of the multitude of American observers that had traversed the Atlantic coupled with British information and the experience of trying to establish a defense system for the United States, one fact had been brought home quite clear. An interceptor capable of locating and destroying enemy aircraft in inclement weather and in hours of darkness was a necessity.

From lessons learned in the skies over England, the Air Corps knew that their night fighting plane would not be a modification to an existing aircraft. It is probably of no coincidence that Brig. Gen. Spaatz, who just earlier had gleaned information on the RAF's night fighter activities as a special Air Corps observer in England, became the Chief of the Air Corps Materiel Division at Wright Field near Dayton, Ohio in October 1940. The major American aircraft manufacturers were operating at capacity and were doing all they could to expand. Hap Arnold was ever pressed to get what he needed to build up the

Air Corps while President Roosevelt was promising Great Britain more and more aid. The result was that quite often the total was greater than the aircraft industry was capable of producing.

History tells us that the barely one year old Northrop Aircraft, Incorporated, of Hawthorne, California, would be the chosen builder of this new craft. But why them? Though Northrop company was relatively new, John K. "Jack" Northrop was a well known aeronautical engineer of great talent. Apparently, a request for a bid on this project was not issued to other aircraft builders. Why sole source? Two factors would seem reasonable to assume. First, the "major" manufacturers were at capacity. Second, the British Purchasing Commission, who had been busy purchasing all the aircraft they could, had approached Northrop concerning a possible night fighter (Northrop would not be the only American manufacturer they would contact). The Army Air Corps no doubt knew of this.

The way that Northrop was contacted was quite unique. Northrop's chief of research, and a leading expert in the use of magnesium in construction of aircraft, Vladimir H. Pavlecka, was at Wright Field in October 1940. He was there helping the Air Corps iron some bugs out of a series of tests in conjunction with magnesium wings that Northrop Aircraft was under subcontract to design and produce with North American Aviation. "Pavi" knew nothing of night fighters or even of the British approaching Jack about such a plane.

It was much to his surprise when the Chief of the Experimental Aircraft Projects, Col. Lawrence C. Craigie called him into his office on October 21. Pavlecka was soon to be the first "Norcrafter" to learn about the P-61:

It must have gotten around Dayton that I was there and where I was from. Somewhere around noon time I was called into Col. Craigie's office. I had never met him before. His first words were,

It was through Northrop Aircraft, Inc.'s contacts with the British Purchasing Commission on the V-72 that talks began concerning the design of a built-for-the-purpose night fighter. Its primary mission would be night air defense for London. (Northrop)

Above: When Northrop Chief of Research Vladimir Pavlecka returned to Hawthorne, California, with the Air Corps preliminary requirements for a Night Intercepter Pursuit, Jack Northrop (above) immediately started conceptualizing. It is interesting to note, though not surprising, that once the P-61 design was a going project, Jack Northrop basically bowed out and concentrated his interests on the flying wing. (Northrop)

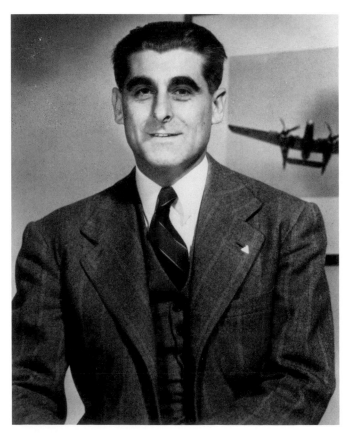

Left: Walter J. Cerny, Assistant Chief of Design, was in on the Northrop night fighter design from the beginning. He accompanied Jack Northrop on the numerous trips to Wright Field in late 1940. (Northrop)

'Now sit down. Don't take any notes, just try to keep it in your memory!'

It was to be an airplane that was to fly at night. I was told nothing about radar, except that there was a way to see and to distinguish other airplanes. That it must have two engines, a man to pilot and a man to operate the device, the guns, and so forth. I was given then a specification almost as complete as any primary specification is given. I was asked to repeat it. I made some errors and was corrected. I was asked to repeat it again. With this I was given a lecture on how important this was, not to play lightly with it, that it is a very serious matter. I was sent out after this.

I was leaving that night on a Boeing Stratoliner – a four engine, supercharged, sleeping airplane. I arrived past midnight in Los Angeles; plans were that I was to see Northrop that morning right away and tell him what I was told. The injunction was not, would we do it or not, the injunction was do it! – that was the point. That was an order.

That morning, October 21st, Jack Northrop met with Vladimir Pavlecka and received the Air Corps specifications. With a minimum amount of rework to his British night fighter design, Northrop was ready to meet with the technical people at Wright Field. On November 5th he, along with his Assistant Chief Engineer, Walter J. Cerny, left for Dayton, Ohio with their proposal.

This aircraft was to be powered with two of the new Pratt and Whitney Double-Wasp engines mounted in low slung nacelles, which tapered back into twin tail booms. The long fuselage, which projected fore and aft of the inner wing panels, housed a crew of three. There was a gunner for the nose turret, pilot, and a radar operator/rear turret gunner. Each turret held four .50 cal. machine guns. With an overall height of 13 feet 2 inches, a length of 45 feet 6 inches, and the wing spanning 66 feet. This bomber-size fighter was to have a tricycle-type landing gear system. For short field take-offs and landings, it had Zap flaps spanning 140 inches. Its empty weight was to be 16,245 pounds and a gross weight of 22,654 pounds. This was the Air Corps "Night Interceptor Pursuit Airplane."

At Wright Field, Northrop and Cerny met with personnel of Materiel Command and the many associated laboratories. Northrop presented his design, designated Northrop Specification 8A, to the Air Corps. From this conceptual material a number of lengthy discussions pursued. At the conclusion of this initial conference, Northrop returned to Hawthorne where he and his design team put many additional hours into incorporating ideas expressed by both Air Corps and those of their own innovations. An interim design of a single tail shoulder wing design was short lived. A modified version of the initial conceptions was agreed upon by the team and Northrop found himself going back to Wright Field in mid-November to present it. In this new configuration an additional gunner's station was added. The nose and tail turrets of the original design had been deleted and in their place was a twin .50 cal. machine gun in the

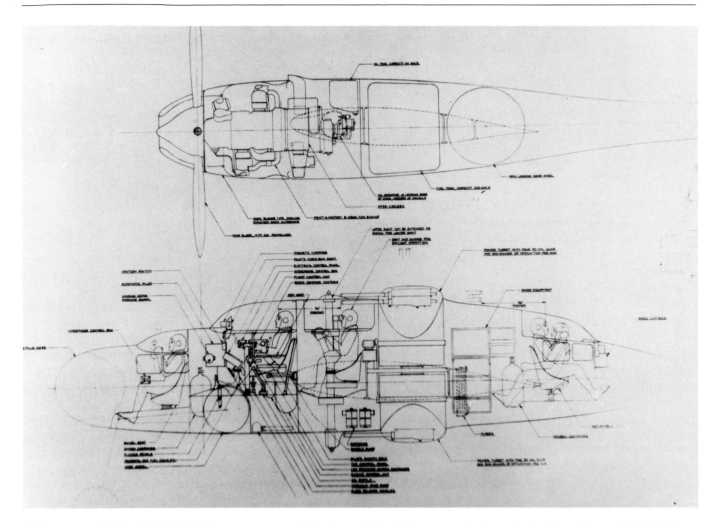

Early conceptual design of the P-61. This four crew, two turret design does not indicate the presence of radar on the drawing and the nose is of metallic construction. (Balzer Collection)

belly of the aircraft and four .50 cal. machine guns in the top turret. The crew now consisted of two gunners, a pilot, and a radar operator. In the nose was located the airborne intercept radar with the structure of the nose now being fabricated from non-metallic material.

Further engineering resulted from these discussions over the new proposal and a further modified design was ready by November 22nd. The crew once again was to a three man configuration: pilot, gunner, and radar operator. The armament changed once again also. It now consisted of four 20mm cannon in the wings, the lower turret had been deleted with the top turret being retained. The wheel base of the aircraft was broadened to 172 inches with an increase of gross weight to a hefty 21,839 pounds.

A letter of quotation was prepared, which included the fabrication of two experimental aircraft which was presented to Materiel Command at Wright Field on December 17, 1940. On January 9, 1941 the Air Corps issued their Military Characteristics of Aircraft for a Pursuit, Night Interceptor under the signature of Maj.Gen. George H. Brett, Assistant to Chief of the Air Corps.

Later that month Brett reported to General Arnold on plans for a "stop-gap" night fighter while the P-61 was being designed and produced. He reported:

Based on a study made during the drafting of Military Characteristics for Night Pursuit Interceptor, it was decided at that time that the most expeditious method of obtaining a "stop-gap" night fighter type would probably be through the conversion of a number of A-20 type airplanes, rather than the introduction of a new type into the picture at this time. However, subsequent studies of the Douglas production picture on the A-20As and A-20s (to be followed at Santa Monica plant by British DB-7s) and the anticipated delays attendant upon completion and organization of the Long Beach plant for our own A-20B production indicate that, *permitting no interference with A-20 production*, the following night fighter situation would prevail.

Under the restricted production capabilities that Douglas was operating, a scheme was envisioned under which a standard service test quantity of 13 could be produced. It was recommended that by taking A-20B parts that would be available in mid-1941 a night fighter variant could be produced. The first airplane was to be delivered in March, 1942, and the last of the 13 by that July. These aircraft would be equipped with AI-10 radar, and a crew of three. Armament would consist of a pair of .50 cal. guns in a top turret and four 20mm cannon in a tunnel under the belly of the fuselage. The cost of the basic A-20B plus night fighter conversion work for all 13 aircraft was estimated at $2,863,263.

In contrast to the Douglas situation, Jack Northrop had greater expansion possibilities over the work then in his shops. He stated that in the event that a contract for 13 service test YP-61s were issued he would immediately divert 125 designers to the project. He promised delivery nine months after receipt of contract for the first experimental aircraft, 10 for the second XP-61, and the YP-61s by 16 months from date of contract, or completion of the XP-61s and YP-61s by May 1942. This schedule was sooner than Douglas could produce their night fighter variant of the A-20B. Like the A-20B night fighter, the P-61 was to be equipped with AI-10 AI radar, but its armament consisted of four .50 cal. machine guns in its top turret as well as four 20mm forward firing cannon.

The British, who were to be included in the initial production of the P-61, were in on the planning. Brett's report stated:

Air Chief Marshal Sir Hugh Dowding has reviewed the proposed Military Characteristics and both the Northrop and Douglas situation. He has expressed the opinion that the Northrop XP-61 design is excellent and meets all British requirements. At the same time, he has covered the Douglas proposal, and is recommending that the British Purchasing Commission drop consideration of the Night Fighter version of the A-20.

The report continues, "The Douglas engineering facilities can be utilized to better advantage by experimental development of: (1) a new light bomber type (initial negotiations now under way) and (2) a 75mm cannon airplane both of which should be available for production immediately following termination of 1st Aviation Objective deliveries in mid 1942." These new designs would soon become the XA-26-DE and XA-26B-DE respectively, the beginning of Douglas' very successful Invader series of attack aircraft. The Invader design team at Douglas was headed up by that company's chief engineer, Edward H. Heinemann.

The Air Corps evaluation considered the proposed delivery dates of the Northrop and Douglas proposals, the capabilities of the two aircraft, and Dowding's comments. The decision was to drop the A-20B night fighter conversion idea and to award Northrop a contract for 13 service test aircraft, as well as the experimental contract which was already in the ratification process. Heinemann and his team at Douglas wasted no time in coming up with a night fighter version of the Invader which would subsequently be designated the XA-26A.

Britain's Dr. Edward Bowen, AI radar expert who had arrived in September of the previous year with the Tizard Mission, was also working through the British Purchasing Commission in investigating mounting AI radar in American aircraft. In a secret letter to the Air Corps on January 29, 1941 he writes:

A British Mark IV AI equipment will shortly be delivered to Wright Field with details of a typical layout in a two-engined fighter.

So far the only models in Service in England have been twin-engined multi-seat aircraft, and it has been found impossible to make a satisfactory fitting to a single engined single seater fighter. We are desperately anxious for an installation in single engined aircraft, and discussions which have taken place between the Bell Aircraft Corporation and the British Air Commission indicate a real possibility of making a workable installation in the P-39. Briefly, the aircraft would be converted to a two-seater by inclusion of a second place in front of the pilot. The AI operator and part of the equipment would be in this space, leaving the pilot free to fly the aircraft and keep a look-out for the target. The Bell Aircraft engineers do not take too unfavourable a view of this proposed lay-out.

We consider the P-39 provides perhaps the only possibility of fitting existing AI equipment to a single-engined machine, and if facilities could be made available, would make a determined effort to see the project through, both on behalf of the Army Air Corps and for ourselves.

We have recently concluded an arrangement with the U.S. Navy in which we helped to install a British ASV set in a Navy PBY. If a similar arrangement could be made in relation to AI in a P-39, we would be glad to help in every way possible. I would be very glad to spend a considerable part of my time on the work, and in addition, there is at present in Canada, an R.A.F. sergeant with several hundred hours' war time experience as AI operator in Blenheims and Beaufighters. He also has experience of installation work and arrangements could no doubt be made for him to give his full time to the P-39 project.

Major B.W. Chidlaw, Chief of Materiel Division's Experimental Engineering Branch at Wright Field responded to Dr. Bowen's letter in early February. He and his staff felt it was not feasible because of the engine-shafting-propeller combination of the P-39 Airacobra. They suggested that if Dr. Bowen still desired to undertake this project that they use one of the Airacobra I's being delivered to the RAF and modify it in England. A mockup was made but apparently no flight articles were produced.

Designing a Night Fighter

By January 30, 1941, the P-61 contract had been approved by the military chain of command including its last stop, the Under Secretary of War. The teams on both sides, military and contractor, were formed. Besides Northrop and Cerny, Fred J. Baum was appointed Project Engineer. Dr. William R. Sears was Chief of Aerodynamics, and aptly assisting them were A.M. Schwartz and Irving L. Ashkenas. For the Army, Capt. Marshall S. Roth from Wright Field was assigned as Project Engineer, and Mr. Mel Robin was assigned as the civilian engineering representative to the program.

Though the initial British night fighter design was now a

British AI radar expert Dr. Edward Bowen, working through the British Purchasing Commission, got some interest from Bell Aircraft in modifying the P-39 Airacobra into a night fighter as shown in this mockup. The US Army Air Corps were not interested in participating in the project. (Bell via Matthews)

U.S. Army Air Corps project, the British were still very interested and deeply involved in the design. Dr. Sears recalls those days, "There was much British involvement. We had RAF officers around the mock-up frequently. I understood that the airplane was, 'being designed to defend England.' The configuration, armament, loiter capability, relatively short range, etc., were all pointed toward the London defense situation."

The two-stage, two-speed, mechanical superchargers which were part of the R-2800 powerplant designated for the P-61 as it was initially designed for the Air Corps gave all the performance required. The thinking in some circles was that the added weight and complication of a turbo-supercharger installation was not necessary. This was not accepted by all, and the team of Sears, Ashkenas and John Wild were very much in favor of

a turbo-supercharged engine. Dr. Sears recalls, "That two-stage geared driven job was really a monster. It required inner coolers and all, and gave only a very moderate critical altitude. We had no choice." As it turned out, this thinking was erroneous and the mistake would not be corrected in time.

The January 30th contract between Northrop and the Air Corps had a price of $1,367,000.00 for which two experimental airplanes and two wind tunnel models, a 1/20 scale and a 1/30th scale, would be constructed. The 1/20th scale wind tunnel model was to be used at Wright Field where high speed and control characteristics tests were to be run. The 1/30th scale freespin model was to be tested at the NACA wind tunnel at Langley Field, Virginia. Though not included in the contract, Northrop would fabricate a 1/8th scale model which would be used at the California Institute of Technology wind tunnel and a Zap wing model to be tested at the University of Washington wind tunnel.

Zap was a very prominent name at the outset of Northrop's night fighter design. During this period Edward Zap, under contract to the NACA, was working at Northrop Aircraft. Numerous Northrop personnel, including Herb DeCenzo, then chief aerodynamist, was assisting Zap in a number of the experiments that he was working on. Incorporated in the Northrop night fighter design was the Zap wing which Northrop was to test at the University of Washington wind tunnel, and the Zap flap which was under test by the NACA at that time. Since the mid to late 1930s, Zap was very interested in increasing the maximum lift coefficient and consequent decreased landing speed by the use of new and improved lateral control and lifting devices, which became known as Zap flaps and Zap circular-type ailerons. The XP-61 of January, 1941, was designed with the Zap wing and Zap flap but did not employ any type of circular arc spoiler or aileron.

In late February, 1941, Gen. Carl Spaatz, who was then chief of the Materiel Division of the Air Corps, and Lt.Col. Monk Hunter went to Wright Field to effect final coordination with the Experimental Engineering Section on all points of the military characteristics of the XP-61 and to discuss a contract of 13 YP-61 service test aircraft. A point of contention had arisen during the pairs visit to Wright Field. The Military Character-

Two aerodynamics authorities at the California Institute of Technology, Drs. Theodore Von Karman and William R. Sears (pictured above), would be involved with Northrop projects throughout the War. Dr. Von Karman would act as a consultant throughout, primarily on the flying wing designs. Dr. Sears joined Northrop Aircraft and became Chief of Aerodynamics. He was involved with the P-61 as well and the flying wings. (Northrop)

istics that the XP-61 was procured under stated the endurance requirements as the "equivalent of two hours at full throttle." GHQ Air Force instigated a "two-hour full throttle" requirement and supposedly coordinated it with Spaatz, Hunter, and the Wright Field representatives. It seems that this "equivalent of two hours" had been interpreted to equal "six-hour at economical cruising." The final sign-off of the YP-61 was in jeopardy because the Office of the Under Secretary of War had recently dictated that no contract would be signed that deviated from the Military Characteristics under which the airplane was being bought. Both Gen. Spaatz and Lt.Col. Hunter knew well of the urgent need of a night fighter, for they had been part of the Air Corps special observers in England during the fall of 1940 and witnessed the devastating effects of the Luftwaffe's night assault upon London. They left the meeting with the Experimental Engineering Section being tasked with determining the equivalent between a two-hour at full throttle endurance vice a six-hour at economical cruise endurance. The alternatives of getting the requirement waived or hanging auxiliary fuel tanks under the wings was also being investigated. On March 10th, some thirty-eight days after the approval of the XP-61 contract, the Under Secretary of War approved a contract worth over five and a half million dollars which called for the construction of 13 YP-61s Night Interceptor Pursuit Airplanes plus one static airframe, without engines and instruments. These aircraft were to be identical to the XP-61s then being developed.

As with any project, Northrop's night fighter also experienced its share of delays and setbacks. In early March 1941, the first major obstacle was encountered when the Army-Navy Standardization Committee decided to standardize on an updraft carburetion for the aircraft's Pratt and Whitney engines. This caused a great deal of anxiety at Northrop due to the fact that their night fighter was designed around a downdraft system. The change would cause approximately 75% scrappage of the work already completed on the engine installation, which would mean about a two month slippage in their timetable. But on the 21st of March, the committee reversed its decision, and the engines with the down-draft carburetion system remained as initially envisioned.

The center nacelle was suspended between two mammoth bar extrusions. These bar extrusions were, at the time, the largest extruded metal pieces manufactured to date. These extrusions connected through the center structure of the fuselage to the wings and supported the huge Pratt & Whitney engines. This twin boom arrangement was not merely a copy of Kelly Johnson's successful P-38 design, as has been thought. This twin boom arrangement was an original part of the night fighting concept, since night fighting combat was to be a head-to-tail affair in that the pursuing aircraft would have to close on the enemy aircraft, and thereby, stay in the slip stream of the aircraft and make positive identification. It was felt the twin rudders would give greater stability to the aircraft.

Many accounts exist of the pilots who were forced to "ride the rudder" of an aircraft to make positive identification before firing. The greenhouse canopy in the aft gunner radio com-

The Air Corps was reluctant to place night fighter business with Douglas Aircraft Co. because of their production problems. Douglas engineer Ed Heinemann, on the other hand, could see multiple applications with their new A-26. The new A-26 Invader was a candidate night fighter. One example, designated XA-26B, would be the only night fighter variant built. (McDonnell Douglas/Harry Gann)

partment was not simply an embellishment for looks on the part of Northrop, as this greenhouse canopy provided a clear field of vision for the gunner-radio operator so that the unwary Widow could not be attacked from the rear. Additionally, the twin rudder allowed one rudder to be in the engine slip stream at all times, even when the aircraft was performing on one engine. This made for much greater pilot confidence in the aircraft and stability of the gun platform.

The aircraft was additionally to have tricycle landing gear, which was fairly new for the day. Lt.Col. Winston W. Kratz had noted that pilots returning from missions during the Battle of Britain flying Beaufighters and Hurricanes of the day were extremely fatigued and indeed scared. Landing a conventional aircraft as any pilot can tell you was a feat in itself. Since the aircraft had literally to be flown until it was tied down to avoid ground looping – an unceremonious swerve off the edge of the runway when brake pressure was applied to one wheel too firmly in one direction. The Black Widow proved to be a joy to the pilot in that if he was able to stick to the main gear on the runway and ease the nose down, he was home free. The tricycle gear would take care of the rest. The P-61 aircraft was to be much heavier than the Mosquito, since it was of all-metal construction. The armor plating was to be of primary importance to the peace of mind of the pilot and for crew safety. Construction of the aircraft was to be semi-monocoque type designed around huge twin radial Pratt & Whitney R-2800s, and the finished product was to look something like an oversized P-38 with a thyroid condition. Its dimensions were indeed those of a medium bomber, wing span over 66 feet and an initial length of 49 feet 4 inches, and a height from ground to stabilizer tip of 14 feet 3 inches.

During the design phase, it was decided that the lower flexible guns, which had been originally planned for the bottom of the aircraft, should be discarded to make provision for more ammunition and increase firepower. The resulting weight of the aircraft, 30,000 pounds, was to be a significant factor in furnishing the highly stable gun platform needed when encountering the slip streams of pursuit aircraft. The auto pilot, or brain, of the aircraft, was deemed an absolute necessity, since night fighting tactics of the intruder type involved long period of tedious waiting and nerve-wracking strain on a pilot. Every system in the aircraft was to have its counterpart back-up except the auto pilot. Its back up was not mechanical; it was that of the human pilot.

A Douglas Design

Douglas engineer Ed Heinemann had been sent to Cuba in December 1940 to work out a problem the Marines were having with their SBD-1 Dauntless dive bombers. On his way back to California he stopped over at Wright Field in Ohio. While there he talked with a Lt.Col. Sims concerning the shortcomings that the Army Air Corps saw in DB-7 (the export version of the AAC A-20 Havoc) in combat flying in Europe. What the Air Corps desired was a modern aircraft to replace the Air Corps' A-20 before the United States was drawn into the war and, in the long term, it was to replace the North American B-25 Mitchell and Martin B-26 Marauder.

On November 5, 1940 the Experimental Engineering Section at Wright Field issued a letter to Douglas Aircraft Company stating that priority should be given to the design of this new aircraft. Ed Heinemann and Project Engineer Robert Donovan developed a preliminary design. A major consideration in the layout of the fuselage was to enable the new aircraft to carry a 75mm cannon. By December 1940 Wright Field believed that this new plane would replace the A-20 in 1942.

Douglas submitted a proposal on January 28, 1941 to the

Materiel Division, Wright Field, for the design of two versions of the new aircraft. One was basically a modern attack plane to replace the A-20. The other was of the same basic design but fitted as a night fighter. Whether Douglas saw the night fighter as an outgrowth of the Air Corps interest in converting the A-20B into a night fighter or as direct competition to Northrop's P-61 is not certain.

Engineering of the new design at Douglas' El Segundo facility continued. Wind tunnel models were produced and data gathered. It was hoped that as a result of an extensive series of wind tunnel tests that were planned that the transition from experimental to production aircraft would be smooth thus minimizing delays and reducing program expenses. A 1/8th scale model was sent to the California Institute of Technology windtunnel in Pasadena, California and at National Advisory Committee for Aeronautics' Langley facility for a comprehensive test program in its 19-foot tunnel, tests of a full-scale nacelle, and tests of large scale wings in the low-turbulence tunnel.

The P-61 in this late 1940 drawing has the basic shape and armament configuration of the final product. (USAF Museum Collection)

One of three wind tunnel models called for in the January 1941 contract for the two experimental P-61s. This is the 1/8th scale model being tested at Caltech's wind tunnel. (Northrop via Balzer)

The engine test stand with the Pratt & Whitney R-2800-25S mounted. Early on in the XP-61 flight test program these engines would prove quite troublesome and would be replaced by the R2800-10 engine. (Northrop via Balzer)

A contract was submitted to Materiel Division in March covering the two airplanes, wind tunnel models and data. The total estimated price was $2,519,793. The Air Corps felt that this seemed to be an unreasonable estimate and further negotiations were conducted with Douglas. Douglas requested that the government consider a cost plus fixed fee contract. Their offer was $2,208,389 plus a fee of 6%, plus the removal of their requested $60,000 per plane flight insurance as requested in the initial proposal. Some time passed before a contract could be signed because of Douglas' refusal to accept a contract without a special clause pertaining to labor shortages and disputes. The government finally relented. They reasoned that because of "greater strength, higher performance, and better crew facilities of the A-26 as compared with the A-20B series" that they would purchase the XA-26A night fighter variant in lieu of 13 night fighter conversions of the A-20B.

Radar Advancements

The Radiation Laboratory at MIT had most of what would be their key people staffed as 1941 opened. Within a few days of the new year, their first 10 cm. radar was mounted on the roof of one of the laboratory's buildings. In two months of ground testing they were successful in picking up echoes from both ground targets and aircraft flying in the area. A version of this equipment was installed in a B-18A Bolo and flown from nearby East Boston Airport on March 10th. Ever improving their equipment, they came to a point where they had an initial design that could be baselined. The laboratory assigned the designation of AI-10 to this equipment. All through the development and testing of their "American-built" radar they had the cooperation and assistance of their British counterparts, in particular Dr. Edward Bowen.

By late spring of 1941 General Chaney of Air Defense Command was requesting the status of AI radar and night fighter aircraft development. The Signal Corps responded that a contract had been let with Western Electric for the production (copy) of 80 sets of British Mark IV-type AI under the Signal Corps designation of SCR-540. They also stated that 75 of these sets were to be installed in A-20Bs. This statement is confusing as earlier in the year the Air Corps, with British approval, dropped the proposal of converting A-20B aircraft into night fighters. In addition to the Western Electric SCR-540 production order, the British were to provide four sets of their Mark IV AI which was to be installed in A-20A aircraft stationed at Wright Field.

To provide limited manufacturing capability for NDRC's

In search of an interim night fighter, the Air Corps pondered modifying Douglas A-20Bs for some time. But Douglas production problems were always a stumbling block. In March 1941 the Air Corps decided to use the money they were planning to spend on the A-20B conversions on the more promising A-26 night fighter. This project would also have its problems. The other versions of the A-26 seemed always to be of a higher priority than the night fighter. The night fighter A-26 project was doomed when the Northrop P-61 night fighter took to the air first. (Air Force Museum collection)

Division D, a Model Shop was established on October 1, 1941, later this would become the Research Construction Company, Inc. RCC was initially under the supervision of Melville Eastham. Successors to this position included E.C. Hutchinson, H.R. Gaither and J.W. Hinkley.

Its function was to manufacture small quantities of both microwave radar components and entire systems developed by the Radiation Laboratory. These systems were used for both Laboratory work and as preproduction units issued to the military service. It also had the capability to produce standard parts not quickly available from other sources. So as not to be in competition with the manufacturing community, its contract stated that it was not to compete with commercial manufacturers but was just to relieve them of the disruptive effect of small quantity production.

Production began one month after its organization and delivery of a small amount of assembly work was made to the Laboratory in December. By this time operations included a sheet metal shop, machine shop, coil winding, engraving radio assembly, mechanical assembly, test, and drafting.

With war lurking over the horizon, the military services were demanding quick delivery of specialized radar equipment for immediate tactical tests. The RCC's operations expanded rapidly, with employment peaking at a work force of 374 people and a plant area of some 66,000 square feet. It added new departments with the increase of the work load. Most Radiation

Laboratory projects saw early production of their electronic marvels come off the RCC production line first. These sets were, for some time, the only ones available to the military and were usually the first to reach combat zones.

The NDRC's Radiation Laboratory at MIT had completed their development work on their AI-10 and were in the process of producing 30 sets. Fifteen of these sets were to be installed in the XP-61 and YP-61 aircraft. One set was scheduled to be turned over to the Western Electric Company. Western Electric was to make refinements, primarily in the area of produceability. At this time the negotiations with Western Electric included an order for 30 of the "refined" sets. This new set was to be designated SCR-520. The report ended with the statement that there were no plans to install any of the AI-10/SCR-520 sets in any of the A-20 type aircraft because "under the best conditions this airplane could not be converted into a night fighter." Then why install the Mark IV/SCR-540 in them? Solely for training purposes?

A couple of other significant activities occurred in June 1941. One of the AI-10 sets was installed in a Royal Canadian Air Force Boeing 247. It was flown to the Fighter Interception Unit at Tangmere where its capabilities were demonstrated for the RAF. During the 247s months of flight tests in England, the AI-10s capabilities were compared with the RAF's AI Mark VIII centimeter radar. It was found that the British radar had the better receiver unit while the American transmitter gave greater

With searchlights gliding through the night skies in search of the enemy, P-61s are seen fending off German bombers in this early illustration. (Wolford Collection)

Lt.Gen. William S. Knudsen (center) of the War Production Board visits Northrop Field. Jack Northrop is on his left and LaMotte T. Cohu, Chairman of the Board and General Manager of Northrop Aircraft, Inc., on the right. (Northrop)

performance. Western Electric in the States would incorporate these findings in their next AI model which would be designated SCR-720.

Also in June the Radar School was established at the Massachusetts Institute of Technology in Cambridge, Mass. under the direction of Dr. Wilmer L. Barrow. The School's purpose was to train a selected group of Army and Navy officers in the principles and techniques of radar. It was intended as a primary course for these officers prior to their attending service schools which would cover the operation and maintenance of specific equipment.

Havoc by Night

On April 2nd, the mock-up board was convened at the Northrop plant. Representatives from the General Headquarters Air Force, Wright Field, the National Defense Research Council and the British Air Commission were present. In general they found the mock-up acceptable. There were, however, a number of changes which they felt were mandatory. The greatest was the removal of the four 20mm cannon from the wings of the aircraft to its belly. They felt that there were two major advantages brought about by this change: first, ease of maintenance and second, improved air flow over the wings. The board also felt that relocation of the armor plates would provide better protection for the crew and ammunition boxes, and also recommended the installation of flame arresters for the engine exhausts which would conceal the aircraft's presence in the night sky. The redistribution of certain radio equipment was also recommended. These changes meant many hours of re-engineering, more tests, and evaluations which added up to about 30 days slippage in schedule, and a cost increase of more than $38,000.

This was not the first major change in the aircraft's design. For as early as February, Materiel Command had desired greater range than that predicted from initial calculations. The aircraft's internal fuel capacity had been increased from 540 gallons in two tanks to 646 gallons in four self-sealed tanks built into the wings. It was approved February 28th. This was not the end; however, for in early March, Wright Field initiated investigations into increasing the internal fuel capacity to even greater amounts and the possibility of hanging external fuel tanks onto the aircraft.

Construction of the two XP-61 aircraft proceeded at a constant rate through the summer months. During this time a number of changes were deliberated of which two were approved in October. The first, and probably most minor, was for Northrop to install government furnished aircraft identification lights. The second, which was approved in mid-month, was for the installation of a pedestal type mount instead of the General Electric ring type for the gun site which was to be used in connection with the aircraft's turret. Northrop desired that

Mockup of the Radiation Laboratory's AI-10 radar. It would be test flown from nearby East Boston Airport on March 10, 1941. (The MIT Museum)

Closeup of the Douglas B-18 Bolo with a clear plastic nose with no framework and the antenna "dish" clearly visible. (The MIT Museum)

The Radiation Lab's borrowed Bolo readies for take-off with AI-10 radar installed. Both airborne and seaborne targets were successfully detected. (The MIT Museum)

change due to difficulties they had encountered in attempting to install the ring type. During that same month, it also became apparent that General Electric would not be able to supply the turret for the first plane under the priority (A-1-B) which the aircraft were procured. It was decided to install a mock-up turret for flight test purposes thus preventing any additional delays.

Night Havoc

Government changes in requirements, manufacturing problems, and the usual design problems that are encountered when engineers are pushing into new technologies were all impacting the P-61s production schedule. Once again the Army realized that steps needed to be taken to develop a "stopgap" night fighter. The Douglas A-20 Havoc seemed to be the only present aircraft in the inventory that could be so used but, as discussed earlier, the Army did not want to add to Douglas' production problems. Someone hit on the idea of possibly using the 59 A-

20s partially assembled then sitting idle on Douglas' Santa Monica field.

The Army had ordered A-20 aircraft with D-2 exhaust driven turbosupercharged R-2600-7 engines and A-20As with the R-2600-11s (no turbosupercharger) in a contract dated June 30, 1939. These aircraft were similar in appearance to the DB-7 export series but were structurally quite different. By the end of 1939 the A-20As were rolling off the production lines, but the A-20 series were experiencing cooling problems with their turbosupercharged Wright engines. Actually both the A-20 and A-20A series were having over-heating problems, but the turbosupercharged Cyclones were having extreme problems. Only four of the 63 A-20 series entered flight test with their supercharged engines. Of these, one was still designated as an A-20 while the other three had been modified for photo reconnaissance operations and became part of the F-3 series. The first A-20 (S/N 39-735) was undergoing flight testing at Wright Field when the decision was reached in 1941 to modify it for the night fighter role.

Installation of British Mk. IV/SCR-540 AI radar in an A-20 aircraft. On the right is transmitting antenna mounted in the nose of the aircraft. In the center is the azimuth antenna which is mounted on each side of the fuselage. On the left is the elevation antenna which is mounted on the top and bottom of the left wing. On the transmitting and azimuth antennas the forward (single) rod is called the Director and the loop behind it is the antenna. For the elevation antennas, the forward rod is the antenna and the rear rod is a Reflector. (McDonnell Douglas/Harry Gann)

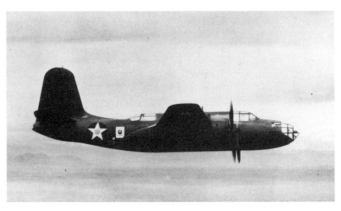

The first A-20-DO, serial nr. 39-735, was the only one of the 63 aircraft procured by the Air Corps with turbosupercharged R2600-7 engines to be completed and flight tested. This aircraft would be modified as the sole XP-70-DO night fighter (retaining its troublesome engines). Three others would be converted into photo recce (F-3) ships while the remaining would have the turbosupercharged R-2600 engines replaced and, similar to the XP-70, be modified into night fighters. (Peter M. Bowers' Collection via Castle Graphics)

The A-20A-DO was ordered at the same time as the A-20-DO, except without the turbosupercharger. These aircraft were rolling off the production line and entering squadron service while only one of the A-20-DOs was in flight test. (Peter M. Bowers' Collection via Castle Graphics)

Modifications to this aircraft included changes in the forward nose area to accept the installation of the AI radar equipment. Initially this was Britain's Mark IV AI, referred to as AI-4 within the Air Corps. The production P-70s would have the US built Mark IV designated as SCR-540 by the Signal Corps. The transmitting antenna was installed in the nose of the aircraft, the azimuth antennae was located on both sides of the fuselage while the elevation antennae were located on the top and bottom of the left wing. The modifications also included the addition of a housing under the bomb bay to accommodate four 20mm cannon and 60 rounds of ammunition per gun. With all this it received the new designation of XP-70. The turbosupercharged R-2600-7 engines were maintained on the XP-70 variant only.

Flight testing of the XP-70 proved it to be a suitable aircraft for its intended purpose (that of a stop-gap machine until the P-61 reached the field). Authorization was issued on October 15, 1941 for the conversion of the remaining 59 A-20s to the new night fighter configuration; these planes were designated P-70.

The XP-70s career would be relatively short lived. It spent most of its time at Wright Field as a flying testbed. In November 1942 it went to Orlando, Florida where the test community as well as the night fighter training organization had a chance to use it. On February 5, 1943 it was involved in an accident at Kissimmee Field, Florida. By the end of March the Air Corps decided it was beyond repair and scrapped it.

The P-70 was like the XP-70 except the radar was Western Electric produced SCR-540A and the non-turbosupercharged R-2600-11 engines (as used on the A-20A model) were installed. Changes to the A-20-DOs to make them into P-70-DOs included a 24 volt electrical system and a 250 gallon leakproof fuel tank in the bomb bay. All standard A-20 armament was removed and four 20mm cannon in a "tub" was attached to the belly of the aircraft. These cannon carried 60 rounds per gun. The forward crew compartment equipment was deleted and the SCR-540 AI

radar set was installed. Also installed was the SCR-274N HF and SCR-522 VHF command radio sets. Also, provisions were made for the future installation of the SCR-515 IFF equipment and more extensive crew armor plate was provided. All these aircraft carried the same armament arrangement as the XP-70. The entire aircraft was painted matt black, as were its early British counterparts of the day. Interestingly enough, Jack Northrop was one of the principal designer engineers of the Douglas model 7B, the forerunner to the DB-7/A-20/P-70 series.

Pilots compartment in an P-70. Unlike the P-61, the P-70 pilot did not have a radar scope. He got his directions verbally from the R/O in the rear. Some P-61 squadrons and their pilots felt that the pilot had enough to do than to try to watch the scope and had them removed from the aircraft. (McDonnell Douglas/Harry Gann)

The 81st Fighter Squadron started its training in August 1942 with 39 pilots and the first group of R/Os to arrive from the Signal Corps radar school at Boca Raton, Florida. Their inventory of aircraft included the three DB-7Bs pictured above, one B-18, and twenty P-70s. (Izenour)

Chapter 3

War Comes to America

As a result of the reports of the Air Corps "observers" and the intelligence that was received through the military attaches stationed at the various embassies, the need to draw up specifications for the Air Corps night fighting aircraft had to be addressed. In a letter from General Arnold to General Spaatz, Chief of the Materiel Division, Arnold lays out his thoughts on the subject:

It is becoming clearer as time passes that the present war in Europe is developing the necessity for pursuit planes of new capabilities and types.

In order to meet requirements along this line which will be imposed upon the Air Force in case we enter any war in the near future, we must start proceedings at once to develop these new types for production at such time as they can be thrown into the factories without slowing up the output.

The radio detector is a necessity for all night fighters. The British search-light plane provides means whereby the radio detector can be far more efficiently used. A larger number of cannon, or .50 or .30 caliber machine guns are a necessity in any night fighter due to the short period of time of contact with hostile aircraft. It would therefore appear that we must develop a night fighter that has a detector and probably the search-light in a lead plane of a flight with heavily armed planes capable of delivering the maximum volume of fire from the other planes in that flight.

The RAF's influence on American planning can be seen quite clear. The "search-light" equipped night fighter is in reference to Great Britain's "Turbinlite" project. When France and Belgium collapsed, Douglas DB-7 aircraft that had been procured by those countries were diverted to England. When received by the RAF in mid-1940, they went to various depots where they were modified to carry British equipment. Initially these aircraft were designated as Boston I's. But many would be converted for night intruder and night fighter roles; these were called Havoc I's.

Of the various night fighting schemes the RAF came up with, Turbinlite seemed to catch the US Air Corps interest. Originally called a Helmore light, it was the idea of Wing Commander W. Helmore who, besides being a pilot, was an engineer. A 2,700 million candlepower search light was installed in the nose of the Havoc, along with the antennae of Mk IV AI, and the power supply for the light was installed in the bomb bay. The added weight of the Helmore light system was so great that all armament was deleted. One could only imagine what the flying qualities of this quite heavy plane with a blunt nose was like.

The operating scenario was that the Havoc I (Turbinlite) would be directed to the area of a target by GCI. Once in range the aircraft took control using its Mk IV AI radar. When within 3,000 feet, day fighters, usually Hurricanes, would form on the Havoc. The Havoc had white lines paralleling the trailing edge of its wings and special formation lights. Then when the formation was within 1,000 feet, the Havoc pilot would turn on the Turbinlite illuminating the target. The theory was that then the faster fighters would go in for the kill. In reality, everyone was blinded by the light; the enemy could easily maneuver out of the light beam, and the system was basically a failure (only one kill was recorded by the 10 Turbinlite squadrons formed by the RAF).

Col. Ira C. Eaker, who would play a commanding role in the Army Air Forces in Europe once the US entered the war, was sent over to England in late October 1941. There were a number of items on the agenda that General Arnold had given him. Among them were: the need of escort fighters for heavy bombers, night fighter operations, and what equipment should the US manufacture and what the British could provide. This was all in the context of a joint British-American effort at defeating the German war-machine.

In Col. Eaker's subsequent report he states:

They (the RAF) believe that there should be a specialized night fighter, probably a 2-engine plane, of sufficient speed to overhaul the

Converted RAF Havocs to the Turbinlite configuration was to be the ultimate in night fighters, or so they thought. The 1st Pursuit Squadron (NF) was planned to be equipped with this type of aircraft. Close-up of the aircraft's Helmore lamp is shown below. (NASM/Smithsonian)

fast night bomber, probably with a 50 mile differential in favor of the fighter. They should have armor forward, but there would be no requirement for armor in the rear. They should have sufficient armament of heavy caliber to knock down the heavy bomber and pierce the heaviest armor. They must have sufficient ceiling to reach all bombers and their engines should be of a type which would obtain optimum performance at the level in which the enemy bombers are operating. They believe the armament would probably be one 40mm, two 20mm and two 50 caliber guns. A certain number of these planes must be equipped with a turbine light. This plane must make provisions for an AI operator. They thought the Beaufighter, now in use as a night fighter, had many desirable characteristics but that a plane of this type should have good stability, greater ease of control in instrument flying and a higher speed. They pointed also to the advisability of having a plane of good landing characteristics on account of the many times when a night fighter has to land with poor visibility. The vision forward in a night fighter is a big feature since the pilot relies on outside vision generally under conditions of darkness and poor visibility for the location of his target after minimum AI range is reached.

Under "Miscellaneous Observations" Col. Eaker remarks:

If, as appears likely, a large portion of bombing is to be at night then night fighters become a definite requirement. Night fighting is a specialized form of aerial fighting requiring specialized equipment and training. It is better to have a night fighter squadron in each fighter group than to have a separate night fighter group. It is best that we should at once organize a night fighter squadron in each of our fighter groups and begin this specialized tactical training without delay.

During his talks with the English, Air Marshal Lynell, Chief of Experimental Development, MAP, suggested that the two countries' air forces would benefit through the exchange of aircraft. The RAF would be glad to provide the US enough airplanes for a squadron if the US would reciprocate with a like number of "new airplanes used operationally in our (the US) service. He thought there might be imminent advantages; for example, an exchange of a squadron of British fighters equipped for night fighting for a squadron of P-38s."

While in England, Col. Eaker worked closely with General Chaney and his staff at the Special Observer Group (SPOBS). SPOBS was the outgrowth of the "observers" that were crisscrossing the Atlantic. It was established as a full time organization in London with General Chaney in command (Chaney also retained command of Air Defense Command for a while). Through the help of Chaney and the staff at SPOBS, the idea of the British providing Turbinlite night fighters and training for American crews was followed up. When the Japanese attacked the Hawaiian Islands on December 7th, project TURBINLITE was already being established. By mid-January 1942, General Arnold had the plans put in motion.

The A-20 equipped 15th Bombardment Squadron (Light), part of the 27th Bombardment Group (Light), stationed at Lawson Field, Fort Benning, Georgia, became the first American night fighter squadron in quite an unusual manner. It was by

This May 1942 picture was taken during the period when the 1st Pursuit Squadron (NF) were undergoing flying training under the guidance of the RAF's 107 Squadron. The event is a party in the RAF Mess at Molesworth when the "student Yanks" were made "honorary" members of the RAF. Two of the squadron's pilots are shown in this photo: Lt. Phillip Henning (third from left) and Capt. William C. Odell (fifth from left). Lt. Henning was later killed in action. Capt. Odell would join the AAF's night fighters, after serving with the 15th Bomb Squadron in England and North Africa, and would eventually become the commanding officer of the 547th NFS in the Pacific. (Odell)

telephone that they were informed by Headquarters, Army Air Force, Washington, D.C., on March 26, 1942, that they were to become a night fighter squadron. It was during this telephone conversation that they were appropriately redesignated the 1st Pursuit Squadron (Night Fighter). It would seem that in the Air Corps planning of the TURBINLITE project that the 15th Bomb Squadron had been selected in late 1940. When the 27th Bomb Group was ordered to the Philippines, the 15th Bomb Squadron was left in Georgia and attached to the V Air Support Command (which would later become the Ninth Air Force). Their new mission was to be part of the new Eighth Air Force in England. They were to receive training by the Royal Air Force in RAF Turbinlite equipped Havocs after which the RAF would provide a squadron's worth of these aircraft to the 1st Pursuit.

For nearly three weeks the squadron took on personnel to bring it up to strength as a night fighter squadron, going from 192 enlisted men and 16 officers to 498 enlisted men and 41 officers. The rapidity at which additional personnel, including night fighter specialists as radar operators and mechanics, were provided to the squadron also indicates that much behind the scenes activity had proceeded that March telephone call. Most of the added personnel came from the 48th Light Bombardment Group based at Savannah, Georgia, which included 20 additional pilots; five were "experienced" while the other 15 were just three months out of flying school. The Foreign Wing of Ferry Command at West Palm Beach, Florida, provided Lt. Peter D. Green and 24 microwave specialists, who had undergone training at the Signal Corps radar maintenance school at Boca Raton,

Florida. The radar operators came by way of the Royal Canadian Air Force. These were Americans that joined the RCAF prior to the US's entry into the war and had been trained in Canada.

On Saturday, April 18th, a train departed Fort Benning, Georgia, with the 1st Pursuit Squadron (NF) as its cargo, 23 cars with personnel and equipment, plus three boxcars and seven flatcars with the unit's vehicles and other equipment. Ten days later they were at Pier 90 of the Port of New York. Among the

personnel of the 1st Pursuit Squadron was Capt. William C. Odell:

On April 29th, the train moved the units personnel from Fort Dix, New Jersey (staging area) to Pier 90 in New York. The scorched 'Normandie' was laying on her side in Pier 88, about 50 feet away. The ship bearing the 1st PS (NF) was a British merchant cruiser, the H.M.S. Cathay, making her first voyage as a troopship. This was a vessel of the Peninsular and Oriental Line, refitted by the Bethlehem Steel Company with armor and black-out equipment. It had two 6-inch guns, four light AA cannon equivalent to our 37 mm, and numerous Vickers machine guns fitted with AA sights. Deckhands were Indian Madagascars. We were at sea on April 30th in a convoy that included the Aquatania carrying 7,500 troops; the Cathay was loaded with 3,000. Our convoy had destroyer escort, and one British aircraft carrier with Swordfish or Gladiator aircraft of the Fleet Air Arm aboard. At this point, there were 23 ships in the convoy, but more were to be picked up passing Boston.

This was the Eighth Air Force on its way to England.

Most of the convoy put into Belfast, Ireland, on May 11th, with part of the personnel debarking the following day. The night fighters were among those who remained aboard. On Wednesday evening, May 13th, they were piloted up Bristol Bay to a berth in Newport Harbor in Wales. The next morning, under the command of Major John W. Griffith, the unit debarked and went by train to their first station at Grafton Underwood Airdrome in the English Midlands. The squadron history for the month of May 1942 states that, "The distinction of being the first men ashore belonging to the first American tactical unit ever stationed in Great Britain goes to Lt. John H. Gravestock." Here, assigned to VIII Ground Air Support Command, they were to start their night fighter training under British tutors.

But the training they received was mostly informal meetings in small groups of 1st PS people and Royal Air Force night fighter/intruder crews on general night fighting subjects as well as Turbinlite operations. Some of the 1st Pursuit's crews were sent on detached service to RAF night fighter squadrons. Those of the squadron who had previous night fighter training, mostly radar operators (additional R/O's joined the squadron at Grafton Underwood), shared what knowledge they had with their fellow American-would-be night fighters. A new Flight Surgeon gave the aircrews a talk on eating foods high in vitamin A for better night vision. They also received lectures on security measures, English customs and mannerisms, money differences, history, and local flying regulations. A number of VIPs from VIII Bomber Command, including General Eaker, also paid them a visit. All flying activities were in two borrowed Boston's and a Tigermoth from the RAF – the 1st Pursuit Squadron (Night Fighter) never received aircraft of its own.

But this all came to an abrupt end in late May, not quite three weeks after their arrival in the British Isles. A letter from the US Army Air Force's Liaison Officer at Number 8 Group, RAF, redesignated the squadron back to their original of 15th Bomb Squadron (L) on May 30,1942. Still assigned to VIII Ground Air Support Command, they were attached to VIII Bomber Command. What had caused this unforseen occurrence? Indications are that it was based on political more than military rationale. In late May, General Arnold was in England with a delegation. Apparently during one of his meetings with Churchill, the Prime Minister needled the General as to when American bombing operations would start. American Independence Day, July 4th, entered the picture at some point during this period. VIII Bomber Command would not have any of their heavy bombers in-theater for a number of months. The only unit in-theater with any bomber training, even if it was "light" bombardment, was the 1st Pursuit Squadron (NF). Whatever the exact details behind this reversal of fortunes, the 15th Bomb Squadron was back in the bombing business. With the change in mission, the radar operators were converted back to bombardiers and the radar mechanics were retrained to communications types, with others being transferred to other Eighth Air Force units.

Though its career as a night fighter unit was short and uneventful, they did go on to make Air Force history. On July 4, 1942, six crews of the 15th Bomb Squadron, manning borrowed Boston III's from No. 226 Squadron RAF, flew with six 226 manned Bostons to strike four Luftwaffe airfields in the Low Countries. This mission inaugurated United States Army Air Forces operations in the European Theater of Operations.

Night Fighter Training

In February 1940, Air Defense command was inaugurated with Brig.Gen. Chaney and Capt. Saville guiding its infant footsteps. By late October, Major Saville had summarized the official plan for air defense in a document entitled "Air Defense Doctrine." It was also in October that Major Gen. Jim Chaney, Saville, and Major Gen. Bart Yount would go to England to "observe" as so many others had previously. After six weeks of taking in all they could of RAF and ground air defense operations, they returned to the US in November. Their report, along with their recommendation that US air defense operations pattern those of the RAF, went to General Marshall. They were given the go-ahead and plans were put into motion. That December Chaney became commander of the newly activated Northeast Air District headquartered at Mitchel Field, NY, redesignated First Air Force a few months later. Also in December, Yount would take on the newly activated Southeast Air District (to become Third Air Force) based Mac Dill Field, Florida. In March 1941, a conference was called in which Chaney and Saville outlined to many general-grade officers, including the commanding officers of the four continental air forces. The theme of this multi-day session was that the American air force had much to learn and there was a lot of catching up to be accomplished.

Another of those many reorganizations within the War Department occurred in March 1942. In this reshuffle a director of Air Defense was created. Assigned to this post was Colonel Saville. By this time Chaney, who had headed the Air Defense Department, was spending much of his time in England, which would become a permanent assignment lasting into mid-1942. A project with the code name of TRIGGER had been inaugurated. This was a plan in which a model air defense sector in the US would be created in the form of the RAF's system and would have RAF personnel assisting in its establishment and in the training of US Army Air Forces personnel.

The condition of the American air defense system was quite lacking in all respects. In late December 1941 British radar expert Sir Robert Watson-Watt was invited to the US to make a personal survey of its air defenses. He found no GCI radar

By year's end the night fighter training program was down to two of the DB-7s (one pictured above), 21 P-70s, three C-78s, and one B-18. The 13 AT-11s so badly needed, and pleaded for so many times, for R/O training were still not in sight. (Izenour)

The second A-20 (serial nr. 39-736) became the first "production" P-70 and was sent to Wright Field, Ohio, for testing (the first A-20, s/n 39-735, became the XP-70). (USAF)

comparable to that in England, that high frequency (HF) radio, which is very poor and static ridden, was still being used in aircraft to ground communication rather than the much improved radio sets operating in the very high frequency (VHF) range. Long range radar stations were poorly located in many cases. Electronic equipment to distinguish friendly aircraft from enemy (IFF equipment) was lacking. And there was no night fighter force. To make sure they had the correct picture, American personnel conducted an independent but like survey at the same time. The results were the same!

To put TRIGGER into motion, Col. Saville instigated planning for a Air Defense Operational Training Unit. This Unit would create an RAF-style air defense network and would include a number of RAF advisors. The "Plan for the Organization and Operations of the Air Defense Operational Training Unit" were drawn up by Col. Willis R. Taylor and approved on March 18, 1942. Saville secured the establishment, through Bart Yount's Third Air Force, of the Air Defense Operational Training Unit. Activated on March 26, 1942, it had its name changed to the Interceptor Command School four days later.

The Interceptor Command School was to be headquartered in central Florida at Orlando. Personnel for the school were drawn from a number of organizations in the area. The Headquarters and Headquarters Squadron and the Signal Headquar-

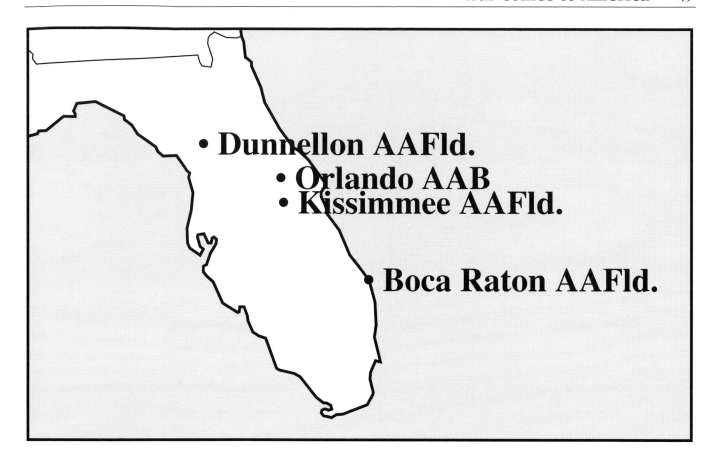

ters and Headquarters Company of V Interceptor Command would provide much of the original manpower, including the Vth's commanding officer, Col. Taylor. These two units of V Interceptor Command had been en route to the Philippines when war broke out and had been ordered back. Also, the 502nd Signal Regiment, AW, the 50th Pursuit Group (Interceptor), and other base service units were integrated into this new organization. On the 29th, Col. Taylor assumed command of the School.

Col. Taylor's plan included a Night Fighter Division under the Fighter Department. The Night Fighter Training Section of the plan broke out training for pilots and for radar observers. The pilots were to receive training via lectures, classes, synthetic operation, and actual operation in night controlled intercepts. This training included familiarization with equipment, procedures, and communications discipline. The Radar Observers were trained in close coordination with the pilot training.

The plan could not be put into action for the lack of equipment, which remained the status for the next couple of months. On May 16th good news came down the chain of command; three Douglas DB-7s (export version of the AAF's A-20) were being transferred to the School. One of the RAF staff at the School was Flight Lieutenant Davis. Davis went to the Link Trainer factory and Wright Field that same week to initiate construction of an Airborne Intercept Link Trainer. In

this same time period, it was decided that one of the squadrons of the 50th Fighter Group (Special) would be given the responsibility of carrying out the night fighter training tasks. On May 28, the 81st Fighter Squadron (Sp) was assigned this responsibility. On the 29th, the School was renamed the Fighter Command School. This was done to indicate the broadening of the scope of its responsibilities, and it was placed under the Commanding General of the AAF. This change was described in an AAF report as:

The mission of the school remained that of tactical training and testing in the field of air defense. It was consequently described as, 'a *school of war* furnishing post-graduate training under operational conditions to key personnel of the Air Defense team.'

With the appointment of the 81st FS(Sp) as the night fighter training organization, a number of personnel who had shown great interest in this field were assigned. On June 10, Maj. Donald B. Brummel, who was "an officer keenly enthusiastic on the subject of night fighters and night fighting," became its commanding officer. Four days later fellow night fighter enthusiast Capt. Griffin D. Davis was assigned. By the 20th, a Night Fighter Department was established under the Fighter Command School and Major Brummel was assigned as its Director, while remaining C.O. of the 81st FS(Sp). Two instructors were soon added to the Department, Lieutenants Robert F. Sugnet and

William M. Copley. Soon following was Capt. Leonard R. Hall. Capt. Hall, another night fighter convert with an electronics background, would become the first radio ("radar" not used at this time) observer (R/O) to be trained in the organization; this being his fourth rating.

Though Brummel had been put in charge and an organization to put the training into action had been established, "higher ups" were to give their assistance. On July 4th Colonel Taylor wrote to Col. Saville, Director of Air Defense, concerning his opinion on night fighter training. The Fighter Command School's unit history states:

On July 4, 1942, Colonel Taylor erected his ideas on the night fighter training into a policy. He felt that the pilots must be brought to a high level of training in instrument flying, blind landings and takeoffs, night formation, night gunnery, operator-pilot airborne interception teamwork, GCI control, and general air defense procedures. Most important was the necessity that all pilots become temperamentally at ease in night operations. Radar operators were to be given operational practice in airborne interception, both with an experienced pilot and with the pilot with whom they would be teamed. These operators should also become highly proficient in flexible gunnery. Maintenance and administrative personnel was to be given a period of working together so as to be able to support the combat crews. Colonel Taylor

recommended that the entire training for night fighter organizations should be given at Orlando because of the location of experienced night fighter personnel and because of the facilities available there.

On the 16th, Brig.Gen. Muir S. Fairchild, Director of Military Requirements, AAF, responded that training in the service and operational tests of night fighter aircraft and airborne radar equipment employed in controlled interception were the School's responsibility. Whether or not all this had any bearing on the matter, the Night Fighter Department was redesignated the Night Fighter Division and it was put under the Fighter Department (somewhat of a reduction in rank it would seem). Don Brummel remained in command but Capt. Griffin D. Davis took over the 81st FS(SP) in place of Brummel, "who was directed to give his full attention to the direction of the Night Fighter Division."

Apparently Brummel and Saville, or their staff, had been in communication since earlier in the year. A flow and training chart for key night fighter personnel had been agreed to by mid-July. This plan called for 17 night fighter squadrons to complete training by August 30, 1943. The first and second squadrons were to be assigned to the Panama Canal Zone and the next two to the Hawaiian Islands. Under this plan trainees were to start arriving in late July. Trained crew output for the night fighter

When the 59 P-70s left Douglas Aircraft's Santa Monica, California, field they headed in three directions. Twenty-five went to Hawaii to equip the 6th Fighter Squadron. The 6th would soon thereafter take them into combat. Twenty-four went to the night fighter training program in Florida where neophyte night fighter crews would fly them. And the remaining 10 would be used in various testing/evaluation programs. (Mc Donnell Douglas/Harry Gann)

trainers was to be about 50 pilots and 40 Radio Observers(I)'s per month. This was to achieve a grand total of 2,012 "key personnel," which included 617 pilots and 495 R/O's.

Radar training for both operation and maintenance had come about somewhat earlier. One of the first students was Col. Dick Ehlert, then a private in the U.S. Army Air Corps:

When the USAAC awoke to the fact that there was in fact a thing called 'RADAR' (Radio Detection and Ranging), they immediately hit the panic switch and said we got to have this. They took a nucleus of personnel from Scott Field, Illinois, which then conducted all radio operation and maintenance training and moved to Morrison Field, Florida. Morrison Field was then, and is now, West Palm Beach International Airport.

Morrison Field was used until April or May of 1942. We went to school in barbed wire enclosed buildings. Security was indeed tight. If you were a student or instructor and got loaded in town, you were immediately bounced out of school. In mid-1942 the government leased the Boca Raton Club, furniture and all, and the school moved to the Club.

When the flying field and the buildings were constructed, the training moved across the highway, but the Boca Raton Club was retained as Officers' quarters. This was pretty good thinking – done on the Field Grade level. They needed this as officers' quarters like a moose needs a hat rack.

Additional information on the early R/O is found in the history of the 414th NFS, the first night fighter squadron to be activated under the Florida night fighter training organization for operational duty:

The observers were members of the first class of A.I. (Airborne Interception) radar observers ever to be trained by the Army Air Forces. The men selected for this pioneer course were hand-picked from a large group of volunteers, first for their scholastic record at the Air Corps Technical School for radio at Scott Field, Illinois, and second for their high physical and mental qualifications. The group was screened through three more competitive examinations before completing their ground training in an advanced technical school at Boca Raton, Florida, and the Air Force School of Applied Tactics, Orlando, Florida, some twelve months later. At this time they were again subjected to physical examinations for combat flying.

The first radar operators arrived from the Signal Corps radar school at Boca Raton, Florida, in August. Also in the month the pilot population in the 81st FS rose to 39. These crews had no dual instrument or dual AI transition training due to a lack of equipment. At this time the 81st had one B-18, three DB-7Bs and 24 P-70s. Aircraft such as the Beech AT-11 were needed for the R/O's dual training. One of the first R/Os to arrive about this time to undergo training was Paul DiLabbio:

We had no instructors and did everything the hard way. Most of the pilots were from observation squadrons and generally were graduates of pilot classes '41-A thru C, with a few new pilot graduates from 42 May classes. All the radar observers were graduates of radio and radar operator and mechanic courses and able to pass a flight physical. All the R/O's were privates except for two officers from the Signal Corps that had been to England as observers of the British night fighters.

After practicing intercepts, the pilots would indulge in low flying techniques – skimming the ocean at Daytona Beach chasing all the bathers on to the beach and then reversing course and chase them all back in the ocean. Or catch a sail boat on one of the many lakes and pull up in a steep climb right over the sail boat and try to spill the sail with the prop wash. There were a few pilots reprimanded and fined for tipping sail boats.

By September the pilot cadre was up to 60, but no additional aircraft. To compound the problem, 30 percent of these aircraft's time was required in support of non-night fighter training requirements (e.g. target towing, radar calibrating, searchlight fighter missions). The one possible bright spot was the arrival of RAF pilot Wing Commander D.V. Ivins and Flying Officer L. Langley, RAFVR. They were fresh from England and would be part of the RAF advisory staff whose job it was to impart their expertise on the fledgling USAAF night fighters.

The night fighters efforts did not go unnoticed. One day in late 1942 they were visited by Col. Earl W. Barnes of the Air Defense Department of Fighter Command School. Captain Hall remembers:

People didn't believe in radar. One day Col. Barnes came down. He was a fighter (day) type. He didn't believe in this magic radar either. I remember Don Brummel telling him that I could vector him into a B-17 at night.

He didn't believe it; he had to be shown. So we checked him out. We told him that he had to fly good formation with the '17. Otherwise you'll come in too fast and overshoot. The tactics were that we would be below the target, keeping it in the lighter part of the sky. This way you could see its silhouette or the rings of its exhaust.

So we went up in a P-70 that night. GCI vectored us to a target. Soon I had it on our AI, so I took over and started guiding Barnes to the B-17. I told him that we were getting into range and for him to throttle back. Well, he didn't. I told him he was going to overshoot. His reply was, 'I don't see anything out there!' All at once he yelled, 'I see him!' I looked up and there were two. We were right under and behind one B-17, closing fast. Barnes throttled back immediately. As he pulled up we hit the bomber's prop wash. It just flipped us – we were in a spin. Boy, I was pinned to the side of the wall. I thought, 'This is it.' But he got it out.

He was convinced. He said, 'I believe it now. I didn't think that there was an airplane in the sky, then all at once, there it was.' It's very horrifying, because when you break up to an airplane at night in total darkness it's not there then it's right on top of you – you've got to believe it.

Class '42-A consisting of 20 pilots and 20 radio observers commenced on September 1, 1942. The pilots received 173 hours of ground school that month while the observers had 92 hours. But they still were unable to receive dual instrument or dual AI training. Neither aircraft capable for this type of training nor the AI Link Trainer were available. Because of this defi-

ciency, the School requested that no additional students be assigned in October.

If things don't work, reorganize! In September, once again, a change in designation; the Night Fighter Division now became the Night Fighter Department (Dark) on the 21st of that month. The 81st FS (Sp) was detached from its parent 50th FG (Sp) and placed under the new department. No miracles were brought about with these changes. The P-70 count had gone down to 23 with the loss of one aircraft in an accident. The DB-7 fleet remained at three and no AT-11 was in sight (it was estimated that 13 were required in order to carry out the assigned training program), though three T-50s were allotted from the September production run, and the B-18 count had doubled to two. Word was also that the AI Link Trainer would not be ready until November. Since early September, P-70 exhaust stack problems and a lack of all spare parts were causing many of the aircraft to be out of commission for extended lengths of time. By the end of October these problems were still a major bottleneck.

October seemed to be a month in which the night fighter organization went through yet more reorganizing. Maybe "shuffle" would be a better word; a shuffle in which someone seemed to be trying to prove the hand was quicker than the eye. Two new squadrons were activated on October 4, the 348th and 349th Night Fighter Squadrons. The plan was for the command structure of the 348th to be established first, so the 349th was attached to the 348th for administration, rations, operations, training and command. At the same time both squadrons were attached to the 81st Fighter Squadron (Special). In actuality, most personnel and equipment were transferred from the 81st to the two newly created squadrons during the first half of the month. On October 22nd, with just 38 enlisted personnel left, the 81st was declared inactive, transferred (on paper) back to the 50th Fighter Group while the two night fighter squadrons were assigned to the Night Fighter Department (Dark). Well, not quite. On that same date the Night Fighter Department (Dark) was once again redesignated the Night Fighter Division and was subordinate to the Fighter Department! The Fighter Command School also underwent a major change this month. On October 27, the Army Air Forces School of Applied Tactics was activated. Under AAFSAT the Fighter Command School and other organizations were integrated, as well as the establishment of an Army Air Forces Board. Initially Col. Taylor of the Fighter Command School served as interim Commandant, but within 10 days Brig.Gen. Hume Peabody was assigned that post. Gen. Peabody had been the Director of War Organization and Movement at the AAF's Headquarters in Washington. Gordon Saville would soon, as a Brigadier General, relocate to Florida and become Director of Tactical Development. This organization, as a special adjunct of AAFSAT, had the task of experimenting with AAF planes and equipment and to decide

Secretary of War Henry L. Stimson, and party, inspect a lineup of aircraft at Wright Field on July 2, 1942. Lined up are a Beaufighter with early microwave AI radar, P-70 s/n 39-736, and a B-17E. Another B-17E is in the background and the tail of a B-25 is sticking out of a hangar. (NASM/ Smithsonian)

Head-on view of the P-70. Quite visible is the fact that the SCR-540 AI radar's elevation antennas are on the left wing only (the upper antenna is somewhat obscured due to the angle of the photo). The distance that the azimuth antennas are away from the fuselage sides can also be seen. (USAF)

upon the most efficient tactical use of each. In this capacity, Saville operated with the Air Forces Board and through the tactical development boards of each of the departments.

Personnel started to be assigned to the new squadrons almost immediately. The first officer to be assigned, was 1st Lt. Paul K. Hutton, who was given the duty of being the 348th C.O. until the 81st's C.O., Major Griffin D. Davis, was transferred in mid-month to that position in the 348th. As October progressed, there seemed to be plans to make the 348th, or at least its command personnel, into a Group. A "Provisional Night Fighter Headquarters" was established with Major Davis as its Commanding Officer. A Major William W. Keith, Jr., who had been the C.O. of the 26th Air Base Squadron at Orlando, was transferred over and given the assignment of Executive Officer of the "provisional group"; 1st Lt. Louie M. Phillips was assigned as "group" A-1 (Personnel), Capt. Charles W. Peckham as A-2 (Intelligence), 1st Lt. Amberse M. Banks as A-3 (Operations and Training) and Capt. Elbridge Teel A-4 (Supply).

With the change of name back to Night Fighter Division, Lt.Col. Brummel remained Director; Capt. Leonard R. Hall was Assistant Director and Officer in Charge of Tactics and Techniques; 1st Lt. Robert J. Rentfro was School Supervisor; 2nd Lt. Raymond E. Karcher had the duty of Projects Officer, and 2nd Lt. Joseph P. Wheeler, a transfer from Fighter Command School, was assigned as Radar and Communications Officer.

Meanwhile, back at Air Defense in Washington, D.C., Col. Saville defined the training objectives for the night fighter program and set them forth as follows per the Fighter Command School unit history:

The 348th and 349th Squadrons were to be used as parent organizations to train personnel under the direction of the Fighter Command School for all additional night fighter squadrons which would normally be activated by the Air Forces to which they were assigned. Key personnel would be available from these sources for each night fighter squadron:

Key Personnel	Number	Source
Combat pilots	15	Two Engine Flying Schools
Radio Observer (S)	1	AAF Technical School No. 2
Radio Observer (I)	13	AAF Technical School No. 2
Radio Mechanic (I)	13	AAF Technical School No. 2

Of the 15 combat pilots allocated, three were to be experienced personnel from tactical units with one having at least two years and the others one year of experience as rated pilots. A total of 15 squadrons were to be activated before September 30, 1943, but it was probable that these figures would be changed. The immediate need was to train key personnel for three squadrons, two of which would go to Hawaii and one to Panama.

The need for the Hawaiian and Panama night fighters was a pressing matter as a Japanese night attack was feared to be imminent. With this mid-October agreement between the School and the Air Defense Directorate, was the stipulation that a total of four qualified radio observers, 20 qualified AI mechanics, 24 pilots, and 18 observer trainees would be furnished by November 30th for service between these two locations. By the end of October, 1st Lt. Robert F. Sugnet of the Night Fighter Division was on his way to Hawaii in advance of the others. There he would immediately assist the 6th Fighter Squadron in becoming a night fighter squadron.

The ambitious training schedule envisioned soon fell into the same snags as all previous plans – insufficient equipment. The plea for 13 urgently needed AT-11 was once again made in early November. By the month's end, the plea was repeated with like results. During November they attempted to squeeze out as much time as possible in 21 P-70s, two DB-7s, three C-78s, and one B-18 for the 104 pilots (half in night fighter training status) assigned. Not only the lack of aircraft but the co-utilization of the aircraft assigned hampered the embryonic training effort. Requirements from the Fighter Command School for target towing flights accounted for 40% of the operational

This 3/4 rear view allows both the top and bottom SCR-540 elevation antennas to be seen on the left wing. It can also be noted that these early P-70s were painted totally flat black. (USAF)

This photo, after an accident in late April 1943, gives a good detailed view of the nose area. It can be seen that the glass in the original A-20s bombardiers nose has been removed and sheets of aluminum has been placed within the frames. (NASM/Smithsonian)

aircraft's availability. Sixty percent of the total aircraft were out of commission for lack of spares and the exhaust stack problem on the P-70s.

Classes '42-A and '42-B graduated on December 9. Each class consisted of 24 pilots and 24 observers. Because of the lack of available aircraft, it was estimated that they received only 80 percent of their flying training; and what they received was considered marginal. The lack of the AI Link Trainers was considered a "serious handicap." In this class was Paul DiLabbio:

When we finally completed the course and graduated, there was no formal ceremony. In fact, the day they gave the R/Os their wings (the old observer wings), I happened to be pulling KP, as I was still a Private. The word was that the Captain wanted to see us, so in fatigues we formed in front of him. He'd call a name, step forward, and sign on the dotted line. Once given the wings, I reported back to KP. About this time the training programs were expanding and a lot of satellite fields were being activated. Now that we had completed training we were assigned to one of the new fields – Kissimmee. Our job was to go out and saw, chop, and drag logs for the revetments that were being put up there. We did this for about six weeks, when we were notified that about 10 crews were to ship out.

We had about three hours notice. We had to catch a civilian DC-3 airliner at Orlando to go to San Francisco. Lo and behold, all the R/O's were going to get promoted – from Private to the new rank of Flight Officer. Technically, we still weren't officers, but warrant officers. So again in Private clothes, we weren't even discharged as Privates, we were sworn in as Flight Officers. We were given gold bars with blue markings in the center. When we arrived in San Francisco, we found out that we would have to do it all over again, only this time we were discharged as enlisted men and resworn in as Flight Officers. After four days in San Francisco we shipped out by a slow convoy for Hawaii.

The training program became quite alive all of a sudden as they entered the new year as Col. Leonard Hall remembers:

We were getting along fine. Then all at once we got a directive from the Headquarters Air Force that Doolittle wanted four night fighter squadrons. He heard that we had a night fighter school going. I think Jimmie Doolittle was in Africa at the time. The British had a night fighter unit in there I guess during the Rommel days. He said, 'I've seen what they've done.' The story that we got was that one night this British squadron shot down, oh, it was six, eight, or ten German aircraft. It just impressed the hell out of Jimmie Doolittle; so he said, 'I want some of our own squadrons.' We didn't have four squadrons trained. We didn't have four crews trained! So in a period of 30 or 60 days we pulled together four squadrons; 414th, 415th, 416th, and 417th Night Fighter Squadrons. We gave them a lot of instrument flying. We made real precision pilots out of them.

January 1943 marked the true beginning of an AAF night fighter training program, for on the 26th the 414th Night Fighter Squadron was activated at Orlando, Florida, the first USAAF night fighter squadron to be organized exclusively as a night fighter from its day of activation. Three more units, the 415, 416, and 417 Night Fighter Squadrons, were activated by February 20. As the meager U.S. night fighter training course wasn't much more than an upgraded instrument course at this time, these four squadrons received only their preliminary phases of training in Florida. Their final phase of training would be carried out under the watchful eyes of the Royal Air Force, the only Allied air force to have acquired extensive combat experience in night fighting. Keeping the RAF's experience in mind, and the destination of these American squadrons being to supplement RAF night fighter units in North Africa, arrangements were made between the USAAF and the RAF for the final phase of training to be accomplished in the RAF Night Fighter Operational Training Units. This was to be a reverse Lend Lease, of both equipment and training. The air echelons of the 414 and 415 NFS arrived in England late on March 31, 1943, while their ground echelons remained in Florida for further training and would sail for North Africa later on.

Detachment 1, 6th Night Fighter Squadron Arrives at Henderson Field on Guadalcanal in February 1943 (in September they will be separated from the 6th and redesignated Detachment 'B' Night Fighter Squadron). (Bradner)

Chapter 4

Winds Execute

The Japanese attack on the Hawaiian Islands on that early Sunday morning in December 1941 should not have been a surprise. Such an attack had been shown possible by the US Navy on three earlier occasions. It was believed in Washington, D.C. that war with Japan would not start until the spring of 1942. Even if "those in charge" were lulled by prevailing theories, the cryptologists in Hawaii were quite busy reading the Japanese encrypted message traffic, including the "winds" messages. It is somewhat ironic that British radar expert Watson-Watt had completed his survey of America's early warning installations and reported in December 1941 of their gross shortcomings, at which time such equipment had detected the incoming Japanese raid on December 7th.

The USAAF's Hawaiian Air Force became quite air defense minded on December 7, 1941. The need for night defense by fighter aircraft was quickly recognized, but it was not until Japanese aircraft incursions to the Hawaiian Frontier at night took place in early 1942 before any positive action was taken. An Air Force report describes Japan's second visit to Hawaii after their December adventure:

In January 1942, three Japanese flying boats, believed to be twin-engined, made an air raid on Oahu, Hawaii. These aircraft, arriving at night, created quite a crisis, as no one had any idea as to the total strength approaching; and certainly a heavy attack could be in the making. Nearly all Army and Navy fighters were thrown in the air, and searchlights and anti-aircraft went wild. Tracers fired from Pearl Harbor lit the sky. Reportedly, three fighters were lost, having crashed as a result of the chaos and vertigo caused by searchlights.

The *Honolulu Advertiser* reported that the air raid must not have been a practice, or the military was getting careless in the way that bombs were handled. One bomb reportedly struck the corner of Roosevelt High School.

The initial night fighter scheme for the Hawaiian Islands was for the Hawaiian Air Force's 15th and 18th Pursuit Groups to provide, on a rotational basis, a squadron to perform night intercept duties. The squadrons in these groups were in the throes of reequipping from the massive losses suffered during the recent Japanese attack. These squadrons were basically equipped with P-40s, P-39s, and a few P-36s.

Neither the equipment nor the pilots who flew them were equipped to fly at night. Fighter pilot training at the time included very little on flying at night. This was done only on an emergency basis. The fighters themselves were not equipped with radar to aid in locating the enemy. They were not really equipped to fly at night. Ground radar was not of much help. The SCR-270 early warning radar was of some help, but could not give altitude information. Ground Control Intercept (GCI) radar was not installed in the Hawaiian Islands.

The outcome was quite predictable. There were instances of multiple fighters trying to take off running into each other. Once airborne the searchlights blinded the intercepting pilots.

(US Navy)

A P-40B Warhawk kicks up a dust cloud as it revs up on the dirt ramp at Wheeler Field in pre-war 1941. Many of these aircraft were lost in the attack of December 7, 1941 including nearly all of the 6th Fighter Squadron's. It would be with this same type of aircraft that the 6th Fighter Squadron would enter the arena of night fighter. (USAF/Hickam AFB Historian)

The 6th Fighter Squadron received 25 P-70s in September 1942. By November they were stationed at Kipapa Gulch on the island of Oahu where they stood alert to protect the night skies of Hawaii. (Alford)

Crew Chief S/Sgt Donaho stands next to one of the 6th FS's P-70s. It wasn't long before the 6th crews started painting the squadron's unofficial "Hoot Owl" emblem on their P-70s. (Alford)

In gunnery practice the P-40 pilots were blinded from the flashes of their .50 cal. guns. Once out to sea on an intercept, it would become a concern for the pilots if they could find their way back. Under circumstances as these, there is also the humor. Like the pilot that ran out to mount his plane during a scramble and discovered that in the dark he had climbed onto the wing of a "dummy" P-40 – his foot went through the wing.

Seventh Air Force (Hawaiian Air Force was so redesignated in early February) then tried the idea of a special composite squadron out of the pursuit squadrons which made up the 15th and 18th Pursuit Groups. Each squadron of these groups would provide two of their experienced pilots to stand night fighter duty on a scheduled rotating basis.

The composite unit idea proved impractical, disrupting the activities of all squadrons involved since they were already short of flight and operations officers for normal duty. The squadron commanders were called to headquarters in June 1942 for a conference as to how to meet the situation. The conference solution was to designate a single squadron as a combination day and night fighter squadron. Lt. James R. "Dick" Watt, commanding officer of the 6th Fighter Squadron, volunteered his unit for this duty. He was offered the base of his choice. He selected Stanley Field, a wing of Schoffield Golf Course. This area lay between Schoffield Theater and Kolekole Pass.

One of the pilots with the 6th FS was then 2nd Lt. Julius E. "Jimmy" Alford. "Tactics for night fighting had to be developed with the P-40B using searchlights and other tactics without the use of airborne radar." Apparently Stanley Field was a classified project at the time.

As a secret airstrip, Stanley Field was created in order that a surprise daylight air attack would not expose the aircraft to the enemy. The fighters were pulled tail-first back under the trees and covered with camouflage during the day while the night fighters were off alert. At dusk, they were rolled out, preflighted and usually pilots on alert took turns practicing interceptions at night. In case of enemy aircraft approaching Hawaii, the fighters which were already airborne would make the first interceptions, and the aircraft on the ground were ready for takeoff if needed. During the daylight hours, they could be airborne in minutes if needed, as the pilots were sleeping within a few hundred yards of the aircraft. They were frequently alerted during bad weather or during Red-alert conditions.

With its lineage dating back to 1917, the 6th Fighter Squadron, commanded by Major James R. Watt, entered the night fighting business in June 1942. It would not be until January 18, 1943 before they would be redesignated 6th Night Fighter Squadron. This unit had always been stationed in the Hawaiian Islands, and now it had the duties of defending Hawaii's night skies. At the time of its change from day fighter to night fighter, the 6th was equipped with the Curtiss P-40B. Since no aircraft were available with AI equipment, two plans of battle were worked out by the "night fighters." The first was a fighter-searchlight cooperative arrangement. The object was for one or more batteries of searchlights to illuminate an enemy aircraft; and the friendly night fighter, who had been orbiting a distance away,

The 6th Fighter Squadron that evolved during 1942 was much larger than the average squadron and was operating as both a day and night fighter squadron. In its day fighter role it had some P-40s and P-39s. (Morales)

Aircraft mechanic Raoul M. Morales stands by one of the 6th's P-70s named "Black Widow" on Oahu, Hawaii. (Morales)

to come in for the kill.

The second method was to work in conjunction with filter centers using SCR-270 early warning radar – the type of equipment that had picked up the incoming Japanese aircraft on December 7, 1941. The "270" equipment was used to vector the night fighter into position behind the enemy, then the fighter pilot would negotiate the kill. One major drawback to this plan was that the "270" could not indicate altitude of the airborne aircraft. To compensate for this defect, the night fighters would fly in groups of three, each at a different altitude. Each pilot would be tuned to the filter centers frequency and fly at the bearings given by the center. Usually an altitude differential was maintained between each night fighter which increased the possibility of visually sighting the enemy.

The "night fighters" found that some day-fighting tactics did not hold true at night. In day fighting you attack your target with the sun behind you. In night air combat it is just the opposite, you attack up-moon. Doing this, your target, and not you, are silhouetted.

The P-70 Goes Operational

By the end of September, all 59 of the allocated A-20s had been modified into the P-70 configuration. They were needed for evaluation and flight testing, training of night fighter crews and an immediate requirement in two critical areas for operational

units. Thirty-two were allocated for operational while the remaining 28, including the XP-70, were of the following disposition: 24 to the Fighter Command School in Orlando, Florida; one to the Air Technical School at Boca Raton, Florida; two to Wright Field, Ohio; and one to the Air Corps Proving Ground at Eglin Field, Florida.

At this time there was still great concern that the Japanese would attack the Panama Canal in an attempt to disrupt that vital link between the Atlantic and Pacific. The 24th Fighter Squadron stationed at Albrook Field in the Canal Zone, then a P-39 outfit, was assigned seven P-70s. Five of these aircraft arrived on September 10, 1942, with the last two arriving on the 13th and 20th. In support of these aircraft the Signal Corps dispatched seven spare SCR-540 radar sets on September 23rd. Virtually no information seems to exist as to their use. What little that is in the 24th FS history seems to indicate not all were ever operational at any one time. One of the aircraft was lost in an accident in September and four of them returned to the US in January 1943, another in February and the last aircraft remained in Panama into July 1943.

Twenty-five of the P-70s arrived in Hawaii during September 1942 to turn the improvised 6th into real night fighters. Change of command took place during this same month when Capt. Sidney F. Wharton became commanding officer on the 14th.

After only three hours of cockpit time, these experienced pilots (in single seat fighters) were ready to become operational

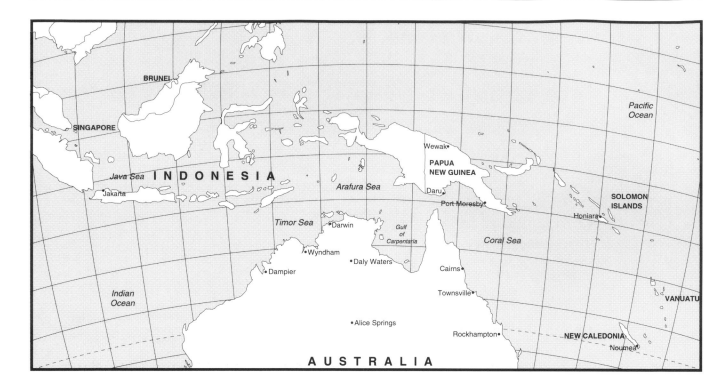

with their new aircraft except for one problem – they had neither R/Os to operate the AI radar, nor radar mechanics to maintain this equipment. This problem was solved sometime later with acquisition of 10 radar mechanics and two Signal Corps officers who were familiar with AI equipment, all from the U.S. Navy's radar school at Hickam Field, Hawaii.

The R/Os had to come from the 6th's own ranks, so the squadron took three weeks off from operational duties, and with

the assistance of the newly acquired Signal Corps officers, started training a number of enlisted men selected from the maintenance, armament, and communications sections as radar operators. Things do not always turn out as envisioned, as was the case with this plan, so personnel were requested from the 18th Fighter Control Squadron, also on Hickam Field. Among the radar operators was Dick Ehlert:

In February 1943 the 6th Night Fighter Squadron's (redesignated "Night Fighter" in January 1943) first detachment was sent out to decimate the enemy. After island hopping and losing one aircraft and crew, the remaining five P-70 arrived over Guadalcanal in the Solomons. Here they make a low level pass prior to landing. (Bradner)

When the 6th FS first received the P-70 they initially tried to make R/Os out of its own ranks. Next they obtained ground radar personnel from nearby units, which worked out much better. A group of Flight Officers trained in Florida as airborne radar operators were sent to the squadron also. They are pictured above during their stopover in San Francisco prior to their long over-water flight. (Hale)

The original personnel of Det. 1, 6th NFS to arrive on Guadalcanal: Back row are enlisted personnel (photo did not include names; Front row (left to right) are: Capt. Ralph E. Jones, unidentified R/O, 1st Lt. James A. Harrell III, Capt Earl C. Bennett (only pilot to shoot down a Japanese aircraft with a P-70 in the Guadalcanal detachment), Maj. Sidney F. Wharton (C.O.), Capt Milton C. Hillebrand, 1st Lt. Ralph F. Tuttle, 2nd Lt. William T. McIvor, 2nd Lt. Jack F. Bradner, Capt. Phillips (flight surgeon), 2nd Lt. Robert E. McDonnell, and 1st Lt. Ralph F. Sugnet (radar maintenance). Note the .50 cal. machine gun in the nose. The 6th NFS installed a pair of .50s in the nose of their P-70s in Hawaii. The idea was to fire tracers from the .50s to help in aiming at a target, then to fire the 20mm cannons once zeroed in. (Bradner)

New living quarters on Henderson Field for the newly arrived night fighters. (Bradner)

All of the enlisted men in this squadron who had attended Radar School at Morrison Field, Florida were notified that they were being transferred to the 6th Fighter Squadron at Kuhuku Field. The 6th had just received 25 P-70s and having been to Radar School we were called into the squadron to operate and maintain this equipment.

What wasn't known at this time by those who decided that we were trained for this task was that all of us had been supposedly trained in ASV (Air-to-Surface Vessels) equipment. This was the equipment used on B-24s for coastal patrol against the German submarines that were operating with impunity and telling success against U.S. shipping along the Eastern seaboard of the U.S. Our training in Night Fighter equipment had consisted of viewing a British training film barely explaining the concept of operation; i.e., how we could detect and track airborne targets with this AI (Airborne Intercept) gear.

We were all given flight physicals and started flying in the P-70s. During this period we usually went up in flights of two aircraft and used each other as targets and interceptor, respectively, during the flying period. A point that is important here is that we had to make up our own pilot-radar operator commentary. We had seen that the British had used the terms 'Port' and 'Starboard' for the turn commands in one training film and by copying some of their terms we were able to set up a standardized commentary. Although it became apparent later, even though we thought we would always fly with the same pilot, we wanted everybody in the squadron on the same general footing. A 'Gentle Port' or 'Gentle Starboard' was a 10 degree bank; 'Port' or 'Starboard' was a 20 degree bank, etc. This method of directing the pilot seemed like a relatively simple and yet an effective system and with a little practice a radar operator would direct a pilot to within a visual sighting of the target, even on the darkest night. We were convinced that we would always be able to see the exhaust patterns of

Pilot 2nd Lt. William McIvor and R/O F/O Willie Coleman survey their new tropical home. (Bradner)

the engines, and then visually shoot the plane down.

Many of the pilots in the squadron were really not too enthusiastic about flying P-70s. The squadron had been equipped with P-40s prior to the 7th of December, and they all wanted to be back in day fighters. The thought of flying in a two place "fighter," a converted attack bomber, didn't quite meet their desires as a fighter. And consequently, many of our "training" missions consisted of buzzing the beaches or the ocean, trying to kick up water spray with the props. This type of training took its toll, and we lost a couple of crews in the month that we started flying. Both of these losses occurred at night, without explanation or known reason.

In November we moved to Kipapa Gulch, just below Wheeler Field and started pulling night 'Alert' with the 70s. The move from Kahuku was hurried slightly by the hole that developed in the runway. The field had been built right next to the ocean out of coral and appeared to have a good solid surface. The construction was such a success that the Colonel who was in charge of the construction received the 'Purple Heart' for his outstanding work. (The Purple Heart was given for outstanding performances – there being no Legion of Merit or Commendation Medal at that time.) Two days following the presentation, the center of the runway started caving in. Water from the ocean was flowing under the runway, and all efforts to fill up the hole proved futile. The hole refused to be filled up. We moved.

Shortly after we arrived at Kipapa Gulch, a Lt. Robert Sugnet of the Signal Corps (1st Lt. Robert F. Sugnet from the Night Fighter Division of AAFSAT in Florida) was assigned to our squadron as a Radar Officer. He replaced three other Signal Corps officers who had been assigned to us, but hadn't had any experience with this equipment. Lt. Sugnet had been to England and had observed and worked with the RAF Night Fighters. His experience with the RAF and his technical knowledge of the equipment gave us a tremendous boost as we were subjects of the 'blind leading the blind' up to this point.

What's A Decimation Or Two?

Project "X." As with any new weapon, the planners in the Pentagon were apt to get carried away with its apparent poten-

tial. The boys in the "five sided puzzle palace" saw the P-70 night fighter as the ultimate weapon. Here was a device that could attack at night without seeing the target and blast the enemy aircraft out of the air. The plan was that just a few of these night attackers in strategic locations were going to so "decimate" the Japanese; that bombing by the Japanese, night or day, was going to become the same as their Kamikaze attacks.

In early January 1943, the 6th NFS was alerted that they would supply two detachments for this project. Admiral King had requested night fighter protection for his South Pacific forces in early February; this was shortly after General MacArthur's earlier request for similar protection for Southwest Pacific forces. General Arnold, apparently thinking the 6th Night Fighter Squadron only possessed 19 P-70s, promised only four of these aircraft for the two requesting theaters.

One of the 6th's Night Fighters' newly created radar operators was Dick Ehlert who related, "We were actually told before leaving Hawaii that we would become a highly mobile force. After we had indeed decimated the night bombing threat on Guadalcanal, we would then be sent to India and eventually into China for another decimation. What the hell, one or two decimations for a half dozen P-70s was considered just about par." They were also told, which might just be rumor or speculation on someone's part, that Guadalcanal was the first target on their mission of "decimation" because it was the personal request of Secretary of the Navy, Frank Knox. It seems that after visiting Guadalcanal, and after having spent two miserable nights in fox holes, that he observed one of the 6th's black P-70s when he came through Honolulu. He inquired as to what it was, and being told that it was a Night Fighter, he then committed a detachment from the 6th to the 'Canal.

Major Sidney F. Wharton, 6th Night Fighter Squadron's C.O., selected five other P-70 crews besides his own and some 20 support personnel to form the 6th's detachment that would go into the Solomons – the first AAF night fighter squadron to see combat. In preparation for their forthcoming entry into hostilities, training intensified. Dick Ehlert recalls:

6th NFS detachment P-70s on Henderson Field. (Bradner)

One of the 6th's Guadalcanal P-70s undergoing minor maintenance at Fighter Strip No.2. Cpl. Dick Ehlert was the R/O on this aircraft. (Ehlert)

With the poor altitude performance of the P-70, the Guadalcanal night fighters looked for a better alternative. Pictured above is the first P-38 assigned to the detachment. First Lt. Ralph Tuttle is on the left and 2nd Lt. Jack Bradner is on the right. In cooperation with ground searchlight units, the P-38 flying night fighters were quite successful in shooting down eight of the high flying Japanese bombers. (Bradner)

"Radio Eye" (radar was classified word) gang: (L to R) standing are Orville S. Merrihew, Benny Benkell, Ted R. Safford, Dick Ehlert, Wayne Frederickson, and Charles E. Magill. Standing are Ed Tomlinson and Raymond A. Mooney. These enlisted men were R/Os and did radar maintenance. The antennas mounted above the tent were for their bench set. They would replace black boxes in the planes and use the "bench set" in an attempt to repair them. The IFF antenna was used to tune their radar frequency and served as a beacon. (Ehlert)

Between April and the unit's disbandment in December 1943, their quarters were at Fighter Strip No.2. Tuttle and Bradner on the steps of Officers Quarters on the edge of the jungle. Behind the quonset was a deep ravine in which about 50 Japanese bodies were in various states of decomposition. (Bradner)

McIvor and Bradner display a trophy. Clothing worn was normal attire for the climate. (Bradner)

Second Lts. Robert E. McDonnell and William E. McIvor stand by the second P-38 inherited by the Guadalcanal night fighters. Markings of the aircraft's nose is from previous owner. (Bradner)

Capt. Ralph Jones was the detachment's third C.O. (Bradner)

During this period we started practicing skeet in an attempt to teach us a little about aerial gunnery. The 70s were going to be further equipped with a pair of 30 cal. machine guns to fire out of the opened rear cockpit and a single 50 cal. machine gun to fire out of the lower access hatch for the rear cockpit. The .30s had a fair effective azimuth coverage as they could be swung from side to side on a single track. The 50 firing through the access door was severely limited in its area of effective firing, and would only be effective against another airplane if that airplane was directly behind and slightly below the 70; this gun could be used effectively for strafing. When these four 20s were fired, the airplane would lose about 20 knots of airspeed. You could feel the bird slow up. Just like dropping the dive boards on jet aircraft.

It would appear that the person making the decision to deploy us to a combat area was unaware of the fact that we as a Night Fighter Detachment could not operate autonomously, or independently, but were completely dependent upon ground radar or ground directed instructions to get into a fairly close proximity of the target aircraft before our airborne equipment would be effective. 'Close proximity' with this equipment meant within two miles maximum. The equipment really wasn't too effective.

On February 18, 1943, we departed for Guadalcanal, with six P-70s and two LB-30s. The plan called for the LB-30s to carry our maintenance personnel and whatever spare parts we would have to have for a 30 day period. Besides providing transportation for the maintenance people and our meager spare parts, the transports were also providing our only means of navigation across the Pacific. We planned stops in Hilo, Christmas, Canton, Wallis Islands, Suva in the Fijis and on to Espirito Santo in the New Heberides. At Espirito Santo we would remove auxiliary bomb bay tanks and reinstall the AI equipment, prior to moving north to Guadalcanal.

Our first three legs were uneventful. Living conditions at Christmas and Canton Islands were rugged. Salt water showers, awful tasting drinking water and food that was not too good. Seems that the further we got away from Honolulu, the worse conditions got. Canton Island had been shelled several times by Japanese submarines and security on the island was pretty tight. There was one coconut palm on the island and a Seabee almost bulldozed that down in clearing the land for additional runway. This was also the highest point on the island, and a lookout was stationed about half way up the coconut palm watching for Japanese warships.

Between Ellis Island and Suva we were forced to penetrate a squall line. Although our pilots had done a little formation flying back in Oahu, none of them were trained to fly a seven ship formation in weather, and this lack of training proved costly. The six P-70s formed two, three flight elements in echelon on either side of the LB-30. This isn't a real good feeling to know that you have to keep a visual contact on your only means of navigation, and there are some real black clouds that you have to go through in the middle of a great big ocean. As soon as we hit the squall line, we encountered the turbulence and that made this formation bob around like corks in a hurricane. Visual contact was almost impossible to keep. You would get a glimpse of the plane you were flying on and hoped it would stay its same relative position after you lost contact in the clouds.

I was in the Number 1 plane in the left echelon. The squadron commander, Maj. Wharton, was in Number 1 on the right. After about three or four minutes, Maj. Wharton decided to move below and directly to the rear of the lead LB-30. He thought that this would allow his No. 2 and 3 man to move closer to the LB-30 and have a better chance of maintaining visual contact. During periods of relatively good visibility, I could look down directly into his cockpit and could see that he was having a most hectic time maintaining his position. I could see him shoving the throttles to the firewall and alternately pulling them all the way back to idle. He was having a difficult time trying to avoid hitting the LB-30 as it appeared that he was going up when the '30 was coming down. I heard him call on the radio, 'I've got to get the hell out of here.' He throttled back and dropped back a little bit, then I saw him push the throttle forward, stand the airplane on its right wing, and go up through the formation. We felt a small bump, and continued on. I could only see one plane on our left wing at this time. A few minutes later we passed the squall line and were out in the clear, but instead of six P-70s only four were visible. The LB-30 started a slow circle, and we heard some radio calls that sounded like they came from the C.O. After radio communications were restored he was given a steer and joined up on us, but we had lost one crew (l/Lt. John E. Meyer, pilot, and Sgt. George D. Pratt, R/O). We never saw or heard anything further from that crew. We spent a night in a converted horse barn at Nandi, and it appeared that the conversion hadn't taken place too long ago. The odors weren't too sweet and most of the flies that lived there with the horses seemed to want to stay.

We arrived at Espirito Santo in the New Heberides without further difficulties. Guadalcanal was just a scant 3-1/2 hours away and this base, 'Buttons,' was a staging base of operations for heavy bombers. It was also well represented by just about every branch of all the allied forces operating in the Pacific. There were sailors, marines, army and GI's from Australia, New Zealand, some French troops, etc.

After removing the bomb bay tanks and reinstalling the radar equipment, we left Buttons for Guadalcanal on the 28th of February and landed at Henderson Field that same day. Either nobody knew we were coming or nobody cared that we finally arrived. We were not greeted or, for that matter, welcomed by anyone. We managed to get cots at Hotel De Gink and ate chow at a mess hall in the same area. The first night we were there we had to tie our shoes to the sides of the cot as it started to rain and the center of the tent became the runoff ditch. After several nights as guests of Hotel De Gink, we managed to scrounge some pyramidal tents that we set up just off the parking ramp at Henderson. This was great during the night, but at about 3:00 a.m. every morning the crew chiefs would start preflighting the airplanes and not only couldn't you sleep through the noise, it was most difficult to breathe in the dust. During this time I lived in a pair of one piece coveralls. Each afternoon a bunch of us would go down to the river, take off our shoes and dive in. I would wash each piece of clothing as I took it off, rinsed it and hung it on the bushes next to the bank. Coveralls, socks and underwear got a daily washing in the river, and I got a bath and a swim. When the swim was over, I put on the same clothes, even though they were still slightly damp and headed for chow.

We had nightly raids from the Japs and one day raid. Either the Japs would bomb Guadalcanal or Tulagi. We could see the anti-aircraft fire at the bombers over Tulagi from Guadalcanal and could see some of the fires the bombers started. 'Washing Machine Charlie' would sit over the island in the searchlights as the 90mm anti-aircraft guns would blast away. It always seemed that the airplanes were just out of range

Most of the Guadalcanal night fighters gather with the remains of a downed Japanese plane and a poster presented to them by the Marines in the Russells. The caption on the bottom of the poster reads: "They let us sleep in Japless peace." (Bradner)

in height. They would be over the island for 30 minutes to an hour, occasionally dropping a bomb. The 'Washing Machine Charlie' handle was given to these Japanese bombers because of the particular sound of the engines. It sounded as though the engines were not synchronized, and this caused a pulsing overtone that sounded somewhat like an old wringer type washer. These raids, although they didn't do too much damage, certainly irritated the troops and prevented them from getting a good night's sleep.

No one could understand why the black birds didn't scramble when "Charlie" came over. Upon their arrival, they found conditions less than ideal, which was to be expected. The runway was somewhat short at Fighter Strip 2 – 3,200 feet; however, they got used to this, but they faced much greater problems, no GCI. There was SCR-270 ground radar which was part of the island's aircraft warning system. Through coopera- tion with the "270" filter centers, operations were initiated much like those performed by the 6th in Hawaii while equipped with P-40s; i.e., the SCR-270 would vector the night fighters in

the direction of the incoming aircraft, and the flight of P-70s flying at different altitudes was suppose to pick up the enemy aircraft on their AI. Not a single kill was made using this technique.

During the second week of March 1943, the detachment moved from Henderson to Carney Field, near Koli Point. From here they would establish their base of operations, after the ground radar station was completed. To aid in the stations construction, a number of the 6th enlisted men were volunteered, among them was Dick Ehlert:

Our main task consisted of digging trenches for the antenna counterpoise for the radio transmitter. The counterpoise was an effective ground for the antenna and consisted of copper wires buried in the sand and emanating from the base of the antenna like spokes in a bicycle wheel. The radiating element of the antenna would be insulated from ground or the counterpoise and fed at the base. The antenna was set on a Coca-Cola bottle, guyed at 120 degree increments and proved to be quite effective. I often wonder how many people knew that the entire

Poster presented to the night fighters by the Marines. The unofficial insignia adopted by the detachment was that of a streetwalker – e.g. night intruder (Disney didn't design this one!) (Bradner)

success of a Ground Controlled Intercept, yea, the first attempted by the United States Army Air Corps depended completely on the strength of an empty Coca-Cola bottle.

The radar station aptly given the call sign 'Kiwi' was just about completed, and we moved back to the Squadron area at Carney Field. We flew a few flights to assist in the calibration of the ground station and from all appearances were ready for business. This is a point that must be noted at this time. This particular airborne/ground system was being committed in a combat area and operated by people who had absolutely no or very little experience. The aircrews had never practiced this, and I doubt seriously if the controllers on the ground had any experience in controlling airborne intercepts. The English had used radar, sound and visual inputs to a combat operations center where they correlated the information on a horizonal plotting table. Strike forces were in the form of flags and symbols moved along course lines and fighters were directed. In this operation, the controllers were going to control directly from the information on the scopes.

We had adapted the Pilot/RO commentary from the RAF and used the terms 'Port' and 'Starboard,' 'Climb' and 'Go down.' One being a one syllable word and the other two. Even garbled it had a chance of being understood. On arrival at Boca we learned that the

R/O had to give a running commentary of commands and position reports of the so-called 'BOGIE.' We were graded and in turn graded the Aviation Cadets on the proper command, inflection, continuity of the chatter. This was strictly ATC for I knew of nobody in the field who did this. The purpose of course is obvious. Any R/O could fly with any pilot and each immediately would be completely understood. Of course, after the Aviation Cadet graduated from Boca he was sent to Hammer Field in California where he was married to his pilot. The pilot and R/O trained together, ate, slept, drank and probably screwed the same girls, and then were shipped out as a team. So this standardized commentary was all for you know what.

We started pulling alert at Carney Field on the March 25, 1943. With five crews, two crews on alert each night, we had the duty every other night. We would each take six hours of being No. 1 – 6:00 to midnight and midnight to 6:00 a.m.

Most of the crews were anxious to get 'Charlie' and in the first couple of nights or week, several got close, but nobody had any success. 'Charlie' changed his tactics just a little. Instead of staying in the lights over the island, he would occasionally try to sneak in just before dawn or at dusk and consequently we started flying patrols during that period. Most of the air warfare was taking place during the daytime.

Because there wasn't any single defense command or commander, all defense forces operated as separate units. The Night Fighters with their ground station, the anti-aircraft batteries with their 90 mm. If the Japs were in the searchlights, the 90mm fired at them without regard for friendly fighters in the area. It is most disheartening having to fly through your own ack-ack, especially since they hadn't hit anything since we had been on the island.

The technique to be employed in the P-70-GCI joint operation was that the P-70 was to attempt to intercept the enemy planes from 50 miles out down to 10 miles from the "gun-defended" area. The P-70 was not allowed in the gun-defended area on the theory that if interception had not been made by that time the enemy was either too high or too fast, and that the best defense was the use of the anti-aircraft guns. Also, reliable communications for control of A-A guns were not available.

In the early morning hours of April 19th, an enemy raiding force was picked up by ground radar. They were headed straight for Guadalcanal at about 22,000 feet. Captain Earl C. Bennett and his R/O, Corporal Edwin E. Tomlinson had the night fighter alert. The enemy aircraft had reached the gun-defended zone before an intercept could be made. The A-A crews didn't have any better luck in destroying the enemy aircraft. As the enemy were about to leave the searchlights, where they had been illuminated for about five minutes, Bennett decided to attack. Observing the air activity from the ground was United Press correspondent William F. Tyree. In a dispatch later sent, Tyree related, "As the Japs approached, the first A-20 (P-70) peeled out of a cloud and went roaring to the attack. . . The fighter pilot delighted listeners on his radio circuit by saying, 'I'll get the first bastard!'" And he did.

While thousands of troops watched, there was a sudden bright orange flash in the night sky and bits of flaming wreckage sprayed out

Aircrews in front of the night fighters Guadalcanal Ready Room with an insignia designed by Walt Disney for them along with the poster presented to them by the Marines. (Bradner)

The 6th NFS detachment's first home on New Guinea was at 3-Mile Strip (3 miles from Port Moresby). Like the Guadalcanal detachment, this group would be separated from the 6th NFS and become Detachment 'A' Night Fighter Squadron in September 1943. (Hale)

like fireworks. The Jap went down, burning all the way. Marines and soldiers danced about joyously and shouted as though they were spectators at a football game instead of a battle of life and death.

It was 0430 hours local, and the crew of Bennett and Tomlinson had just made the first AAF night fighter kill. Dick Ehlert recalls:

An interesting facet about that first 'kill.' The 'Canal was under command of the Navy at the time. The Navy wanted to award their 'Silver Star' to Bennett. The Air Corp wanted to award their 'Silver Star' to Bennett. They bickered back and forth for a couple of weeks, and the problem was never solved. It just faded away, and Bennett didn't get zilch.

During this period, the night flying activities of the Japanese were quite sporadic. There just wasn't anyway in which you could guess when they would be over. Their air losses in daylight operations were quite heavy. We would be given operational summaries almost daily and could see that they were losing quite a number of planes and crews.

For nearly three weeks things had been quiet around Guadalcanal. I hadn't had a 'Box Top' since the 20th of April. A 'Box Top' in our jargon then was a combat mission where you got fired at or where you fired. Ten Box Tops equalled one Air Medal .

About this time we received three more crews. One of the new R/ Os was a Flight Officer, a new rank that we were seeing for the first time. It seems that the R/Os position was being given the same prestige and responsibility as Bombardiers and Navigators and consequently, should be either Warrant Officers or Commissioned Officers.

Washing Machine Charlie became active again in mid-May. On the 13th 'Charlie' came over again and dropped a number of bombs on Carney Field for the first time. One bomber was knocked down by a P-38 (day fighter). Three of our P-70s were up but didn't get any. It looks like the Japs will get active at night again, as it is coming into the period of a full moon. They are not too much different than us. It's a lot more fun flying at night with a full moon than on a dark night.

We moved again on 27 May, to Fighter Strip No. 2. We were set

up pretty good, living in Dallas huts and subsisting with a Navy Fleet Air Base Unit. These Dallas huts were prefab sectional buildings that could be constructed in single units or in multiple units. They had a plywood floor and were screened in, and for Guadalcanal in mid-43 were quite plush. We had swapped a portable gasoline pump for a small electric generator, wire, sockets and light bulbs and had electric lights. When we moved, the lighting system went with us. We would have moved the Dallas huts, but the Navy kept watching us too carefully.

1st Lt. Jack F. Bradner was one of the 6th's pilots on Guadalcanal. In a combat intelligence interview of June 1944 he vividly describes those early months of operations:

At the beginning of their operations at Guadalcanal in night fighting with the P-70s SCR-540 (the British Mk IV had been replaced in most of the P-70s) AI radar, there was no GCI station and the outfit for awhile relied on the ground radar, then being used as the aircraft warning system, to vector them. However, this radar (SCR-270) could not receive or transmit altitude of enemy aircraft to the pilots. This presented a real difficulty which was compensated for in part by certain air tactics which were developed. The SCR-540 AI with which all P-70s were then equipped was unpredictable. It continuously cut out at high altitudes.

The outfit shortly started to use the P-70 as low cover on beachhead landings and as low cover for our PT boats, very active at this time in blockading Kolombangara Island. During these operations the AI was not installed and the altitudes they flew at varied between 500 and 2,500 feet. Next, the detachment was issued new P-70As equipped with bombays. These ships were to be used in intruder missions, in strafing and bombing Jap supply dumps, AA and searchlight positions, and barges. The missions were highly successful, severe damage being inflicted against the enemy. Jap airstrips were harassed nightly. In these harassing missions, as well as intruder missions, all AI was removed for security reasons.

P-70A "Stygian Pigeon" of the 6th NFS on New Guinea in the summer of '43. The two upper .50 cal. machine guns have been removed and the ports that the barrels came through have been covered up. (Hale)

While the night fighters were based at 3-Mile Strip, they quite often stood alert at 7-Mile because it had a longer runway and less hills around it. Later they would use 12-Mile and go to the other side of the island to Dobodura. Above is the detachment's "Tomcatin." (Hale)

It was soon found out that the Japanese knew the radio frequencies for the GCI controllers and had a trick up their sleeve. On a number of occasions, the Japanese would imitate the GCI controller and give the interceptor night fighter erroneous information. Lt. Jack F. Bradner relates a personal incident concerning a Japanese radio traffic interception in a report to Hammer Field: "GCI on Guadalcanal had just scrambled Bradner . . .' Keewee from Bradner – how do you receive me – five by five?' The answer came back instantly in fair English but recognizable as a Jap voice, 'Bradner, this is Keewee. I receive you five by five. Orbit save.' Orbit Save meant 'discontinue intercept.'"

The 6th's detachment initial responsibilities were to stand dusk to dawn alerts, with no patrols. The night fighters would be scrambled only when an unknown aircraft was detected on the GCI, usually about 30 miles out. Then the P-70 would be scrambled and vectored into position for the attack.

Soon after the GCI station was put into operation two problems were experienced, the lesser one being the low level of proficiency of the personnel. The other was much more serious. The island's high mountains, 8,000 feet, were a major problem. Due to the poor location of the equipment (poor location by "the book," but there was no better place on Guadalcanal), permanent ground echoes were caused by the surrounding mountains. As the proficiency of the GCI operators increased, the problems with the ground echoes were overcome to some degree.

About a month after the detachment arrived, a second flight of three additional P-70s with their crews joined them. For almost four months the P-70 operated as interceptors, but they were found to be operationally unsuitable for this mission. The AI equipment in the P-70 continually failed at high altitudes, which gave the aircraft a limited service ceiling of around 22,000 feet. It took about 45 minutes for the P-70 to climb to 27,000 feet, and it could not always reach this altitude. It didn't take the Japanese long to figure our shortcomings, because they started to come in at 30,000 feet, impervious to attack by the P-70s. During this period, the night fighters would close in on the Japanese intruders only to have the radar go out as the Japanese were coming into range.

Although the performance of the night fighters on Guadalcanal had been quite dismal, Thirteenth Air Force, to which they were attached, realized the great potential in this new arm of America's fighter force. In a report of mid-June 1943, the Thirteenth's commander, Maj. Gen. Nathan F. Twining, outlined the operations of a P-38 augmented night fighter force:

Upon receipt of warning of impending raid it will be the duty of Fighter Control to scramble planes and to alert an additional flight of the same strength. Fighter Control will keep GCI Control constantly advised of bearing and distance of raid. When raid approaches within sixty miles, Fighter Control will turn control of P-70s over to GCI Control. If AI contact is not made by the time target is within ten miles of Lunga Point, GCI Control will direct P-70 to original orbit point and Fighter Control will control searchlights and interception by P-38s. As a recapitulation of the above, GCI Control is responsible for directing

On March 19, 1943 the 6th NFS's Detachment 2, under the command of Capt. Warren G. Hornaday, left on its island hopping flight to the Southwest Pacific Area and New Guinea. This flight of six P-70s was accompanied by two LB-30s carrying ground crew, supplies, and doing the navigating. (Hale)

P-70s within sixty down to ten miles of Lunga Point. Fighter Control is responsible for directing searchlights and P-38s within ten miles of Lunga Point, and in addition, is responsible for control of anti-aircraft artillery. These responsibilities are not overlapping. Close coordination and thorough indoctrination of the above procedures will prevent confusion between Fighter Control and GCI Control. Common sense application of these principles and a few dry runs will eliminate any bugs.

The following recommendations are based on the assumption that forty minutes warning of raid has been received. Action to be taken in event of less warning is shown in the paragraph above. 1 - Dispatch one P-70 to orbit the eastern tip of Santa Isabel Island and to climb at maximum rate to its ceiling. 2 - Dispatch one P-70 to vector 270, to climb at maximum rate for a distance of fifty miles and there orbit at its ceiling. This latter plane will be located about ten miles south of Russell Island and may be kept in this position by GCI operator. 3 - Dispatch two P-38s to climb at maximum rate, one to 20,000 feet and one to 17,000 feet, orbiting around a filtered searchlight located about ten miles on bearing 210° from Lunga Point. Fighter Control will keep GCI Control informed of distances and bearing of a bogie. When bogie approaches within sixty miles GCI Control will vector the nearest P-70 on interception course and attempt interception using standard recognized procedure for GCI. The other P-70 will be used as a reserve force in event of a following raid. If the first P-70 has picked up target on AI screen and is able to reach target altitude, it will be allowed to follow target across the defended area, closing and firing as soon as possible. If however, target has not been picked up on AI screen by the time it is within ten miles of Lunga Point, GCI Control will direct the P-70 back to its original orbit, and will notify Fighter Control that long range interception has failed. Fighter Control will then release searchlights for action. Illumination of target may be announced by ground observer located close in vicinity of Fighter Control or may be seen by P-38s. Fighter Control will then order all but three lights out of action and notify P-38s that target is illuminated. The P-38 at 20,000 feet will fire on any target above 20,000 feet, the P-38 at 17,000 feet will fire on target below 20,000 feet. Target will be passed along by searchlights

so that three and only three lights illuminate it at any time. If target is not shot down before passing out of range of searchlights, interception attempt will be made on outgoing course by GCI, using P-70s. The P-38s will be returned to orbit light. In event of a raid which seems directed at Florida Island, only P-70s will be used. The reason for this is that searchlights on Florida Island cannot be controlled by Fighter Control. It is essential that information concerning speed and altitude be given to intercepting planes.

Operation of P-38 – Searchlight team in conjunction with P-70: When unsatisfactory results were obtained with the P-70, the following plan was put into effect: The P-70 was used as in par. 3 above. The following technique is used in operation of the P-38 Searchlight team: A low-intensity light with a red filter was installed one mile from the outer edge of the target area to be used as an orbit point for the P-38. Anti-aircraft fire is controlled as the situation warrants. Strict rules have never and will never be laid down as to when or if to shoot, or to hold fire. The guiding principle of AA control is that the P-38 has first priority on the target if it appears that he might reasonably be expected to intercept it when and if illuminated. During the Jap's approach to the area, as much information as possible as to his speed, altitude and course are transmitted by radio to the fighter. Searchlights are always released for action and illuminate without further orders any target within their range. The fighter may then either see the target in a cone of searchlights or may be advised by radio that the target is illuminated. From then on, as in other aircraft interceptions, the fighter uses his own initiative.

None of the P-38 pilots currently being used for night interception have had any special training for this work. Informal discussions with them have been held in which certain approaches, rates of closure, night blindness, extra-foveal vision, gun sights, etc. have been discussed. The cellophane filter on the P-38 gun sight is a deep red and was cut out by hand from a piece of photographic filter. Its main purpose is to dim the light in the gun sight. It is placed in the sight itself so that the light from the reticle to the reflector is filtered! Thus, the vision is not hampered but is improved because of decreased glare.

Equipment: A standard P-38G was used in these missions, the only special equipment was the above mentioned red cellophane which was placed over the gun sight to minimize glare. The guns were loaded; one armor-piercing; one incendiary; one tracer.

Suggestions made by pilots operating P-38s at night are listed below: When you see the target take your time and come into position slowly; pull right up behind target at his speed. In that manner you can get a perfect set-up shot. Watch your distances they are hard to judge. Keep yourself oriented with orbit light and other landmarks. Once target is in lights, get into position quickly – but not fast – and you have him 'cold turkey.' Conserve fuel as much as possible as you may get caught in subsequent raids and have to remain aloft for a considerable length of time.

So in June the 6th's night fighters started receiving their Lockheed P-38Gs. Compared to the P-70, the P-38G had a speed advantage of over 30 mph and an operational ceiling of 10,000 feet greater. In time to climb, the '38 reached 25,000 feet in 11 minutes compared to the Havoc's 33 minutes duration; 30,000 in 15 minutes, as the P-70 struggled to 27,000 in almost

Because of the poor altitude performance of the P-70, the 6th NFS detachment on New Guinea obtained two P-38Gs and modified them into night fighters. (Hale)

A close up of one of the P-38 night fighters shows the SCR-540 antennas mounted on the nose of the Lightning along with flashhiders on the guns. (Hale)

45 minutes.

After arriving at Fighter Strip 2, the 6th detachment was told that the P-70s were being retired and that the pilots were going to start flying P-38s. The P-70 just wasn't the plane for the job; a low altitude attack bomber with added radar equipment and four 20mm cannon just couldn't be a high altitude night fighter. They tried stripping the P-70s to get more altitude, but this didn't make an appreciable difference. A phenomenal altitude (for the P-70) of 29,000 feet was reached, but the plane was just hanging on the props. Try a five degree banking turn, and the plane would lose 300 feet of altitude.

The night fighter-searchlight cooperative would work like this:

A P-38 would be on alert and ready to scramble when given the word from the local filter center. As enemy aircraft are picked up by the local GCI, the P-38 is scrambled and vectored to an orbit point. Here it waits until the searchlights have illuminated the enemy aircraft. Usually the searchlight battery which is equipped with radar picks up the aircraft first, then other lights illuminate the aircraft; a three-intersection beam being preferable. With the enemy aircraft intensely illuminated, the P-38 would come in for the kill. The theory was that the "friendly" AA would cease fire either when the Jap reached his bomb release point or on command of the night fighter pilot. But, ". . . the ack-ack seldom stopped and to secure the kill, it would usually be necessary for the pilot to enter right into the ack-ack in pursuit of the enemy aircraft." Capt. Earl C. Bennett, Jr., stated, ". . . this didn't bother them (the night fighters) too much for they felt relatively safe in our own ack-ack." He did come away once with flack holes in a boom of his P-38. In this type of operation, the detachments P-38s accounted for seven enemy aircraft destroyed.

The first night fighter squadron kill with a P-38 was accomplished on June 16 when Lt. Charles E. Van Bibber successfully destroyed a Japanese "Hap." Eye witness to this kill was Newsweek South Pacific correspondent William W.

Boddie:

I was up on Guadalcanal during several air raids, and I assure you that a faster man than I for getting into a foxhole never hit that island. Nor a man who was more viciously attacked by mosquitoes. I saw a P-38 night fighter shoot down a Mitsubishi bomber. His tracers came out of the blackness like a long line from a Roman candle and went completely through the Jap plane, which burned like a flare in the sky. He got the bomber three times on the way down, and perhaps it sounds like young Mussolini, but I never saw a more beautiful sight in my life.

A group of us were sitting on the side of a dugout watching; and when the bomber began burning, there were cheers like a football game. You did not think of the six or seven Japs who died; or if you did, you remembered that the Jap had jettisoned his bombs – he was caught by seven or eight searchlights – close enough to the dugout to shake it considerably. You feel a very personal war against those babies on Guadalcanal.

Not a single 6th NFS P-38 was lost while flying through the friendly antiaircraft fire, but very strained relations developed between these two branches. Of interest to note is that only "friendly" naval vessels were harder to call off than the anti-aircraft boys when firing on friendly aircraft.

With the inauguration of the P-38 searchlight teams as the main night defense of the area, most of the P-70s were converted to night intruders. The P-70 had not been allowed to fly over enemy held territory on previous occasions due to security restrictions placed on its radar equipment. As an intruder the SCR-540 was removed. The R/O was retained and an aerial gunner was added to the crew. Twin 30 cal. machine guns were installed to be fired from the rear top turret, and a single 50 cal. machine gun was mounted as a "tunnel gun." To give it a bigger punch, six bomb racks were added which enabled the P-70 to carry 600 pounds of high explosive ordnance. These aircraft were supplemented by later model P-70As having bomb bays a couple of months later. A number of the unit's P-38s were modified to carry a single 500 pound bomb adjacent to its auxiliary fuel tank for intruder work.

Munda and Rendova had been taken by the Army and Marines and action over or near Guadalcanal had dropped off considerably. During the last week of July, "Charlie" snuck in one night and dropped a string of bombs on Fighter Strip No. 2, near the night fighters area causing several casualties. The Jap's tactics had changed considerably, due primarily to the P-38s operating at night. Instead of coming in above 30,000 feet and just sitting over the island in the lights, "Charlie" was now forced to come in on the deck to avoid radar, drop his bombs and get out.

The Japanese weren't going to give up easily in their battle for the Solomons. They had pushed hard to reinforce their battered garrisons on Guadalcanal and surrounding islands. The US military presence – submarines, PT boats carrier and land based aircraft, and surface ships – all made daylight operations suicidal for the Imperial Navy. A very standard practice in the Pacific areas of this conflict was Navy PT boats and night fighters joining forces in their efforts to exterminate the enemy.

First the PT boats started to have an effect against Japanese shipping. To counter this the Japanese started sending out slow-flying float planes. These "floats" as they were referred to would spot the wake caused by the PT, drop flares in its vicinity, and then make firing passes on the PT. To counter this, the Navy and the night fighters of Detachment "B" worked together to counter this threat. Jack Bradner, a P-38 pilot that joined the night fighters on Guadalcanal when they started using P-38s, recalls an experience he had:

We took off from Munda to cover three PT boats that were operating in the Ferguson Passage area. My radar operator was F/O Willie Coleman. This was to be a set-up to lure one of the Japanese fighters up. The PTs made a 'bogey bait' run through the passage, but no enemy aircraft appeared, so the next step was for the boats to spray the Kolombangara coastline with .50 cal. fire. Not long after this, a Mitsubishi F1M2 'Pete' float biplane flew into the vicinity. As the enemy pilot lined up for a pass, our P-70 came in full throttle for a 90 degree deflection shot, without any visible results. Seconds later, I had put our fighter back into position, at point blank range of 150 or so feet. We boresighted the enemy biplane, but only one of the 20mm fired. The target did a quick Split-S and shot back. Contact was lost. All of the action took place at under 2500 ft. Weather was good with visibility up to three miles. I am sure that we got the float plane! The Captain on the PT boat stated that he saw the enemy go down, but we never received credit. I guess it doesn't matter, because after this mission, float planes never bothered the PTs again.

In early September 1943, Capt. Ralph F. Jones initiated the unit's role in intruder tactics with an attack on Kahili Airdrome located on Bougainville Island. Dick Ehlert remembers those days of late 1943 very well:

After Rendova and Munda Islands were secured the next logical

hop in the island hopping war was Kolombangara and some well planned leaks told the Japanese that this is just exactly what the Yanks were going to do. The Japanese started reinforcing Kolombangara with some of their best troops by barge, at night from Bougainville. The PT boats from Rendova operated against the barges. The Japanese sent in some 'Dave' float biplanes to try and sink the PT boats, and we were called upon to give night cover to the PT boats.

After the success the P-38s were having against the Japs at night, we removed the AI equipment from the P-70s and installed a Navy ASB-3 radar search set. This set had two Yagis, transmitting and receiving antennas that were mounted at the end of the wings. These antennas were rotated about 90 from a dead ahead to a beam position and allowed search either ahead of the airplane or to either side, and were controlled hydraulically from the rear cockpit. There was no capability of telling the relative altitude of an airborne target. We used this equipment to search out the Jap barges. We also installed absolute altimeters for use on intruder missions over Bougainville.

September 16, 1943 marked the end of the Guadalcanal detachment as elements of the 6th Night Fighter Squadron. This unit, originally designated as "Project X," was now to be independent of the 6th Night Fighter Squadron and designated Detachment "B" Night Fighter Squadron and assigned as an independent unit of Thirteenth Air Force.

As Detachment "B" Night Fighter Squadron, their first aerial victory came a few days later in the early morning hours of September 21st. Flying a P-38, 1st Lt. Henry Meigs II made a spectacular exhibition of flying when he made visual contact with attacking enemy bombers over Guadalcanal. Within 60 seconds two Japanese Betty bombers were plummeting towards earth as two great balls of fire. Major General Nathan F. Twining, Thirteenth Air Force commander, personally decorated Meigs with the Silver Star for this feat.

One of the more successful intruder missions in the South Pacific was carried out by Captain Ralph F. Tuttle. Captains Tuttle and Bennett were flying low over Japanese held territory in order to avoid detection by the enemy's ground radar and preserve the element of surprise upon any targets of opportunity that they might find. They passed over a Japanese airfield where Tuttle observed five torpedo bombers lined up in a neat row. What more could he ask for? One of the bombers even had its landing lights on; probably readying for a mission. Capt. Tuttle lined up with the five and made a very effective firing pass in which each of the bombers was observed to have been destroyed. While he was still in the process of bringing destruction upon the bombers, Tuttle observed a number of barges being off-loaded at a nearby dock. Still in the same firing run he fired at the barges; which exploded almost immediately, indicating they were probably loaded with fuel.

November was a very active month for the Guadalcanal night fighters. They started off on the 1st by providing night cover over the task force and landing barges during the Bougainville landing operations. Dick Ehlert was very busy modifying their remaining P-70s for intruder operations:

We put another ASB-3 Radar Set into Aircraft 52 and took out the

AI equipment. We scrounged these sets from the Navy and it was tough trying to get all the components and the cables. Most of the equipment came from wrecked aircraft at Munda and I spent several days there just scrounging this equipment. We got our absolute altimeters in the same manner. Lt. Van Bibber got 'Photo Joe' day before yesterday. The Japanese started sending a photo recce version of their Zeke over the island just about every day right around noon. Lt. Van Bibber followed him past the Russells and about half way to Munda, flying right behind him and low. The Jap seemed to think he was free and clear of the Yanks when Lt. Van Bibber, just pulled the nose up and let him have a burst. One burst and he blew up.

At 2400 on December 15, 1943, Detachment "B" Night Fighter Squadrons were disbanded. Some personnel and equipment on Guadalcanal were transferred to the newly arrived 419th Night Fighter Squadron. Other Detachment members were assigned to different units in their area and a few returned to Hawaii and the 6th Night Fighter Squadron.

Southwest Pacific Sojourn

Shortly after the departure of the 6th NFS's "home grown" night fighter pilots and R/Os departed for Guadalcanal, the Florida-trained night fighter teams arrived and joined up with the 6th NFS at Kipapa Field. With this new group was newly promoted Flight Officer Paul DiLabbio:

We stayed there (at Kipapa) for six weeks doing additional training and helped train the enlisted R/Os in the squadron. The pilots were still young then and bets were always made as to who could land the shortest. Kipapa was built in the middle of a sugar cane field with a deep drop at the one end. As you can probably guess, the winner of the shortest landing was the one pilot who lost his gear by not clearing the drop. We got all of one weekend in Honolulu before shipping out.

On March 19, 1943 the 6th's second detachment started its long trek across the Pacific. Under the command of Capt. Warren G. Hornaday, a flight of six P-70s and two LB-30s (carrying support personnel and equipment). One of the LB-30s would be in the lead while the other would be "tail end Charlie." Their sojourn took them to Christmas Island, Canton Island, Wallis, Nandi, New Caledonia, then to Brisbane, Australia and finally Townsville. Weather was good all the way. The only mishap occurred as they arrived in Townsville. The P-70 with pilot Fred Secord and his R/O Carl Hale experienced a gear malfunction – his gear wouldn't come down. Lt. Secord tried to shake it loose by going through some violent maneuvers, but to no avail. His only real alternative was to make a gear-up landing, which he did perfectly. The problem turned out to be a loose hand crank in the nose wheel well which jammed the gear.

The 6th's detachment, minus Secord and Hale who would spend some time there overseeing the repair of their plane, left Townsville and proceeded on to New Guinea. Their destination was "Three-Mile" strip (Kila), which was located three miles

from Port Moresby. Arriving there on April 1st, their landing was somewhat nerve rattling for these stalwart night fighters. The runways at Three-Mile were covered with pierced metal planking, and this was their first experience in landing on it. They hadn't been warned beforehand, so were unawares of the great noise made as their tires touched down. It really made the ol' adrenalin flow!

"Ran into our first bottleneck," remembers Paul DiLabbio of their time of arrival on New Guinea, "Night fighters-no one really trusted us and rumor had it that MacArthur wanted to use us for low level night attack against shipping."

One of the 6th's pilots, John Florence, was there in the beginning:

With the five P-70s, our mission was to intercept enemy bombers sent over the installations around Port Moresby at night. These attacks were so sporadic and our capability so limited that patrols were out of the question, so we would scramble one plane when radar picked up an enemy flight coming over the Owen Stanley range or down the coast (By the time we arrived in Port Moresby the Japs had been driven back from the Kokoda Trail and the ground fighting was in Buna and Dobodura on the north coast of the island). We would stand alert at Jackson airdrome (Seven-Mile) to which we would fly 2 or 3 planes from Three-Mile each evening and return the next morning. Reason was the shortness of the runway at Three-Mile and also the hills at each end of the runway. Seven-Mile was longer and had better approaches for night operations.

The first fatality on New Guinea was that of the detachment's CO, Capt. Hornaday, and his R/O, F/O Howard M. Krause shortly after their arrival. Hornaday was flying under the hood in a practice flight. He and an accompanying P-70 flown by John Florence entered a thin layer of clouds. When Florence came out of the clouds Hornaday's P-70 was nowhere to be seen. It was later learned that an antiaircraft battery on the cost observed Hornaday's plane spin into the sea. Florence recalls: "Evidently, he looked out while in the cloud layer and became disoriented." Capt. Robert W. McLeod became CO of the detachment.

The same lack of cooperation was experienced by the 6th Night Fighter Detachment on New Guinea with the searchlight batteries as was experienced by the Guadalcanal detachment. But here, the P-70s were under orders not to enter the 12 mile radius of the anti-aircraft's zone of fire. The question was whether the anti-aircraft should have a free field of fire, or if it should be curtailed to give the night fighter a chance to make the kill. Though the anti-aircraft won its own way, it did not bring down a single enemy aircraft during the detachment's stay.

The detachment soon were sending three of their P-70s to Horanda airstrip near Dobodura on the north side of the island to stand alert there also, this was quite an effort for a unit with just five aircraft. Conditions at Dobodura were quite primitive. The landing strip was sod. The personnel there lived in tents located on the edge of the jungle. The floors of the tents were elevated about six feet above the ground. They were entertained at night by a variety of jungle sounds.

The New Guinea detachment came up against the same problems as had plagued the Guadalcanal detachment, poor GCI coverage and poor P-70 performance. The Owen Stanley mountain range behind Port Moresby created a constant ground echo. The GCI operators proficiency was quite good when the detachment started their operations, but replacement personnel who arrived later proved to be unsatisfactory. The performance of the P-70s in general and that of its communications and radar equipment was found, once again, to be lacking. It took the P-70 45 minutes to reach an altitude of 25,000 feet, and even this was not always obtainable.

In an attempt to increase their airplane's performance, the 6th's New Guinea detachment set about to modify their quite inadequate P-70s. All armor plating was removed, along with the rear guns, B-17F propellers were installed, as were P-38 fuel booster pumps. Capt. Robert W. McLeod, who was a member of this unit, reports that "these changes were helpful and did improve the performance capabilities of the ship," though by their lack of success and further experimentation attempted, it would seem that the P-70 never did meet the requirements of an acceptable night fighter aircraft in any way.

The one and only confirmed air victory of the New Guinea detachment came late on May 15, 1943. Lt. Burnell W. Adams, pilot, and F/O Paul DiLabbio, R/O, were one of the crews on alert duty at Port Moresby. Lt. DiLabbio tells of this intercept in a report he made at Hammer Field, California, about a year later:

Nips were reported coming over in elements of two. We weren't high enough to intercept when they made their first run. The controller, Captain Ball, vectored us to the other side of the anti-aircraft ring from which we were flying – a good guess – Nips came out at about 19,000 feet heading Northeast, and we were given about three or four vectors, which then placed us behind and above. This gave me a contact about 18,000 feet on the scope, about 4,000 feet below us and 40 feet to starboard. I then said 'contact' to Lt. Adams and gave him the general route. When I told him to 'steady' we were about 5,000 feet and in a general dive, going 350 mph, IAS, and just about the same level. I started to give Adams degree correction to the left, but Adams reported back 'Tallyho', which placed us about 1,000-1,500 feet behind, with the Nip a little to our left. The tail gunner of the Nip evidently saw us at the same time for he opened fire, but the bullets went over my head. By this time Adams had turned into the Nip and fired a burst which silenced the gunner and evidently wounded the pilot because the Nip turned into a general dive to the right. Adams then followed, fired another burst which hit the gas tanks, the fuselage and the wings. By now the craft was ablaze. He (Adams) fired another burst, and the Nip plane blew up. We were now about 15,000 feet – we watched enemy aircraft go to 3,000 feet – another explosion.

While Adams was firing and trailing this Nip the other enemy aircraft in the element had made a general climbing turn to the left. He was about 5,000 feet away, about 20 degrees above us and about 30 degrees to our left. But try as I did, I couldn't reach Adams on the interphone, so I gave up and watched him get the other.

Shortly after Lt. Adams' kill, the Japanese discontinued sending their raiders over at 18,000 feet and started coming in at between 24,000 and 29,000 feet; which proved to be a problem for the night defenders. At these altitudes the P-70s radar equipment would usually work only intermittently, and quite frequently, would fail completely. Bad weather would give false indications on the radar or cause the picture on the scope to fade out completely. The VHF radio equipment used in the aircraft at this time was at an early stage of development and did not function well. The aircrews relied on their HF communication gear most of the time. But there was a great problem with this – the Japanese could monitor the HF frequencies that the GCI-P-70 crews were using. The Japanese, who usually came over in two plane raids, each plane spread 10 to 15 minutes apart, would start taking evasive action as soon as they heard the GCI controller start vectoring the interceptor.

"Herk" Adams and fellow pilot Samuel V. Blair both transferred out of the unit because of their frustration over the P-70s performance. Adams would attain six more victories as a day fighter pilot and Blair would be credited with seven.

At both of their bases on New Guinea, the 6th's responsibilities were to stand dawn to dusk alerts, no patrols. The night fighters would be scrambled only when an unknown aircraft was detected on the GCI, usually about 30 miles out. Then the P-70 would be scrambled and vectored into position for the attack as in the kill recorded by Lt. Adams and R/O DiLabbio. Unfortunately, Lt. Adams' kill was much the exception than the rule, due to the P-70s poor performance capabilities.

Like their fellow detachment on Guadalcanal, the New Guinea detachment was separated from the 6th Night Fighter Squadron and designated Detachment "A" Night Fighter Squadron.

By October 1943, out of frustration, the unit began experimenting with the idea of converting a P-38 into a night fighter. A P-38G was appropriated and Lt. Melvin Richardson, one of the pilots and the squadron's engineering officer, went to work on it. A SCR-540 AI radar set, probably removed from one of the P-70s, along with HF and VHF radios were installed in a belly tank. A second seat was added behind the pilot and the radio sets were wired to the pilot's and R/O's location as well as a scope for the R/O. It was found that even with the additional weight that the P-38 could climb to the same altitude as the P-70 in about 10 minutes vice 45 for the P-70. It was also capable of greater altitudes than the P-70. A second P-38G Lightning was also modified. For this gallant effort, Richardson and a radar mechanic who assisted received the Legion of Merit award.

Testing of these new night fighter aircraft had only just begun when an advanced element of the newly arrived 418th Night Fighter Squadron arrived at Dobodura on November 15, 1943. Detachment "A" Night Fighter Squadron was attached to the 418th shortly after their arrival. By the end of November Detachment "A" Night Fighter Squadron was disbanded. Some personnel were sent back to the States while the remainder were scattered among the other organizations within Fifth Air Force.

Chapter 5

Mediterranean Adventure

The air echelons of the 414th and 415th Night Fighter Squadrons bid farewell to their ground echelons. Their training at Orlando had been minimal. They had no idea of how to prepare for the English equipment they were to fly and maintain. Besides the aircrews, the air echelons were comprised of the maintenance and ordnance officers and key enlisted personnel. It would be up to these experienced men to teach those in the ground echelons once they rejoined in North Africa.

What had the night fighters learned during their stay in Orlando? The squadron history for the 417th gives us a hint at it:

For 4 1/2 months at Orlando and Kissimmee, our pilots had practiced at night flying. Anywhere from 140 to 30 hours in the P-70, twin-engined fighter-bomber, America's version of the night-fighter. Transition flights, navigation problems, target missions with fighter planes, GCI, AI, calibration flights, and some plain and fancy flying mixed in. Their course included about 25 hours link trainer time, for instrument flying must be second nature to the night-fighter. 'Seat of the pants' stuff doesn't work with a seven or eleven ton ship on a pitch-black night! Palm Beach, Miami Beach, Daytona Beach, Leesburg, Titusville, Tampa, Melbourne, Gainsville, even the Bahamas, Key West, all of Florida and surrounding waters, familiar names to the men in the black P-70s with the big yellow numbers. Lots of flying and lots of fun! Joe Leonard opening his top-hatch to help pull out of a spin, then fighting to close the hatch the rest of the way in! Nice cool work there, Joe! 'Chick' Hooton deciding he wanted to stop in a hurry, and finding out that the emergency brake apparatus really did work! Those poor tires. The two P-70s (pilots still officially unknown) who got caught buzzing, almost driving a poor Mrs. O'Donnell and her car off the road, resulting in the Banana River Naval Air Station reporting, 'Two Army P-70 type planes made strafing runs on this station and through

seaplane landing area at 1920 and 1938 at an average altitude of 40 feet. Planes very dark color, observed from air leaving in direction of Orlando.'

The air echelons of the 414th and 415th NFS sailed aboard the SS Empress of Scotland, which was originally the Empress of Japan, on March 23, 1943. A pleasure cruise it wasn't. Conditions were crowded and the food was not something of which you would request seconds, though this was typical of the many such voyages that were occurring between America and Britain. They arrived in the early afternoon on March 31 at Liverpool where they debarked and boarded their train for Cranfield.

The air echelons of the two American night fighter squadrons arrived at the RAF station at Cranfield, Bedfordshire late at night on the 31st. They were then transported by their RAF hosts from the nearby train station to Cranfield, a pre-war airdrome of great beauty. Here they found magnificent brick and stone buildings and hangars and many comforts which included WAAF "bat-women" who would take care of their quarters, make their beds, shine shoes and miscellaneous services.

The 415th NFS's unit history for April has a somewhat humorous perspective on the cultural differences between the Americans and the British:

We find that the differences between the American and British languages are sometimes embarrassing, sometimes amusing and often confusing (such words as "shag" and "keep your pecker up" had sexual inferences on one side of the Atlantic while on the other side it was quite the opposite). One of the British customs which is new to us is eating four meals a day. Besides breakfast and lunch we have tea at 1600 (4.00 p.m.) and supper at 2000 (10.00 p.m.). Another custom of which we don't disapprove is the six day working week.

Capt. Gordon Timmons of the 415th NFS in North Africa. (Gray)

Cool desert dress was always appropriate. George Fors, on the left, was "winner of the money," so states the back of the photo. (Hagen)

Business started immediately. To train the Yanks, the squadrons were split up according to their work sections and sent to the appropriate RAF station where they would learn the English equipment and methods of operations and maintenance. The pilots and engineering section operated out of nearby Twin Woods; the radar observers went to Usworth Ur Sunderland, Durham. The armorers trained at West Malling, while the engineering and radar maintenance worked with RAF Operational Training Unit Shops at Cranfield. All of the squadron's gunners were transferred out as the Bristol Beaufighter, which the Americans would be equipped with, did not have a requirement for their services.

The American pilots found they had quite a task in transitioning from the P-70 which they flew in Florida and the Beaufighter that they were destined to fight in. The 414th NFS history gives a good bit of insight into this matter:

This transition was made exceptionally difficult and unusually dangerous because of the widely different characteristics of the two aircraft. The technique of handling the tricycle geared P-70 is much more easily mastered than is that of handling the conventionally geared Beaufighter, which requires constant attention to the controls during the entire take-off and landing operations. The slightest pilot error at these times results in a ground loop. The location of the gas line on

Beaufighter aircraft presents further hazard when such an accident occurs. Situated at the rear of the engine and forward of the fuel tank, the line is invariably broken when the ship's undercarriage collapses. Fire and explosions are the all too frequent results.

On the day British pilots commenced to train air crews of the 414th Night Fighter Squadron, experienced aviators of the Battle of Britain admitted without exception that the Beaufighter was the most difficult of all British airplanes to fly.

The British made their program as comprehensive as was humanly possible and undoubtedly employed additional patience in their efforts because these trainees were Americans. Since the British flying training program is based largely on British equipment, graduate crews of the Royal Air Force enjoy the advantage of reaching the 1500 to 2000 horse power class of airplane in much the same manner as Americans do through primary, basic, and advanced. However, by comparison to British trained crews, the conversion problems of the 414th Night Fighter Squadron were multiplied many times. To effect the conversion from a P-70 to a Beaufighter, pilots had to unlearn more habits and learn more new techniques in flying than would have been the case in changing to any other airplane. It was necessary for them to master a new engine completely foreign in both design and operation. The airframe was vastly different in construction, balance, and airfoil characteristics from that of any aircraft they had flown in the United States. They were unfamiliar with thumb-controlled air brakes and the technique of landing a heavy conventional geared airplane.

One of the first and most vivid problems faced by pilots of the 414th Night Fighter Squadron was the use of thumb controlled brakes in place of toe brakes. From the first day these pilots had stepped into an Army plane to the day they entered the Beaufighter, they had used the toe brake. They had to forget their first flying-life habit and master a new coordination. They were obliged to understand the Beaufighter airframe thoroughly in order to keep from unduly straining the gear, empennage, and controls in taxiing, taking off, landing, and maneuvering in combat. They could not taxi with the ease they had formerly been used to because the Beaufighter had slick tires, airbrakes, and a heavy tail that would whiplash at the slightest laxity in control.

Handling the throttles and getting maximum performance from the sleeve-valve Hercules engine required a complete change in conception of control for American trained pilots. The increase in inertia within the engine, the lag in response to the throttles and the cooling of this differently cowled engine all offered new problems. On take-off they had to start down the runway straight and use throttle control because the rudder was not effective until the Beaufighter attained sixty miles per hour; in other words, rudder control required not only anticipation but also intuition. Power and air-foil characteristics were the important factors in rendering the acceleration and 'feel' of the Beaufighter on take-off vastly different from the American counterpart. Because the speed of the Beaufighter in going over the end of the runway is slower than that of the P-70 by thirty to fifty miles per hour, and because of the ship's built-in stability characteristics, pilots found it necessary to 'fly' the Beaufighter on take-off.

After becoming airborne the speeds of the Beaufighter compared favorably with those of the P-70. However, the lag between control surface pressure and reaction to that pressure was greater in the Beaufighter. Because Beaufighter trim controls, particularly rudder and aileron, were much less sensitive than those on the P-70, the former seemingly could never be trimmed to fly 'hands' off.' Although the facility of the Beaufighter in changing its attitude of flight became an advantage in aerial and intruder combat maneuvering, American pilots beginning to fly this craft felt that they did not have full control of the ship and were ill at ease. A common feeling among night fighters, which resulted in the transfer of some men back to American equipment, was expressed by a pilot of 250 combat hours when he stated that only during his last twenty hours did he really know that he had the Beaufighter 'all buttoned up.'

At Twin Woods vigorous calisthenics were indulged in every morning. The pilots flew 25 transitional hours in Blenheims and then checked out in their Beaufighter Mk VI aircraft, which were equipped with Mk IV AI. The schedule was that half of the pilots spent the morning of each day at ground school, conducted at Cranfield by the RAF, then flew out of Twin Woods in the afternoon, while the remaining pilots worked a reversed schedule. The observers at Usworth had four hours of class and flew in Avro Ansons for four hours, logging about 35 hours total time while in training. The 414th's history describes what the R/Os were challenged with:

Upon changing over to British type Mark IV A.I., which was carried in the first Beaufighters that were assigned to the 414th, the

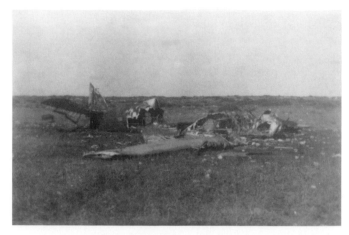

Desert remains. No matter where the night fighters went, there were always the remnants of war. (Gray)

The 414th NFS aircrews rejoined the ground echelon at Reghaia, Algeria on July 8, 1943 after completing their training in Great Britain. Smoke arises from two of the 414th NFS's Beaufighters that crashed on take-off from Reghaia. Scenes like this would be all too common to the AAF's Beaufighter squadrons in the Mediterranean. (Jenkins)

difficulties encountered by the observer in presenting to his pilot a verbal picture of position and movement of the enemy or target aircraft in relation to his own plane were slightly alleviated due to the technical improvements of this British set over the SCR 540-A. However, these improvements were only minor, and the observer was still confronted with the very annoying limitation of the gear caused by the fact that ground echoes restrict the range of A.I. coverage to the height of the fighter plane above ground. This, together with the enemy's devices for tail warning and his methods of jamming our radar, called for many long and tedious practice flights by each crew with the observer and pilot perfecting their running commentary, methods of approach, overshoot, and attack on low flying targets. Many of these flights were also carried out in joint practice with the ground radar stations until our teams gained a degree of professional skill and confidence which later proved ample to cope with the enemy's cunning tactics near Corsica.

As April 1943 came to a close, so did the first phase of training. The different elements of each air echelon gathered at Cranfield and prepared to transfer to their next station where the air echelons would operate as a unit. The 414th NFS air echelon was transferred to Valley Airdrome, Anglessy, Wales and the 415th went to Heathfield, Scotland. At their respective bases

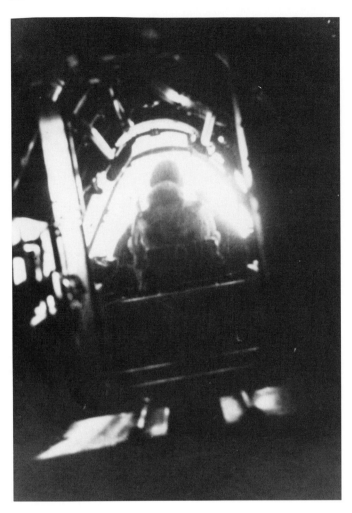

Inside the Beaufighter, looking towards the pilot. (Jenkins)

Three men boarded the Edinburgh Express in London and settled themselves in a small compartment. They were strangers, and none seemed willing to speak.

They rode in stony silence for about another hundred miles. Then one of the trio, a gentleman in his late 50's, spoke up:

'Name's Hathaway Parkinton-Jones. Brigadier General, Retired, Coldstream Guards. Married, two sons, both barristers.'

The express roared on for another hundred miles before the silence was again broken. This speaker was also in his late 50's and was also the very model of a proper English gentleman.

'Name's Reginald Cooper,' he said. 'Brigadier General, Retired, Queen's Own Fusiliers. Married, two sons, both surgeons.'

The third occupant, a non-descript little man, was not impressed with his fellow passengers. As though anxious to get it over with, he said, 'Name's Jenks. Chimney sweep, retired. Single, two sons, both brigadier generals.'

The first leg of their trip was a short one to Portreath on the southern tip of England. There the crews stayed overnight. During that time their Beaufighters received their final servicing. The crews were up early on the morning of July 1 and started on their long flight to Gibraltar. The flight was long and tiring. It was a welcome rest after flying some 1,250 miles in cramped quarters. After lunch they took off for "the Dark Continent." It had just before dark when they landed in Algiers. The following morning Brig.Gen. Elwood R. "Pete" Quesada, commander of XII Fighter Command, paid the night fighters a visit. To welcome them, he invited the commanding officers and flight commanders of the night fighter squadrons over to his house for dinner that evening.

each unit was assigned 12 Mark VI Beaufighters. By mid-month they were checked out in their mounts and moved on to other bases where their operational training would be concluded.

The 415th moved on to Prestwick and the 414th to Honiley. At Honiley the 414th greeted the 416th Night Fighter Squadron who, along with the 417th, had just arrived from the States. The 417th had been assigned to Ayr, Scotland. Unlike the preceding AAF night fighter squadrons, the entire 416th and 417th squadrons had been sent to Britain for their final phase of training. Their training for the next two and a half months would be like their predecessors.

In the morning hours of June 30 the 414th's and 415th's crews bid farewell to the RAF personnel that had been attached to them during their training. They loaded all they could in their aircraft and headed for Portreath on the first leg of their journey to North Africa. From Honiley, the 414th took off as a squadron, formed over the field, then made a low pass over the field (some of the pilots being low enough to chew up parts of the grass field) as they headed south.

The men of the 415th NFS left the British Isles with more than British training and British aircraft. There was also a little British humour as illustrated by the following:

Armament personnel of the 416th NFS load ammunition for the Beaufighters .303 in. wing guns. Note the Mk. IV AI radar antenna mounted on the wing's leading edge. (USAF)

When the night fighters arrived the Northwest African Air Force (NAAF), which was composed of British air units and the US Twelfth Air Force, had just completed their victorious campaign over the Axis forces on Pantelleria and Lampedusa and were initiating operation HUSKY, the invasion of Sicily. These first missions were against airfields on the islands of Sicily and Sardinia and on mainland Italy.

July 3rd was a day the night fighters were looking forward to for about two and a half months – they were complete squadrons again. The 414th NFS joined up with their ground echelon at Monastir, Tunisia, while Capt. Gordon D. Timmons and his 415th NFS joined it at Rerhaia, Algeria. The ground echelons had been in Algeria since about May 10th. During their long wait the mechanics of the 414th got some "hands-on" time with Beaufighters as the RAF's 255 Squadron at La Sabala II in Tunisia took them under their wing for a couple of weeks.

Though night fighters were under British control, the British gave Major Arden W. Cowgill, the 414th NFS CO, a free hand to develop his own tactics, evasive actions, etc. With the Sicilian campaign just starting, most of the night fighters' missions were of convoy escort and cover. It was one of these type missions that the 415th NFS flew on its first operational flight on July 5. This one was a patrol flight of the Sousse harbor area south of Tunis.

On July 10 the 415th lost their first aircraft in North Africa (two pilots had been lost in Beaufighter training during their stay in Great Britain). One of the Beaus piloted by Lt. Jordan had just landed when the engine caught fire. Both Jordan and his R/O escaped without injury, but the aircraft was a complete writeoff. Less than a week later Lt. Konosky had an engine quit on him as he was taking off. Konosky crash landed his craft and both he and his R/O got out unscathed. Yet three days later Lt. Harold F. Augspurger crashed in making an attempted landing at Teleigma. The Beau burned, making the third one lost in July. Fortunately, both crew members escaped uninjured. All four Twelfth Air Force night fighter squadrons would have such problems with their Beaufighters, especially with ground looping.

On July 23 both the 414th and 415th NFSs sent crews to the field at Protville, near Bizerte, for a week's tour of duty. It had been observed that there was considerable enemy transport activity between Sardinia, Corsica, and Italy. These crews would be part of operation PANTHER, which was to destroy as many of these, and any other enemy aircraft, as they could intercept during sweeps of the Tyrrhenian Sea. Both squadrons' detachment would see action when they flew their first mission the next day – and with the same enemy aircraft.

On this mission, Major Arden Cowgill and Lt. Billie White of the 414th NFS and Capt. Nathaniel H. Lindsay with F/O Austin G. Petry as his R/O represented the 415th. At 7:25 a.m. a German He 115 was spotted some 45 miles east of Olbia. Lindsay made the first pass at the Heinkel setting the starboard engine afire. Major Cowgill went in next. The Heinkel went into a dive and was observed breaking up as it went into the sea. The Air Force awarded the victory to Lindsay and Petry.

The 414th NFS received their first Beaufighter fitted with the much improved Mark VIII AI was received on October 7, 1943. This radar did not suffer from ground returns as severely as the older Mark IV.

The 415th NFS erect maintenance stands in preparation of many hours of work needed to keep their Beaufighters fighting. (Gray)

The ground crews of the 416th NFS serviced the squadrons' Beaufighters in the afternoon in preparation for that night's missions. (USAF)

A Luftwaffe Messerschmitt Bf 109 that is no longer flyable but proved of interest to the Allied airmen who always wanted to know more about the enemy aircraft they were up against. (Gray)

Cantania Airfield, Sicily, as it looked when the 415th arrived in September 1943. (Gray)

The Protville detachment flew sweeps with no contact for the next few days. On the 27th, the 414th had three Beaufighters in the air. An Italian SM 82 bomber-transport was spotted some 60 miles west of Monte Circeo. The three Beaus gave chase for about 10 minutes when Capt. Charnley K. Atwater was in position dead astern of the enemy and opened fire. Next, Lt. Francis B. Clark was in position, also dead astern, opened fire, moving from that position to the port side while firing. Return fire from the SM 82 hit Clark's plane. F/O Cortina, flying as Clark's R/O, had one of these shells explode in front of him. Fortunately, though rather disconcerting, neither man was injured. The Italian crew managed to ditch their craft in the sea. Three of the crew were observed to climb out on the wing and get into a dinghy. Atwater and his R/O, F/O David L. McAbee, received credit for the kill. Unfortunately for Clark and Cortina, the enemy fire that they had absorbed had damaged their hydraulic system and Clark was not able to get his landing gear down. He made a belly landing from which both crew members were able to walk away.

The night fighters ended July with the 414th NFS getting their second victory. Lts. John E. Patterson and George J. Holbig were on a sweep when they observed an Italian transport some 50 miles off the northeastern coast of Sardinia. Holbig and his R/O, F/O Irving Wohl, attacked the transport from port astern. They saw their fire hitting the port engine, fuselage, and tail. The aircraft seemed to ditch, but no one was seen to get out.

The 415th's first month of combat had their enthusiasm dampened with the loss of one aircraft and its R/O. On July 26 one of their Beaufighters piloted by Lt. J.E. Jennings and F/O W.K. Price, as his R/O, were with a second squadron Beaufighter when they were jumped by a Bf 109. The German attacked both planes, causing severe damage to Jennings.' Only Jennings was able to get out and parachuted into the Tyrrhenian Sea area and was later rescued.

The 416th NFS moved in September also; in their case it was to mainland Italy. Here "Honeychile" is serviced at Grottagile, Italy. (USAF)

Dense smoke covers a good portion of the airfield after one of the 416th's planes crashes while landing and catches fire. The pilot and R/O crawled out of the wreckage unhurt. (USAF)

Harris Cargill, Brewer, Darwin Brake, and Jim Doudna at the "Finger Inn." All were of the 416th except for Brewer who had been with the 416th until he was in a serious airplane accident during their training in England. At the time of this photo, Brewer was flying with Air Transport Command. (Hagen)

In August the Twelfth Air Force's night fighter strength doubled. Fresh from the British Isles the 416th and 417th Night Fighter Squadrons arrived. Under the command of Capt. Amberse M. Banks, who had taken over command in late June, the 416th NFS arrived at Algiers for a short stay. By August 17 they were located at Bone, Algeria where they became operational. To help the new arrival, the 415th NFS at La Sabala, Tunisia sent representatives from each department of the squad-

ron for a two week stay with the 416th. Unlike the 416th, which would be stationed at six different fields before the year ended, the 417th arrived at Tafaraoui, Algeria on August 8th and would stay there into January. Maj. Joseph T. Ehlinger, the 417th's C.O., soon had his squadron integrated into the night fighter force.

The 415th was credited with its third and last aerial victory while on the African continent on August 16. First Lt. Robert E. Walber and F/O Emmett B. Faison, Jr. encountered and destroyed a modified Italian Z 1007 during the early morning hours.

Capt. Earl T. Smith of the 414th NFS received credit for that squadron's one victory in August while he was on an "administrative" flight. The action report tells a good story:

On August 18 Captain Smith took off from Taher to return to base after making an administrative flight to this airdrome near Djidjelli. Riding in the observer's seat was S/Sgt Bryant, while Lt. Walker, a student pilot with the squadron, rode behind the pilot's seat. As he was crossing Bougie Bay, Captain Smith noticed an unfamiliar aircraft east on the deck. His suspicions aroused, he went down to investigate, at which time the aircraft turned north. Giving chase it was soon determined that the aircraft was a Ju 88. After a chase of several minutes the Captain closed to attack, but to his dismay found that his cannon was jammed. He was forced to make the attack with his machine guns, and only four of these were found to be serviceable. Return fire was drawn from the German plane, and a few ineffectual hits were scored on our Beaufighter. Finally, after a 45-minute chase, Captain Smith was forced to turn back, and he left the enemy aircraft with one engine smoking. The claim sent in was one Ju 88 probably destroyed.

A few nights later Lt. White and F/O Kirschenbaum were sent out on an Air-Sea rescue mission from Taher. Lights from a dinghy were seen, and fixes were taken from different heights. The crews on this dinghy were picked up later, and discovered to be German. They had been at sea for a number of days, and suffering from exposure were unable to give any authentic information at first. Later, when they were sufficiently recovered it was definitely established that they had been shot down by a Beaufighter on the afternoon of August 18 in the area where Captain Smith had his combat. Thus the 'probably destroyed' was taken down from the scoreboard, and a 'destroyed' put in its place.

In mid-September the 414th's Maj. Arden Cowgill was assigned to the 63rd Fighter Wing at Rerhaia, Algeria. Taking over command of the squadron was Maj. Earl T. Smith. In an intelligence interview conducted in May 1944, Maj. Cowgill's experiences were capsulized:

Major Cowgill's outfit arrived in North Africa in July 1943, and shortly thereafter the first all-American Night Fighter mission was carried out. Once assigned to combat duty, the squadron continued to operate in close coordination with the British, who handled all operations. Major Cowgill was left with a free hand to develop his own night fighter tactics, evasive action, etc. It was at this time that the foundation was laid for our own night fighter tactics, independent of the RAF. He remained as CO of the 414th in North Africa operating in and around Oran, Algiers and Bone and accomplished intruder missions near Bizerte. For a while and it is reminiscent of many instances in this war, equipment was inadequate and obsolete. The Beaufighters and radar had been superseded by improved models but these could not be obtained. It wasn't possible with the Mark IV equipment to operate effectively below 3,000 feet altitude. However, with obsolete equipment and only 12 aircraft the squadron managed to fly some 400 combat hours per month. Red tape was overcome and the American night fighters were supplied with the latest Mark VIII equipment (in October 1943); now they could operate effectively below 3,000 feet altitude and down to 500 feet.

Major Cowgill had flown 67 combat hours which included three intruder missions prior to leaving the squadron.

When US troops entered Messina, Sicily on August 17, 1943, the Sicilian Campaign was officially over. The next move would be the invasion of Italy. To give the Allied forces night protection on Sicily, the 415th NFS was transferred to that Mediterranean island on September 3. The scenery was quite different from their previous North African setting. Here they were nestled among the ever present almond groves. They soon found that they were only a 15 minute walk to a beautiful, crystal clear swimming hole along the coast of the Ionian Sea.

In October the 414th NFS started transitioning from Mark IV to the Mark VIII AI radar. The differences in these equipment is described in a report made by that squadron:

In October 1943 the 414th observers were confronted with transition to the improved British A.I. Mark VIII. This new type equipment, while possessing conspicuous advances over the Mark IV, had many limitations and used an entirely different method of target presentation. To realize the problems confronting the observer, it must be understood that since this set provided for low-level scanning, it would therefore pick up false targets from mountains and islands. Remarkable skill and intuition were required on the part of observers in order to distinguish these false 'blips' from the genuine. On many occasions they lost and regained their contacts four or five times before they completed the interception. Whenever the 'bogey' struck out in the general direction of any hilly land or an island, the genuine 'blip' would be surrounded and almost obscured by these ground echoes, even as far as thirty-five miles out over water. Demonstrating a high degree of determination, 414th observers proved their versatility and adaptability by mastering completely the new techniques for operating this set and became 100% operational on it within one month.

The 415th's two month stay at Cassibile was ended due to inclement weather. Their living area, dispersal area and runway were all unpaved, flat, and very poor drainage. Neither man nor machine were equipped to operate under these conditions. Though no enemy aircraft were claimed, the 415th, as well as the other AAF night fighter squadrons in the Mediterranean area, provided protection for the fleet and beach heads.

On November 2nd the 415th arrived at Cantania, Sicily. Because of the poor conditions back on Cassibile, it took the squadron most of the day to get their aircraft free of the mud and into the air. One aircraft was so mired down in the mud that it was temporarily left behind. On the 11th, the 414th left North Africa and set up operations on Sardinia, leaving the 416th and 417th on the African continent.

In November the 417th NFS got their first aerial kill. The squadron history vividly describes the action:

Using an elaborate system of pathfinders and previously selected assembly points, and taking advantage of poor weather which afforded cover and concealment, the German Air Force began striking at troop and supply convoys moving towards Naples and Bari. Large forces of Heinkel 177s, Dorniers, and Ju 88s, carrying radio-controlled bombs, repeatedly attacked these allied convoys at dusk or during the hours of night only. During the entire period, planes of the 417th [Night Fighter Squadron] met every enemy attack in its assigned area and either drove off the bombers, or reduced the enemy attempt to ineffectual impotence. As an example of the tenacity and determination with which aircrews of the 417th kept faith with their responsibility, an attack may be cited which took place on the night of November 11, 1943. A large force of Heinkels, Dorniers, and Junkers attacked an important eastbound convoy 20 miles northeast of Arzu. Lt. C.(Clarence) Richard McCray, pilot of a Beaufighter (Lt. Robert D. Hamilton as R/O), after a determined pursuit to head off the attacking bombers, discovered that both engines of his plane were over-heating badly. Although he realized that either or both of the engines might quit at any moment, he nevertheless maintained his pursuit and shot down one Dornier 217 into the sea. Although low gas supply and faulty engines would have

Take-off in late afternoon. Soon the sun would be down and these 416th Beaufighters will be on station over Allied convoys, troop installations, or on station and awaiting GCI directions to intercept an incoming target. (USAF)

"Fluff" of the 416th NFS stands idle during the day. The night fighters' shift usually started just before sundown. (USAF)

justified an immediate break-off, he still refused to leave the engagement. Disregarding the flashing danger signals on his panel, he searched for other enemy bombers until he found another Dornier, giving it several long bursts. This plane was later verified as probably destroyed. Lt. McCray (now Major) was later awarded the Air Medal for his courageous action.

Capt. Harold L. Price, a former member of the 414th NFS, reported his squadron's activities, including their kill in November, in a combat intelligence interview at Hammer Field in Fresno, California in late May 1944:

In November 1943, the squadron moved from North Africa to Sardinia and, at this time, engaged heavily in search radar interception from the southern coast of France to the Anzio beachhead. The German bombers followed this general path to the beachhead and were usually caught in the close vicinity of Elba Island off the west coast of Italy.

Once based at Sardinia the 414th [as with the other AAF night fighter squadrons in that area] was equipped with the new British Mark VIII AI which is the approximate equivalent to our SCR-720. Formerly when using the Mark IV AI in North Africa trouble had cropped up. The German, once warned, could employ evasive action and slip away. He was aware of the Mark IV's limitations and usually hit the deck to cut the Mark IV's range to a minimum. However, the new AI was deadly stuff, making it extremely difficult for the Hun to evade. Hitting the deck, he no longer could effect a get-away for the AI range down here was not appreciably changed to permit this. The squadron worked in constant close cooperation with the GCI stations. It was well developed system with both stations and operating personnel exceptionally good. The stations could obtain a 90 mile range provided the Hun was no lower than 7,000 feet. The range of the AI Mark VIII was eight miles.

The 414th, like the 417th, would also claim an aerial victory in November. The Coastal Air Force would report, "The enemy launched another attack in Bougie Bay, timing it an hour and a half before sunset. One [troop] transport [of the Allied convoy in that area] was hit by an HS glider-bomb and sank with heavy

Field maintenance is performed on one of the 414th's Mark VIII AI equipped Beaus at Elmas. With a constant shortage of operable aircraft, the maintenance personnel had to be quite resourceful. (Jenkins)

loss of life due to the high seas running at the time. A very heavy toll was taken of the strike force." Both day and night fighters of the Allied air forces went aloft and accomplished the destruction of numerous enemy bombers. Among the Allied defenders was a crew from the 414th NFS consisting of 2nd Lt. Francis B. Clark (pilot), 2nd Lt. Abraham M. Goodman (R/O), as well as a Lt. Allemand. They successfully intercepted and destroyed an He 177. The combat report adds a few more details:

On November 26th 1943 Lt. Goodman was riding as observer with me on an administrative trip to Algiers. Lt. Allemand of 346 Squadron was a passenger. We passed a convoy near Bougie at 1615 hours when the R/T told of enemy formations approaching from the north. We turned north on an intercepting vector climbing from 7,000 to 12,000 feet. By the time we reached the vicinity of the convoy the first wave had attacked. We could see French Spits mixing it up with them and later learned there were English Beau's & P-39s. We spotted a big one about 10 miles away going full speed for the deck and gave chase. After ten minutes we caught him just in the base of a broken cloud layer around 2500 feet. Some miles back from a quarter view Allemand and I had identified the long nose, two nacelle etc. as a He 177. Now we could also see two glide bombs along outside the engines. He went into a slow starboard turn, so at 300 yds. with 10 deg. deflection I gave him a long burst with cannons and machine guns

raking him from outside the left nacelles through the fuselage to the right nacelle. Oil and pieces of the ship, one of which could have been an engine cowl or escape hatch flew past and both engines were on fire as we ducked into the clouds for a second. Dropping down on a parallel we saw him jettisoning fuel and one of the radio controlled bombs shaped like a plane. One man bailed out. We closed to 250 yards firing him again in both engines; this time he started losing altitude and I think the fuselage was on fire. Then for good measure we went in a third time to 100-150 yards leaving the whole ship a mass of flames as it dived into the sea. Another man parachuted just before the ship hit and exploded. We circled twice but couldn't see any signs of life so climbed for a fix and headed for Reghaia.

Captain Price of the 414th NFS reported on the types of missions that the night fighters flew in his 1944 combat intelligence report:

The few intruder missions, about three per man in the squadron, were largely limited to attempts to seek out and hit the German radar stations on the Balearic Islands. Intruder missions were not attempted on a large scale due to security restrictions placed on the Mark VIII AI. These restrictions regulations prohibited flying the Beaufighters closer than a ten mile band along the western coast of Italy. The 415th, however, based at Naples, did do a great deal of intruder work but here

A trio of 416th Beaus make a low pass while the officer on the right seems to be giving hand signals. (NASM/Smithsonian)

the squadron was equipped with the old Mark IV AI which had no security restrictions to limit them.

The night fighters were used as convoy escort and cover when the weather was too bad for the day fighters. The Beaufighters being a much better instrument ship could make use of its AI in day time and come through the worst weather, where a day fighter was really up against it. The squadron carried out a continual training program and when covering a convoy, two ships were always sent up to work a practice interception. Patrols and alerts were maintained at all times. The squadron had alert shifts and at any time during these shifts four pilots, R/O's and ships would always be ready to go.

Comments on German bombing tactics:

The Germans seldom came over at high altitudes such as the 30,000 foot level the Japs are using. In bombing convoys, the Jerry came over on the deck. For hitting harbor or shipping areas his altitude was between 10,000 and 15,000 feet. Their formations would vary. Sometimes they sent as many as 30 or 40 aircraft. In the great majority of attempted bombings (the Germans knew night fighters were protecting the area) they would jettison their bombs and head for home. At one time, 30 German bombers attempted a raid on the harbor facilities and shipping at Algiers. When they got within five miles of the coast and became aware that night fighters were operating over the target (radio intercept) they dropped all their bombs and headed for home. From prisoners captured and questioned it has been determined that the German fighters are deathly afraid of Spitfires in the day and the night fighting Beaufighters. They high tail it for home or take violent evasive action as soon as they know your presence."

German evasive methods and tactics:

The Germans employ 'window' which clutter up the GCI and AI scopes. However, Captain Price stated that 'window' isn't too difficult for an experienced R/O to recognize. It remains in the area dropped for quite a long time, drifting with the wind. On the GCI and AI tubes it looks like a little sausage with fuzzy edges. It does, however, take a well-trained, experienced R/O to call it and avoid following it around.

The Germans are using some type of airborne AI in the rear of bombers as a means of warning against closing night fighters. It appears to have a range between 2,000 and 3,000 feet and works very satisfactorily. As soon as they pick up one of our night fighters, they begin immediate evasive action. The squadron (414th NFS) first ran into this in December 1943. It was an out-growth of the terrific beating the Germans took in the air action around Bizerte – an attempt and seemingly successful one to develop some means of protection against our night fighters. The usual evasive action employed by the Germans was to hit the deck in an attempt to short range the allied AI. This was rather successful until the squadron was equipped with the new Mark VIII AI.

The American night fighters had their baptism under fire in 1943. They were now veterans and ready to meet anything the enemy could throw at them. 1944 would open with a bang with the Anzio landings, and the night fighters would be in on the action.

Wind tunnel testing continued throughout the war in an effort to refine the Black Widow. Here a technician adjusts the 1/8th scale model in the Caltech wind tunnel. (Northrop via Balzer)

Chapter 6

Nocturnal Primitives

On December 7, 1941, the Japanese attacked Pearl Harbor and the United States of America was at war. By the 24th, a Letter of Intent was initiated which called for 100 P-61 series airplanes and spare parts. A supplement to the contract dated January 17, 1942, provided for an additional 50 aircraft. Yet another supplement was approved on February 26th which superseded the prior two contractual documents ordered 410 examples of this new night fighter. Under this agreement 50 aircraft were called for under a second Lend Lease Program and 360 aircraft for the U.S. Army Air Corps. Under these contracts, $7,136,689.56 was chargeable to Defense Aide and $55,656,178.57 to Air Corps Appropriations. The delivery schedule was set up under this agreement calling for 12 aircraft to be delivered in April, 1943, to the RAF under Lend Lease, 45 to be delivered in May, 1943, of which 38 were under the Lend Lease agreement and seven for the Air Corps, and 45 additional aircraft to go to the Air Corps between June and December 1943 with the remaining 38 aircraft to be delivered to the Air Corps during the month of January 1944.

The red letter day of May 26, 1942, scheduled first flight of the first XP-61, was fast approaching. Though it seemed that the aircraft would meet all expectations, the road had not been smooth. At the beginning of the year a directive had been issued by Materiel Command which stated the P-61 project would experience a three week delay due to Northrop's sub-contract work on the A-31 Vengeance dive-bomber. Upon further investigation by Materiel Command they determined that the War Department directive which they were following did not apply to Northrop.

The XP-61 had been scheduled to have the AI-10 experimental radar which was being developed at the Radiation Laboratory at MIT to be installed. However, in order to make the experimental aircraft as close as possible in configuration to the production aircraft, it was decided that the SCR-520 production radar, which was being manufactured by the Western Electric Company, would be installed instead. Partially due to

this change in plans it would not be until early April 1943 when a XP-61, the second aircraft, would receive the initial radar equipment. There were possible propeller problems in the wind also. In February 1942 the propeller division of Curtiss informed the Army and Northrop that propellers would not be available for the experimental aircraft. As a replacement, Hamilton-Standard propellers would be installed on the XP-61s initially. All was not bad news, for the day before the Widow's first flight, the Army Air Forces drew up a letter contract calling for 1,200 P-61s. These aircraft would be produced by Northrop at a government facility at Denver, Colorado. Shortly after awarding this contract it was reduced to 1,000 and by late July the contract was renegotiated downwards to 207, all of which would be produced at Northrop's Hawthorne, California plant.

The big day, May 26, 1942. It was late afternoon when veteran test pilot Vance Breese took the first XP-61 on its maiden flight leaving the Northrop Field runway at 4:37. Flight time was very short, fifteen minutes, during which all preliminary evaluations seemed satisfactory. At the conclusion of the flight, Breese is reported to have exclaimed to Mr. Northrop, "Jack, you've got a damn fine airplane!" The plane which flew this day was not much like those that would be flying in combat some two years hence. This was an aircraft without radar, with a dummy turret on top, Hamilton-Standard propellers, partial Zap flaps, and conventional ailerons. Breese, who Northrop had contracted with for the initial test flights only, was soon replaced by John W. Myers.

Myers, who had been a lawyer, found his interests was in the flying game while at Lockheed Aircraft. Jack Northrop who had known of John Myers through legal matters in the past contacted Lockheed Aircraft in Burbank and made arrangements for his release and subsequent employment with Northrop. Myers was retained as a consultant test pilot with Lockheed throughout the war. Subsequent flights of the XP-61 by Myers revealed stability problems in its present configuration and numerous problems with the experimental R-2800-25S engines. Numerous engine failures had been experienced and from the

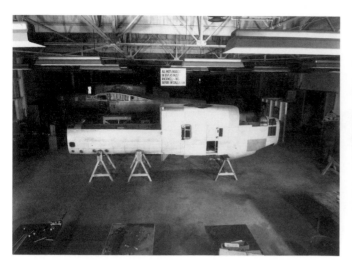

Progress on the crew nacelles of the two experimental P-61s is shown in this February 1942 photograph. First flight for the first XP-61 was only three months off. (Northrop via Balzer)

Close up view of the welded magnesium boom. Magnesium welding techniques were developed by Northrop's Chief of Research, Vladimir Pavlecka. (Northrop via Balzer)

Oxygen bottle installation in the XP-61. Oxygen quantity was greatly increased in the production planes. (Northrop via Balzer)

occasions. He remembers one encounter that Myers had with a canopy:

John had developed a skill most good test pilots should have. That's a very artful, dynamic, way of kicking ass if things went wrong. And they frequently did. I remember one case in particular. This was the XP-61. The cockpit arrangement and canopy release mechanism was different than on the production planes that followed. It was a one piece canopy and the whole thing was supposed to come off in one fell swoop. We were doing our cockpit check prior to a test flight one day. I was looking at my things that I had to do and John was checking over the cockpit. All of a sudden he looked down at the canopy release mechanism. And he said to me, 'Do you think that thing will release?' I said some reassuring thing like, 'Beats the hell out of me!' And John gave it a real good pull and nothing happened. It didn't budge. Then he gave it another, harder pull, and it still didn't budge. So then he got himself cocked around in the cockpit and got his foot up on something, maybe the instrument panel, and gave it one hell of a jerk, and nothing happened. By then you could see the temperature rise – John was obviously PO'd. We got out of the cockpit, and he stomped into the flight office and proceeded to do a number on that flight department, like you have never seen. I have always admired that characteristic, never perfected it myself, but, pretty handy thing to have.

John did it in a nice way. They still ended up respecting him and they knew they had their work to do. It took the crew, the engineer, and I don't know who else to get that canopy off of there. It took four crowbars, two on each side. It was a disaster! If old Vance Breese had known that he'd have upped his fee, I think.

Early in the flight test program Northrop had decided to replace the partial spans Zap flap with full span flaps for two reasons, the first and probably greatest were mechanical problems which were hampering production and installation of the Zap flaps. Second, full span flaps would improve short field landings and take-off. To improve longitudinal stability the horizontal stabilizer and elevator were redesigned. John Myers recalled his early flights in the XP-61:

evaluation made by Pratt & Whitney, the engine manufacturers, it was determined that the cause of their troubles was oil and gas being trapped in the engine crankcase. The aircraft was grounded in July during which time the -10 version of the engine was installed in place of the -25S.

Hugo Pink, one of Northrop's flight test engineers on the Black Widow project, flew with John Myers on a number of

Above and left:
Turret installation in the XP-61 shortly before rollout. (Northrop via Balzer)

The aircraft initially had Zap flaps on the inboard portion of the wings only. It had the jury-built aileron (standard type) system and an elevator with an offset hinge. The reasoning for the offset hinge type was that as it was unported it would take care of the tremendous negative pitching moment that was anticipated that the flap would produce when they were put down. The result of this thing was that the airplane was pretty violently unstable in the longitudinal mode. So unstable that if you got very far off of your trim speed you just weren't strong enough to handle it. The faster it went the more it wanted to dive, or the slower it went the more it would want to loop.

Northrop Aircraft had been involved in the National Advisory Committee for Aeronautics (NACA), the predecessor to NASA, experiment with a Sikorsky OS2U-2 airplane at Moffett Field where it had been reconfigured to use full span Zap flaps and different configurations of circular-arc spoiler ailerons. So to enable the P-61 to utilize maximum trailing edge space on the wings for flaps, it was decided to use the circular-arc type spoiler device for lateral control. Small conventional ailerons would be used to give the pilot "feel."

A NACA report describes some of the background and engineering involved:

A spoiler-type lateral-control system has been developed for use on the Northrop P-61 airplane. The lateral-control system is to be used with large-span flaps and consists of a thin circular arc spoiler, linked with a short-span plain aileron located just outboard of the spoiler. This unconventional lateral-control system has been accepted with enthusiasm by the pilots who have flown the airplane. They particularly

appreciate its characteristics at high speed. The combination of light forces, favorable yawing moment, and low wing torsional moments, make it a very effective, easily applied control. The control available at and through the stall is also remarkably good, although this characteristic may be attributed, in part, to an exceptionally good wing stalling pattern rather than entirely to the use of the spoiler type aileron. In the landing configuration, the lateral-control effectiveness increases automatically with the extension of wing flap so that powerful control is available during the approach. There is, however, a decrease in effectiveness for the first four per cent of the wheel travel with a resultant tendency for inexperienced pilots to over control slightly at low speeds. The fact that the aileron can be fully used at the stall, however, more than compensates for this loss of effectiveness with flaps down and greatly enhances the airplane's landing performance.

In the case of the Northrop design, landing and approach performance were deemed of sufficient importance to warrant an attempted solution of the fullspan-flap problem. The choice of the lateral control

The second XP-61 receiving its engines. (Northrop via Balzer)

XP-61 number one shortly after rollout. The two experimental models would sport their overall black paint scheme only for a short time. They would be in natural metal finish for most of their careers (unlike the 13 service test aircraft which would maintain their black finish). (Tinker AFB via Campbell)

Contract test pilot Vance Breese revs up the XP-61's engines prior to first flight from Northrop Field in Hawthorne, California, in May 1942. (Wolford)

arrangement to be used was largely a matter of picking the lesser of a number of evils, in view of the limited success of installations and schemes tested up to that time. A review of the possibilities, however, showed that in regards to adequacy of control and mechanical simplicity, the spoiler-type lateral control device had the advantage over slot-lip ailerons, drooped ailerons, plain ailerons in combination with retractable flaps, or any of the other devices enjoying current favor. As a matter of fact, the only question mark concerning its successful application to an airplane was its very erratic hinge moments – a fault also appearing in some of the other possible systems. Accordingly, the retractable aileron was chosen as the most likely to succeed. The ways and means used in obtaining satisfactory hinge moments and effectiveness are given herein.

It soon became apparent that the solution of the hinge-movement problem would be perhaps the most difficult. Researches conducted by the National Advisory Committee for Aeronautics finally had produced a stable hinge-moment variation for a modified circular-arc spoiler, but only through the use of various vanes, vents, and passages some of

them apparently quite critical. Even then, the resultant pilot forces were unacceptably high, and no satisfactory method of trim control was available. Preliminary tests in the Northrop wind tunnel directed toward the possibility of obtaining stable hinge moments with a system in which the center of rotation and the center of the arc were not coincident showed no promise. Pressure measurements corroborated the speculation that the extending hinge moments, existing near the flush neutral position, were due to the negative pressures acting on the exposed edge of the scoop (These extending moments, when combined in an unsymmetrical mechanical system, produce unstable pilot forces). While these extending moments were not directly proportional to the upper-surface of the scoop, nevertheless, their magnitude could apparently be greatly decreased by a reduction of this area. It was decided, accordingly, to minimize the inherent instability of the scoop by the simple expedient of reducing its thickness as much as possible.

It was thus possible to provide lateral control with very little attendant pilot effort, and there remained only to build into the system a positive centering tendency, some means of trim control and some

The interior of the XP-61's pilot's compartment. (Northrop via Balzer)

degree of pilot 'feel.' Since these properties are all, of course, available in the conventional lateral control, one solution of the difficulties enumerated was to link to the scoop system a complete conventional aileron of small span. This compromise system, moreover, consisted of components the characteristics of which were sufficiently explored to allow routine aerodynamic calculations. Its advantages more than outweighed the loss of wing flap attending the use of a small conventional aileron. There now existed a reasonable certainty that a 90 per cent full-span flap could be made to work with a relatively small amount of development time.

In the interests of a continuous wing flap and also as a concession to conservatism, it was decided to locate the conventional 'balance' aileron at the wing tip. A preliminary wheel-force analysis, neglecting the scoop contribution, indicated that a plain-flap aileron occupying the outer wing bay, having a chord of approximately 15 per cent of the wing chord and a maximum throw of 25 degrees, would supply forces in the neighborhood of 80 pounds wheel force at 80 per cent of maximum indicated level flight speed. The scoop located adjacent to the balance aileron and at approximately 70 per cent wing chord, to insure acceptable time-lag characteristics, was laid out.

The results of this development program indicate, to some degree, the success obtained with this new lateral-control arrangement. Another indication is the universal enthusiasm with which pilots have accepted

this unconventional control.

The scoop vibration that occurred inside the slot during the preliminary flight tests can be eliminated by closing the lower-surface slot. Closing the slot had little effect on the control flaps up, but with flaps down, the effect was detrimental unless the flap slot was sealed.

This change in flap and aileron configuration required an entire restructuring of the trailing edge of the P-61's wing. As the first XP-61 was being modified, the second P-61, which was still under construction, had its wings restructured to this new design also. In November 1942, the second XP-61 was rolled out at the Northrop factory; and some days later, on the 18th, it made its first flight. This was the first flight of a XP-61 with full span flaps and spoiler type ailerons. During the test flights of the second XP-61 some difficulties were experienced which caused the pilot to use excessive amounts of energy when operating the rudders. It was felt that the restructuring of the wings and horizontal stabilizer brought about certain aerodynamic changes which in turn now caused these difficulties. By changing the shape of the leading edges of the rudders, this problem was overcome.

Vibrations were experienced with the new circular-arc

spoilers when they were in the stowed position. John Myers recalls:

Initially the spoilers travelled in a slot that completely penetrated the wings from the top side to the bottom. The spoiler would extend upward from the top of the wing, then it would go down underneath the wing, and as it came underneath the wing it would more or less port. We ran into a series of problems with this slot running all the way through the wing. One was high speed vibrations. The spoilers were constructed out of magnesium. The air currents through the slot would cause a resonance that would just destroy the spoilers. Several times I had to land with the aileron controls completely locked because the spoilers had shattered. It really caused no real problem because the airplane had very good directional stability, plus with the twin engines it was easy enough to keep the wing up and make a successful landing. The ultimate cure of that is to put a plate over the slot on the underside of the wing, stopping the air flow through the slot.

The Army Air Forces' Project Officer, Lt.Col. Marshall S. Roth, visited Northrop Aircraft in mid-June during which time

Northrop test pilot John Myers prepares to take off in one of the experimental Widows. Myers' duties not only included those of test pilot but he had to go to the Pacific where he had to "sell" the P-61 to the AAF night fighter squadrons stationed there who had no training in that aircraft before deploying overseas. (Northrop)

Because of the engine problems with the initial R-2800-25S engines, they were replaced by the R-2800-10 series early in the XP-61's flight test program. (Northrop via Balzer)

Northrop learned much from a contract it had with NACA where they experimented with unique control surfaces on a Navy-Sikorsky OS2U-2. Famed aeronautical engineer Edward Zap was a consultant on this project. (Northrop via Balzer)

he test flew the XP-61 in its original configuration. In general he found that the airplane handled on the ground and in flight very much like the North American B-25. He reported that he felt that prior to the time the first YP-61s were delivered to the Materiel Command the airplanes would be satisfactory in every respect. His major concern was in longitudinal stability:

The airplane is longitudinally unstable and subject to large changes of trim with power. At the present time the Northrop Aircraft Corporation is redesigning the horizontal tail surface as well as the elevator. This will decrease the cord of the elevator approximately twenty inches and increase the cord of the horizontal stabilizer a like amount. It is believed that sufficient elevator will remain to handle the airplane satisfactorily. It will be recalled that the large elevator was installed on this airplane to overcome the diving moment caused by full

span Zap flaps. Since these flaps are not to be installed on future airplanes, the large elevator is no longer necessary. The new elevator will be fastened to the horizontal stabilizer conventionally, instead of the larger type now installed.

Even with the new R-2800-10 engines the P-61 was still experiencing some power plant difficulties. Capt. Leonard Hall, Chief Radar Officer in the USAAF Night Fighter Training Program, accompanied the training program chief, Col. Don Brummel, to Northrop Field frequently during the P-61s early days. Hall still recalls quite vividly when he went up with Northrop test pilot, Myers, for the first three or four flights they would end with an engine failure and single engine landing. John Myers remembers the engine failures, "It later developed that through some series of developmental improvements that they (Pratt & Whitney) had cut the oil consumption down and this resulted in oil starvation to the master cylinder. The master cylinder would freeze, and of course, the rod would keep going and all of the articulating rods would try to wind up in the pocket of the master cylinder – the engine would just come apart with great rapidity." The engineers from Pratt & Whitney were quick to analyze the problem facing them and correct it by adding oil jets in the engine.

Between December 4th and 8th, 1942, the Engineering Board of Inspection (the "689 Board" so-called) was conducted on the second "X" ship at the Northrop plant. Representatives from Wright Field and the Night Fighter Training Program participated in this exercise. The Board was quite concerned that the gun blasts would affect the front and rear canopies, access doors and nose wheel landing gear doors. So great was their concern that special firing tests were begun on the 18th. The Board also suggested changes and additions that were considered improvement items. Among them were windshield wipers, auxiliary fuel tanks, dive brakes (which were scheduled

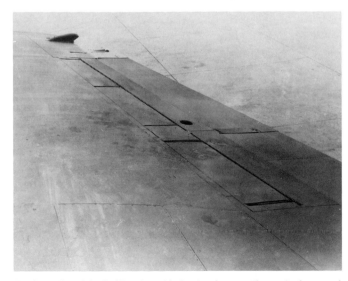

Trailing edge of the P-61's wing with the circular arc ailerons in the stowed position. (Northrop via Balzer)

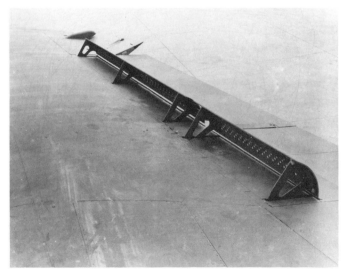

Circular arc ailerons in the extended position. These "spoiler" type ailerons enabled the Widow to out turn nearly any aircraft that it met in combat, almost hovering below stall speeds. (Northrop via Balzer)

for about the 201st aircraft) dual controls for the YP-61s so a second pilot sitting in the gunners position could fly the aircraft while in training, and a Monica (a British designed tail warning device).

Army Airborne Radar Development

Besides the development of long-wave radar for ground based systems by the US Army Signal Corps laboratory at Ft. Monmouth, New Jersey, there was also the Signal Corps Aircraft Radio Laboratory at Wright Field that served the Air Corps/Air Forces in matters of airborne radio, navigation, and later radar and like systems. The ARL's mission was not that of basic research; for this it looked to other research agencies both within the military and the civilian sector. What the ARL did was to apply the engineering research required after a basic

Wright Field's Project Officer, Lt.Col. Marshall S. Roth, sits in the pilot's seat of an XP-61 with Northrop test pilot John Myers behind him giving him his cockpit check. (Northrop via Balzer)

The second XP-61 made its maiden flight in mid-November 1942. The first experimental P-61 would spend most of its life in California whereas the second article would spend a good bit of its time at Wright Field in Ohio with the AAF's flight test crews. In this photo it is shown shortly after arriving at Wright Field. (USN via National Archives)

development had been accomplished to assure producability of the equipment.

The US Army's, and in turn the ARL, view of the need for airborne radar is summed up in the fine publication (US Government Printing Office) UNITED STATES ARMY IN WORLD WAR II, The Technical Services, THE SIGNAL CORPS: THE TEST (December 1941 to July 1943:

Here and there along the coasts, ground radar stood guard to alert the guns, searchlights, and interceptors of the defense stations against the approach of enemy aircraft, but airborne radar had yet to go into action. The nation's defenses were eager for it, because the attack upon an outlying territory had made continental targets seem fearfully vulnerable. The country was primarily apprehensive of carrier-based attack, but the threat of long-range submarines to coastwise shipping became the dominating menace. To meet either threat, radar was what was needed. Moreover, it must be radar which was not obliged to accept the conditions imposed by the attacker, as even the most mobile ground radar had to, but which move out to find him. To acquire this

degree of range and mobility, radar would have to be installed in airplanes.

Between the elementary work that had been accomplished in the United States prior to the Tizard Mission visit in September 1940 and the information Sir Henry Tizard and his party brought with them, the Army, and particularly the Air Corps, new they needed airborne radar. From the same document referenced above:

AI sets, as developed to meet the vehement demands of the U.S. military air organization, were radars of relatively short range which, installed forward in pursuit planes, enabled the pilots both to 'see' a bomber several miles ahead and, by centering the bomber's reflection in their oscilloscopes, to hunt it down. The ARL had two types well in hand by 1942. The first was a long-wave model, calibrated at about 200 megacycles. This was the SCR-540 (Note: SCR means 'set complete radio'), a copy of the British AI-IV. It was not a very good set. For one thing, its one and a half meter wavelength required large external

Above and below: the XP-61, the B-25 Number One (NA-62), and the XA-26A. These aircraft are quite close in weight and dimensions.

	Span	Length	Empty Weight
XP-61	66' 0"	48' 11"	19,487 lbs
B-25	67' 6"	54' 1"	16,767 lbs
XA-26A	70' 0"	52' 5"	25,600 lbs

(Northrop via Balzer, North American via Avery, USAF Museum)

antennas, a bane to aircraft design. All through the last half of 1941 the ARL and Western Electric had difficulty in adapting this American copy of a British set to American airplanes. They were still having trouble as 1942 began. In January, Western Electric samples of SCR-540 components failed vibration tests and had to go back to the factory for modifications. By March the first 80 sets under contract were supposedly so nearly ready that Colton, Acting Chief Signal Officer during General Olmstead's westward tour, set up a priority list for their delivery to radar training schools. Yet only five sets arrived. And in each of them a single component, the General Electric inverter, failed in high altitude tests.

Not until the late spring of 1942 had Signal Corps' copies of the puny British AI-IV (long wave) begun at long last to come off Western Electric's production lines as SCR-540. Only 580 sets had been ordered; no more were wanted, so the AAF had asserted in May. Late in June the AAF issued a priority schedule for delivery of the first SCR-540s: to Navy, 3 sets; to the ARL, 1 set; to the Douglas Aircraft Company, 1 set; to the Hawaiian Department, 3 sets; to the Signal Corps School, 6 sets; to the Western Electric Training School, Kearny, New Jersey, 5 sets; then 6 more sets to the AAF Technical School No.

2. Finally, after all the above had been delivered, 59 sets would go to the Douglas Aircraft Company.

By October 1942, therefore, America's first air intercept radar, the SCR-540, was obsolescent. Further, it suffered from many defects. Maj. James W. McRae, charged with the Airborne Radar Section in the Radar Branch of the Office of the Chief Signal Officer, reported concerning SCR-540s which had been installed in P-70s at the Orlando air base, Florida, that though, 'the external appearance and general impression created on first examining the SCR-540A equipment is one which augurs well for the future . . . unfortunately it is not borne out in practice.' He attributed many breakdowns to inferior materials used in its construction, especially in the cables interconnecting the components of the radar. He noted defects in the cathode ray tubes which were 'seriously astigmatic,' so that accurate focusing of target echoes was impossible. Some breakdowns he blamed upon bad installation (as in the case of the VHF command radio, SCR-522) and others he attributed to poor workmanship or even sheer carelessness on the part of crews.

The Aircraft Radio Laboratory's other AI set, the SCR-520, employed microwaves ten centimeters long, in the frequency range

Components of the SCR-520 Airborne Intercept radar manufactured by Western Electric Co. (Hall)

Maj.Gen. William Knudsen and Gen. H.H. "Hap" Arnold were frequent visitors to the various war production facilities around the country. General Arnold had many a headache in trying to get an operational night fighter and ordering the correct type and quantity of airborne radar for the Army Air Forces. (Northrop)

around 3,000 megacycles. It was a much better radar and became available sooner than the SCR-540. When the Tizard Mission brought over the cavity magnetron and asked American help toward designing workable radar circuitry for it, London had just then defeated the Luftwaffe day raids and was awaiting Germany's night bombers. Faced with the need for a better air intercept set than their long wave AI-IV, the British sought it in microwave equipment. As soon as the Bell Laboratories could produce the new magnetrons for generating powerful microwaves, the Radiation Laboratory had gone to work on a ten-centimeter AI (AI-10) and had come up with a model of it early in 1941. Tested at the ARL, this model attained considerable success despite its awkward bulk. Though heavier – it weighed about 600 pounds – than the SCR-540, the new ten-centimeter SCR-520 used a compact dish-like transmitting and receiving antenna array, two feet in diameter, which could be mounted wholly within the plane's nose. In performance, this microwave AI radar gave more distinct reflections from targets and suffered far less interference from undesirable ground reflections. Taking a page from British success with equipment built in a laboratory, that is, 'crash-built,' the Signal Corps had ordered a number of sets from Radiation Laboratory's own shop, the Research Construction Company, and had already began receiving them. Meanwhile, the ARL went ahead toward the construction of hundreds of SCR-520s on contracts with Western Electric, which, in December 1941, had delivered a preliminary production model.

In Air Forces demands, however, AI was receding in priority. Submarines, not airplanes, were bringing the war to the Western Hemisphere, and the Air Corps, which in 1941 had wanted what applied to the war situation of 1941, but which had been obliged to wait for the planning and manufacture of this equipment, now had the same problem in a 1942 situation. General Arnold, chief of the Army Air Forces, was confronted with a double embarrassment. In the first place, he was not getting antisubmarine equipment. In the second, he was getting air interception radars. He had asked for them, but now found he had no airplanes ready for them. Here was the Signal Corps, offering more sets of the newest and best AI radar than the AAF knew what to do with. Quietly store them, or something, Arnold advised his Director of Air Defense, Col. Gordon P. Saville, lest the Signal Corps return with interest the accusations which the Air Forces had been in the habit of lodging with the top Army command. 'The first thing you know,' Arnold wrote, 'we will have a complaint being registered by the Signal Corps to the Secretary of War. Isn't it possible to take the AI-10s and put them in storage in our own warehouses, or do something along that line, so that the Signal Corps won't have reason for their present feeling of 'what's the use of producing these sets when all we do is store them away.' (Note: 86-Hq AAF R&R CG [H.H.A.] to Dir of Air Defense, 11 Feb 42, sub: Status of AI-10 Cm prod and instl. AAG 413.4-G C Com Equip. Saville had noted in a routing and record sheet to Arnold on 10 February that the delivery schedule of the AI-10s was anticipating the production program for the P-61, the new heavy fighter designed to take it. The smaller SCR-540 [AI-IV] could be fitted into existing A-20 light bombers, and used for training only. In same file).

Most of these SCR-520s were destined to be delivered, not as AI's, air intercept radars, but as air-to-surface-vessel sets. They would be converted into SCR-517s, to serve in the capacity which the immediate needs of the war most urgently demanded – aircraft search for enemy submarines.

The XA-26A night fighting Invader in flight. This aircraft was armed with four .50 cal. machine guns in an upper turret that could be fired by either the R/O or pilot and four 20mm cannon in a tub similar to the P-70. (Mc Donnell Douglas/Harry Gann)

About four months prior to first flight, the Air Corps informed Douglas Aircraft Co. that there would be no orders for their night fighter variant of the A-26. The XA-26A housed the AGL-1 radar in the nose and was powered by two R-2800-27 engines. (USAF Museum)

No sooner did the airmen begin to receive this highly complicated airborne equipment than dire difficulties respecting maintenance arose, difficulties touching all airborne radar alike, IFF and ASV as well as AI. Two Signal Corps lieutenants who had served in England as members of the Electronic Training Group and who were now contributing their experience to the ARL recommended to Colonel Bayer, the chief of the Radar Division at the laboratory, that each Air Corps squadron be assigned maintenance men who could make minor repairs on the spot. In their opinion, each squadron should adopt the British practice and set up a maintenance section of a score or so men equipped with the "megger" (which was a special device to test insulation), together with test set I-48, the multirange volt-ohmmeter TS-189, and

suitable signal generators and oscilloscopes. Colonel Gardner, director of the laboratory, agreed, excepting only the signal generators and oscilloscopes which he believed should be reserved for maintenance work at depots.

Test and maintenance equipment constituted but one trial. Another, especially severe in airborne radar, was training equipment. Airborne radar required that operators be well trained, or else the costly equipment was useless. Yet to train men in actual flight was out of the question. There were not enough airplanes, and what radar existed was desperately needed for patrol and combat operations. The answer lay in sets which could simulate airborne operation in a classroom. The British had devised such radar trainers. The ARL, also, had long before

As the P-61 went into production, Northrop expanded in both people and facilities. The photo on the left is an aerial view of the camouflaged plant. The photo on the right is proof that it rains in southern California. (Northrop)

asked the Link Aviation Devices Company, manufacturers of the well known Link trainer for pilots, to develop a radar crew trainer, RC-110, to train men in AI (SCR-540) operation. But before production of the trainer had begun, the 540 itself was becoming obsolete for air intercept, being replaced by the much larger microwave AI radar, the SCR-520, which called for a quite different trainer set. Because this new radar was already well developed, Colonel Marriner was able to cancel further work on the development of the 540 trainer (c. 22 Oct. 42).

When factory production began in late spring, the Air Forces set up priorities for the first deliveries: the first two sets to the Northrup Aircraft Corporation and thereafter one to Western Electric (the manufacturer), one to the Douglas Aircraft Company, thirteen to the Air Forces Technical School No.2, six to the Signal Corps School, and four to the Signal Corps Maintenance School at Kearny, New Jersey.

Night Invader Takes to the Air

In late April 1941 a mock-up inspection was held. By May the delivery schedule called for the XA-26 bomber to be delivered in June 1942, the XA-26A night fighter in September, and the XA-26B "destroyer" in October. At this time Wright Field was trying to decide whether the "A" would have airborne interception (AI) or automatic gun laying (AGL) radar installed.

A cost plus fixed fee contract was finally approved on June 2, 1941 by the Under Secretary of War at an estimated cost of $2,083,386 plus a fee of $125,003. On the 9th Change Order 1 was added which added the installation of one 75mm cannon on a third version which was designated the XA-26B. This added $541,773 to the contract. A production contract was awarded in October 1941.

In July 1944 Northrop held a "Name a Black Widow" contest for two Black Widows purchased by Northrop employees in the Fifth War Loan Bond drive. Boyd Lee Ashton's winning suggestion was HADES LADY. Ashton picked this name because he felt "She'll give 'em hell!" FIRST NIGHTER was Albin A. Johnson's winning submittal. He came up with this name as it was the name of his favorite radio program at the time. (Northrop)

As time went on the Production Engineering Section at Wright Field was busy debating what variations they wanted. Much centered around a common airframe with interchangeable noses with varying sizes and numbers of guns; the night fighter version slipped to fifth on their list. In the meanwhile, Douglas was experiencing delays in producing the experimental versions due to delays in procuring components.

First flight of the XA-26 was originally scheduled for January 15, 1942 but it was slipped to July 1st because of the production delays. Complete information on the turrets did not reach Douglas from the Air Corps until May 2nd. Besides disrupting the experimental aircraft construction, the production effort was also impacted. On July 10th the XA-26 took to the air for the first time. In September Douglas was informed by the Air Corps that there would be no production quantities for the night fighter version. The XA-26A night fighter version's first flight occurred on January 27, 1943.

Family Day at Northrop Field and Lt. Callahan and daughter in the cockpit of FIRST NIGHTER, with the planes log book, shortly after the dedication ceremonies. (Northrop)

A play on names – Northrop employees Tom Pratt and Leonard Whitney play with the prop of a Black Widow's Pratt & Whitney R-2800 engine. (Northrop)

Capt. Paul R. Zimmer, newly returned pilot from the 421st Night Fighter Squadron in the Southwest Pacific Area, is introduced to an audience of Northrop personnel by Northrop test pilot John Myers. (Northrop)

Chapter 7

Night Force

The Army Air Forces School of Applied Tactics (AAFSAT), under the command of Brig.Gen. Hume Peabody, replaced Fighter Command School in November 1942. Under AAFSAT, the Air Defense Department commanded by Col. Earl W. Barnes was responsible for both fighter training and air defense of the entire AAFSAT "War Theatre." Col. Brummel and his Night Fighter Division came under Col. Barnes' jurisdiction. This reorganization was to increase the scope of all tactical training avenues.

By mid-1943 the night fighter program had more than doubled. On April 1st the 418th and 419th Night Fighter Squadrons were activated, followed on May 1st by the 421st Night Fighter Squadron. The training cadre needed bolstering, so on June 1st the 420th Night Fighter Squadron was activated as the third night fighter training squadron.

Men who had served with the RAF and the Dominion forces and those who saw combat with the USAAF in the early war days were coming home to impart their knowledge of combat tactics on the new night fighters. Reorganization of the training program was in the wind again. Up until this time the training of night fighters was under the jurisdiction of one of AAFSAT's elements. On July 15, 1943 Night Fighter Division became the 481st Night Fighter Operational Training Group which consisted of three training squadrons, the 348th, 349th and 420th Night Fighter Squadrons.

The command of this new night fighter training group was assigned to Lt.Col. Winston W. Kratz who had returned from Europe that past March. Col. Kratz' previous assignment had been that of Eighth Air Force assistant operations officer. Col. Kratz recalls of those early days:

I left for England on the last day of May 1942. Only four of us went over in that particular air transport; and our flight – as I recall – was Washington to Nova Scotia to Greenland to Prestwick to Northolt Air Base near London. It was a matter of interest that upon our arrival at Northolt, where we were met by the station commander, several squadrons of Spitfires were just in the process of landing from a sweep over France. This sight of course gave all four of us a feeling at long last of actually being part of the war effort.

I was assigned to Eighth AF Headquarters as liaison officer with the planning group under Sir Sholto Douglas, then RAF Fighter Commander, which was doing the initial planning for fighter dispositions in connection with the Normandy Invasion. While doing liaison work, I was befriended by a Scotsman, Air Vice Marshall MacGregor, who was kind enough to take me down to Manston which was England's most forward base in the Dover area. I had discussions with several Night Fighter pilots; and since I knew that at the time we had no operational Night Fighter Squadrons in existence, I wrote up quite a report for the VIII Fighter Commander stressing the importance of our getting into the night fighter business. I did not at that time know that a program was already afoot at Orlando for the creation of fourteen night fighter squadrons.

The Fighter Commander, Gen. Hunter, asked Gen. Spaatz to hear the report, and I duly read the report and had quite a long discussion with Gen. Spaatz, Gen. Eaker and Gen. Hunter. As a result of this, I was assigned to RAF 605 Squadron which was located on the Channel Coast in the vicinity of Bagnor Regis. Our runway ended virtually at the water of the English Channel. This was a very active base. 605 was a Night Intruder Squadron equipped with Havoc aircraft.

I was then sent to 23 Squadron for operational training on the Mosquito. After being checked out on the Mosquito I was sent back to 605 Squadron which was being re-equipped with Mosquitos. After a very brief and rather uneventful operational tour in the Mosquito flying from Ford Airdrome, I was sent to Orlando around March 1, 1943, to become chief of the Night Fighter Division at AAFSAT. This division was growing so rapidly that we were soon upgraded to Group status.

Opposite:
"Black Widow," one of the five P-70s that Detachment "A" NFS turned over to the 418th NFS on New Guinea in December 1943. (Ross)

Lt.Col. Winston "Winkie" Kratz returned from his duties within Eighth Air Force in England where he was exposed to RAF night fighters to take over the USAAF's night fighter training program. (Kratz)

Al Lukas was one of a gang of Americans that returned from England at the time Col. Kratz did to help form an American night fighter program. Lukas had left college in 1939 to join the fight in Europe under the "British sounding" name of Harry Gerald Hamilton and obtained a seaman's passport as a Canadian citizen. In a trek that took Lukas and a friend through southern France, North Africa, and imprisonment on a number of occasions, Lukas finally made it to England. As a Pilot Officer he flew night intruder missions in Havocs in the 418 Squadron (RCAF). When America entered the war, P/O Lukas joined the Eighth Air Force and flew Spitfires for awhile before being sent back to the US to enter its night fighter program. (Kratz)

The lack of knowledge of the US Army Air Forces about Night Fighter matters was literally appalling, and my experience in this area was certainly not very great. However, it was obvious that our pilots were going to need much more thorough instrument training, and such a program was immediately instituted.

Possibly our biggest deficiency was in the training of radar observers who were then using the English Mark IV aircraft interception equipment. These young student observers had to fly in the back seat of a P-70, which was a version of the A-20, and training of observers on a basis of one observer per aircraft totally over-taxed our facilities. Consequently, we asked for and received ten or twelve C-45s, in which aircraft we were able to place several observer positions with one instructor to attend the several observers being simultaneously trained. This tremendously increased the efficiency of the R/O primary training program. In the fall of the year we received two YP-61s for evaluation and gunnery tests.

Among the returning veterans who would be under Col. Kratz was Maj. William C. Odell and 1st Lt. Paul H. Baldwin, both coming from the European Theater of Operations. Maj. Odell was with the 15th Bombardment Squadron, designated for a short time as the 1st Pursuit Squadron (NF), in England and North Africa. He flew with them on their first mission, which was also the USAAF's first combat mission in Europe. Returning to the U.S. in May, 1943, Odell was assigned to AAFSAT but was given command of the 420th NFS upon its activation in June 1943.

Lt. Baldwin had been among a group of U.S. Army electronics specialists who were sent to Great Britain in 1942. Their mission was to first study the RAF's radar work; then to assist the RAF operationally. While in England, Baldwin was attached to the RAF and had flown combat missions with both the Coastal Command and a RAF night fighter squadron. Baldwin was fully qualified as a combat radar observer having been through the RAF's ground radar school at Yatesbury, England; and RAF airborne radar school at Prestwick, Scotland. Upon his return to the States he was assigned for a short time to the US Army's ground radar school at Boca Raton, Florida. From there he was assigned to the 481st NFOTG where he became the group's Chief Training (radar) Observer.

With its initial cadre of experienced personnel and a handful of aircraft, the 481st and its three training squadrons were in business. This new night fighter training organization suffered from a lack of facilities and aircraft as many new units before them. When the Night Fighter Division of AAFSAT became the 481st NFOTG there were three squadrons already in training; the 418th, 419th and 421st NFS. The 481st's primary aircraft for training purposes were about a half dozen Beach AT-11s which were used in R/O training and a handful of P-70s for the pilot – R/O to train as a night fighter team. By using all means at his disposal, including a number of trips to Washington, D.C., Col. Kratz managed to get additional aircraft.

By late 1943 a real night fighter organization was in full operation. The 348th NFS at Orlando AB was conducting the initial phases of the training program, instrument flying, and at Kissimmee Army Air Field the 349th was carrying out transi-

Night fighter trainees in Florida. The use of red lensed goggles prior to night flights and the eating of carrots as a steady diet were part of the training program. As with most training programs, the red goggles and carrots were non existent on the battlefields of World War II. (Odell)

Night fighter training personnel and visitors. From left to right are exRAF veteran Al Lukas (note RAF wings), in doorway is Major William R. Yancey (C.O. of the 349th NFS), officer in bush jacket is from the Polish Air Force, drinking beer is Czech night fighter ace of the RAF F/L Carol Kutelvasher (26 victories at the time of the photo), and officer on far right with Coke is Lt.Col. William C. Odell (C.O. of the 420th NFS and past member of the 1st PS[NF]). (Odell)

tion training, while the 420th was providing operational training at Dunnellon AAFld. In November the training program forged ahead even further with the first YP-61s arrival from the AAF's testing and evaluation units which were also in Florida. The 422nd NFS, which was in the midst of its training for overseas deployment, was the first unit to receive training in the Widow prior to going into a combat area. Orders had come down from the Pentagon for Col. Kratz to step up the training and to produce one combat ready night fighter squadron per month. To meet this demand, another squadron was activated on the 24th of November 1943; the 424th NFS. The 424th NFS joined the 481st NFOTG headquarters and the 348th NFS at Orlando where it performed its training functions.

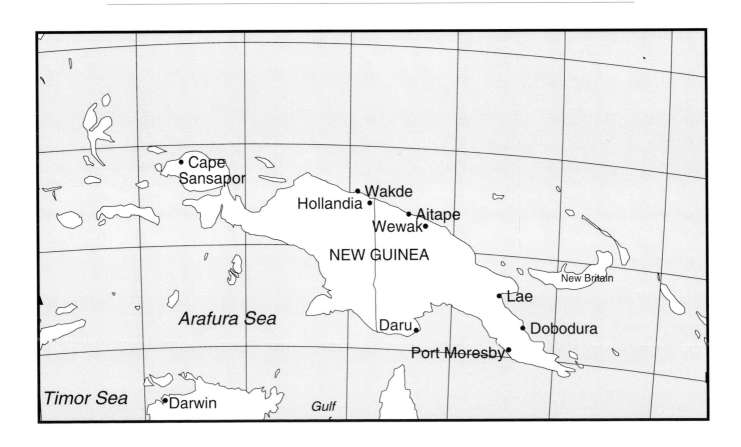

Nipponese Nemesis

Even after their gallant efforts, Detachment "A" Night Fighter Squadron gave up on further attempts to make the P-70 into an interceptor. Like their fellow detachments on Guadalcanal they turned to the best available aircraft, the P-38. In October 1943, two P-38Gs were converted to two-place night fighter aircraft. SCR-540 radar together with the HF and VHF communications equipment was installed in a standard belly tank. For the painstaking work put into this modification Lt. Richardson and a radar mechanic received the Legion of Merit Award.

Testing of these new night fighter aircraft had only just begun when an advanced element of the newly arrived 418th Night Fighter Squadron arrived at Dobodura on November 15, 1943. Detachment "A" Night Fighter Squadron was attached to the 418th shortly after the new squadron's arrival, but by the end of November Detachment "A" Night Fighter Squadron was disbanded. Combat operations of Project "X" were coming to an end during the latter part of 1943. Detachment "B" on Guadalcanal welcomed the arrival of the 419th Night Fighter Squadron on November 15 under the command of Capt. John J. McCloskey. The 419th set up operations on Fighter Strip 2 along with Detachment "B" and training flights were begun in an endeavor to bring the squadron up to "combat ready" status. A week after the 419th's arrival, Capt. McCloskey was making a routine approach to Fighter Strip 2 upon completing a training flight when something malfunctioned and his P-70 crashed, killing him instantly. With Capt. McCloskey's death, joint command of the 419th and Detachment "B" was given to Major Ralph F. Jones, who was at the time Commander of Detachment "B." This joint command situation did not last long, for on December 15, Detachment "B" Night Fighter Squadron was disbanded with all personnel and equipment being assigned to the 419th Night Fighter Squadron.

In late January 1944, Detachment "A" of the 419th Night Fighter Squadron was sent to Torokina on Bougainville. From their new base the 419th Night Fighter Squadron's mission was to protect Allied forces in the northern Solomon Islands and to harass the enemy forces that still remained in the area. Both P-70 and P-38 aircraft were initially used at this forward base, but within a couple of months all P-70s were relieved of operational duties. Detachment "A" stood night alerts on Bougainville, Green and Treasury Islands, while Headquarters detachment stood duty on Guadalcanal, Russell Island and at Munda on New Georgia, and most of these alerts were very uneventful. During the daylight hours, the P-38s flew in strafing and bombing missions against the Japanese forces which remained in the Solomons. Though their skills as night fighters were getting slightly rusty from a lack of use, the 419th was becoming quite proficient at dive bombing. A flight of two or three P-38s on this type mission would come into the target area at around 9,000 feet and dive to about 3,000 where they would release their 1,000 pound general purpose bombs. Their accuracy became truly remarkable, and it was a most unfortunate target that presented itself to these "bored" night fighters.

The night fighter strength of the Fifth Air Force was

Lt. John H. Striebel had flown Havocs as an RAF pilot against the Germans over such distance places as France and Malta. After serving in the AAF night fighter training program he would go with the 550th NFS into the Pacific war. (Kratz)

Lt.Col. Kratz and F/L Kutelvasher beside one of the 348th NFS's P-70s. Many Allied night fighters paid visits to the AAF's night fighter training establishment to give of their experiences. (Kratz)

First class to graduate, July 14, 1943. (Kratz)

In December 1943 the 419th NFS arrived on Guadalcanal and relieved Detachment "B" NFS. Capt. Al Lukas is pictured in the cockpit of one of the P-38s that the 419th inherited. (Lukas)

One of two A-24s used by the 419th NFS on Guadalcanal as an instrument trainer. Pictured in #302 are Capt. Al Lukas in the front seat and Lt. Don Dessert in the rear. (Lukas)

increased with the arrival of the 421st Night Fighter Squadron at Milne Bay, New Guinea, on January 4, 1944. This was a full T/O & E unit of 438 enlisted men and 40 officers who had received complete training in the business of nocturnal battling and were ready to practice their skills. Except for one problem – they had no steeds to ride into battle, and it was almost three weeks later before they received their first aircraft, a single P-38.

In late January an advanced party of the 421st Night Fighter Squadron was sent to Nadzab, New Guinea where their initial operations as a fighting unit was to begin. The rest of the squadron, and their one plane, followed on February 1, 1944. With only one aircraft it was almost impossible to do anything.

The camp site was established, perimeter defenses were established (these men were trained in French Foreign Legion style self-defense) to thwart any attacks by Japanese ground forces. Many ground classes were held to keep up their proficiency.

Not until mid-February did the 421st Night Fighter Squadron receive two additional aircraft, another P-38 and a tired P-70. With such "strength" it was time to get into the action. The first mission flown by the 421st was a dawn weather reconnaissance flight on the morning of February 25, 1944. This was just the first of such flights, many of which were in cooperation with Navy PT patrols.

It would not be until mid-April before the 421st had a strength of eight aircraft, four P-38s and four P-70s. Their

A P-70A of the 419th NFS. These aircraft were soon removed from the night interceptor role by the 419th and assigned to intruder and PT boat cooperative missions. (Harry Gann Collection)

sentiments are brought out in a report of mid-July 1944:

> The major difficulty in using the squadron effectively has been a lack of understanding on the part of higher headquarters as to the purpose and means of operation of night fighters, and assignments of airplanes to the squadron.

The 421st did not have a monopoly on this lack of adequate aircraft situation. When the 418th Night Fighter Squadron arrived at Dobodura, New Guinea, the five P-70s and two modified P-38Gs "night fighters" of Detachment "A" Night Fighter Squadron, became their aircraft. Five additional P-70s were picked up in Brisbane, Australia, over the next couple of months. Morale was given a boost when four P-38Js were received from the 10th Service Squadron, but this euphoria was short lived. In January, 1944, the "Js" were taken away from them and replaced by war weary P-38Fs and G. By the end of January their aircraft strength stood at ten P-70s and six P-38s, all of which should have been retired from service long ago.

Col. Carroll C. Smith, who commanded the 418th Night Fighter Squadron remembers the first P-38s his unit received:

> We started using P-38s because so many of the day fighter people were not trained to fly instruments during their hurried training program, and our boys were quite good at instruments, for that time. We could fly at night without killing ourselves, which was rather remarkable in those days, so we started flying P-38s. We would relieve the day fighters in time to get home before dark, then we would patrol over Wewak and Alexishafen and places like that. Then we started doing searchlight co-op, also with the P-38s. It's rather a thrilling experience if you haven't tried it before on a good black night. Trying to figure out which searchlight is going straight up is rather hairy, so pretty soon you learn, if you survive, without paying any attention to

trying to outguess which one is going straight up. You rely on your instruments and flying combat by instruments. Otherwise, you just can't make it.

Prior to this time the 418th's mission consisted of night alerts; night patrols in the areas of Dobodura, Port Moresby, and Finschhafen on New Guinea and over Kiriwina Island, and early morning P-38 missions. Four of the unit's P-38s were assigned to cover the convoy which landed the Allies at Saidor on January 2, 1944. The detachment of the 418th operated from the strip at Finschhafen and flew their patrol from 6:00 to 8:15 in the morning hours. This mission proved uneventful for the 418th as the Allied landing took place with a minimum of problems.

Col. Smith reminisced some years later:

> I think we probably did more for the night fighter business in getting people to understand the state of the art, and what radar could do and couldn't in our little sphere of influence at that time. We were, I won't say frowned at – we were sort of country cousins, we were in separate squadrons. We didn't have a group or a wing to look after us, but we managed to shoot down a few flamers there. That came down with great spectacular success and focused attention on the fact that we were indeed better, and so we started getting at least some help. At least the type of support that you need. But we were kind of orphans. I can't speak for how it was in the European theater. I think they were attached to wings or groups there, but in our particular area, Fifth Air Force for example, had one night fighter squadron – me. Groups and wings had Lt.Cols. and Cols. and so forth, and I was a Major. And just on the normal competition for things you could not compete very well, so you ended up becoming very, very adept at thievery. So we stole our way into success pretty much.

A 421st NFS P-70A at Nadzab, New Guinea. With its six .50 cal. machine guns the 421st found, as did the other P-70 equipped night fighter squadrons in the Pacific, that it was better suited for night intruder work. (Hernandez)

However, mid-January the squadron started seeing action. The squadron's first air victory was claimed by their commanding officer, Major Carroll C. Smith, while flying a dusk fighter sweep on January 13, 1944. Smith and Lt. Harold B. Wittern were flying in the Madang and Alexishafen area when Smith spotted a Val dive bomber approaching the Japanese-held air strip at Alexishafen. Bringing his P-38 into position, Smith gave the bomber three bursts of fire, the last being at around 400 feet altitude, sending the enemy down to its destruction. Smith recalled later:

When I finally hit it, the only way I hit was that I got to point blank range. You see the amount of gunnery practice we had was almost nil. I had one of my very finest officers, a fellow name of Sorbo, almost quit flying because on about two or three successive nights he went up and fired and couldn't hit anything. But what could you expect? He hadn't had any practice. We just didn't get any gunnery training before we went overseas. On about the third session I told them that what I did was just get to point blank range. So you fly through some debris, at least you stand a better chance of hitting him. He finally got one, and his morale changed, and he did real well.

The following day two of the unit's P-38s went out on strafing missions. Their first target was a 100 foot, two-masted Japanese ship near Palos Point, and the P-38s scored direct hits on the doomed ship. On their way to the enemy held airstrip at Alexishafen they strafed an enemy encampment and a camouflaged native canoe. Upon their arrival at Alexishafen, they found a number of aircraft on strip number two which they proceeded to rake with their gun fire. The results were one Sally confirmed and eight or nine probables.

"There was kind of a humorous side when we were doing P-38 work", Col. C.C. Smith remembers:

At the time a fair amount was being done and some lieutenant came up to me one evening and said that he was slated to go home, and he was a P-38 pilot from a day fighter outfit nearby. He had received commissions from his commander to come and fly a few more sorties with us. We were desperately needing P-38 pilots at the time. So I guess I fell for it, primarily because we did need them. So I checked and found out that he was indeed qualified. I let him fly the sortie that I was going to fly because I had a number of things to do. I rescheduled myself and flew the next sortie which relieved him. Wouldn't you know, that little son of a gun went up and shot down two before I could get off the ground? Talk about good timing, or bad from my standpoint, depending on how you look at it. He had four before then, and he ended up getting two that night.

Towards the end of January, Lts. Richard B. Ferris and Edward E. Craig were flying their P-38s on a patrol to Hansa Bay when they spotted a "Sugar Charlie" (1,000 ton Japanese freighter) off Condor Point. Apparently the Japanese had spotted the P-38s also because they started to take for the lifeboats before Craig and Ferris started their attack. During their third strafing run, the ship exploded bursting into a fierce fire. During this same mission, they strafed a wooden barge as it was discharging enemy troops.

Once again the old problem between night fighter and anti-aircraft came up; this time between the 418th Night Fighter Squadron and the ack-ack at Finschhafen. A great deal of trouble developed between these two units during January and February which resulted in direct hits on two of the 418th's P-38s and one of its P-70s. Major Smith, the 418th Commanding Officer, made an investigation and found that the major causes for the lack of coordination was two fold. First, the Controllers at Finschhafen were found to be very inexperienced; and secondly, just plain carelessness. Captain Paul O'Brien, an experienced Controller and once a member of the 418th Night Fighter Squadron in the States, was sent to Finschhafen. Capt. O'Brien's assignment seemed to clear up the situation. Fortunately, no injuries were sustained by the 418th's aircrews.

In mid-March the 418th received movement orders once again. The unit spent most of the latter half of the month packing up their camp at Dobodura, and by the 28th of March all members of the squadron were at Finschhafen, their new base of operations. Their new camp site was well under way becoming habitable.

The first half of April was very uneventful, and night patrols staging out of Saidor were flown in the Cape Croisilles and Karkas Island areas. Around mid-month intruder missions were flown over the Hansa Bay and Alexishafen area as this was the beginning of the full moon period. A good explanation of just what "intruder" work is, is given in the 418th Night Fighter Squadron Unit History:

Intruder work was started in England and was proven highly successful there. It deals with the night fighters' staying aloft over enemy dromes, waiting for the return of their bombers, also the strafing and harassing of the enemy troops at night. Being strafed in the daytime is quite a sensation in itself, but being strafed at night is the most horrifying and nerve-wracking experience that could possibly happen to anyone. Were it not for the fact that we still remember the enemy at

Another 421st P-70A. This one is staging out of Wakde Island prior to flying a night intruder mission against enemy positions in the north. (Hernandez)

A P-70A, with the 418th NFS emblem on its nose, at Port Moresby, New Guinea. This aircraft is another leftover from Detachment "A" NFS. The sensor's knife cut out the azimuth antenna on the side of the fuselage. Lts. Buck Young and William F. Ross (left to right) pose for the camera. (Ross)

One of two P-38Gs modified by Detachment "A" NFS which was also turned over to the 418th. Lt. Richardson and a radar mechanic received the Legion of Merit Award as a result of their work on these planes. (Ross)

Pearl Harbor and his other treacherous deeds, one could have a sense of pity even for the Nip. In pursuit of this type of work, 1st Lt. Gilbert P. Eissman not being satisfied with his usual bomb load of four 250 pound bombs, and his Observer, R/O Walter Fradin, loaded the rear cockpit of the P-70 with six 20 pound fragmentation bombs which he fused by hand and passed to S/Sgt. George L. DeHaven, Jr., Aerial Gunner, who dropped them at the command of Lt. Eissman when luscious targets of opportunity were spotted. This proved quite successful in addition to being great sport, and was adopted by all crew members of the organization. We do not advise this; however, for general practice, because fusing bombs by hand is not conducive to long life.

Not all was serious business in the jungles of New Guinea. One evening after Lieutenants Leon O. Gunn (418th Night Fighter Squadron Operations Officer) and Frank M. Dubasik had consumed several bottles of Hock, Burgundy and stronger intoxicants they struck upon the idea of mud baths "for health's sake." The idea apparently caught on because it resulted in the dunking of all the 418th's officers in a convenient mud hole which was nearby. A former officer of the squadron, Lt. Walter A. Weinberg, had the unfortunate pleasure of visiting his old unit on this momentous day. Weinberg had the pleasure of enjoying the mud bath twice. A correction should be made, one of the squadron's officers was absent at this time, Major Smith, Commanding Officer, was away having dinner with some friends. A vigil, though unsuccessful, was kept for his return. The author of the squadron's Unit History states, ". . . we felt that there is something lacking in Major Smith's life that will be remedied in due time."

450 AAFBU· 26· DEC· 44·G·1212· COCKPIT OF P·61 B
HAMMER FIELD, CALIF. CONFIDENTIAL

Chapter 8

Anatomy of the Lady in Black

I t was feared that the blast effect of the powerful 20mm cannon combined with the four .50 calibre machine guns of the P-61 would cause such severe vibrations that it would structurally weaken the aircraft under actual flight conditions. The extremely fragile construction of the thin framework of the greenhouse type canopy needed to be reinforced. Structural weaknesses were found in the nose gear door and in certain access doors also. These areas were strengthened and steel skins replaced aluminum alloy construction. Stronger springs were required to keep the nose gear doors in the up position when the cannon were fired. Blast tubes extending the barrels of the 20mm cannon were placed on the guns, which moved the muzzle blast forward of the nose gear door structure. It was also found that these blast tubes aided in hiding the muzzle flash, as well as extending the detrimental vibration effect forward of the critical area. Problems with latching the hatch on top of the pilot's canopy and the addition of bullet proof glass also dictated the necessity of restructuring the greenhouse canopy.

The gunner, who sat aft of the pilot, was to be in an elevated position so that his field of vision would be completely unhampered forward and to the side of the pilot who sat immediately in front of him. Both pilot and gunner had no armor plate on the X and Y models. Perhaps the inclusion of the armor glass alone would have strengthened the structure sufficiently to enable the guns to be fired without detriment to the existing structure. However, this point is mere speculation, since the blast tubes worked quite effectively and seemed to clear up the problems for the moment. Later in combat it was found, much to the dismay of Northrop Aircraft, that the hinged emergency escape hatch immediately above the pilot's position had a tendency to be blown off and the R/O's tail cone tended to implode during dives approaching 400mph. However, for the moment, it appeared as if the problems with the structural design of the canopy were solved.

During the period of design and modification of the airframe, the SCR-720 radar was being rapidly put into production by Western Electric and Bell Telephone Laboratories. The SCR-720 AI radar design was a highly complicated affair, since the maze of black boxes required skills and levels of an electrical engineering degree to operate them. The SCR-720A and 720B sets were developed almost simultaneously. The A configuration was used on American aircraft while the B was for British usage. Both models were quite similar. Towards the war's end, improved models, C and D, for American and British usage respectively, were installed in operational night fighters. The primary function of these radio sets was to aid in the interception and ranging of other aircraft. It could also be used as a beacon or homing service on the host aircraft, a navigational aid, or used in conjunction with the interrogator-response equipment for identification of friendly or foe aircraft. The system operated on four different ranges at 26,000 feet, 10 statute miles, 20 statute miles and 150 statute miles. The scan ranges of the SCR-720 equipment were limited to 180 degrees forward (90 degrees on either side of the aircraft of dead ahead) or 180 degrees to the rear if the equipment was so modified. The SCR-720A equipment required a 10 ampere, 115 volt, 400 cycle alternating current transmitted on a frequency of 3,300 megacycles, varying as little as plus or minus one per cent. Heat given out by this system was intense, yet the system was not up to the heat emissions of the German or British sets. The SCR-720 emitted a "cone" of energy forward of the aircraft as opposed to a ball of energy, or blirp of energy, emitted by the British or German system. This cooler operation was part of the superior design of the SCR-720A which used the magnatron tube. The development of this super-secret device by Radiation Laboratory radar

Opposite:
R/O's compartment in the P-61. (Hughes via Thompson)

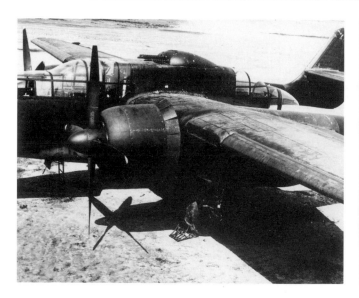

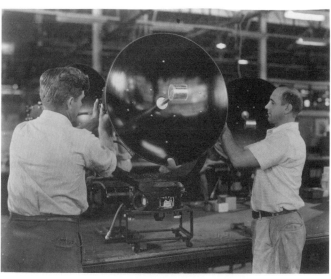

Vibrations that were caused when the turret was rotated or the guns elevated was always a problem within the test community – though the combat troops seemed to have no problem with it. Here an XP-61 is being used in the making of a Signal Corps movie entitled "Airplane Turret." (USAF)

SCR-720 antenna is adjusted by Western Electric Company personnel prior to delivery to the Signal Corps. The SCR-720 was initially installed in the Black Widow by AAF personnel but later as production accelerated Northrop personnel performed the task. (Western Electric Co.)

Very seldom seen is the installed radar in the P-61. (Northrop)

design engineers as well as the extremely complicated installation of this maze of black boxes necessitated installation at secret facilities located at Wright Field, Ohio.

In February 1943, the first YP-61 came off the Northrop lines, its 12 sister ships were scheduled to be completed within the next four months. To handle all of the production flight testing and some of the experimental work, Northrop Aircraft started up field operations at Ontario, California. From this field Major Marshall S. Roth, the Air Force's Project Engineer, flew the second XP-61 to Wright Field on April 15, 1943. At Wright Field it would be the first Widow to receive its "black boxes."

That same summer test pilot John Myers and Northrop project engineer Fred J. Baum, flew the first YP-61 to Wright Field. John Myers unknowingly, and ironically, found an unknown weakness of the Widow's anatomy. During a routine stopover for fuel in Arizona, the 110 degree heat of the summer sun boiled the black paint plexiglass radome of the Widow, literally causing it to liquefy. On the subsequent take-off the radome collapsed causing the lucite tail cone at the rear of the aircraft to be literally blown out, thereby creating a monumental draft. The aeronautical charts and extraneous bits of paper were sent swirling in the ensuing whirlwind, but Myers effected a routine landing. The result of this experience caused the redesign of the radome and preparations for the redesign were begun almost immediately. The remaining YP-61s and early production P-61As received the same plexiglass radome, whereas subsequent production models were to receive a laminated fiberglass nose which was not as sensitive to heat as was the plexiglass variety. Subsequent efforts to reduce the intense heat of the radome necessitated either not putting the paint on the radome or applying a liberal coat of white paint on the forward portion of the aircraft.

In the next few months, all 13 YP-61 aircraft had rolled off the assembly line. Three of the initial YP's were assigned to Vandalia, Ohio, where they would undergo an accelerated service test program. On July 8, 1943, the first XP-61 was

Many contrivances were tried in attempts to eliminate the turret/guns vibration "problem." Here airfoil sections have been placed over the gun barrels on the inboard end. It would be the higher requirements for the Boeing B-29 project that would cause the turret to be eliminated from most of the P-61s. (Northrop via Balzer)

officially accepted by Army's Materiel Command, with the 13 YP-61s being accepted between August 1943, and early September of that year. The majority of these aircraft were assigned to Materiel. One was retained at Northrop Field for factory training while five went to Ohio. Three of the Ohio Widow's were at Vandalia while two, along with the second XP-61, were at Wright Field where they underwent tests and evaluations by the armament and radio laboratories.

Air Proving Ground Command was quite concerned in late August, 1943 that they had not received a P-61 to evaluate. In a letter from Lt.Col. Joseph D. Lee, Jr., Acting Director of Tactical Development, AAFSAT to Col. O.P. Weyland, Chief of Allocations & Programs Division, Office of the Asst. Chief of Air Staff; Operations, Commitments & Requirements dated August 30, 1943:

It is understood that this aircraft is now undergoing accelerated service tests at Vandalia, Ohio; however, it has not as yet been submitted to the Army Air Forces Proving Ground Command for operational suitability tests. Advance information on the performance of this aircraft has not been such as to warrant its tactical acceptance without being evaluated for the Army Air Forces Board by the Proving Ground Command.

It is felt that if action is expedited towards sending this aircraft to the Proving Ground Command for operational suitability tests, these

YP-61s being assembled at Northrop's Hawthorne, California, plant in mid-1943. (Northrop via Balzer)

The first YP-61 took to the air in February 1943. Completion of the remaining 12 articles would continue through the summer.

By early 1943 the black paint had been stripped from the experimental Black Widows. Northrop painted the cowls and spinners of their flight test aircraft a orange-yellow. (Northrop via Balzer)

Unlike the (now) silver experimental and flat black service test Widows, the first production aircraft were painted olive drab over gray. (Wolford)

Northrop test pilot John Myers checks out Lt.Gen. Millard F. Harmon, Commanding General of US Army Forces in the South Pacific Area, in a P-61A. (Northrop)

tests can be conducted simultaneously with the accelerated service tests, thus the tactical use of the aircraft will not be delayed if it is found satisfactory.

Within a week the first of three YP-61s arrived at Eglin Field, Florida.

Hints of the existence of the P-61 had trickled through the ranks of the Army Air Forces personnel. Many people were anxious to learn more of the super-secret Black Widow, as well as perhaps get an opportunity to fly this machine. For the moment the aircraft was to remain secret.

After the delivery of the YP-61s had been completed, it was found that when the defensive top turret was rotated about the azimuth or elevated and fired, severe buffeting problems arose when the aircraft was in flight. Again, it looked as if the Widow's sting would be severely lessened by the deletion of this essential defensive armament. Subsequent design changes were to practically eliminate this buffeting problem. In the interim, numerous experiments at solving the problem such as

deletion of two of the inboard machine guns were tried. This procedure proved to be only limited improvements. Dr. William R. Sears of Northrop Aircraft had even thought of placing a sub-wing type structure on top of the turret creating a downward pressure upon the turret.

Dr. Sears recalls of a "coolie hat" type vane they tried:

In the first flight it inhibited the buffet all right, but it broke off. Dick Ranaldi (Northrop test pilot) wanted us to placard the vanes, 'Please Return to Northrop Aircraft.'

Northrop P-61 project engineer Fred Baum remembers:

The original turret was a dome and caused buffeting as determined in the wind tunnel. It was streamlined in the straight ahead configuration which eliminated this condition completely until the turret turned to about 45 degrees off center. Both from front and rear. No rearward buffeting occurred. Though it did occur in the side position and it was not severe. Vanes and deflectors were tried to

Putting together the P-61. First two photos show the coming together of the inner wing. In the first photo the oxygen bottles are visible in the aft section where the boom is attached. As the crew nacelle progresses along the assembly line wiring, tubing, and electrical components are installed by a bevy of assemblers (opposite, top left). Photo four of this series (opposite, top right) gives a good look at the dolly on which the crew nacelle is carried until wing mate takes place. With so many of the male workers being inducted into the military services, the once all-male assembly force became quite integrated with female workers during the war (below left). After wing mate, the engines are installed (below right). The overview of the assembly bay gives a bird's eye view of the major assembly cycle. (Northrop)

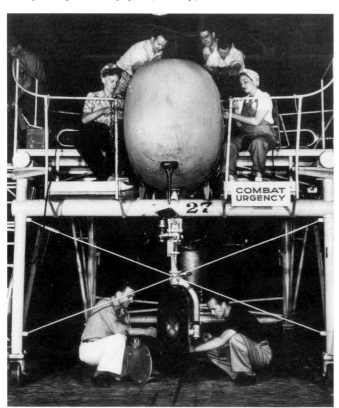

improve the air flow, but with little improvement. Side firing beyond 30 degrees was not very practical anyway. We had very severe blast buffeting in the forward position when all four guns were fired. This was a muzzle blast effect from the four .50 Cal. guns that shook the structure just forward of the gun muzzles and originally caused severe structural damage. The situation was corrected by using steel skin on heavy steel channels on the fuselage top just forward of the turret. We

had the same blast problem from the 20mm cannon on the belly and had to go to steel nose doors and structure around the gun muzzles.

A complete redesign of the top turret structure was eventually to eliminate the buffeting problem to an acceptable level. The ensuing problem with the rotation of the top turret coupled with the scarcity and high priority of the top turret mechanism, which

were also used on the Boeing B-29, supplied by the General Electric Company, caused the deletion of a great majority of these turrets from the "A" production aircraft, as well as the first half of the P-61B model production. Many of the turretless P-61s were modified at Air Force depots in the Pacific theatre to carry four fixed .50 calibre machine guns in the dorsal turret's location. In some instances, the turrets were removed and long

range ferry tanks with a protruding dome-like structure were placed in the crew nacelle cavity.

The P-61 was starting to be noticed. General Roth recalls:

Shortly after the performance tests were completed, General Arnold visited Wright Field and in company with Oliver P. Echels viewed the airplane on the flight line. At this time, it was complete with

Practically from the beginning it was realized that the Black Widow needed longer legs. The aircrews in the field realized this even more as they switched from area defense to intruder missions. As the operational squadrons made modifications in the field, Northrop carried out experiments back home, much of which was incorporated in later production models. Different sizes, shapes, and combinations of external fuel tanks were first tried out on wind tunnel models (opposite page, this page, above, below). Then they were tried by the flight test community – first with two external tanks and then four. Both standard 165 gallon tanks and the much larger 310 gallon tanks were attached. If fuel tanks and bombs could be carried externally, couldn't smoke and chemical dispersing tanks be carried also? They could, but in one experiment over Northrop Field the wind shifted and the dropped chemicals landed on houses, washing, and cars. A sticky mess in more than one way. (Northrop)

turrets and installed guns. General Arnold remarked, 'Who is responsible for this assortment of built-in head winds?' General Echels was proud to announce to General Arnold that the speed tests conducted on the XP-61 exceeded by one mile the Northrop guaranteed performance.

Captain Fred P. Jenks, production project engineer, commented that:

The P 61 is an honest airplane. It has no mean tricks. In acrobatics such as loops, spins, Immelmann's and fast turns, it behaves as a pursuit plane should. Its stalling gestures are near perfect.

Air Force studies concluded late in the war would cite the P-61 as the most maneuverable AAF fighter; it also proved itself

against U.S. Navy fighter aircraft. All did not agree however. In a letter from Brig. General B.W. Chidlaw, Chief, Materiel Division to Colonels R.C. Wilson and Brentwall, he said:

I notice in copy of cablegram No. 5208 dated November 9, 1943 that Eglin Field does not think very much of the P-61. This is almost in direct contradiction to a cable from AAFSAT of about a week ago which was very laudatory in its tone toward the P-61.

Wish Colonel Wilson would see some of the Fighter people down in OC&R and attempt to get these two outfits together. At least an indication of what the trend on this airplane may be.

With the training of the night fighter squadrons begun, the need for the P-61 was urgent. The Army Air Corps had placed an initial order for 200 P-61As. Lend Lease of P-61 aircraft to Britain was cancelled by this time; though they were still quite interested in the Widow's flap and spoiler system. Mr. W. Tarlo, Chief Patents Division, British Air Commission and Air Vice-Marshall R.B. Mansell, RAF, British Air Commission, negotiated for some two months before obtaining a full set of drawings from Northrop with AAF consent.

The first P-61A rolled off the assembly line at Northrop Aircraft in Hawthorne, California in October 1943. Along with 36 of its sister ships, these aircraft had the four .50 calibre machine gun dorsal turret with the inherent defect of the buffeting problem when rotated. The remainder of the initial batch of the 200 P-61s had the turret deleted.

The first of these P-61 aircraft weighed 29,007 pounds empty with dorsal turret. With the dorsal gun turret deleted, the aircraft weighed 27,490 pounds. An interesting point is that despite the 1,500 pound differential in weight, the top speed of the aircraft with the deleted gun turret was increased only three mph. The stalling speed with flaps down and wheels down and 1600 horsepower rating in each of the R-2800 engines was 75mph with the gun turrets, and 78mph without the gun turret. The flight characteristics of both turret and non-turret models were excellent. Full control of the aircraft could be maintained with one engine out, full gas load and all crew stations occupied with no apparent difficulty. The aircraft could be stalled with one engine out and only a noticeable shudder would occur when the aircraft would drop slightly below the horizon and level off to normal flight position. The aircraft could be slow rolled with one engine out in the direction of the dead engine. This proved to be a favorite trick of the P-61 pilot.

Mr. Hugo Pink of Northrop Aircraft relates one of the most spectacular of all P-61 Black Widow tests that gives evidence to the tremendous structural integrity of this aircraft. While Mr. Pink kept close watch on the fuel flow meter during a routine fuel consumption test both engines stopped. The huge propellers were feathered and a deathly silence filled the aircraft with only the on-rushing wind outside being heard. The test pilot, Alex Papana, had feathered the useless engines, banked sharply into an emergency landing at Mines Field below. The Widow picked up speed almost as rapidly as her altitude decayed.

Papana forced the airplane into a crab position in an effort to slip the huge plane onto the emergency taxi strip. One problem – two North American B-25s were warming up for take-off on that taxi way. Skillfully, Papana slipped the right wing of his aircraft over the B-25 wing before the unbelieving eyes of the novice B-25 pilots. Still in the crab angle, the mighty right main gear of the Black Widow sheared off, then the left main gear and nose gear were torn away. The radome shattered and the P-61 acted like a huge plow scooping up dust and sand in the open crew nacelle. Pink states he was somehow out of the aircraft and running between the booms before it stopped its incredible slide. Papana had to be dug out literally with shovels.

The first P-61s that were coming off the assembly line were painted in conventional daytime camouflage schemes of olive drab with neutral gray undersides. Many discussions arose about the most suitable form of paint camouflage to be used on night fighter aircraft. The British had preferred a flat black paint and used it to great success, as had the Germans. These aircraft, however, when illuminated by the searchlight beams appeared to have a white outline. The olive drab camouflage configuration was of no greater success than the flat black. Finally, a satisfactory solution of the painting scheme was arrived at by the National Research Committee which conducted tests at Eglin Field, Florida in the fall of 1943.

Three aircraft were to be used. One was to be in standard daytime camouflage of olive drab with neutral gray undersides; the second was to be painted a flat black similar to the finish used by the British and German aircraft. The third aircraft was to be painted glossy black, a novel innovation of the day. These aircraft were to be flown over Fort Barracuas, Florida, through a barrage of searchlights. The olive drab and matte black aircraft were spotted easily in the searchlight beams, but the glossy black aircraft surprisingly enough had reflected the white beams of the searchlight and seemed to be almost invisible. This cloak of invisibility was essential to night fighting techniques and of even greater value for night intruding.

The observers at Fort Barracuas reportedly called back to the base which dispatched the three aircraft to request the glossy black aircraft to be sent over, when in fact the aircraft had already flown past. Thus, the Fort Barracuas barrage of

A P-61A-1 in pristine factory finish takes to the air from Northrop Field, Hawthorne, California. Only the 45 P-61A-1s, most of which went to the Pacific, would have the turret. It would be 355 P-61s later when the turret would be seen again in the middle of the B-model production. (Wolford)

The use of night binoculars in the AAF's night fighters was developed by the night fighter training units early in the program. They combined the gun sight with 5.8 power night glasses and could be swung down in front of the pilot's eyes with a simple hand movement. With the pilot's canopy hatch up, the binoculars are viewed in their stowed position. (Northrop)

searchlights had entirely failed to see the invisible glossy black aircraft. At one point during this early period of development the finish applied to the inside of the Black Widow was matte black. However, after a full day in the sun, the interior was untouchable. The insides were thereafter left the normal zinc chromate or medium green finish.

The flame dampers and flash hiders worked so well that the P-61s in service reached a high degree of invisibility. One particular account from Europe states that two of these aircraft were known to have loitered near German air fields and waited for returning bombers to land. Upon the P-61s initial entry into the pattern, they were given a green light to land by the German control tower who thought they were friendly aircraft. The P-61s continued their loiter operations outside and waited for the returning bombers. As four German bombers entered the landing pattern, the Widows indiscriminately blew them out of existence while remaining completely undetected themselves; neither their engine exhaust flames nor the guns when fired at the enemy aircraft were observed.

These first P-61As that were coming off the assembly line had a top speed of 370 mph and a ceiling of 30,000 feet plus. Beginning with the P-61A-5, the 46th and subsequent aircraft, the Pratt & Whitney R-2800-65 series engines were used. This boosted the horsepower rating to 2,250 horsepower and was even greater for the P-61A-10 aircraft which utilized water injection.

So secretive were plans for the development of the P-61 that the general public was not to learn of the existence of the P-61 officially until January 8, 1944, when she made her official debut over the Los Angeles Coliseum at a joint Army-Navy war show. The some 75,000 observers who saw the mysterious black ship for a brief instance that day thought perhaps this was the largest pursuit that they'd ever seen. Indeed, they were correct. However, had the general public been more aware, they would have had a better look at the P-61. At least, the readers of a certain comic strip created by artist Leslie Turner. The P-61 appeared in his comic strip "Wash Tubbs" six days after the Los Angeles show. No doubt Turner was inspired in using the

The night binoculars are in the forward position. This photo illustrates their initial installation in a YP-61. The sight presented a row of illuminated dots which were lined up along the wingspan of the enemy aircraft. (Hall)

There were many war bond drives during the war. A placard is being installed in a P-61 which states that the aircraft was purchased through war bonds by Christian Brothers College of St. Louis, Missouri. (Northrop)

P-61 from seeing them fly over his Orlando home. Plus, his daughter Joy married 1st Lt. Ernest P. Luke, Engineering Officer of the 422nd Night Fighter Squadron which was undergoing night fighter training at the time. The Widow's first appearance in publication caused repercussions throughout the War Department. His reasons behind its use was that he thought it would have been announced before his syndicated comic strip appeared and that no other airplane he knew of fitted the needs of this then current story line.

Specifications for the XP-61 looked so good on paper that Materiel Command had ordered 13 YP-61s only 28 days after the original contract was signed for the XP-61 on January 30, 1941. However, with all its innovations and novelties, the P-61A was found to be inadequate by aircrews who later flew the aircraft. Common complaints were that the aircraft did not have enough speed, altitude and other shortcomings which were brought to the attention of the Air Intelligence contact center unit at Army Air Force Redistribution Station No.3, Santa Monica, California. Maj. Carroll C. Smith (who was the highest scoring AAF night fighter ace) from the 418th Night Fighter Squadron, 1st Lt. Lloyd Muldrem of the 417th Night Fighter Squadron, and 1st Lt. Paul A. Smith, the first AAF night fighter ace, pilot of the 422nd, all gave their evaluation of the P-61. The general consensus was that the P-61A was a very satisfactory aircraft for the mission it was designed to do. The greatest fault, however, was a lack of sufficient speed and request for more powerful engines with turbo-superchargers.

With regard to the top turret, the unanimous opinion existed that this should be eliminated, due to the extra weight and little use for defensive weapons on the aircraft. The canopy should be streamlined and strengthened, since it was very fragile and would rip off at excessive speeds obtained in a dive. The tail structures should be reinforced since the tail booms tend to wrinkle up on a pull-out at excessive high speeds. Greater internal fuel capacity was needed to increase the range of the aircraft and for loiter time on station. Improved diving characteristics and perhaps dive brakes would be a useful addition to the aircraft. Instrument lighting, which was of the indirect black light type, was requested to be changed to the red post lighting used on more conventional aircraft. The greatest complaint was lack of sufficient aircraft parts, spares and replacements and the need for highly trained radar technicians who could repair the radar on the aircraft rather than simply replace black boxes. Further, the radar observers should be trained in troubleshooting problems that might arise on the radar system in flight. Repairs and extra equipment as well as test equipment were sorely needed.

First Lieutenant Paul A. Smith had remarked earlier that, "I have never known of an enemy aircraft shot down by the use of radar without visual perception. Since the standing order is no aircraft would be fired upon without positive identification first." The majority of the night fighters, aces as well as other pilots, agreed that this was an onerous task to be placed upon the pilot.

Northrop Aircraft listened intently to the demands and requests of the night fighter aces and ground personnel who had voiced complaints about their aircraft, so much so that the P-61B was introduced in July 1944. The P-61B had incorporated many of the suggested combat improvements such as greater fuel capacity. The total fuel capacity of 636 gallons in the P-61A's was augmented in the late P-61A-11s by the addition of two dropable 165 gallon fuel tanks mounted on electrically operated wing pylons raising the total fuel capacity of 966 gallons. On the P-61B, provisions were made for four external stores pylons which could accommodate four 310-gallon tanks, or four 1,600 pound bombs, making a grand total maximum fuel capacity of 1,876 gallons. The P-61B was approximately eight inches longer in the nose section than its P-61A sister ship. The new P-61B had incorporated the tail warning radar unit as well as standard identification friend or foe (IFF) SCR-695 equipment.

The cartridge ejection doors of the 20mm cannon on the P-61A were constant sources of trouble and caused frequent jamming of the ejection mechanism of the 20mm cannon. These doors were eliminated on the P-61Bs and replaced by a simple open slot to allow ejection of the cartridge directly into the aircraft slip stream. The hydraulically operated landing gear doors were also supplanted by a smaller, more compact mechanical door mechanism. The smaller door was similar to that of the B-25 in that the main gear doors opened to receive the landing gear and closed immediately after the landing gear had retracted or extended fully, leaving only a small external gear door to allow extension or retraction of the main gear strut. The primary reason for the change was due to heavy field operations caused accumulation of mud and extraneous debris in the landing gear openings when the gear were extended. The cowl flaps were also changed on the P-61Bs to facilitate the cooling of the R-2800 engines.

Perhaps the most novel innovations of the P-61B were the night binoculars at the pilot station as well as an installation of a radar scope (the "B" scope) for a visual presentation of the radar picture for the pilot's use. This did not make the pilot less dependent upon his radar observer but simply enabled the pilot to fully appreciate the radar observer's problems with tracking

The news release for this photo states: "The newest 'pledge' of Gamma Phi Beta on the University of Southern California campus – the Black Widow P-61 night fighter, poses with twenty sorority sisters. Name of the plane is 'Gamma Girl.' It is one of the two Northrop Black Widow P-61 night fighters for which money was raised through a War Bond drive conducted by the sorority. Second of the Black Widows, world's largest and most powerful pursuit planes, has been named 'Gamma Phi Beta.'"

The P-61 was the integration of airframe, armament, radar, and powerplant. All of these major elements added up to a rugged, dependable, forgiving aircraft. The Pratt & Whitney R-2800 series engines were not only powerful, but they could take a good bit of battle damage and get its crew home. (Northrop via Balzer)

These large flaps are what gave the Widow its superb short field take-off and landing capability. (Northrop via Balzer)

a fleeing aircraft. Additionally, this system could be used as a backup system as well as navigation purposes by the pilot.

The night binoculars were unique since with these pilots could shoot accurately and see approximately five times as far at night as a pilot without the advantage of night binoculars. The binoculars were mounted on a track above the pilot's head along the left side of the canopy and could be stowed in an up position or could be pulled along the track and adjusted to eye level when locked in place. The night binoculars were a combination of 5.8 night glasses and optical gunsights mounted on gimbals to prevent vibrations during flight. When the pilot was ready to use the night binoculars he simply swung them into the position immediately in front of his head at eye level and locked them. All manipulation and movement of the night binoculars could be accomplished with one hand operation, allowing full control of the aircraft while locking the binoculars into position. The optical gunsight of the night binoculars consisted of a row of horizontal illuminated dots, four in number. The pilot simply aligned these dots with the wing of the aircraft being pursued. The inner dots were ten mills apart and the outer dots 70 mills apart. Thus enabling the pilot to scale the enemy's range with remarkable accuracy.

The light features of the instrument panel of both P-61A and B were not the post system used in most aircraft of the day, but were another novel innovation of Northrop Aircraft. A fluorescent lighting system above the aircraft instrument panel enabled the pilot to see the glow of the instrument dials thereby reducing eye fatigue during long periods of blackness and eyestrain encountered by the pilot during long period of aircraft loiter or on target. However, the pilots still preferred the red, more conventional lighting system, which simply flooded the instrument panel with red light, thereby preserving the night vision of the pilot. The reason for the fluorescent system was to reduce possibility of detection from the ground or air since this system could only be seen from the aircraft cockpit. All P-61A and B pilots were required to be so familiar with the controls and

gauges of the aircraft that they could pass a blindfold test before operational use of the aircraft. These tests were conducted at all intervals during a night fighter pilot's tour.

The P-61B was approximately 350 pounds heavier than the P-61A. The first 200 P-61Bs did not have the top turret. However, starting with the 201st P-61B, the first P-61B-15, the GE dorsal turret containing four .50 caliber guns were reintroduced, since the buffeting problem had been severely lessened by redesign of the structure, and the B-29 priority had been reconsidered; the latter was the major factor. This turret could be controlled by either the gunner or radar observer but fired by all three – pilot, radar observer or gunner. The four 20mm cannon offensive armament remained in the exclusive control of the pilot.

The fully loaded weight of the P-61B with four 310 gallon external drop tanks, which tripled the range of the aircraft, increased ammunition and complete crew of three was 37,091 pounds. This raised the critical engine speed to 137mph and raised the stall speed to 95mph, which was still docile for an aircraft of this size. Restrictions were placed on the aircraft, however, of diving speeds of 495mph indicated with a do-not-exceed speed of 405mph at 20,000 feet. Aerobatics with the aircraft were strictly forbidden when the increased equipment, four 310 gallon fuel tanks, was installed. Normal maneuvers such as half rolls, slow rolls, loops, Immelmanns and limited inverted flight were permitted.

The P-61B would seem to be the solution to the night fighter pilot's problems. Indeed, complaints such as lack of sufficient heat at altitude were considered by Northrop in the installation of larger heaters for the crew nacelle as well as a new gun camera system and internal fire extinguishes in the aircraft. One of the great complaints of the pilots was the inability to gauge the absolute altitude of the aircraft at night, particularly at low altitude, 100 feet or less. Northrop came up with the absolute altimeter or ideal altimeter which made low-level, minimum visibility flights possible. This system was so effective that the 426 NFS crew of Frederick A. Cliby, R/O, and his pilot, Capt. John Pemberton were amazed to find how low they had flown after returning from a low-level strafing mission of Japanese positions. They had strafed a convoy of trucks carrying troops and knew they had flown extremely low, but neither realized their proximity to the ground that night. In the routine post-flight walk around inspection, both men were astounded to find embedded in the ventral surface of the boom a portion of a human skull. They had hit one of the Japanese troops who was unfortunate enough to be in the wrong place at precisely the wrong moment – standing in back of one of the troop transports. So the radar had to be accurate within 10 feet or Cliby and company would have become an integral part of the landscape.

Actress Janis Paige, elected "Black Widow Girl" by pilots of the deadly P-61, adopts a suitable pose for pin-up purposes.

The black in Black Widow was added on the P-61A-10 series and was carried throughout its production. A number of tests showed the glossy black to be better that flat black or the OD over gray schemes when in the beam of a searchlight. Early stealth! (Pratt & Whitney)

The caption to this photo reads: "An expert archer, Jeanne Haverhill doesn't spend all her time with the bow and arrow. She works on the production line that turns out the deadly Black Widow night fighter."

Chapter 9

Pacific Adventure

Guarding America's Pacific frontier during the hours of darkness was the 6th Night Fighter Squadron. After the disbandment of its detachments in the combat zones of the Pacific during the latter days of 1943, the 6th's sole purpose during the first half of 1944 was to protect the night skies of Hawaii. Most of its P-40s and P-39s were replaced by P-47s, but the P-70 was still the only night fighter to be had. Appropriately, the 6th Night Fighter Squadron was to be the first unit to receive the Black Widow as they were the first American night fighter squadron to enter combat, and the first to make a night fighter kill.

To assist the night fighters in their transition from the makeshift to the first "built-for-the-purpose" night fighter, Northrop Aircraft sent specialists out to the theater of operations. In March 1944, the team of John W. Myers, M. Scott Johnson and Dan J. Collins left from Hamilton Field in northern California for the Pacific. John Myers was Northrop's Chief Engineering Test Pilot and had many hours in the Widow, including some of the first flights in XP-61 number one. It was Myers' job to instruct the pilots in the handling characteristics of the P-61, and to demonstrate these. Scott Johnson and Dan Collins were service experts. Upon their shoulders were the tasks of instructing in the maintenance of these aircraft, and working out the early "bugs" that were bound to pop up in the field.

Collins was assigned to Seventh Air Force, under which the 6th Night Fighter Squadron operated. Upon their arrival in Hawaii, John Myers and Dan Collins started working with the 6th Night Fighter Squadron immediately. Scotty Johnson had been assigned to the Thirteenth Air Force and went on to Guadalcanal where the 419th Night Fighter Squadron had been stationed for some time.

Myers found that he had an additional job to perform, to "sell" the Black Widow to the crews. Their makeshift night fighters had performed poorly. They just couldn't see how a fighter the size and weight of a medium bomber would perform any better, if as good. The night fighters had a Missouri attitude, "I'll believe it when I see it." Myers knew that he had a real job of selling on his hands. As soon as the first '61 was assembled and checked out, Myers took the big bird up to show what it could do. Along with him sitting in the gunners position was Major Victor M. Mahr, the 6th Night Fighter Squadron's commanding officer. With all of the 6th watching from the sidelines, Myers made a short take-off. Then to show the versatility of this bomber-size fighter he went through his routine:

This was the kind of thing that was always fun. The typical fighter pilot thought this airplane was a monstrosity of course. I had perfected a little routine that took just about three minutes. I would make a very short take-off and climb up to a chandelle, back across the field at a very low altitude, loop right off the deck, then Immelmann. Coming out of the Immelmann, I would feather the left engine, the critical engine, come down and across the deck again and do three rolls into the dead engine right off the deck and land.

At one point Myers checked his passenger for his reactions, he found Major Vic Mahr non-commital. At the end of the performance, it was quite different. It impressed Mahr, for as Myers looked over his shoulder again to check the Major's reaction, there was Mahr with a grin that went from ear to ear. As a climax, John Myers brought her in on a short field landing. Mahr's first words were, "That does it! I've seen everything!" After this, each and every pilot was taken for a ride.

All of the initial deliveries of the P-61 were by surface ship. Both American and Canadian ships, cargo and aircraft carriers, transported the P-61 overseas. Here a cocooned Widow has been transported from Northrop Field in Hawthorne to the port at Long Beach, California. (Northrop)

Here three cocooned Widows are tied down on the deck of a cargo ship. The outboard wing panels and propellers will be reinstalled at a depot near the receiving operational night fighter squadron. (Northrop)

The 6th Night Fighters would use the rest of May and part of June to check out in their first (real) night fighter before sending a detachment into combat. Myers' job in Hawaii was completed and he left to join Scott Johnson on Guadalcanal.

Scott Johnson was present for the unloading of the first P-61s from the transports onto Kukum Pier on Guadalcanal on May 3, 1944. On the 8th, Marshall Holbrooke of Pratt & Whitney arrived; and with the assistance of these two technical representatives, the 38th Service Squadron began assembling the P-61s. Within six days of the Widow's arrival, the first ship was brought to the 419th flight line on Fighter Strip No.2. At 4:00 o'clock in the afternoon of May 12, Major Emerson Y. Baker, C.O. of the 419th, along with Northrop's Scott Johnson,

made the first flight of a P-61 from Guadalcanal. Two days later John Myers arrived:

I was flown to Guadalcanal where I was to introduce the Black Widow to the 419th NFS. We arrived late in the day. I went to the Commanding General's tent, a guy named Barnes (Brig.Gen. Earl W. Barnes, XIII Fighter Command). I paid my respects. He said that he was expecting me to test fly the first airplane assembled there the next morning, and that he would like to ride with me. Well, what the hell can you do when the commanding general asks? So I said certainly.

The General had built it up as quite an event on the 'Canal. I don't know how many thousands of men were standing around waiting for this. The Japanese had been raising hell with our troops; they weren't

A P-61 Black Widow is being unloaded from a Navy barge onto the dock at Hickam Field, Oahu, Hawaii. (USAF)

First Widows arrived in Hawaii on January 19, 1944. Once unloaded, the P-61s were taken to the Hawaiian Air Depot where the protective cosmolene coating is removed. (USAF)

The transformation can be seen between the P-61 in foreground where the stripping process has just begun and the background P-61 which has completed its first phase of being put back into operational condition. (USAF)

All cleaned up, now the outboard wing panels need to be reattached. In-theater modifications will be made to these aircraft before they are delivered to the 6th Night Fighter Squadron. (USAF)

doing a lot of damage, but they were keeping them awake all night. A bomb had been dropped one night earlier, and had landed in an ammo storage area. There were continuing explosions for about 48 hours. People were kind of sensitive and thought anything that would clear the skies at night was good.

I got out to the plane the next morning, and Scott (M. Scott Johnson, Northrop Tech Rep) and I gave the airplane a once over. The General arrived at the appointed time and got into the seat behind me. I started up the engines and started down the taxi way. When we got to the end of the taxi way, there was a P-38 with its engines going. Over the interphones inquired, 'Mr. Myers, do you see that P-38?' 1 said, 'Yes, sir.' 'That's a stakeout.' 'Stakeout?' 'We want to see what your airplane will do. When you're satisfied that your plane is in good condition, rock your wings three times, and we'll join in mock combat over the field.' He didn't know it, but I had tested for Lockheed, and I knew the '38 just intimately. I knew its limitations, and of course, those of the Black Widow.

So over the field I rocked my wings, and we broke off. I just slaughtered that poor bastard in the '38 because I knew exactly what he couldn't do, and what I could. I finally wound up just about putting the Widow's long nose between his tail booms. Barnes was so funny. At one point he said, 'Get him, Myers! He's going to Immelmann, damn it, he's going to Immelmann! Get him!' It was then that I just about put the nose between his booms, he dropped his wheels – it was all over, very melodramatic.

Then Barnes said, 'You see all those men down there?' I said, 'Yes, sir.' 'Well, they're expecting a little demonstration.' 'You mean I can flat-hat?' 'What do you think they're there for?' So with the commanding general, I put on my demonstration. Everything went just absolutely beautiful; until I feathered the left engine.

When I did my first roll, right on the deck, into the left engine, the hatch came off and went into the right engine. The prop tract on the right engine became quite wide, and I couldn't unfeather the left engine. Well, there I was with the commanding general. We had lots

The 6th Night Fighter Squadron is not any too sad to turn in their Douglas P-70s for the new Northrop night fighter. Though the 6th will again go into combat as a night fighter, they will continue the dual role of day fighter within the Hawaiian Islands. In 1944 they switched from the Bell P-39 for the Republic P-47D Thunderbolt for day fighter operations. (Morales)

of inertia. I didn't have to use much power to get around and make a landing, just as if it had been scheduled for them.

Within the month he had taken each of the 419th's pilots up for orientation/instructional flights. As with the 6th Night Fighter Squadron, the '61 had to be "sold" to these crews. Overall, they felt it was a very good aircraft, and the only criticisms were its relative short endurance (about three hours) and its performance above 20,000 feet seemed to be somewhat lacking.

The 6th NFS's Capt. George Mulholland (below) inspects the pilot's area in the Widow. On the pilot's instrument panel is the SCR-720 radar scope for the pilot's use. In practice, the pilot left the "scope" work for the R/O while he flew the aircraft and worked towards making a visual I.D. of the target being pursued. (Thompson for Mulholland, Northrop via Balzer for three cockpit photos)

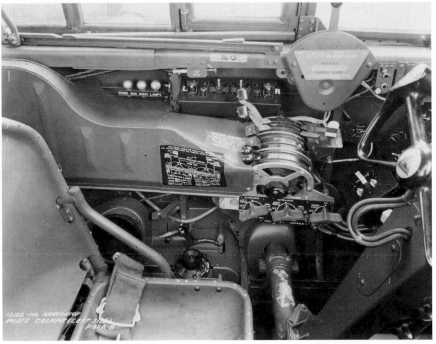

Alerts were discontinued at Munda and the Russel Islands and these crews remained on Guadalcanal for the transition training. Detachment A at Torokima on Bougainville remained there for most of the month providing night alerts from that base as well as Treasury and Green Islands. Myers spent a short time on Bougainville before he and Johnson continued their South Pacific travel to Brisbane, Australia.

Toward the end of the month, Detachment A was recalled from Bougainville, and a big push was put on to ready the squadron for action in an area of greater opportunity. Only one combat mission was attempted during May with their new aircraft. On the 31st, Major Baker along with Capt. R.F. Sugnet (R/O) and S/Sgt. H.R. Masek (gunner) flew to Green Island in preparation for a possible night intercept. A Jap flying boat was expected to come up the Buka Passage from Rebaul, but it never appeared. While the Northrop representatives were working with the 6th and 419th Night Fighter Squadrons, P-61s were arriving at Brisbane, Australia, via sea transport. These aircraft were to be supplied to Fifth Air Force's two night fighter squadrons on New Guinea. 1st Lt. Willard F. Hall, Engineering Officer, and 12 enlisted men of the 418th Night Fighter Squadron left their base at Finschhafen on New Guinea and went to Brisbane to assist in the assembly of the Widows.

418th Night Invaders

A commanders meeting at Fifth Air Force headquarters in late April 1944. Maj. Carroll C. Smith of the 418th Night Fighter Squadron decided to use this opportunity to put forward an idea of his. He felt that the 418th wasn't being used to its potential with the P-70s and P-38s it was flying. As a night intruder squadron flying B-25s they could make a much greater effort to the winning of the war. Smith related:

Northrop's John Myers was dispatched to the Pacific theaters to help the 6th, 419th, 421st, and then 418th Night Fighter Squadrons transition from their other aircraft to the P-61. Myers, along with Dan Collins and Scott Johnson, helped in instructing the in-theater depots to reassemble the P-61 and assisted the squadron maintenance personnel. The Black Widow technical representatives patch is shown in the second photo of this series. As can be seen, living conditions were somewhat sparse. There was also death and destruction around them. (Wolford)

First P-61 assembled and flown on Guadalcanal. Once checked out, the 419th Night Fighter Squadron would take their new craft into combat. (Johnson)

A 419th NFS Widow undergoing routine maintenance on Guadalcanal. The white 300-series squadron aircraft number on the side of the crew nacelle just forward of the cockpit was unique to the 419th. (USAF)

I knew of some "H" models that no B-25 unit wanted for they had only single pilot controls and a useless 75mm cannon in a tunnel where the co-pilot would have been. Our squadron was not being utilized in any really useful way and we felt with our night flying ability we could do a good job of night intruding with these aircraft.

While at the commanders meeting I tried to convince Brig.Gen. Ennis C. Whitehead (who commanded Fifth Air Force, Advance Echelon) to give me 12 of the B-25s. He at first said no, but General Kenny overheard my request and after some discussions General Kenny told General Whitehead to give me 12 aircraft. It was understood by General Whitehead and myself that we would use them as night intruders and as such the gun turrets would be useless as well as the cannon.

We removed the turrets and 75mm cannons and mounted forward firing 50s instead. We had 14 forward firing 50s plus waist guns for the radio operator and gunner to use. General Whitehead had not really wanted to give us these aircraft and I suspect he was a bit annoyed for

ExRAF night intruder pilot, now Captain in the AAF, Al Lukas, on the left, stands next to one of the 419th's newly arrived Widows. The squadron had been quite active flying intruder missions with their P-70s and would continue this type of flying with the P-61. (Lukas)

one of our early missions was a noon raid on Rabaul. This was our one and only daytime raid. It was a 12 plane raid. We lost no one. We were not trained at all in formation bombing and over Rabual I am sure the Japs thought if they let us alone we would kill ourselves.

In mid-May the 418th was ordered to move to Hollandia, New Guinea. The ground echelon made the move immediately, leaving most of the flying types at Finschhafen to fly their few aircraft (mostly P-38s and P-70s) up later. Then word came from higher headquarters that plans had been changed. Verbal orders were received from V Fighter Command for the air echelon to move immediately to Port Moresby. Here, their weary aircraft were turned in to the Replacement Pool, and transition training was started in B-25Hs. They were to be "night intruders" and the B-25s were to be used permanently instead of the P-61s. This came somewhat as a surprise to Lt. Willard F. Hall, engineering officer of the 418th, and 20 enlisted men who were at Brisbane in preparation to transition over to P-61s. The flight crews, Lt. Mervin E. Lyall, ordnance officer and 38 enlisted men, as well as the personnel that had been in Australia were all sent to Port Moresby for transition training into the B-25s. The crew of the 418th's B-25s would consist of pilot, navigator-observer (the R/O's job now), radio operator/ gunner, and rear gunner.

On June 8, 1944, Major Smith and two other crews flew to Wakde Island in preparation to running night raids in the Geelvink Bay area. The crews would fly in shifts against the Japanese in an attempt to keep them awake all night as well as damaging their war-fighting capability. Smith and his crew flew the first mission that night against the Babo Airdrome. They fired some 6,000 rounds of ammunition on strafing runs and dropped nine 100 pound paradone bombs. Capt. Leo O. Gunn, executive officer, and his crew were to fly the next shift. Bad weather precluded their reaching their target and they returned to base with a full bomb load. Lt. Richard F. Day and his crew, flying the third and final shift of the night, were able to reach their target and bomb and strafe it.

B-25s of the 418th NFS being prepared for a night mission. Quite often they would fly to a forward airstrip during the day and fly night intruder missions around sundown. (Ross)

To increase the firepower as night intruders, the 418th Night Fighter Squadron traded their P-70s for B-25Hs. Some of the nose guns and side guns are visible. Not required for their mission, and to reduce weight, the top turret was removed. (Crain)

But the Japanese returned the favor to the 418th. At 4 o'clock in the morning the enemy bomber dropped his bombs down the Wakde strip. What would he hit but Capt. Gunn's bomb laden ship. When it exploded it in turn destroyed Major Smith's B-25 that was parked on one side of it and damaged a B-25 on the other side beyond repair. The Japanese attackers destroyed 18 aircraft on the raid on Wakde. Intelligence reports later estimated the 418th's attack on Babo to have destroyed about 14 enemy aircraft.

The next mission was on June 19th. The entire squadron was airborne for this daylight raid. Their destination was Wide Bay some 30 miles south of Rabaul, New Britain. They took off in such bad weather that their fighter escort could not accompany them. Their mission was to destroy field gun emplacements, bivouac areas, and radio towers. The squadron history reports on this mission:

What would become the 418th NFS's unique squadron tail markings was initiated with their B-25s. These markings consisted of a yellow moon and star which represented the night. The blue stripe with white border was a reverse slanting Bar "sinister" and according to the squadron's self appointed expert on the rules of heraldry represented "Bastard Ancestry" – the night fighters were treated like such at a family picnic by the rest of the theater military, so it seemed appropriate to the 418th. (Ross)

William F. Ross in the cockpit of his B-25 "Blues in the Night." Standing next to "Blues" is navigator-R/O Raymond L. Duethman. With this aircraft Ross and Duethman flew 28 combat missions and destroyed two Japanese ships and about 20 barges. (Ross)

The mission did prove humorous because it turned out to be quite a rat race that will long be remembered. A gunnery pattern was set up, and everybody conformed to this pattern with the exception of two ships which flew exactly opposite to the pattern, resulting in ships meeting head on and waving to each other from a safe distance. These two culprits have never identified themselves and for good reason too. If at any time in the future their identities are discovered, they will be given a G.I. shower bath and a manual to read on aerial gunnery. The mission was completed in spite of this without mishap, and all ships returned.

Unlike the above recorded missions, the other missions flown in June were not quite as eventful. Night harassment missions were flown against Wewak, Dagua, and But airfields as well an other installations in the surrounding area. They also flew cooperative missions with PT boats. The B-25s would fly as "bait" in luring enemy anti-aircraft to fire at them. When fired at, the PT boats, who were stealthing along the shore, would open up on the gun emplacement firing on the aircraft. This was accomplished with a great measure of success according to Naval intelligence reports.

"Louisiana Lullaby" on Kwajalein Atoll. Here the newly P-61 equipped 6th NFS makes a fuel and rest stop on their way to Saipan Island. (USAF)

In July raids were carried out against air strips at Moemi, Babo, and Sagan. Two injuries were incurred, but under quite different circumstances. On one, Cpl. Robert Nelson was wounded in the right foot when the aircraft he was flying in was hit by flak. In another incident, as the B-25 was taking evasive action, a gunner was thrown off balance and broke his ankle.

Enemy coastal shipping was also an inviting target for the night intruders. On one of these missions around Soembroko Island Lt. Richard Day and his crew spotted a lugger. After making two bombing and strafing passes, the lugger was left afire and badly listing (later confirmed destroyed). Upon returning to base Lt. Day found his hydraulics were shot away by the enemy flak he had encountered. With hydraulic fluid rapidly dissipating, S/Sgt Lowell E. Eich and Sgt. Welmar Z. Smith were able to acquire enough "fluid" from urine and coffee to pump the wheels down and lower the flaps so the B-25 could safely land. The squadron's history reports, "They particularly recommend coffee with lots of sugar and cream in it so as to increase the viscosity of the hydraulic fluid."

Pilots and R/Os that hit the Halmaheras, Netherlands East Indies in August 1944. From left to right are: (squatting) Kerstetter and Ayres; (standing) Burke, Foster, Sorbo, Ross, and Duethman; missing is Dubasik. (Ross)

Ahead of the aircrews of the 6th NFS, Lt. Jack Pabst, a controller assigned to the 6th, landed on Saipan with the 4th Marine Division and set up a mobile GCI station at Violet Field (code name) at Magicienne Bay on the southeast side of the island. Flanking Lt. Jack Pabst in this photo are fellow controllers Charles Townsend on his left and Steve Puskar on his right. (Pabst)

The first P-61 of the 6th NFS comes in for a landing on Saipan, in the Marianas, on June 24, 1944. Bystanders and P-47 Thunderbolts greet the 6th. (USAF)

Touchdown – the 6th has landed. Soon the enemy will feel their presence. (USAF)

Other barges, ships, and a schooner also fell victim to the 418th in July. One gunner was seriously wounded by flak and died shortly afterwards in the hospital. One B-25 was lost but the crew, unhurt, was located and brought back to base. In early August they experienced further losses. Two gunners were killed on one raid and a B-25 was shot down in another with the loss of the entire crew. Their work was dangerous. But even with these losses, these night fighters were creating even greater losses on the enemy. On August 18th this all came to a sudden end. They would soon be transitioning to the P-61.

The Widow's Sting

The next Allied advance was to the Marianas, whose strategic importance to the AAF was as a forward base for their long range B-29s. Bases were to be established on the islands of Saipan, Tinian and Guam from which waves of Superforts would strike at the home islands of the Japanese empire. To protect these B-29s during the hours of darkness, the 6th Night Fighter Squadron sent out a detachment of night fighters.

Under the command of Major George W. Mulholland, six P-61s, aircrews and support personnel were dispatched to Saipan. The first wave of Marines landed at Saipan on June 15, 1944, and with the 4th Marine Division was Lt. John G. Pabst, a Fighter Director of the 6th Night Fighter Squadron. Soon after the landing he had their first mobile GCI station set up and ready to operate.

The 6th Night Fighter Squadron's Widows arrived at Isely Field on Saipan on June 21st with their first mission being flown on the 24th. On June 30th the first Japanese aircraft would feel the sting of the Widow. On board the P-61 was 2nd Lt. Dale F. Haberman piloting the craft and F/O Raymond P. Mooney on the scope. Haberman would later recall that historic encounter:

Sgts. Jerry K. Lucas (facing camera) and Leroy F. Miozzi of the 6th NFS load 20mm ammunition in preparation for a mission from Saipan. These men served as armorers by day and gunners by night. (USAF)

Onlookers surround the Widow while in the background is a bombed out Japanese hanger. What somewhat resembles a turret is a long range ferry tank that was installed in Hawaii. (USAF)

With its special long range fuel tank removed, and guns reinstalled in dorsal position, this 6th NFS Widow is prepared to fly against the Japanese night marauders. (USAF)

We were vectored on the bogie at 7,000 feet with Mooney insisting that we had two targets in formation on our scope. We chased them for 7,000 to 23,000 feet over a 25 minute period and never did get quite to their altitude. I also forgot the radio and left it on 'Transmit' so the whole intercept was heard over the entire Saipan area.

Admiral Hoover allegedly enjoyed the mission Pilot/RO conversation immensely. At any rate, I finally got a visual on the bogie, a Betty with a Zero on her right wing turning toward the island up much higher than we were. I pulled the Widow up on her tail and nailed the Betty in the port engine, while the Zero flipped over and came down on our rear with us in a full stall, high blower, engines at 300 degrees C and throttles over the stops.

We wound up going straight down. Mooney looking up the Zero's gun barrels telling me to twist port or starboard to make the Zero's gunfire miss. We left him like he was in reverse. He also disappeared from the Condor base scope so we don't know what happened. I saw the Betty finally explode near the island, also witnessed by the entire area and suddenly realized we were buffeting badly and were way over the redline. In those days we called it compressibility. I pulled her out at 1500 feet and since nothing seemed bent or broken we landed. Subsequent inspection found nothing wrong and a report was submitted to Northrop.

On July 6 at 11:00 p.m. a 6th NFS P-61 piloted by 1st Lt. Francis C. Eaton, with 2nd Lt. James E. Ketchum (R/O) and S/Sgt W.S. Anderson (observer-gunner) took off to relieve the swing shift.

The 6th NFS officer personnel on Saipan. Front row: Lts. Robert Phillips (P), Don Evans (P), Jean Desclos (R/O), James Ketchum (R/O), Ray Mooney (R/O), Nick DeVita (R/O), Stan Marks (Eng.), Robert Robbennolt (P), and F/O Dan Hinz (R/O). Second row: F/O John Szpila (P), Lt. "Hap" Haberman (P), Doc Braham (Flt.Sgn.), Capt. Milt Hansburg (Radar), Capt. Mark Martin (P), Capt Si Bock (Sup.), Lt. Ernest Thomas (P), F/O Tom Boyle (R/O), and F/O Richard Phillips (R/O). Third row. Lts. Bob Ferguson (P), Jay Watts (Arm.), Charles Ward (R/O), Wes Reynolds (R/O), F/O Al Borges (R/O), Lts. James Crumley (P), Myrle McCumber (P), Frances Eaton (P), John Acre (R/O), and Dale Laney (S-2). (Pabst)

They weren't airborne but a few minutes when ground control radioed them a bogey had been detected; Bluegrass 53 (code name for Lt. Eaton's crew) was vectored 120 degrees. This maneuver brought them too close to slightly trigger-happy "friendly" surface vessels. Anti-aircraft fire from the ships were too close for comfort, which forced Eaton to put his aircraft in a sharp diving, banking turn. Again ground control called, "vector 040, bogey at 8,000 feet altitude." Now Eaton had to gain altitude. "Vector 360 degrees." The incoming enemy bomber was only four miles from the Widow now. "Vector 120 degrees." Now Ketchum had a blip on his scope, the enemy. Tensely, Sgt. Anderson was straining his eyes trying to make a visual contact with the bomber somewhere in the endless darkness.

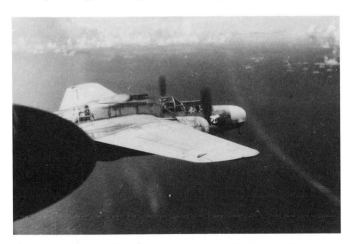

Pilot 2nd Lt. Dale F. "Hap" Haberman and R/O F/O Raymond P. Mooney patrol in their P-61 "Moonhappy" which is a contraction of Moon(ey) and Hap(py). The 6th NFS was one of the few squadrons to receive the turret equipped P-61A-1 model which usually carried a gunner. (Haberman via Thompson)

The first P-61 kill by the 6th NFS is appropriately affixed on Haberman and Mooney's P-61 after their victory over a Japanese Betty on June 30, 1944. (USAF)

The distance is closing. Eaton's mind is working: "Have to drop flaps, don't want to over-shoot. Too fast, too fast, have to S-turn." "Two miles to target," Ketchum calls out over the intercom. 600 feet. "There he is," visual contact. Slightly to port and at the same altitude is a Japanese Betty. No results are seen from the Widow's first barrage of gun fire. The Betty starts turning to the left and more lethal lead is spewed by the '61. Direct hit in the left wing. Closer, closer, closer. Eaton now has his black beast dead astern of the Betty. The Widow shudders with the roar of cannon and machine gun fire.

In a great ball of fire the Jap exploded, forcing the Black Widow to make an evasive maneuver to avoid collision. On its way down, the Betty exploded once again, sending shock waves through the night sky. The Widow had just gone through its "baptism of fire."

The 6th set up their operations at Aslito Field while Isely Field, across Magicienne Bay from them, would be the home of the 73rd Bombardment Wing, the first of the XXI Bomb Command's B-29 wings to arrive in the Marianas. By early April 1945, the remaining four B-29 wings would be operational from their bases on Tinian and Guam.

The 421st, based at Nadzab, New Guinea, started sending crews to Brisbane in late May to check out in their new aircraft, a welcome replacement. When John Myers and Scott Johnson arrived at Brisbane, they found some P-61s had been assembled and flown, all this without factory assistance and almost no technical information. John Myers later stated:

It is forever to the credit of the men of the service squadrons that they had both the will and the ingenuity to do this. And it's just as much to the credit of the boys who got in and flew the ships without even a pilot's instruction book. Naturally, there were some misunderstandings all around, and in most cases, they weren't able to get the most out of

the ship. It didn't take us long to iron out these minor difficulties, and then the boys went for the Widow in a big way.

From Australia John Myers went to New Guinea and then Wakde Island where he demonstrated the P-61's ability to the 421st Night Fighter Squadron. As at previous bases, the Widow's ability to turn inside any aircraft around, single engine performance, and short field take-off and landing capability won the confidence of the onlooking flyers.

The 421st's night fighter pilots had learned their lessons well, and they drew their first blood with the venomous sting of the Black Widow on the night of July 7, 1944. 1st Lt. Owen M. Wolf and his crew, 2nd Lt. Byron N. Allain (R/O) and S/Sgt. Donald H. Trabing (gunner), were one of the crews standing alert duty. Their official report reads:

Scrambled by Fighter Sector, I took off immediately after sounding of red alert and stayed at a minimum altitude on a course Southwest from Owi Strip and to avoid friendly A/A (anti-aircraft). I climbed rapidly to 10,000 feet on a SSW heading. GCI called in a vector, and I proceeded on this course, but bad weather obscured the radar scope so that no contact was made.

Next I was vectored on a course parallel to and ahead of the bogie. At the direction of the Radio Observer (Allain) I throttled back, turning slightly port so that the enemy plane, if it continued on its course, would cross in front of the nose of my plane. By this time my plane was out of the range of the GCI Controller, but I requested and received permission to continue the search visually and through my own radar equipment.

On a general westerly heading I searched the area for about five minutes, slight rain hampering the sighting. GCI ordered me to return then if I had no contact. I asked for a few minutes more and received permission. Suddenly a blip appeared on the radar scope at 0055/K,

A recently received P-61 of the 421st Night Fighter Squadron. Northrop test pilot John Myers and famed aviator Charles Lindbergh would fly to the Mt. Hagen area of New Guinea in this plane in what would become a quite memorable experience. (Wolford)

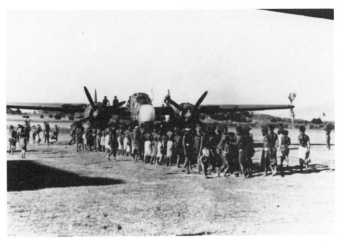

The above photos give some idea of what it took to pull the P-61 out of the New Guinea mud on Mt. Hagen. (Wolford)

and the Radio Observer took control of the course of the 'Queen.' He directed the ship on a gentle turn to the port and then to the starboard bringing my plane directly behind and below the tail of the enemy plane. At that time we were one mile behind the bogie at 6,500 feet.

Throttling back at the direction of the Radio Observer so that we would not overshoot, I closed quickly on the enemy plane. The plane was a twin-engine bomber with tapered wings and a thin fuselage, apparently a Sally or a Dinah. The exhaust pattern, bright orange, was distinct and visible. It extended below each nacelle at an angle of 45 deg. to the rear and 65 in width as viewed from behind.

Upon obtaining a visual on the plane, I throttled slightly forward and opened fire with all eight guns. At a range of 150 yards the first burst scored a direct hit on the starboard engine of the Japanese plane. The engine flamed and part of the fuselage exploded, throwing fragments into the path of my ship and slightly damaging the underside of my fuselage and the port spinner. I continued to press the attack, firing long bursts.

I could see the 20mm exploding against the enemy plane, and the tracers of the 50 cal. entering its outline. The aircraft suddenly flamed and fell off into a steep dive. I followed directly on its tail, continuing to fire, until my indicated air speed reached more than 400 miles per hour.

The enemy plane crashed in the water along the beach on the Southwest of Japen Island. It exploded when it hit the water, and I could see both the engines thrown to the shore. There was no return fire from the enemy plane as it was apparently unaware of my presence until the attack. None of the enemy aircrew was seen to parachute.

There were numerous civilian "tech reps" in the Southwest Pacific Area helping the Army Air Forces crews get the most out of their aircraft. For Northrop Aircraft was John Myers who flew the P-61 Black Widow as if it was part of him. At the same time Myers was on New Guinea with the night fighters, Charles A. Lindbergh was there showing the P-38 fighter jocks how to

The 421st NFS, like most of the other AAF night fighter squadrons, put their personal adornments on their Widows. This widow adorned Widow belonged to Capt. William T. Bradley, C.O. of the 421st. (Noyes)

"Nocturnal Nemesis" of the 421st NFS. Like all of the early Pacific AAF night fighter squadrons, the 421st had not had any previous training in the P-61 prior to receiving it in the combat area. (Burdue)

As the sun goes down, the night fighters go to work. (USAF)

get the most out of that plane. Bill Bradley, C.O. of the 421st NFS, knew Lindbergh and invited him over to their quarters on Owi Island. With the help of Bradley and Myers, Lindbergh was checked out in the P-61. On his first attempt to solo, Lindbergh nicked a 55 gal. oil drum with a prop. First flight was put off for another day. Lindbergh would later describe the Widow as, "An exceptionally fine plane."

In the heart of the Owen Stanly range, lying WNW of Lae, New Guinea, is Mt. Hagen. Virtually untouched by civilized man, it has been described as an almost "Valley of Shangri-La." Before the conclusion of his mission in the Pacific, Northrop's John Myers and a Widow load of passengers, which included Lindbergh, flew to this near-paradise to visit with the Australian Commissioner-in-charge, Captain Blood.

It was a short grass field that they were headed for, the elevation was around 7,000 feet. As Myers was making his approach, Lindbergh, who was sitting on the ladder behind Myers, noticed that the P-61 escort aircraft, which V Fighter Command insisted upon, was right on top of them – ready to land on top of them. Lindbergh advised John Myers of this, and they took off across country like a "bat out-a-hell!" The 421st NFS pilot landed a little long and ran out of runway, ending up in deep mud.

It had been raining hard just prior to their arrival, and as the big fighter came to a stop, the heavily laden landing gear sank deep into the mud. A native celebration was in process, and seeing that it would be impossible to get the plane out on its own power, Myers asked assistance of the two tribal chiefs to supply the manpower to move the mud embedded airplane. The chiefs agreed with the stipulation that they would be given a ride in the big bird. It took a multitude of natives to get it out. With one chief in the gunners seat and the other in the aft compartment, Myers gave them a real ride – Immelmanns, slow rolls, buzz jobs over the heads of their tribes, dives, etc. Though the fellow in the gunners compartment wanted no more to do with the Widow after they had landed, he probably saw too much from his vantage point, neither chief would have any trouble for the rest of their lives, since they had touched the hand of God in their wild ride.

Myers then saw a disturbing sight. A number of wrecked aircraft at the end of the landing strip. It seemed that it was easy enough for aircraft to land on this 2,800 foot strip, at 6,500 feet altitude, but the take-off was another situation. Lindbergh and Myers knew that they were in a very good plane when they found that she used only about half the length of the runway when they departed.

As with all new weapons systems, problems were beginning to show up once the Widow had been operationally flown in the field. Scott Johnson, one of Northrop's tech reps in the Pacific recalls some of these initial teething troubles:

One of the first problems I can recall hitting us on Guadalcanal (419th NFS) as we were unpacking the airplanes in preparation for assembly was the condition of the 20mm ammunition boxes. In an effort to use non-critical materials these were made from a pressed fiber material which it turned out had a great affinity for moisture. Immediately upon receipt of the aircraft in the tropics these boxes were found to have withered down into a 'mass of mess' resembling a smashed milk carton. We then locally designed and made replacements of stainless steel. Equivalent changes were subsequently made in production. As I look back on the problem, the recovery made, and the performance of the local Service Squadron in manufacturing the replacement boxes was an outstanding accomplishment.

At first fuel siphoning from the fuel vent outlets (which were located at the wing root adjacent to the crew nacelle) presented a problem. Due to the location of the vents, when siphoning occurred fumes and sometimes raw fuel was introduced into the crew nacelle. Siphon breakers were incorporated, and we moved the vent outlet to the lower aft portion of the crew nacelle to solve this problem.

Due to the high humidity of the tropics, we were at first plagued with problems with aircraft radar due to arcing and shorting in the electrical connectors. At about this time we had just solved a problem of arcing and burning of the spring contacts on the end of the 'cigarettes' of the connectors to the spark plugs on the R-2800 engines by the packing of the cavity with Dow Corning silicone grease. We moved this solution over to the airborne radar system connectors and for all practical purposes solved that problem.

Another problem associated with the airborne radar was a problem of maintaining pressure in the electronic tanks and avoid high altitude arcing. The electronics of the radar system, involving high voltage, were contained in tanks which were sealed and then charged with air on the ground to a pressure slightly above sea level pressure. It was extremely difficult to maintain perfect sealing so we were often plagued with loss of the air charge and the subsequent arcing at altitude. The seals and sealing methods were improved, and we also incorporated an airborne pressure system utilizing the pressure side of the engine-driven vacuum pumps as source of supply. This system was incorporated on a number of our aircraft and proved to be quite satisfactory.

On the subject of radomes, the first ones were frosted plexiglass left unpainted. This configuration of frosted plexiglass stood out like a beacon at night, and we subsequently painted ours to create a new problem. With the dark paint on the plexiglass, under the tropic sun, the radome would become hot enough to sag down to interfere with the radar dish. We then had to make and use covers to protect the radome while on the ground. The plexiglass section was confined to a rather small part of the removable nose section itself. The rest of the removable nose section from the mounting at the fuselage bulkhead to the plexiglass was a magnesium structure. The next version was a complete fiberglass removable nose section. With this version we did not need to protect the nose with a cover while on the ground.

Chapter 10

Training and Politics

Night fighter training under the 481st Night Fighter Operational Training Group was finally in full swing. The Florida war theater had turned out three fully trained night fighter squadrons in 1943 and by year's end three additional squadrons were in training, the latter squadrons were the first to check out in the much anticipated Northrop P-61 Black Widow. But it seems that the powers-to-be just can't leave well enough alone.

With the coming of the new year came a change of scenery for the night fighter training establishment. They were given their walking papers to leave Florida and to set up operations in California's San Joaquin Valley. Their main operating base would be Hammer Field near Fresno; but they would soon expand out to fields at Bakersfield, Delano and Salinas as well as gunnery practice near Van Nuys, northwest of Los Angeles in the San Fernando Valley, as well as Hayward in the East Bay area near San Francisco.

Of the four squadrons in training as the move commenced, the 422nd NFS remained in Florida and marked time until they received their overseas orders. The 423rd and 425th NFSs went along with the training troops to sunny California. From the time of their arrival, a squadron a month was activated. The last night fighter squadron was the 550th which was activated on June 1, 1944.

Overseeing the training was still Lt.Col. Winston Kratz at Group with Lt.Col. Griffith D. Davis providing instrument training with his 348th NFS, the 349th under Lt.Col. William R. Yancey performing transition training, and the final phase, operational training, being provided in the 420th NFS. Commanding the 420th was Lt.Col. William C. Odell who had gone to Europe with the 1st Pursuit Squadron (NF) in 1942 and saw a good bit of combat flying A-20s with the 15th Bomb Squadron. He would soon relinquish his command to take the helm of the 547th NFS when it was activated and lead that unit in its battle

with the Japanese. To round out the training units, the 424th NFS under Major Hubbard K. Gayle was providing replacement crews for the operational squadrons in the combat theaters.

Not that "Winkie" Kratz didn't have enough to keep himself busy, but still more changes and assignments, were soon to be. The 481st was just settling down with three months of hard work in their new home when the word came down that the present training organization would be disbanded and in its place would be a much different organization. Under the command of Col. Ralph A. Snavely, the 319th Wing would oversee night fighter training as well as other responsibilities. Under the 319th Wing was the 450th Army Air Forces Base Unit (AAFBU) which was the operational training unit. The 451st AAFBU was the replacement training unit. Under each of these AAFBUs were two types of squadrons designated as A, B, C, etc. and T-1, T-2, T-3, etc. The 450th and 451st, along with the night fighter staff at 319th Wing, replaced the 481st NFOTG and the four night fighter training squadrons using the same air fields. Gunnery and other assistance were provided by the 441st AAFBU at Van Nuys and the 403rd at Hammer.

Mosquito And Other Tails

Col. Kratz would soon find himself at General Arnold's emissary on night fighter affairs, traveling around Europe, the Mediterranean, and the China-Burma-India theaters. One of his trips would be to England where he was about to assist the AAF in replacing the P-61s of the 422nd and 425th NFSs with British Mosquitos. The dealings with the British and the use of their Mosquito night fighter by the AAF had a long and involved history.

In late 1942 the Army Air Forces new that they needed to get help from the British. On December 16th Col. Robert W.

Opposite:
P-70 #313 "Deanna" gets last minute adjustments prior to a training mission. (Thompson)

In late 1943 the mainstay of the night fighter training program was the P-70-DO. Most of these aircraft assigned to the training program had their SCR-540 AI radar replaced by the SCR-520 microwave AI radar. (Soukikian)

Harper, Assistant Chief of the Air Staff, A-3, wrote Group Captain John W.F. Merer of the British Joint Staff Mission in Washington, D.C.:

General Arnold has asked me to look into the matter of how the Air Ministry would react to releasing the A-20s allocated to the United Kingdom under the pending agreement for calendar 1943.

As you probably know we are considerably concerned as to obtaining night fighters for our North African effort and our P-61s remain in the uncertain status always surrounding untried production scheduled for future delivery. Further possibilities out of our A-20 production have their definite limitations in view of the firm commitments known to us both.

It is the understanding of our people that the RAF will be somewhat pressed for Spitfires for 1943, and although RAF requirements for A-20s remain unfilled, the question of relative need might work out in favor of releasing A-20s to the Army Air Forces in return for the release of certain Spitfires by the Army Air Forces to the RAF. As you probably know, Spitfires are scheduled for delivery to the Army Air Forces under the pending agreement.

Major Burt tells me that you are well disposed toward obtaining an expression from the Air Ministry upon the principle of such an exchange and I would appreciate your advising me of the Ministry's reply. Details as to scheduling the exchange can be worked out, I believe, after we know where we stand on the principle.

Pressure from the Pacific commanders for the War Department to provide night fighters increased the need for British assistance. In a memorandum for the Joint Chief of Staff Maj.Gen. George E. Stratemeyer, Chief of the Air Staff, recaps the situation:

1. Since receipt of Admiral King's letter of February 3, 1943, relative to the need of night fighter aircraft in the South Pacific, a pressing request has been received by cable in the War Department from General MacArthur for a night fighter squadron in the Southwest Pacific, and consequently it is believed the problem in the two theaters may be discussed at one time.

2. Further, General Arnold has cabled in to the War Department subsequent to his conversations with Air Chief Marshal Portal that 'it should be borne in mind that we cannot send Beaufighters to any night fighter unit we may operate in the South Pacific.'

3. Distribution under original plans of adoption of the Army Air Forces' existing night fighter aircraft (P-70s) now in Hawaii to the South and Southwest Pacific was held up pending the reaching of an Agreement with the British relative to night fighter protection in North Africa where the political situation and the possibility of concentrated night bombing attacks made the matter one of paramount importance.

4. There are nineteen (19) P-70s in Hawaii at this time, and it is believed that immediate dispatch of four (4) to the South Pacific and four (4) to the Southwest Pacific is desirable at this time. Augmentation of this initial force can be made when forty (40) A-20s under modification at this time to be night fighters are completed.

5. Arrangements are on their way to completion between the British and the Army Air Forces for the British to equip and complete the training of Army Air Forces night fighter units required in the European Theater of Operations until such time as the Army Air Forces receives from United States production adequate aircraft and other equipment. Consequently the A-20's being converted above will be available, other than those required for training, for use in Pacific Theaters.

6. Mobile GCI (Ground Control Intercept) equipment will become available to the Army Air Forces in the United States about March 15, 1943. Sufficient VHF (aural communications) equipment for the control of aircraft was shipped from the United States (Bendix) to Guadalcanal on February 5, 1943.

7. The Army Air Forces will provide adequate ground personnel to operate the four (4) P-70s mentioned above in each of the South and Southwest Pacific Theaters.

II. Recommendation.

It is recommended that:

a. Four (4) P-70s be sent from Hawaii to each of the South and Southwest Pacific Theaters as quickly as arrangements are completed for their operation in those areas by the Army Air Forces.

b. Representatives of the Army and Navy be designated to determine which Service will have mobile GCI (Ground Control Intercept) equipment to be made available to the South Pacific at an earlier date and that the first available be sent to that Theater.

c. No request to be made on the British to furnish one (1) night fighter squadron to the South Pacific.

Stratemeyer understated the number of P-70s that were in Hawaii at the time. From the above, additional light is shed on the two detachments of the 6th Fighter Squadron that went to Guadalcanal and New Guinea on their first leg to decimate the Japanese.

In May 1943 the first two of four American night fighter squadrons were in the British Isles being trained by the RAF in Beaufighter VI aircraft. America didn't have the P-61 and it had been determined that the Yank units going to the Mediterranean would be better served if equipped and trained by the British. The C.O. of the 414th NFS didn't agree. In a memo to Eighth and Twelfth Air Forces as well as the Director of Air Defense and Air Service Command, Maj. Arden W. Cowgill wrote:

It is urgently requested that immediate action be taken to replace the Beaufighter VI Aircraft that the Night Fighter Squadrons now in operational training in England, are equipped with.

These aircraft are obsolete for Night Fighter operations, and all comparative British Squadrons are being changed to more modern and faster equipment as soon as equipment can be produced.

The 414 and 415 Squadrons are now equipped with this type aircraft, and the 416 and 417 Squadrons will receive the same type of equipment.

In three weeks of operational training, there has been considerable maintenance troubles of which the most serious are:

(a) Engine change, starter parts fell into accessory section during operation.

(b) Engine change, cylinder hold down studs pulled out of crankcase.

(c) Engine change, loss of oil pressure, main bearing on crank shaft lost oil seal.

(d) Tail frames and fuselage are being damaged by vibration caused by vibration of tail wheel. Will develop into structural failure unless corrected.

(e) One ship a wash-out resulting from hard landing at night. This plane stalled on right wing about 20 miles per hour faster than normal resulting in a very difficult plane to land or take off.

(f) All V.H.F. Radio equipment was rebuilt 1133G types and very unserviceable; has been changed to rebuilt ____G which is some better, but still far below safe operational standards.

(g) Planes were equipped with both old and rebuilt; also some new Mark IV A.I. equipment. This equipment is far below operational use and is an obsolete type; is not used for operational purposes except where Mark 7 and 8 is restricted. This type of equipment has been used for instructional purposes at Orlando, and now is being replaced with modern American make.

5. From the pilots point, and this should be given very careful consideration, there are several difficulties encountered, of which the most prevalent objections, are:

(a) Very hard airplane to fly, resulting in early pilot fatigue.

(b) Unstable and difficult to fly on instruments, almost impossible to do so until great amount of flying time is put in, on this type of equipment.

(c) Plane very heavy on controls, requires a large amount of time for change of power and airspeed. Center of balance will shift at different speed and power setting. Plane can not be recovered from spins without a great loss of altitude.

(d) The armor and protection for pilot and observer will not stop 30 cal. fire. Is of no use except protection from flak fragments ahead of plane.

(e) The British turn and bank has caused considerable trouble on instrument and night flying.

To augment the P-70/A-20/DB-7 fleet were a number of YP-61s and Beech AT-11 Kansans used in airborne radar intercept training for the R/Os. (NASM/ Smithsonian)

Another P-70 with a "nose job." Night fighter pilot trainee 2nd Lt. Herman Ernst stands prepared to go on a practice mission. Lt. Ernst, a member of the 422nd Night Fighter Squadron, would go on and have five German aircraft plus a V-1 accredited to him while flying in the European Theater of Operations. (Ernst)

(f) The ship is very unmaneuverable and requires almost all the strength of a pilot in making steep turns or coming out of a dive.

6. Planes are too slow for Night Fighter Operational use. There is no enemy aircraft operating in this area that can be caught by Beaufighters. All British Squadrons are now equipped with or are being equipped with Mosquitos within the next two months. All squadrons in active area and operation are now so equipped. The normal indicated top airspeed of the planes with which this squadron is equipped, at full throttle and RPM, is 280 miles per hour. All enemy aircraft use evasive action and speed that put it completely out of the speed range of a Beau VI.

7. This Aircraft is far below American standards in construction and maintenance facilities. The ship is hard to work on and service or repairs are a hard slow process. The British system of a daily inspection is used and requires three hours to pre-flight the ship. There is a constant replacement of rivets, screws and small bolts, due to vibration and structural flexing.

8. The ship has severe ground loop tendencies, and has resulted in the loss of one ship and damage to landing gears on three others.

9. Single engine operation of this plane is wishful thinking at its best. It will maintain altitude, but no ability to climb or maneuver. There are no full feathering props on these ships. The plane crabs in flight on one engine and instrument flying or control of flight by instruments is impossible. All pilots and crews have been ordered to leave the plane if at night and over land on single engine operation. During daylight, a crash belly landing would be possible.

10. In comparison with American equipment, both airplane, VHF and AI, it is the opinion of the technical specialists in this organization, that is not equal to our products in serviceability and operation.

11. I have been informed by representatives of the Air Ministry that the present equipment will be replaced after two or three months in the African Theatre by Beaufighter VI with the British Mark 8 AI.

12. In view of the above information, it is requested that the above

replacements be stopped, and the American Night Fighters Squadrons be given American equipment, both plane and equipment.

13. The American Night Fighters P-70 are comparable type, and can be fully equipped and ready for operation before the British equipment is available. With the Douglas Aircraft Assembly Depot and Army Depots this conversion on A-20B can be done in Africa from present planes there.

14. Recommend Aircraft and equipment in attached letter.

So went America's reverse lend lease of night fighter equipment. The AAF crews were never won over by the Beaufighter, but a shortage of equipment persisted through 1943. In a

The somewhat cramped R/O's quarters in the P-70 is illustrated in this picture. Note that the R/O's plexiglass canopy has been painted over. (Ernst)

The practice of "personalizing" their aircraft was started in training and embellished overseas. Here Lt. John Anderson of the 422nd NFS has personalized a P-70A of the 348th Night Fighter Squadron. This aircraft, as with a number of P-70As, has had its radar removed. The replacement of the plexiglass panels in the bombardiers nose by sheets of aluminum is quite clear. When installed, the SCR-540's azimuth antenna would have been in the center of the plate just forward of the 348th's emblem. (Anderson via Thompson)

First P-61 lost in an accident was YP-61 serial no. 41-18884. Lt. Steve Izenour was ferrying the aircraft from Florida to Wright Field in Ohio when he made an emergency wheels up landing in a corn field about 60 miles north of Atlanta, Georgia. Izenour heard that the crew nacelle was salvaged and modified into a gunnery training simulator. (Izenour)

September memo between the Fighter and Air Defense Branch and the Requirements Division (both within Operations, Requirements and Commitments) it was stated:

1. There is no existing requirement at this time for the Mosquito airplane as a fighter-bomber.

2. While there is a need for night fighters both in training and in the Pacific theaters, it is not believed that twenty Mosquito night fighters could be efficiently employed to meet this requirement. It is understood that the construction of the airplane prohibits its use in the tropics, and if this airplane is not to be used in combat, it should not be introduced in the night fighter training program.

3. There are presently four American night fighter squadrons in North Africa equipped with the British Beaufighter airplane. If no other use is found for the eighty Mosquito airplanes, we should determine whether or not an exchange can be made for the sixty fighter-bomber Mosquitos to provide, instead, sixty additional night fighters. If it is found that this can be done, we should then query the Twelfth Air Force to determine if they can use Mosquito airplanes in their night fighter squadrons instead of the Beaufighters. It is not considered advisable to open this subject with the Twelfth Air Force until more information is available as to all possible uses of these airplanes.

4. No further action will be taken by this Branch pending additional information from the Requirements Division.

The night fighter establishment in Florida commented that same month to the OC&R Division:

1. Request that American Night Fighter Squadrons be equipped with DeHavilland 'Mosquito' aircraft.

2. Due to the delay in production of the P-61 aircraft, considerable efforts have been made by members of the 481st Night Fighter Operational Training Group in cooperation with representatives from Wright Field and Washington, D.C. to convert A-20G aircraft for night fighter use in such a manner that fire power of at least six 50 calibre machine guns firing forward could be procured and that also SCR 720 could be used (Note: this is P-70B effort. ed.). Additional modifications were made in the way of providing such an aircraft with paddle props, booster pumps for all tanks, and stripping of armor plate and rear firing machine guns in order to procure better performance. Unfortunately, none of these compromises has resulted in a truly high performing night fighter aircraft.

3. YP-61 aircraft are now being delivered to the 481st Night Fighter Operational Training Group. It has been found that this aircraft has many disadvantages as a night fighter, among them being short radius of action due to limited gas capacity and high gasoline consumption, too many fittings, brackets and so forth, which retard forward vision, buffeting caused by the power turret guns when in certain positions, lack of speed at sea level, etc.

4. Members of this organization have flown the 'Mosquito' in combat and know it to be an excellent night fighter aircraft. The 'Mosquito' is fast both in altitude and at sea level, has a high rate of climb, has considerable range, has splendid fire power, and accommodates SCR 720 perfectly. The British have made tests of the 'Mosquito' equipment with 720 and have found the combination highly satisfactory.

5. It is believed that while the P-61 may develop into an adequate night fighter, that the 'Mosquito' is at present a far superior aircraft for this purpose, and it is strongly urged that sufficient 'Mosquito' aircraft be procured to supply the 418th, 419th, 421st, 422nd, 423rd, 424th, 425th, 426th, and 427th squadrons, some of which are now forming in

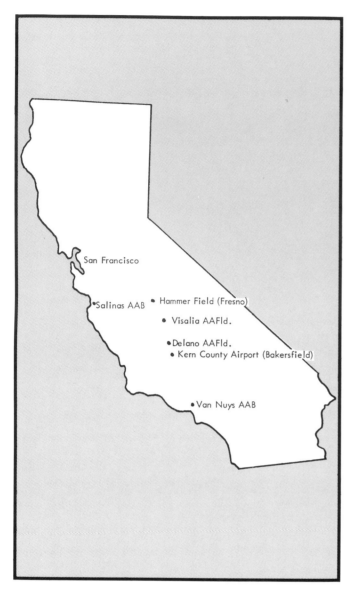

AAF Night Fighter Training Centers
California

On October 29, 1943 Brig.Gen. Mervin E. Gross, Deputy Asst Chief of Air Staff (OC&R) wrote to Maj.Gen. Barney M. Giles, Chief of Air Staff, concerning the inadequacies of both the P-70 and Beaufighter and the need of the Mosquito to equip the AAF night fighters:

1. The enemy has demonstrated that when our day fighter makes his daylight raids too costly he will resort to night bombing raids against our airdromes and other vital targets. To meet this threat we must have specially trained units, equipped with night fighter aircraft incorporating radar and capable of locating and destroying enemy night bombers.

2. Seven Night Fighter Squadrons have completed training and are deployed and equipped as follows:

> North Africa - 4 Sq Beaus
> Pacific (1 flt Hawaii, 1 flt SOPAC, 1 flt SWPA) - 1 Sq P-70
> Enroute to South Pacific - 1 Sq P-70
> Enroute to Southwest Pacific - 1 Sq P-70

3. Three OTU-RTU Squadrons, equipped with the P-70, are presently in operation. Three combat squadrons, also using the P-70, are now undergoing training, and four additional combat squadrons are scheduled to complete training by 1 July 1944. This will give us a total of fourteen Combat Squadrons and three RTU Squadrons.

4. Neither the P-70 nor the Beaufighter is a satisfactory night fighter. Informal reports from Orlando and Eglin Field indicate that the

Col. Guy Kirksey, commanding officer of Hammer Field, California, welcomes Lt.Col. Winston W. Kratz, commanding officer of the 481st Night Fighter Operational Training Group, on Hammer Field's flight line. (Kratz)

Orlando, and the remainder of which will be activated here, together with sufficient additional 'Mosquito' aircraft to supply the 414th, 415th, 416th, and 417th Night Fighter Squadrons which are now serving overseas and which are presumably equipped with Beaufighters.

6. If procurement of sufficient 'Mosquitoes' for the above out-lined purposes is not possible, it is recommended that many squadrons as possible be equipped with 'Mosquitoes' and that the remainder be equipped with P-61s. This will provide some of the squadrons with a high-classed night fighter aircraft for both defensive and intruder operations, and will provide other squadrons with the P-61 to ascertain the abilities of the P-61 as a night fighter.

7. It is requested that at least three 'Mosquitoes' equipped as night fighters be assigned to this organization for the purpose of operational training and also for use as comparative performance tests with the YP-61.

Though the night fighter training organization left Florida in early January 1944, the 422nd NFS remained behind to finish out their last few weeks before being sent to the Ninth Air Force in England. Pictured here is the 422nd's C Flight. From left to right are: Dorner, Allee, Tierney, Smith, Bost, Koehler (flight commander), Anderson, and Morgan. (Tierney)

P-61 has demonstrated excellent characteristics and should be supplied to both the combat units and the training units as soon as possible. We could well use two hundred P-61 airplanes today if we had them.

5. The latest available production estimates are as follows:

Nov	Dec	Jan	Feb	Mar	Apr	May	Jun	Jul	Aug	Sep	Oct	Nov	Dec
3	7	12	13	25	35	45	50	50	50	50	50	50	50

Production at the rate of fifty per month can be accomplished without interference to any other scheduled production, and every effort should be made to reach this rate as early as possible.

Recommend that the attached R&R be signed and forwarded to Asst Chief of Air Staff, Materiel, Maintenance and Distribution.

That same day General Giles wrote General Arnold:

1. For your information, I inspected and flew the YP-61 at the National Airport on 28 October and was quite pleased with it. The flying characteristics are excellent and are designed to meet the special requirements for night fighting.

2. Night fighter operations are currently being performed in the U.K. solely by the British, and in Africa jointly by the British and Americans. When we move to the continent we will probably have to provide our own night fighters; we will certainly have to provide them in India, China, and the Pacific.

3. The enemy has demonstrated that when jour day fighters makes his daylight raids too costly he will resort to night bombing raids against our airdromes and other vital targets. To meet this threat we must have specially trained units, equipped with night fighter aircraft incorporating radar and capable of locating and destroying enemy night bombers.

4. The P-70, which has been engineered by modifying the A-20, has been our only night fighter and has proven unsatisfactory. Its use has been necessary, however, pending the development and production of the P-61, which was designed specifically for this work.

5. The P-61 is superior to the P-70 in every respect. It incorporates our latest developments in night fighting radar equipment and mounts four fixed 20mm guns and a power driven turret with four caliber 50 guns.

6. Northrop is scheduled to produce 780 of these airplanes by the middle of 1945, which can be done without interference to other scheduled production. I think it advisable to continue this program without change.

Hinging on a lot of these discussions was whether or not the P-61 could do the job. Only the XP-61s and YP-61s had been tested to date. This was brought out in a memo of October 31st from the OC&R troops in Washington, D.C. to the AAF Board in Florida:

Reference P-61 Night Fighter, General Craig desires tomorrow, 1 Nov 1943, that the story of the Night Fighter Program, to include statement of requirements for Night Fighter Squadrons to fight this war and the airplane with which to do it, be furnished to him.

Col. Kirksey and his staff greets Lt.Col. Kratz and his staff at base headquarters. Some of the Hammer staff would be integrated into the night fighter training program. (Odell)

Three of the major players in the California night fighter training establishment. From left to right: Lt.Cols. William C. Odell, C.O. of the 420th NFS, Winston W. Kratz, commanding the 481st Night Fighter Operational Training Group, and William R. Yancey, C.O. of the 349th NFS. (Odell)

Two veterans who brought much to the AAF's night fighter training: Capt. John Striebel on the left and Lt.Col. "Winkie" Kratz on the right. Both had served in Europe, Striebel with the RAF prior to the US's entry into hostilities and Kratz while assigned to Eighth Air Force. Col. Kratz would travel to Europe, the Mediterranean, and the CBI as the chief of night fighter affairs for the AAF. (Kratz)

The information submitted to him reference the P-61 states that it is better than the P-70, etc., but General Arnold has asked to what extent it is better, can it catch the present and anticipated German and Jap bombers at all operating altitudes and other similar questions?

Suggest data from Eglin Field and Orlando concerning performance and suitability of the P-61 be procured by teletype or other means to be included in this story. A decision reference the P-61 must be made soon and the complete story must be given to General Craig as outlined above before General Arnold will discuss it.

The next day the AAF Board replied:

Furnishing information of YP-61 retel conversation Col. Wise to Colonel Lee of Army Air Forces Board as follows. This information recd from the Night Fighter Group Orlando Air Base and has not been checked or approved by the Army Air Forces Board. It is considered general and tactical in nature since all operational suitability tests are being conducted by proving ground command who furnishes you desired information direct. YP-61 great improvement over P-70 and Beaufighter as night fighter. Pilots this sta consider YP-61 to be most suitable and safest to fly night fighter in existence. Aircraft not quite up to speed and climb of Mosquito but presence of power turret with automatic gun laying and automatic sighting appears to make up for any comparative deficiency in performance. Exhaust flames are entirely too bright and reflect on pilots wind shield which impair night vision. Same can be seen from head on as well as from the rear thus impairing the elements of surprise. Adequate armor protection is provided pilot and crew. Radio equipment consists of 2 522A receiver transmitters, 720B radar RC 36 interphone 695 IFF 729 Beacon IFF receiver Detrola beam receiver. All satisfactory for combat use. Severe buffeting is encountered when turret guns are in certain position but Wright Field is working out solution this problem. Combat weight of aircraft 28,000 pounds however wing loading is only 41 pounds. Aircraft easy to taxi and has good view all around while on ground. Handles well at normal speeds. The slow speed lateral control not entirely satisfactory for present YP-61 aileron spoiler combination had dead spot for about 30 degrees rotation of the control wheel at speeds below 125 miles per hour. This is undesirable but can be tolerated until improvements are made. Controls at all speeds much lighter than those of P-70. Rate of roll is approximately twice that of P-70 and rate of turn is very good. On several tests P-61 could out turn P-70 from head on to tail on at 180 degrees. In comparison with the Mosquito the P-61 is believed to have a slight but definite edge in maneuverability. Stall characteristics of the aircraft are superior. Landing run to clear 50 foot obstacle is 1,200 feet. Take-off to clear 50 foot obstacle is 1,250 feet minimum. Aircraft is excellent to fly at night being very smooth and stable. Pilots visibility for night searching appears only fair with bullet proof glass and plexiglass combination however it is believed the P-61A using bullet proof glass as a forward part of the wind shield will be much better. Front gunners vision very bad due to distortion induced by present plexiglass wind-shield arrangement. Rear gunners vision satisfactory for sighting of turret. Endurance of the plane without external gasoline tanks is 3 hours at normal cruise. Plane can be equipped with 4 300 gallon external tanks or 4 2,000 pound bombs. YP-61 best speed is 372 at 22,000 feet. Northrop believes 400 miles per hour at 26,000 feet possible with water injection and improved supercharger ducts. Ser-

A YP-61 warms up for a training mission from a sunny California airfield. In the background are a number of P-70Bs that joined the training program in 1944. The YP-61 was used as a pilot trainer with controls in the gunners position for a second pilot as well as a trainer for the pilot-R/O team. (USAF)

vice ceiling 30,000 to 32,000 feet. Absolute ceiling approximately 37,000 feet. Initial rate of climb 2,800 feet per minute decreasing to 1,100 feet per minute at 20,000 feet. Time to climb to 25,000 feet 17 minutes from start of takeoff. Aircraft is slow to accelerate in dive. Plane gives promise of being fairly easy to maintain. Flashes from 50 caliber turret guns are so brilliant at night that they completely destroy the pilot and gunners night adaptation. Further firing tests will be made upon arrival of night binoculars to determine if they provide any additional shielding from gun flashes. 20mm gun flashes are not visible to pilot. It is the general opinion of the Night Fighter Division Air Defense that the YP-61 is an acceptable night fighter and is a great improvement over the modified A-20. Reference information on oxygen system of P-70 1939 series is equipped with low pressure system made up of three bottles. 1942 series has a high pressure system of 8 bottles. A-20G aircraft also has high pressure system of 8 bottles. in order to install 3 bomb bay bottles in the P-70 one must change the location of the oxygen bottles, that includes the 1942 series P-70 or the A-20G. It doesn't pertain to the 1939 series. Two bomb bay tanks can be installed without moving the oxygen system.

In a follow-up memorandum to General Craig from within the War Department dated Nov. 2, 1943, the second paragraph reads:

2. Specific comparison tests between the P-70 and P-61 have not been run, but preliminary reports from Orlando and Eglin Field show that the P-61 is superior to the P-70 in every respect. Pilots at Orlando, who are familiar with British night fighters (Mosquito and Beaufighter), consider the P-61 the most suitable night fighter in existence. It is not quite up to the speed and climb of the Mosquito, but the power turret and automatic gun laying and automatic sighting appears to make up for any comparative deficiency in performance. Handling characteristics are excellent. It is more maneuverable than the Mosquito and has superior stall characteristics, with very smooth and stable flight characteristics.

By December 1943 Col. William F. McKee, Deputy Asst. Chief of Air Staff for Operations, Commitments & Requirements wrote:

1. This R&R will supersede the breakdown of type total by model of the approved AAF Requirements for 1944 submitted to General Jamison on 23 October by Commitments Division, Allocations Branch, and will also supersede memorandum of 10 November, subject, 'AAF Aircraft Requirements for 1944' insofar as each refers to Mosquito aircraft to be obtained from British and Canadian sources.

2. The attached chart states the total current AAF requirement for Mosquito aircraft, with breakdown by model. Explanatory notes

A few P-61As, as the one on the left, were assigned to night fighter training. Along with the Douglas P-70, shown in the background, were some A-20s as "Pandora's Box" assigned to training the night fighters. (Soukikian)

A P-70A, less its transmitting antenna, bristles with eight .50 cal. machine guns in its nose. (NASM/Smithsonian)

regarding the deployment of and negotiation for each model are included.

3. The present agreement provides for delivery of forty (40) Canadian unarmed bombers, forty-three (43) British fighter bombers and one hundred two (102) British P.R. models. Attention is particularly invited to the additional requirement for night fighters presented in the attached chart. The unsatisfactory performance of the P-70 and the delayed deliveries of the P-61 both contribute to the inadequate availability of American-built night fighters. It is recommended that every effort be made to obtain (after study of the performance characteristics of the various British models which may be available) competent Mosquito night fighters for use in the European and Mediterranean theaters, thus expediting availability of P-61s now urgently needed in the Pacific.

4. For your information, the Arnold/McCain/Courtney/Portal agreement allotted one hundred twenty (120) Mosquitos to AAF during 1943 and representatives of RAF delegation have unofficially advised representatives of AC/AS, OC&R, that the British contemplated allotting ninety (90) Mosquitos to AAF during first six months of 1944 – a total of two hundred ten (210) aircraft until 30 June 1944. As revised at present (exclusive of night fighter requirements), the agreement calls for delivery of only one hundred thirty-seven (137) aircraft in the same period. It is suggested that the reduction of seventy-three (73) articles from the original schedule may be used to good advantage in negotiating for night fighter models.

There were a number of Mosquito variants to choose from. A Lt.Col. J.A. Gibbs of OC&R Requirements Division documented his findings in a memo on December 4th:

1. We have been called upon to decide what model Mosquito night fighter we would like for re-equipping our night fighter squadrons in North Africa and England (note: there were none in England at this time, see charts notes below. ed.). We have no way of knowing whether or not we will receive this British equipment however. Allocations is preparing a request for sufficient Mosquito night fighters to equip three squadrons in U.K. and bring four squadrons in North Africa up to T/O strength.

One of the youngest AAF night fighters, 1st Lt. Robert M. Blackman. Blackman joined the RCAF and became a night fighter pilot at age 16 or 17. He flew night fighter combat in England for about a year prior to transferring into the AAF. Pictured here in the cockpit of a P-70, he was an instructor in the AAF's night fighter training program. Later he would go into the Southwest Pacific Area with the 547th NFS and would have two confirmed victories prior to being killed in action on an intruder mission in the vicinity of Manila, Philippine Islands, on December 31, 1944 – he was not yet 21 years old. (Odell)

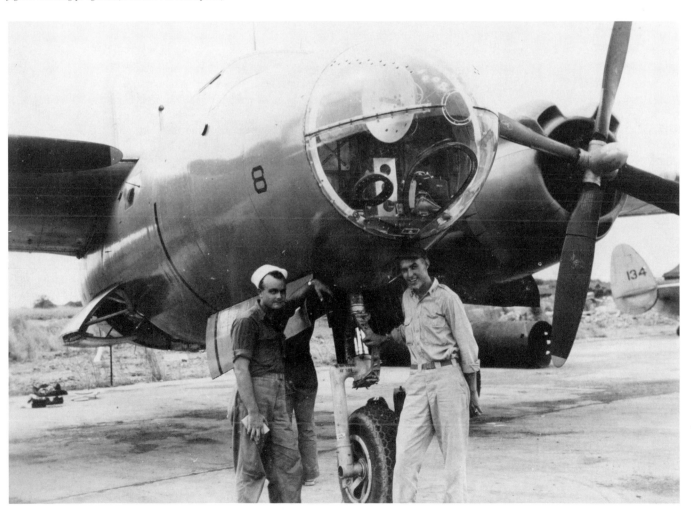

A couple of Navy-Martin Marauders with radar installed in the bombardier's compartment to be used in R/O training and for target towing. On the left Lt. Robert G. Graham is picking one of the Marauders up from the Navy. To the right is how one of the Martins looked once integrated into the AAF's night fighter training program. (Graham via Thompson)

2. The best available information on British equipment which I have had access to has been obtained from Air Intelligence officer. The information is not too much in detail but after carefully considering the data now available I recommend the following order of priority for Mosquito night fighters:

a. Our first choice – Mosquito XIV night fighter (two 1,370 horse power Merlin 73 engines). No performance figures are available on this Mosquito equipped with the Merlin 73 engine, however, Mr. Thomas of the British Air Commission lead me to believe that the Merlin 73 was the best Mosquito high altitude engine now in quantity output. The Mosquito XIV is equipped with AI Mark 8 radio equipment. This equipment is the best currently in production in U.K. but is not quite as good as our 720 set.

b. Our second choice for night fighters should be the Mosquito XV high altitude night fighter version, equipped with two 1,370 horse power Merlin 73 engines. This airplane is a new high altitude pressure cabin fighter, which when equipped with VHF air to air homing, and AI Mark 8 radio equipment would be a night fighter version. Present armament as a night fighter is not known. This airplane has an operational ceiling of over 40,000 feet.

c. Our third choice – Mosquito X if it can be equipped with AI Mark 8 radio equipment. This Mosquito has two 1,370 horse power Merlin 73 engines, is equipped with high altitude pressure cabin, is a development from the night fighter VI and is considered the fastest long range night fighter in the world. First production began in 1943.

d. Last choice is the Mosquito XIII night fighter, which is equipped with two 1,405 horsepower Merlin 23 engines. This airplane equipped with these engines has low performance and is only a low altitude night fighter. It is possible that this will be the only Mosquito that the British will give us. However, I feel it is not as good as our P-70.

3. If the above meets with your approval, Allocations will be notified of the above desired priority in order that they may go ahead and request sufficient models from the British.

An attached chart to the memo had the following notes of interest:

"Sad Sack," a P-70A-2 of the 348th Night Fighter Squadron helped train neophyte night fighters in Florida and California. (NASM/Smithsonian)

As training progressed in 1944, the YP-61s turrets either had the guns removed or the entire turret assembly was removed as shown on aircraft 41-18878. Most of the P-61s going into the field did not have the turret at this time. (Esposito)

(a) There are now four (4) AAF Night Fighter Squadrons in the Mediterranean Theater partially equipped with Beaufighter aircraft which are short to the extent of 34 airplanes from their authorized strength. The December allocation (of Mosquitos) is calculated to eliminate the current shortage by equipping 2 of these squadrons with Mosquitos. The 1944 allocations are for attrition replacements for both the Beaufighter and Mosquito Units, thus permitting a gradual conversion of the Beaufighter squadrons to Mosquito aircraft.

(b) The 422nd Squadron is committed to the U.K. as of 1 Feb 1944 (actually arrived 7 March 1944. ed) The January allocation is for unit equipment and reserve for this squadron and subsequent allocations represent attrition replacements.

A Marauder in formation with a number of A-20/P-70s on a training flight. (Graham via Thompson)

As Northrop designers were hard at work on their night fighter design, additional production contracts were received for the Vultee Vengeance in June 1941. This time it was for the Air Corps A-31 variant. (Northrop)

A mainstay of the night fighter training program in 1942 and 1943 was the Douglas P-70. These aircraft followed the RAF night fighter paint scheme of the time of overall flat black. (Mc Donnell Douglas/Harry Gann)

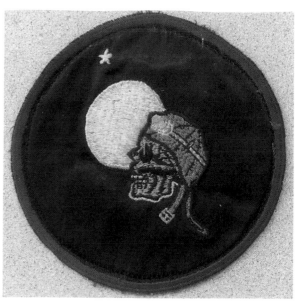

Above and left: The official emblem of the 348th Night Fighter Squadron and a variation that was used on flight jacket patches and on the squadron's aircraft.

The official emblem of the 349th Night Fighter Squadron and a variation.

Wheeler Field as it appeared in the Fall of 1941. This serene scene would be turned to death and destruction in just a couple of months. The P-40Bs and P-36s seen here equipped most of the pursuit squadrons then stationed on Oahu in the Territory of Hawaii, including the 6th Pursuit Squadron. (Garrett via Thompson)

The only mishap on the flight to New Guinea was when the P-70 flown by Lt. Fred Secord, with F/O Carl Hale as R/O, couldn't get the nose gear to extend as the flight came in to Townsville, Australia. Bouncing the plane hard as they touched down on the main gear didn't work. Nor did a half loop or inverted flight. A gear up landing on the gravel field was accomplished. The aircraft had minimal damage and the crew got away unscathed. The plane is shown after repair had been accomplished at Archer Field, Australia. (Secord)

Left: Lt. Fred Secord and his P-70 "Dusty." Lt. Secord recalled that on their way to New Guinea the P-70s and their very secret radar was always under guard when they landed to refuel or rest. On one of their stops an Aussie soldier came over to Secord's plane. Secord was in the plane completing some paperwork when the soldier asked him what the thing sticking out the nose of the plane was. Secord wondered for a moment. He couldn't mention radar. So he explained that it was a harpoon and that their was a giant spring inside the nose cavity of the fuselage. That when they got close enough to a Japanese plane that he would fire the harpoon. The Aussie soldiers comment was, "What you Yanks won't think of next!." (Secord)

A bit of field maintenance. 6th NFS detachment P-70 gets an engine change at 3-Mile Strip on New Guinea. (Secord)

A P-70A taxies out on 12-Mile Strip. The "A" model contained six .50 cal. machine guns in the nose, an upper rear single flexible .50 cal. machine gun that the R/O could fire, and a lower rear single flexible .50 cal. machine gun that a radio operator/gunner could man. It did not carry the four 20mm cannons as did the original P-70-DO configuration. (Secord)

A bird's eye view of 12-Mile Strip. By the time the night fighters arrived on New Guinea the Japanese ground forces had been driven back from the Kokoda Trail and the ground fighting was around Buna and Dobodura on the north coast. (Secord)

1st Lt. Frederick H. Secord named his P-70 "Dusty" after the dusty wheels up landing he had on a gravel airstrip in Australia. (Secord)

"Black Widow," a P-70A, was the aircraft of Capt. Robert W. McLeod, the detachment's commander. (Secord)

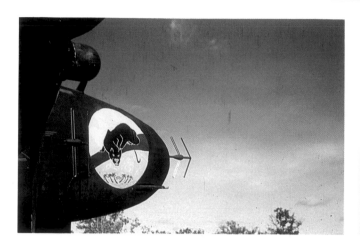

A close up of the 6th's P-70-DO which left Douglas with only four 20mm cannons to which the 6th NFS added to .50 cal. machine guns in their aircraft shortly after receiving them in Hawaii; probably accomplished at the Hawaiian Air Depot at Hickam Field. (Secord)

The 6th NFS detachment on New Guinea, redesignated Detachment "A" Night Fighter Squadron in September 1943, was disbanded in December. Its aircraft on hand at the time were turned over to the newly arrived 418th NFS and most of the crews returned home. Though the detachment destroyed only one enemy aircraft in the air, their presence discouraged many. Like most of the AAF night fighter squadrons to come, they did more intruder missions than air defense sorties. (Secord)

P-70A "Shirley Ann" of the AAF's night fighter training organization. (DiLabbio)

A P-61A-1 flying over southern California. Under right lighting conditions the plexiglas radome, which was left unpainted when it left the factory, would be translucent and the features of the parabolic radar antenna could be distinguished. (Wolford)

Above and below: The P-61 Black Widow. (Wolford)

A B-25 of the 418th NFS flying to a forward airstrip to stage from for upcoming strikes at distant enemy airfields and shipping. (Bradley via Hernandez)

Most of the production Widows went to the operational areas. Only a few were allocated to the training organizations. (Wolford)

Above: An olive drab over grey P-61A-1 glides through the California skies. Visible in this picture is the aircraft's red serial painted on the aft portion of its boom. (Wolford)

Above right: A trio of Black Widows fly over the central California San Joaquin Valley in a daylight flight. (USAF)

Right: A P-61A-1 dips its wing over southern California. Gunnery training was carried out from Van Nuys Army Air Base northwest of Los Angeles. (Wolford)

426th NFS personnel work on one of their recently received P-61 at their Madhaiganj, India base. The chipped paint is not from wear and tear but from the removal of the protective tape applied to protect the aircraft from salt water damage while aboard ship. (Le Fever via Thompson)

"I'll Get By" flown by Capt. John Wilfong and R/O Lt. Glenn Ashley. Wilfong and Ashley, pictured on the right, got one of the few night fighter victories in the CBI when they successfully intercepted a Japanese Lily bomber on November 21, 1944. (LeFever)

Skipper Bill Bradley of the 421st NFS stands proudly next to his P-61 on New Guinea. The 421st was pleased to receive their Widows in replacement for their P-70s. The euphoria soon wore off as realities set it – higher headquarters didn't know what to do with night fighters. (Desclos)

The 6th NFS night fighter team of 1st Lt. James C. Crumley and 2nd Lt. Jean B. Desclos stand alongside their P-61 "Husslin' Hussy" on Saipan. From this island the 6th flew combat air patrol, stood alert in anticipation of night intruders, and assisted lost and damaged AAF bombers get back to their home fields. (Desclos)

"The 'Virgin' Widow" of the 6th NFS on Saipan. The word "virgin" was overpainted with red stripes after the crew got a confirmed kill. (Donnelly via Thompson)

Opposite and this page:
In living color – Ninth Air Force night fighters.
(USAF)

A P-70 of the 481st Night Fighter Operational Training Group on a training mission off the coast of Florida. (AAF)

Both the flight test community and the operational crews felt there were areas that the P-61 needed improvement. These included turbo-super-charged engines to enable them to catch the faster enemy fighters, speed brakes to prevent them from overshooting a target as they were making an interception, and greater fuel capacity. The latter was taken care of both as field modifications and on the production line with the addition of pylons to hang external fuel tanks. (Wolford)

The first XP-89 flew on August 16, 1948. When the Scorpion arrived at Muroc, the Curtiss-Wright XF-87 had already been there for six months. Northrop not only had to prove themselves, but were in competition with a competitor who had been flying previously. (Northrop)

"Wabash Cannon-Ball IV" of the 425th NFS was flown by the squadron's commander, Lt.Col. Leon "Gilly" Lewis. (Anderson)

The P-38M started coming off Lockheed's Dallas modification line in the summer of 1945. The night fighter training program under the 319th Wing at Hammer Field, California, had been training in modified P-38Js in anticipation of the receipt of the "Ms" and subsequent deployment to the Pacific. (NASM/Smithsonian)

The remains of a Ju 88 shot down. Note the radar operators equipment in the photo below. (Conway via Campbell)

Both the Junkers Ju 87 dive bomber and Fieseler Fi 156 "Storch" (Stork) liaison aircraft gave the night fighters quite a challenge. It was from the night fighters attempts to intercept these types of aircraft that the "fighter brake" concept came from. (Campbell collection)

The Junkers Ju 290 was used for both transport and long range maritime reconnaissance. (Campbell collection)

A P-38 of the 421st returning from a daylight flight. (Bradley via Hernandez)

A flight of 6th NFS P-61s over Kagman Point on Saipan. (Desclos via Thompson)

The 421st NFS moved up from the Philippines to Ie Shima in early August 1945. Here one of the late P-61Bs received by the 421st awaits the night's mission. (Chew via Thompson)

Oakley Allen of the 339th Fighter Squadron with his F-61 at Kisarazu, Japan in 1947. (Allen via Thompson)

"Husslin' Hussy" of the 6 NFS on Saipan with pilot Jim Crumley in the cockpit. (Desclos via Thompson)

The 416th followed in the steps of the 417th. They were redesignated the 5th Fighter Squadron on that same November 9th and came under the control of the 52nd Fighter Group. As with the 2nd FS, they too were transferred with the 52nd FG back to the US less personnel and aircraft. Pictured above is a P-61 of the 416th NFS at Horsching, Austria, in August 1945. (Dickey via Thompson)

A similar action was taking place in the Pacific as in Europe. At the end of the War there were 10 night fighter squadrons (including the two in the CBI). A number were inactivated at war's end and others joined the ranks of the inactivated until there were only three left in February 1947; the 6th, 418th, and 421st Night Fighter Squadrons. Shown stationed at Wheeler Field in late 1945 are the P-61s of the 6th NFS. (Hahn via Thompson)

Like their counterparts, the Pacific night fighter squadrons were also redesignated. In February 1947 the 6th, 418th, and 421st Night Fighter Squadrons became the 339th, 4th, and 68th Fighter Squadrons, respectively, and came under the command of the 347th Fighter Group. A quite worn F-61 (the "P" for pursuit being replaced with the "F" for fighter) of the 4th Fighter Squadron on Okinawa. (Umbarger via Thompson)

Next to come under ADC was the 325th Fighter Group headquartered at Hamilton Field near San Francisco, California. (USAF via Anderson)

With the war ended, most of the AAF's night fighters were scrapped over seas. Many P-61s were turned to scrap metal in such places as New Guinea, the Philippines, Germany, and, as pictured above, on Okinawa. (Horton via Campbell)

The end of World War II marked the end of piston engine combat aircraft. Also, the pioneering night fighters, as specialists of combat in the dark, would soon become the standard for all fighters. The night fighter would evolve into the all-weather fighter, and eventually all fighters would be radar equipped and capable of operating in all weather conditions, day and night. As so often happens, their was a gap between drawing board and fielding of the new jet night/all-weather fighters. To fill this gap, the last World War II era fighter, the North American F-82 Twin Mustang long range escort fighter, would be pressed into this additional role. (Thompson collection)

Symbol of the new jet Air Force, the Northrop F-89 Scorpion. A new chapter begins. (Northrop)

(c) The 423rd Squadron is committed to the U.K. as of 1 April 1944 (actual arrival 17 April 1944. ed.). The March allocation is for unit equipment and reserve for this squadron and subsequent allocations represent attrition replacements.

(d) The 425th Squadron is committed to the U.K. as of 1 May 1944 (arrived 26 May). The April allocation is for UE and reserve for this Squadron and subsequent allocations represent attrition replacements.

In reply to a letter from General Giles, Air Marshal Courtney wrote on January 21, 1944:

My dear Barney,

I refer to your letter dated 15 January, 1944 (copy attached for easy reference) on which I wrote 'agreed.'

I believe I may have inadvertently misled you as to the date when the four U.S. Squadrons can be re-equipped from Beaufighters to Mosquito. The position is that a number of British Night Fighter Squadrons in the U.K. are still equipped with the Beaufighter and I believe you would agree that they should have priority over Squadrons in the Mediterranean theatre. The Mosquito Night Fighters are coming through very slowly and I am afraid that it will not be possible to begin the re-equipment of the Mediterranean Squadrons until the second half of the year. In the meantime, however, we can maintain these Squadrons with Beaufighters.

I therefore ask you to agree that priority should be accorded to the re-equipment of the U.K. Squadrons and that the re-equipment of your four Squadrons in the Mediterranean should be effected as early as possible in the second half of the year.

s/Yours sincerely
Chris Courtney

Messages started flying all over the world. In an OC&R memo dated February 4, 1944 it was stated:

On General Giles' recent trip, the subject of the AAF night fighter squadrons was discussed with General Eaker and Air Marshal Slessor. They both concurred in the fact that the 4 AAF night fighter squadrons should be maintained even at the expense of rolling up some of the RAF night fighter squadrons now in the Mediterranean. This is in accordance with the exchange of letters between General Giles and Air Chief Marshal Courtney on the allocation of aircraft (night fighters) from the RAF to the AAF.

Three days later a follow-up memo:

In view of the information contained in Comment #1 (memo above), all allocations of P-61 aircraft to the Mediterranean are being cancelled. This will eliminate projections totaling sixteen (16) aircraft, and will enable acceleration of other commitments by that amount.

Meanwhile, the four AAF night fighter squadrons in the Mediterranean were suffering from poor performance and attrition of

A formation of P-70As from Salinas Army Air Field fly over California's Salinas Valley. Salinas was one of a number of satellite fields used by the night fighters. (NASM/Smithsonian)

their Beaufighters. The following memo was submitted to General Craig:

1. A message from the Mediterranean Army Air Forces Caserta, Italy (No. __ 6996, dated 22 March) states that Beaufighter aircraft being flown by the USAAF squadrons are obsolescent and that the RAF has informed them that Beaufighter production has been discontinued. This cable requests immediate action to alleviate the current situation and provide suitable equipment.

2. The four (4) USAAF night fighter squadrons in MTO are now equipped with forty-eight (48) Beaufighters. The authorized strength for these four squadrons; is forty-eight (48) unit equipment plus twenty-four (24) reserve for a total of seventy-two (72). Aircraft now on hand, therefore exactly equal unit equipment requirement and provide no aircraft for reserve.

3. While in London arranging Lend-Lease schedules for 1944, General Giles and Air Marshal Courtney reached an agreement whereby the RAF would support USAAF night fighter units in MTO. This

Night fighter training does not stop when the sun goes down. Night fighters with their flying gear in order make their way to their aircraft for a practice night mission. (Odell)

Left: The business end of a night fighter; the end that many an unhappy prey saw in the last moments of its life. The hole between the four .50 cal. machine guns is where the transmitter antenna for the SCR-540 is installed. (NASM/Smithsonian)

The P-61 was the plane the night fighters wanted, but it wouldn't be available before the first four American squadrons would be dispatched to the Mediterranean theater. (Northrop)

Britain's De Havilland Mosquito was a plane that the Americans wanted. The Beaufighter-equipped MTO squadrons wanted them in place of their Beaufighters and the AAF, at least the test community, felt that it was a better plane than the P-61. Political maneuvering was going on on both sides of the Atlantic. (Campbell)

agreement is quoted in part in attached draft of message to General Eisenhower.

4. Recommend authorization be granted for dispatch of attached message.

General Giles responded to the situation by writing Air Marshal Sir William L. Welsh at the British Joint Staff Mission in Washington on April 1st:

Dear Air Marshal Welsh:
General Eaker has cabled stating that the Beaufighters being flown by U.S. Army Air Forces night fighter squadrons in the Mediterranean are obsolescent and are in a general worn out condition.

I realize that the U.S. Army Air Forces and the Royal Air Forces squadrons in the Mediterranean are supplied from a common pool and I have agreed with Air Marshal Portal in a general plan to give preferential treatment as regards equipping the night fighter squadrons in the U.K. with the newer types of planes. However, I am frankly worried that our forces in the Mediterranean will be placed in a highly vulnerable position if we don't take some positive steps at once to furnish them with sufficient modern night fighters. Our units are equipped with enough airplanes to provide them with unit equipment, however, they have no reserve aircraft. I concurred in Air Marshal Portal's request that the allocation of Mosquito night fighters to the Mediterranean be deferred until such time as the night fighter squadrons in the U.K. were equipped, however, it was my definite understanding that our squadrons would be maintained with Beaufighters to the extent of their unit equipment, reserve airplanes and that they would be provided with sufficient attrition airplanes to keep the units equipped with aircraft that were not obsolete or worn out.

General Eaker has been advised that the matter of the equipment for these squadrons is being taken up with the Air Ministry through the R.A.F. Delegation here in Washington and I would appreciate your advising us as to what Air Chief Marshal Courtney has planned for sustaining these units.

Again Giles wrote Air Marshal Welsh on May 25th:

Dear Freddie:
At the time of our conversations last January, an agreement was reached in regard to Mosquito Aircraft required by the U.S. Army Air Forces for the period 1 January 1944 - 30 June 1944, and a tentative agreement made for the period 1 July 1944 - 31 December 1944. These agreements were made a part of CCS 495.

Due to the production of Mosquito night fighters and the need for this type aircraft in the United Kingdom, no deliveries have actually been made to our squadrons in the Mediterranean. These squadrons are still operating on Beaufighters that are far from satisfactory. The P.R. Mosquitos have been delivered on a reasonably satisfactory schedule.

Our requirement for night fighters still remains, and I should like to submit a bid for their supply to our squadrons and reaffirm our agreements as regards the delivery of the P.R. type as follows:
a. Mosquito Night Fighters
Period 1 July 1944 - 31 December 1944 - 90.
Period 1 January 1945 - 30 June 1945 - 36.
b. P.R. Mosquitos

Period 1 July 1944 - 31 December 1944 - 42*
Period 1 January 1945 - 30 June 1945 - 36.
*Plus any undelivered portion of the 60 scheduled for delivery in the first six months of 1944.

I should appreciate your submitting this bid on our behalf to Air Chief Marshal Portal and using your best efforts to obtain a commitment to meet this requirement in full.

The Air Marshal replied on June 9th:

My dear Barney,
I have now had a reply from Courtney to the request for Mosquitos contained in your letter dated 25th May.

As regards night fighters he considers that ultimate distribution of whatever quantity is available for the M.A.A.F. should be left to Eaker and that it would be wrong to tie his hands by making specific allocations either to the U.S.A.A.F. or R.A.F. squadrons under his command. I understand his present intention is to re-equip, alternately, one of each until all are completed and although it seems unlikely that more than four will be re-equipped by December I know that Courtney will provide as many aircraft as is consistent with necessary maintenance of the U.K. night fighter squadrons. I think you will agree that it is best to leave this matter to Eaker's discretion.

Your bid for 42 P.R. Mosquitos in the second half of this year and for 36 in the first half of new year can be met, and this letter constitutes acceptance of the commitment.

There quite often seems that those testing aircraft, or any system, and those that operate it in the field have differing opinions. The P-61 was no exception.

WAR DEPARTMENT
CLASSIFIED MESSAGE CENTER
INCOMING CLASSIFIED MESSAGE

SECRET
PRIORITY

From: CG Strategic Air Forces in Europe, London, England
To: War Department
No: U 63574   13 June 1944

To Arnold signed Spaatz U 63574.

Tests here indicate P-61 will not prove satisfactory night fighter against most German night bombers presently used primarily because of speed limitation. Vandenberg is worried that 9th Air Force may not be able to take over night defense at scheduled time because of this limitation. It has been suggested that water injection and 150 grade fuel may improve this situation. If this is impractical or does not allow sufficient improvement, information is requested as to the possibility of procuring sufficient late model Canadian built Mosquitoes for substitution in night fighter units. Should this be possible, request an

Bristol's Beaufighter night fighter was what the AAF's first night fighters would fly against the German and Italian air forces. From the beginning, during their training in Britain, the night fighters wanted something else – even the P-70. (Campbell)

estimate of delay caused by training and modification (Training air ground crews) on this type airplane.

End

General Arnold replied on the 14th:

To Spaatz signed Arnold rewired U 63574 dated June 13.

Water injection and use of grade 150 fuel in P-61 are both practical but increased performance will not be sufficient to make the P-61 effective against fast German bombers. Water injection now going into production aircraft increases top speed only 10 miles per hour. No action will be taken to provide kits for aircraft in service unless requested. P-61 has not been tested in this country with grade 150 fuel but it is believed that little, if any, increase in performance will result. Canadian built Mosquito is an unarmed bomber type and extensive modification would be necessary to convert this aircraft for night fighter use. We are negotiating with the British Air Commission to secure 36 British built Mosquito night fighters for your 2 squadrons. Estimate your squadrons would require 6 weeks training to become fully operational on Mosquito aircraft.

End

The test between the Mosquito and the P-61 flown by the Ninth Air Force's 422nd and 425th Night Fighter Squadrons crews was proved out in the English skies as told in the next chapter. But the Mediterranean troops were still struggling with the Beaufighter, with not a single Black Widow in sight. On June 17th General Giles once again wrote Air Marshal Welsh:

Dear Freddie:
Thank you for your letter of June 9 with reference to Mosquito aircraft for the Army Air Forces.

I am glad to know that our bid for the P.R. aircraft can be met.

As regards night fighters for the MAAF, I feel that we should have a schedule of the proposed allocation by the RAF to the Mediterranean Theatre and would like you to ask Courtney to provide us with this schedule in order that our planning people will have some idea of what is going to take place.

A new high priority requirement for Mosquito night fighters has been cabled us by the 9th Air Force. The 9th Air Force has three night fighter squadrons, presently being equipped with P-61s, all are committed to the defense of our installations on the Continent. Tests of this airplane in the U.S. indicate that it will not be a satisfactory night fighter against the German night bombers, because of speed limitations and some time will elapse before modifications will sufficiently improve its performance. The 9th Air Force with a little more than half again as many aircraft as the RAF Expeditionary Air Force, has only these three night fighter squadrons while the RAF has 6 night fighter squadrons and two additional as reserve in the ALGS. In addition to these eight squadrons, the Metropolitan Air Force has thirteen night fighter squadrons. I feel that the air units engaged in support of our expeditionary forces should have the best equipment available and that the USAAF squadrons charged with the defense of our installations on the Continent should be equipped with Mosquito night fighters until such time as the P-61 has been improved.

Therefore, I wish to place a bid on behalf of the Army Air Forces for 60 additional of the latest type of Mosquito night fighters for equipping and maintaining during the last six months of 1944 two of the three AAF squadrons in the Allied Expeditionary Air Force. This in my opinion is deserving of a priority higher that accorded RAF squadrons assigned to the ADOB. An analysis of this requirement is as follows:

> 24 airplanes for 2 squadrons
> 12 airplanes for reserve for 2 squadrons
> 24 airplanes for attrition for 6 months at the rate of 2 per _____ squadron per month
> 60 total airplanes.

On July 21 Col. J.B. Gordon, Asst. Adj. Gen. of the US Strategic Air Forces in Europe, wrote General Arnold:

Summing up the Night Fighter situation in this Theater, the following information now furnished by the Ninth Air Force through General Vandenberg is believed pertinent.

a. The P-61, as a result of operational use over the beachhead and recent tests, is believed the best available airplane for assignment to the two (2) Night Fighter Squadrons in the Ninth Air Force. It is considered that the installation of water injection on all P-61s, both in this Theater and on production aircraft from the States, will provide adequate operational speed. The installation of external fuel tanks should be expedited in order to improve the range of this airplane. Maneuverability however, as well as present armament, is considered adequate for the purposes for which the airplane is to be utilized. It is expected that the above mentioned modifications will provide satisfactory performance and also should enable favorable comparison to the new British Mark XXX Mosquito. It is therefore requested that the planned flow of P-61 aircraft to this Theater be maintained until such time as operational results prove this particular model of airplane to be unsatisfactory for its planned utilization.

2. In addition to the above, the unavailability of the British Mosquito, due to deficiencies in their planned production, as well as increased activity of RAF Night Fighter Squadrons combating the flying bombs, removes any possibility of employing the Mosquito for some little time.

3. In view of paragraphs 1 and 2 above, it is quite evident that the P-61 is the most logical Night Fighter airplane available for our use at this time. Every effort will be made to study and improve the performance and operational use of this airplane, especially in view of our desire to utilize American equipment whenever and wherever possible.

After all this "jockeying around" the only American night fighter squadron to receive the Mosquito was the 416th NFS in the Mediterranean.

Chapter 11

Across the Atlantic

The first American night fighter to reach the ETO, excluding the 1st Pursuit Squadron (Night Fighter), was the 422nd Night Fighter Squadron. They had the distinction of being the first night fighter squadron to receive training in the P-61 Black Widow prior to going overseas, and the last squadron to complete their night fighter training in Florida. The other night fighter squadrons that were still going through their training when the 422nd departed for Europe were transferred, along with the entire AAF night fighter training program, to new bases in California during January 1944. Upon their arrival at Charmy Down, England, on March 7, 1944, they found themselves lacking an element that every combat squadron deems necessary – aircraft. This condition would prevail during their two month stay at Charmy Down. Ground schools were conducted, and as much flying as possible was flown in the squadron's two aircraft, an Airspeed Oxford and Cessna C-78, plus any aircraft that could be "borrowed" from nearby units.

Following close behind the 422nd Night Fighter Squadron was a number of replacement personnel. In this party was Flight Officer Robert F. Graham, an R/O to be assigned to the 422nd Night Fighter Squadron once they reached England. Bob Graham found the voyage across the Atlantic quite enjoyable:

A bunch of us went over on the Queen Elizabeth; must have been about six or eight crews. That was kind of funny. The Liz being a British boat, and the British were very rank conscious usually. We were the only Air Corps detachment on board. All the rest were infantry, field artillery and so forth. So naturally being Air Corps we got the best deal anyway, and then they found that all the R/Os were flight officers. Now, a flight officer in England was pretty well up the ladder, so we got put four to a big stateroom whereas captains and lieutenants were down in the hold. Of course, no one said a word about

that, especially a flight officer. We set up a big poker table in the middle of the room, and we played poker all the way across. The life of Riley, we really had fun.

Fresh from their night fighter training in sunny California, and the first to complete its training at the new training facilities, the 423rd Night Fighter Squadron joined the 422nd at Charmy Down on April 17. IX Tactical Air Command, to whom these two squadrons were assigned, was not engaged in night operations at the time, which might account for the cool reception that the night fighters received. IX TAC was not prepared to receive them, much less to train them.

Warning orders for an impending move were received by the 422nd on the first of May, with the actual order to move coming shortly thereafter. On the 6th of May the actual move was made to their new station at Scorton, England. Here there were numerous AAF and RAF aircraft which would be at their disposal for flight, navigation and AI training. Also, rumors were rampant concerning P-61s having arrived in England. On May 10th Col. Oris B. Johnson, Commanding Officer, along with Captains Edward S. Page and George W. Reynolds, and Lt. Ernest P. Luke flew to the depot at Speke to find out for themselves. These latter officers were the 422nd's Intelligence, Operations and Engineering Officers respectively. The rumors were true, for lined up on the field were eight P-61A-5s. They were given a high priority and were promised their aircraft around May 20th.

English Widow

These were not the first to reach Great Britain. A P-61A-1 had arrived on March 21 for Royal Air Force evaluation. This was

The first Widow to reach Europe was this P-61A-1 seen on the ramp at the depot at Speke in April 1944. Oddly enough this was not for the AAF night fighters but for the RAF to evaluate. The AAF night fighters would get their first Widow, a turretless P-61A-5, about a month or so later. (Northrop University)

quite understandable because the British had initially contacted Northrop prior to the AAF's interest had been sparked. As a matter of fact, after the Northrop night fighter became an AAF project, the RAF was to share in the initial production quantity in which it was to have received 50 of the first 57 aircraft under Lend Lease.

The RAF kept this plane in their possession until February 22, 1945 when it was returned to the AAF. The P-61A-l series, as this one was, was powered by the R-2800-10 engine. These power plants are of a lower rating than that of the R-2800-65 which powered the P-61A-5 and subsequent aircraft. The

English were not very impressed by the plane's performance; but then they were not very impressed with much that wasn't English.

Put to the Test

On the 23rd, the first Black Widow arrived at Scorton, thus the 422nd became the third AAF night fighter squadron to be equipped with this aircraft. It had been 77 long days since the 422nd arrived in Great Britain, and morale had never been as

R/O Robert F. "Shorty" Graham, on the right, was a replacement who came over in relative luxury to join the 422nd NFS in England. As a flight officer, Graham was not very high in the AAF's "pecking" order, but in the RAF it was a different story. Since his ship was British, he was treated as a British Flight Officer. With Graham is Lt. Robert G. Bolinder who would be Graham's regular pilot and be teamed with Shorty Graham on four of the five victories Graham would participate in. (Graham)

A 422nd NFS family portrait. Standing are some of the pilots with their R/Os squatting in front taken in England in May 1944. From left to right is Donald W. Allee (R/O Richard Heggie, Jr. not in picture), Paul A. Smith and Robert E. Tierney, Thomas H. Burleson and William P. Monahan, Leonard F. Koehler and Louis L. Bost, and John W. Anderson and James W. Morgan. (Tierney)

Lt.Col. Oris B. "OBie" Johnson, C.O. of the 422nd NFS, in the cockpit of his "No Love! NO NOTHING!" The receipt of their Widows was bitter sweet for the night fighters. After months of waiting for their aircraft, they no sooner received them that it looked like they were going to be taken from them and replaced by British Mosquitos. (USAF)

Maj. Leon G. "Gilly" Lewis, C.O. of rival 425th NFS and "Wabash Cannon Ball IV." Nos. I and II were Martin B-26s which Lewis flew in the Pacific. Number III was an earlier P-61. (AAF)

high as it was this day. The rest of the month and early June was spent getting reacquainted with the P-61. The RAF loaned experienced night fighter personnel to aid in the tutoring; the American R/Os hadn't looked at a radar scope since Christmas. Because these aircraft were not equipped with turrets, all gunners were transferred to other units, mainly the A-20 equipped 423rd Night Fighter Squadron which indicated they were going to operate in a manner different from the other two night fighter squadrons.

The all-over glossy black paint scheme had been determined superior to the olive drab and gray that the 422nd's

Widows were. The RAF was contracted to perform a repaint of some of their aircraft. It seems that most of the aircrews managed to get their radomes painted. The crews had a choice of nose colors, which probably wasn't part of the original bargain. James F. Postlewaite recalls:

We got all our noses sprayed on a RAF base in England; they being the radar kinds. They sprayed lead to the underside of the radome to reduce the ground scatter out of the radar. Our radar was pretty sensitive, and this would take out the clutter from the ground. Well, everybody had different colors, some had red, brick red noses. You'd

The crew of "Plenty Peed Off!! "Patootie III" are Capt. Russ Glasser on the left and Lt. Bill Tripp on the right. Glasser was instrumental in the plot to get the first P-61 modified in the 425th NFS by having the R/Os equipment moved from the back of the crew nacelle to the gunner's compartment. (425th NFS collection via Anderson)

Lt. Alvin E. "Bud" Anderson is photographed in front of "Fearless Fosdick." As a replacement pilot, Anderson did not have an aircraft assigned to him and his R/O but had to share other aircraft because of the squadron's shortage. "Fearless Fosdick" was not one that he flew; it was being used as background for a number of photos being shot on this particular day. (AAF)

have this lead bottom, and then the fellow would ask you what you wanted for a paint job. I've forgotten who started this; so we happened to go in one day, and he didn't have too many dark colors. All he had were the light ones, so we took the yellow one and away we went. It was quite outstanding. When we brought it back, I thought O.B. Johnson (squadron C.O.) was just gonna flip. Oh, you could see that airplane 20 miles away in the sky in the daytime. And do you know at night, in the black night, I've run into that airplane. I couldn't see it, and I've run right in and smacked my head on it.

As it turned out, things weren't so bad. I flew wing for O.B. Johnson one of our first times we pulled the maneuver of taking off before the day fighters came back. Well, it was real great, about 4,000 feet you know, that's a real tight formation. He was screaming about that yellow nose as we were headed towards Germany before the sunset. I didn't feel any better about it than he did because you could see us coming. That night he stirred five of them up. I chased them all over the Bonn airdrome, and we didn't even get to see one; but I got the green light at Bonn airdrome from the tower to land. We wanted to catch them in the landing pattern; it had been one of their tactics to shoot Allied airplanes in the landing approach with the wheels in the down position, when you're sort of helpless. They had no lights, no nothing, and were sinking. They were probably Fw 190s and were going fast, but we never saw them.

The Ninth Air Force's third night fighter squadron, the 425th NFS, arrived at Charmy Down on May 26, 1944. Their inactive period was relatively short for on the 12th of June they also were sent to Scorton where they were checked out in the P-61.

The European based Black Widows did not have the dorsal turret. With the empty gunners position, and feeling that two sets of eyes looking forward were better than one, the 425th NFS hit upon the idea of moving the R/Os position up forward. They enlisted the assistance of Northrop technical representative Rulon V. Harmon in this endeavor. With Harmon, the squadron's engineering and chief radar officer as well as Capt. Russell Glasser (a pilot with a graduate degree in mechanical engineering) set out to draw up a plan detailing all that had to be accomplished, create a set of drawings, and make a cardboard mockup of the installations to check its fit in a P-61. To actually get the modification accomplished took some clever scheming on Glasser's part. Russ Glasser once recalled his part in this escapade:

We drew up plans for the changeover and went up to Ninth Air Force to propose the change. They were turned down because Ninth felt that the airplanes could not be kept out of commission long enough to make the conversion, being needed for combat missions that were scheduled. They felt that the change was not worth the time and money required – the 425th disagreed and went on with their plans. I checked with the engineering officer at Burtonwood, a major repair depot in England. They agreed, but the plane needed a reason to be down for about two days. I scheduled time, promising that they would have a valid reason to keep the airplane down that long.

So when it became time to have the props magnafluxed (required every 50 hours) on my plane, I flew it to Burtonwood. I came in for a landing about 50 feet too high. Did what was an apparent stall, caught it just before it hit the ground and made what to me was a normal landing, but to the control tower it looked practically like a crash landing. I then called the tower and asked if everything looked all right. They said it looked like I was minus one piece of the airplane and

Herman Ernst's P-61 "Borrowed Time" at Hurn Airdrome in July 1944. Behind the P-61 are some Mosquito Mk. XVII's, against the likes of which the Widow had to prove itself. (Ernst)

Another of the 422nd's Widows. Note how unlike "Borrowed Time" the invasion stripes on this ship are. They are only on the lower surfaces of the boom and wing. The grey beneath the radome is a thin spray coat of lead to reduce ground clutter. (Stegner via Campbell)

Both the night fighters and GCI crews had to become much more proficient and work out tactics among themselves before any thought could be given to entering combat. In this effort to become combat ready, the 422nd NFS, 425th NFS, the 75th Station Complement and RAF night fighter specialists worked hard, though some competitive friction arose between the two American night fighter squadrons. This friction brought bold comments from the men as, ". . . there isn't any field large enough to hold both the 425th and ourselves," according to a 422nd Night Fighter Squadron operations report.

In the photo above Lt. Stan Woolley of the 425th NFS supervises the painting of his ideal on "Mah Ideel." Below is the end product. Bob Llovett was Woolley's R/O in "Mah Ideel." (Woolley & Stegner via Campbell)

should have it checked. So I wrote up a Form 5 stating that it needed a landing gear strut and wing examination and had it towed into the hangar.

While the props were being magnafluxed, we installed the radar equipment in the gunner's position. The change increased the speed, depending on the airplane, from 15 to 20 mph at cruise. The center of gravity was changed 15 inches forward. The angle of flight at cruise was changed from a slightly nose up to a slightly nose down attitude. It made a remarkable difference.

We then persuaded the chief engineering officer from Ninth Air Force to fly both the converted and regular models. He then authorized the change. He was so impressed that he completely forgot the circumstances under which the conversion had been made.

To aid the 422nd and 425th Night Fighter Squadrons in becoming operational, there was a menagerie of aircraft at their disposal which included A-20s, P-47s, a Hurricane and Wellingtons.

Trained as night fighters in P-70s and P-61s, the 423rd NFS found themselves as night photographers. The A-20J photo Havocs were quite similar to the P-70s the pilots had flown during their night fighter training in Florida. (423 NFS/155 PRS Assoc. via Campbell)

The Havoc's engines rev up as the ground crew make it ready for an upcoming night mission. (423 NFS/155 PRS Assoc. via Campbell)

Lt. Gordon Hulse in the cockpit of "The Robert E. Lee, II." A few days after this picture was taken Hulse along with navigator Lt. William Levenworth and gunner Claude Whiteman were out on a mission when the plane was badly shot up. Whiteman bailed out but Hulse and Levenworth were killed while attempting a crash landing. (McKeon)

As mid-June faded into the past, the 422nd was starting to shape up into a real combat ready unit. Lt.Col. Oris B. Johnson, realizing his aircrews needed some realistic training to prepare them to meet the foe, made arrangements with a RAF Halifax unit at Croft. The arrangement was for the 422nd Night Fighter

Squadron to fly day and night intercepts against the RAF bombers. During these training exercises the bomber crews honed their skills in evading attacking Luftwaffe night fighters while the AAF night fighters polished their night interception tactics.

The 422nd NFS unit history goes into detail concerning these joint training exercises:

The daylight tactics were designed to give the 'Big Friends' a real workout in evasive tactics, but at the same time it piled up the time to the credit of the 'Blip Jockeys.' The night exercises (Bulls Eye) were damn good practice. The Halifaxes would take-off on a three-legged flight, covering the greater part of Northern England and Scotland. We were given an area to defend and GCI would vector us into the stream. 'Window' and evasive tactics were used by the Bomber Boys. When we got within minimum AI range and in position for the kill, we would so signal by flipping on the navigation lights; while the tail or other gunners flashed a light if they had us in their sights before our lights went on. Such was our success that it tended towards an underestimation of the Huns abilities as well as a feeling of over-confidence on our part, best expressed by the remark, 'The number you shoot down on one sortie depends largely on how few rounds you have fired to make the kill.' Little dreams of glory, but it looked so easy. There must be a catch to it. Also PIs (Practice Intercepts) were attempted with the target taking the most violent evasive action, which the Widows were capable of, and that was plenty. The stars over Yorkshire saw some rugged interceptions, but it was the best kind of practice.

The 422nd's ego was greatly deflated after a visit by Brig. General William L. Richardson, C.G. of IX Air Defense Command, on June 21st. The American night fighters in England had come under his command just the day before. It seems that the General left the impression that the night fighters would be subordinate to the anti-aircraft units, and whose sole responsibility would be to protect areas and installations in the rear areas.

The 422nd Night Fighter Squadron had received their first P-61s just 35 days earlier when on June 27, Colonel Winston W. Kratz of the 481st Night Fighter Operational Training Group

Like their ex-night fighter comrades, and the rest of the Army Air Forces' aircrews, the 423rd NFS/155th PRS aircrews decorated their war machines in a variety of ways, though the main theme seemed to have a female in mind. (423 NFS/155 PRS Assoc. via Campbell)

and a Colonel Henry Viccellio from the Operations, Commitments and Requirements Section of the War Department arrived at Scorton Airdrome, England. The purpose of Colonels Kratz and Viccellio's trip was to determine the suitability of the P-61 for combat operations in the ETO and the readiness of the 422nd and 425th Night Fighter Squadrons. To carry out this combination operational readiness exercise for the squadrons and suitability test for the P-61, a detachment of six P-61s with three crews from each squadron was sent to the RAF airdrome at Hurn. This site was chosen due to its close proximity to the Normandy beach head. While at Hurn, this composite detachment was attached to the 125th Newfoundland Squadron. Col. Kratz was in charge of the evaluation exercise while Colonel Johnson of the 422nd was detachment commander.

Jim Postlewaite remembers well those doubtful days of late June and early July 1944:

You bet, we took our wings off and went into O.B. and laid them on the table and said if we don't fly the '61 we all quit and walked out.

And then we had to make a test between the '61 and the Mosquito. Northrop's technical representative took O.B.'s airplane and screwed the props down so they wouldn't fly off and put Norm Williams and Doyle in as the crew. They went up, and they took that Mosquito apart.

There was some thought within War Department of scrapping the Black Widow in favor of Britain's night fighter version of their Mosquito. The idea of changing from their newly acquired '61s for Mosquitos did not sit well with the men of either the 422nd or 425th Night Fighter Squadrons, upon whose shoulders the fate of the Widow rested. The 425th's squadron history's comment on this bad news was:

Somewhere, apparently, someone whispered to a General big enough to count that the P-61 type aircraft was not what it was cracked up to be; that the Mosquito Mark XVII, the famed British "Mosey", was the better aircraft for night fighting purposes. Apparently the General stood aghast for a moment and then, falling weakly into a swivel chair, gasped, 'Gad'! 'We must demand an investigation.' With which a bevy of full Colonels leaped to their feet, and saluting, said, 'We Concur.'

The evaluation demonstration of the two aircraft took place on July 5, 1944 at RAF Station Hurn. The 422nd's Unit History relates it this way:

On the 5th, the long awaited test with a Mosquito (Mark XVII) was laid on at 1600. Squadron Leader Barnwell of 125 Squadron and his R/O vs (1st Lt. Donald J.) Doyle-(F/O Norman N.) Williams. The P-61 more than exceeded even our wildest hopes, being faster at 5,000, 10,000, 15,000 and 20,000 feet; out turned the Mossie at every altitude and by a big margin and far surpassed the Mossie in rate of climb. We could go faster and slower up or down. Faster than the pride of the British – a most enjoyable afternoon!

A memo to Lt.Gen. Hoyt S. Vandenberg, Commanding Officer of the Ninth Air Force, from Fighter and Air Defense Branch, OC&R; subject: Report of Operational Test of the P-61, July 7, 1944 in the ETO, stated, "Mosquito and P-61 were approximately equal in performance with the P-61 being slightly faster." In their follow-up report, Kratz and Viccellio reported that the P-61 had proven itself adequate to cope with Ju 88s, Do 217s, and He 177s. It also stated that the Widow was slightly faster that the Mosquito Mk XVII at all altitudes tested, which was up to 20,000 feet, and that it could out climb the Mosquito and was able to turn inside it in aerial combat.

There always seemed to be some doubts within the War Department as to the suitability of the Widow and they seemed to be driven in their attempts to get Mosquito night fighters. Col. Kratz who had just learned first hand the feelings of the Ninth's night fighters and witnessed the P-61s performance pitted against that of the Mosquito, recalled an earlier similar experience:

I was in General (Carl) Spaatz's office along with Mr. Robert A. Lovett, then Assistant Secretary of War for Air. We wanted to know whether or not the P-61 should be produced in quantity. Mr. Lovett was very much in favor of it. General Spaatz was not. He said he had the performance troops (at Eglin Field, Florida) in the P-61 and the Mosquito, and they found the Mosquito to be better; and he had arranged for the AAF to get 200 Mosquitos.

I asked Gen. Spaatz if he couldn't have a competition. I had an informal competition. I flew the P-61, and someone else flew the Mosquito; and we tried climbs, etc. I was very elated at the results and sent back this report to Gen. Spaatz. The P-61 was then mass-produced. A couple of months later a more formal contest was held using the test pilots. I'm sure they could get a great deal more out of the '61 than I could and probably a test pilot could get more out of a Mosquito. The same thing happened.

I'm absolutely sure to this day that the British were lying like

The crew of Lt. Clifford Mackie (pilot), Lt. Vernon Redd (navigator), and Sgt. William McKeon (photo gunner) had a very rough mission over Germany. As Lt. Mackie was attempting to bring the stricken A-20 in for a crash landing, they crashed into a P-47. Sgt. McKeon was out first and attempted to free Lt. Redd, but he was too entangled in the wreckage. In the first photo a number of ground personnel have joined the rescue and were able to extract Redd. Sadly, Lt. Redd died the next day. The next two photos are of the damaged nose area of the A-20 and of the P-47. This was Sgt. McKeon's 24th and last mission (he had flown 50 missions previously in B-17s of the 352nd Bomb Squadron, 301st Bomb Group). (McKeon)

Pilot Lt. Herman Ernst in the front seat and his R/O, Edward Kopsel, riding in the back as usual, were the first 422nd crew to get a victory when they shot down a V-1 on July 15, 1944. (Ernst)

Lts. Garth Peterson (pilot) and John Howe (R/O) were the first to strike pay dirt for the 425th NFS when they destroyed a V-1 on August 5, 1944. (425th collection via Anderson)

troopers. I honestly believe the P-61 was not as fast as the Mosquito, which the British needed because by that time it was the one airplane that could get into Berlin and back without getting shot down. I doubt very seriously that the others knew better. But come what may, the '61 was a good night fighter. In the combat game you've got to be pretty realistic about these things. The P-61 was not a superior night fighter. It was not a poor night fighter. It was a good night fighter. It did not have quite enough speed.

From Guns to Cameras

In the dark of night an A-20J taxies out onto the runway. The green light is given; with a deep-throated roar the aircraft takes-off into the darkness. The plane circles the field and straightens out for his destination. Target ahead! The gunner is alert in his turret, the navigator is passing on positions to the pilot. Over target now; the flash bombs are released; 23 seconds are counted off, and the camera releases.

The above mission was not flown by a photo recon squadron, in name at least, as one might conclude. It was the 423rd Night Fighter Squadron, who never flew as night fighters in the combat area; and who would become a photo reconnaissance squadron some five weeks after entering the European Theater of Operations.

Activated on October 1, 1943, the 423rd Night Fighter Squadron begun its training at Orlando, Florida under the command of Maj. Joe G. Gillespie. Training was carried out, without aircraft, at Orlando until late January 1944 when the night fighter training program was moved to California. The 423rd arrived at Kern County Airport, California, on January 29, when ground training was carried out in P-70 and A-20 aircraft. With their training accomplished, the 423rd left California in late March for the Camp Joyce Kilmer, N.J., staging area. On April 5th they boarded H.M.T. Arundel Castle for their voyage to Europe. Debarking at Glasgow, Scotland on April

Herman Ernst poses with his crew chief shortly after the V-1 kill. It is interesting to note that though the V-1 victory stencil has been added to the aircraft, only the "H.E." of H.E. Ernst has made it. (Ernst)

17th, they trained to Charmy Down, Wilts, England the same day.

Soon after their arrival in the ETO they started training again, this time in night photographic work. On May 18, 1944 they were transferred from IX Tactical Air Command to the 10th Photographic Reconnaissance Group. On 20 May they moved from Charmy Down Airdrome to Chalgrove Airdrome, Oxon. A few days later four crews from the 33rd PRS (10th PRG) were assigned to the 423rd on detached service to aid in their training in night photography.

Modifications were made to the 423rd's A-20J to enable them to carry K19 vertical cameras and flash bomb racks in their bomb bays. Dr. Harold Edgerton of Massachusetts Institute of Technology developed the lamps that would be used for this specialized night photography. They were good for almost an unlimited number of flashes!

Operations commenced for this night fighter-turn-night photographer squadron during the early hours of D-Day. In support of the invasion, four crews were sent to photograph German troop movements in six target areas on the Cherbourg Peninsula. The first mission was a good one as all made it back to base. The one A-20 which was equipped with the Edgerton lamp achieved good results whereas the other crews had timing and altitude difficulty with their flash bombs.

On June 22, the 423rd Night Fighter Squadron was redesignated as the 155th Photographic Reconnaissance Squadron. The 155th PRS would continued in its role of night photography for the remainder of the war. The night flying training as night fighters would serve them well as night photographers.

Into Combat

With the question whether the Ninth Air Force night fighters were going to be equipped with the Mosquito or Black Widow settled, the night fighters could now get down to the real business at hand. In mid-July a detachment of the 422nd Night Fighter Squadron was sent to Ford Airdrome where they were to chase the V-1 Buzz Bombs. These missions were code named Anti-Diver patrols. The V-1s were referred to as "Divers" because they would dive towards the ground when they ran out of fuel. The proper way to destroy these nasty machines was to fire into its pulse-jet engine. If you fired into the fuselage of the drone, you had a great possibility of it exploding in your face.

On the night July 15th, 2nd Lt. Herman E. Ernst along with his R/O, F/O Edward H. Kopsel, were on the lookout for these fast moving craft. Soon the controlling GCI station had one on their screen and were vectoring the night fighter team to an intercept position. Because of the V-1s greater speed, the P-61 had to gain enough speed for the intercept by going into a slight dive. Lt. Ernst was directed into a position from which he could begin the attack. As he descended through the clouds he heard distraught sounds from F/O Kopsel sitting in the back of the crew nacelle, the tailcone had "disintegrated." Later it was discovered that the differential in pressure when the P-61 was in a dive would cause an implosion of the plexiglas tailcone. This occurred on a number of early P-61s; and when the AAF and Northrop were made aware of this, field modifications were made to strengthen the tailcone as well as changes on the Northrop production line.

Ernst and Kopsel were given another opportunity the next night. They were at an altitude of 3,000 feet when Lt. Ernst spotted four V-1s approaching the English coast line. He got his plane in position to dive at the first missile when an RAF Mosquito, also attacking the same V-1, interfered with his attack and Ernst had to abort. With other V-1s in sight, Ernst positioned himself for attack on the second Buzz Bomb. Diving from 5,000 feet, his air speed indicator was soon approaching 350 mph. Closing in to 2,000 feet, Ernst sent a salvo of 20mm cannon fire at the robot. Still closing, he was soon closing to within 900 feet of his target. He fired his cannons again. This time hits were observed on the propulsion unit. The Buzz Bomb went into a steep dive, exploding before going into the Channel. "I wish I could remember the name of the crew", Bob Graham, ex-422nd R/O, reminisced:

They got in behind this buzz bomb off of Cherbourg. They were in perfect position; they slid in behind it, and the R/O was reading its range: 600 feet, 500 feet, 400 feet, shoot 300 feet, 200 feet aw forget it; and about that time the pilot opened up. About that time the

1st Lt. Raymond A. Anderson (left) and 2nd Lt. John U. Morris, Jr. (right) were the first crew in the 422nd to destroy an enemy aircraft when they successfully intercepted a Ju 88 on the night of August 7, 1944 (J. Anderson via Thompson)

The 422nd's team of John W. Anderson and James W. Mogan pose in front of their P-61 "Tennessee 'Ridge Runner.'" (J. Anderson via Thompson)

The 422nd NFS moved onto the European Continent when they left their English hosts and relocated to Maupertus (A-15) airfield in France in late July 1944. Shark-nosed "Jukin' Judy" and "Husslin' Hussy" are captured in the camera from a fellow 422nd P-61 crew on their way to their new field. (USAF)

propulsion unit blew up; boy, smoke and fire and everything else came out! When they got down on the ground, the R/O just looked at the pilot, turned his back on him and walked off.

The night fighters liked the idea that the Buzz Bombs didn't fire back, but they soon learned that they were dangerous in their own way. One of the other 422nd NFS crews chasing these pilotless craft were Capt. Tadas J. Spelis along with his R/O, F/O Eleutherios (Lefty) Eleftherion. Flying with them on their July 20th Anti-Diver patrol was the 422nd's intelligence officer, Lt. Philip M. Guba, riding in the gunner's seat. Capt. Spelis was pressing the attack hard. He was firing as he closed to within 450 feet from the V-1. His gunnery was right on the mark, it exploded! Being in such close proximity, the explosion threw the P-61 out of control. They bounced around like a tiny ship at sea in a storm. With much effort, Spelis was able to regain enough control to get them back to base safely. Afterwards an inspection of the aircraft showed both ailerons badly scorched, the fabric on the left rudder and left half of the elevator was burned away, the other half of the elevator and right rudder was badly scorched, and many holes and dents peppered the P-61.

V-1s were not the sole property of the 422nd NFS. The 425th was in on the action also. For four days in a row in August they got one a day. The team of 1st Lt. Garth E. Peterson and 2nd Lt. John A. Howe (R/O) got one on the 5th and 6th. Then Capt. Francis V. Sartanowicz and 1st Lt. Edward M. Van Sickels turn came on the 7th. It was almost 2:30a.m. when Lt. Sartanowicz sighted an incoming V-1. Its flight path was in an easy decent but it was going quite fast, around 300mph. The P-61 and its crew had sufficient height above the Buzz Bomb so they could gain the speed necessary to get within firing range. When Sartanowicz was about 600 feet from the Bomb, he gave a burst from his 20mm cannon. He was right on target! The cannon fire went right into the propulsion unit. The V-1 lost power and dove into the English Channel harmlessly.

The next night the 425th's last V-1 kill almost ended with disastrous results. On patrol were 1st Lt. James L. Thompson and his R/O, F/O Joseph E. Downey. Lt. Thompson spotted the fiery exhaust of the V-1s pulsejet engine coming across the Channel. This "V" weapon was traveling at about 350mph at about 1,800 feet. Diving on his target, Lt. Thompson pulled out of his dive on the tail of the V-1 and fired at quite close range.

As the bomb exploded, Thompson was pulling the '61 up. This good piloting, or luck, averted the Widow from being destroyed also.

The Allied invasion of the Normandy beachhead had been secured. Enemy forces were being pushed inland from the coastal region. As the Army ground forces advanced, the supporting tactical air forces had to keep up. The 422nd Night Fighter Squadron, under the control of IX Tactical Air Command, was assigned the duty of providing night protection for the First US Army. The 422nd NFS arrived at the captured German airfield at Maupertus, near Cherbourg, France, in late July; it wouldn't be until the last of July before the last aircraft and crews would arrive from detached service in England.

Now the 422nd was to oppose an enemy who could give battle, and return shot for shot. By the early morning hours of August 7 the night fighters were going to get their most probable of probables. Their record in France so far was two probables, both on August 6.

According to Jim Postlewaite, Maj. Churchill K. Wilcox, the 422nd's Weather Officer, was a real asset to the squadron:

Churchill was a great weatherman. He was in our tent one night, and we asked him how the weather was, and he said, 'Man, it's gonna be clear. 'I had just walked in, and I asked him, 'Hey, Churchill, how's the weather?' He replied, 'It's clear as a bell out.' So I retorted, 'You'd better bring a knife along to cut the fog.' I think that night we lost two airplanes, and they had to bail out. There was no place to land, but it was typical weather. But I must say that he really was a good weatherman.

The 422nd's first sighting of an enemy aircraft came on August 4th when a Ju 88 was spotted, but an intercept was not made. The next night 1st Lt. Eugene D. Axtell and F/O Joseph F. Crew intercepted a Do 217. In the pursuing battle Axtell was able to get some good deflection shots off. The Do 217 had returned some accurate fire and dove through the clouds out of sight. They felt this was a kill, though it couldn't be confirmed. That same night 1st Lt. Lewis A. "Sack" Gordon and 1st Lt. Creel H. Morrison intercepted a Ju188. In their fight, Gordon and the German went from 9,000 feet down to 2,500 feet. At this point the Ju188 went into a spin (Gordon hadn't fired a shot). Gordon, like Axtell, also felt they had destroyed the enemy craft but it too couldn't be confirmed because of cloud cover. Of this latter

The 425th's new home at Vannes (A-33N), France, was located on the southern border of the Brest peninsula. This ex-Luftwaffe airdrome included bullet riddled buildings and a number of German aircraft in various conditions of damage and disrepair. (425 NFS collection via Anderson)

action, the 422nd's squadron history states:

Almost immediately the overcast was illuminated by an explosion and the same time a Mossie pilot called control and asked which one of our chaps (meaning RAF) had gotten a kill. Despite this, 21 Scctor disallowcd the kill on the grounds that it was ridiculous to presume a victory when no shots had been fired.

Finally a confirmed kill came on August 7th when 1st Lt. Raymond A. Anderson, pilot, and 2nd Lt. John U. Morris, Jr., R/O got on the tail of a Ju 88 over the Bay of Mt. St. Michel. The intercept was right on the mark. Lt. Anderson fired his 20s and the enemy blew up in mid-air. No confirmation problems this time.

That same night, a team that would eventually receive credit for five kills, had a real close encounter. 1st Lt. Paul A. Smith and 2nd Lt. Robert E. Tierney were on patrol when Tierney picked up a blip on his scope. Receiving directions from Tierney, Paul Smith set his course to intercept the target. He had to get close enough for a positive visual identification to be made before a shot was fired. As he closed in, he was able to identify it as a Bf 110. At this same time the German apparently realized he was being stalked as he began taking evasive action. The Messerschmitt tried to turn away from the P-61 but the Black Widow with its tight turning radius had no problem staying with him. It wasn't long before they were both standing on their wing tips. It was an eerie sight as both crews looked at each other as they pivoted around the same axis. Soon their wings hit. With this impact both planes went out of control

momentarily. When Smith regained control, the German was nowhere to be seen. After landing, an inspection showed scrapings of the Bf 110's paint on the leading edges of the P-61s wing.

Movement once again. As August came to a close the 422nd moved to Chateaudun. Their short stay at Maupertius

425th's C.O. "Gilly" Lewis discusses an upcoming mission with his R/O, Carl Soukikian. "Souky" might seem somewhat out of place navigating Maj. Lewis around the darkened, enemy filled night skies over France. It had been only a few months since the dancers at the Latin Quarter, the Brown Derby, and the Fox and Hounds in Boston had crowded around the orchestra stand to hear the Gypsy violin of young maestro Jean Carl Soukikian.

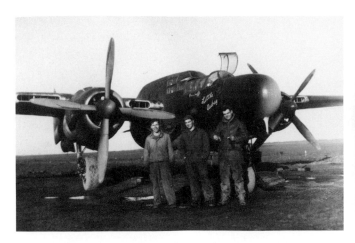

Another "Little Audry," this one belonged to the 425th's Lt. James Thompson and F/O Joseph Downey. They were credited with the 425th fourth and last V-1 to be shot down. The new black paint job doesn't seem to be quite complete when this photo was taken. (Downey via Thompson)

The night fighter team of Stan Woolley and Bob Llovett of the 425th pose next to "Norma Dea." (425 NFS Assoc. collection via Anderson)

had been fruitful for the night fighters. They had rung up a score of three enemy aircraft confirmed destroyed, four classified as probably destroyed, and one damaged. They bid a bon farewell to the Cherbourg peninsula.

The 422nd's sister squadron in the Ninth Air Force, the 425th Night Fighter Squadron which was attached to the XIX TAC, was making its effect felt also. They remained at Scorton, with detachments at Hurn and Ford Airdromes, until mid-August. While there they modified their P-61s to carry the radar observer at what had been intended as the gunner's station, immediately behind the pilot. As with the 422nd, turret equipped Widows were not foreseen in the near future, and the gunner position was surplus.

They too chased the Buzz Bombs around southern England. They tallied a score of four confirmed and two others claimed but not given credit for (damaged or probables). The night fighter team of 1st Lt. Garth E. Peterson and 2nd Lt. John A. Howe held the 425th's record of two destroyed.

Their stay in England was shortened due to the XIX TAC's movements, which were in support of Patton's highly mobile Third U.S. Army. The 425th Night Fighter Squadron moved to the continent, arriving at Vannes, France, on August 18th. The aircrews with their Black Widows arrived shortly thereafter. They were barely settled in when "all hell" broke loose. The 425th's history retells this tale:

On Sunday evening, August 27, an excited, red faced lieutenant

of Cavalry arrived in camp and informed Major Lewis that thousands, literally thousands of Germans had broken out of the Lorient trap at Belz; that they were headed this way; that he, the Lt. of Cavalry, desperately needed some air support; and could we furnish it? Could he substantiate his claim? He could and apparently did.

This was strictly not SOP. Skipper Lewis looked about him – into the expectant faces of the pilots and men clustered about him. 'Combat at last,' those faces said. 'What the hell are we waiting for. Let's go!'

The Skipper could see he'd have one disappointed gang on his hands if he said no, and besides – weren't the Jerries headed this way? – And wasn't our airfield in danger? – And didn't he, the Skipper, want to go even worse that the rest? 'Okay. Let's go.'

This being a daylight ground support mission, the R/Os were not required. The planes were armed and in the air within 15 minutes! Enemy positions were soon under attack. The 425th found the enemy and were really in the war.

They made numerous strafing runs at gun positions, areas of troop concentration, and convoys in the Belz area. Within a half hour they had completed their mission and returned to base. A report by the 86th Cavalry Reconnaissance Squadron stated that a 155mm battery had blown up when the attacking P-61s exploded a nearby ammunition dump; that the Belz FFI reported that the attacking night fighters had killed many and injured others as well as shooting up nine gun positions and five houses. During the attack, a P-61 piloted by Lt. Nelson Willis struck a telephone pole. The plane crashed, killing Willis.

Chapter 12

Oriental Adventure

The 427th NFS in the Mediterranean Theater of Operations

In the fall of 1943 AAF leaders saw an opportunity to pursue their idea of using Russian bases as stopover points in "shuttle" missions. These missions would enable either Fifteenth Air Force bombers operating out of Italy to fly, or Eighth Air Force from England, to fly raids against targets deep inside Germany and its conquered lands and then fly a shorter distance into the USSR rather than making the longer, and dangerous, return trip to their point of origin. In Russia, they could refuel and rearm and on their return trip additional targets could be hit.

This was also an opportunity to show the Russians that the Americans were helping them fight "their" enemy. But the Americans were not schooled in the Russian way of doing business. Quite often what seemed to be an agreement really wasn't and the Russians were in no hurry to play the American's game. Both Foreign Minister Vyachlesav M. Molotov and Russian leader Joseph V. Stalin had to be dealt with; a tact that the US leaders didn't develop, nor understand.

The Combined Chiefs of Staff gave the AAF's General Arnold approval to pursue his plan in October 1943. FRANTIC, the code name given to this project, was put forward to the Russians. Maj.Gen. John R. Deane, who headed the US military mission in Moscow, accompanied by Brig.Gen. Hoyt S. Vandenberg, first briefed the British, who were not overly enthusiastic about the idea, and then went on to Moscow. The Russians seemed to give the okay, but nothing was happening. During the Tehran conference of December 1943, American Ambassador W. Averill Harriman as well as Col. Elliott Roosevelt (the President's son) pressed for action from the Russians. All to no avail.

In February Stalin apparently gave the order and things started to move ahead. The AAF would not receive the number of bases it desired nor their location. Somewhat distant for the Air Forces purposes, the three bases were not far from Kiev. All three bases had been decimated as an outcome of the Russian defense against the invading Germans. Much had to be accomplished before they could become operational. On June 2, 1944, the first shuttle mission was flown, the honors going to the Fifteenth Air Force. The mission was quite successful and plans for further missions were soon in the works. The Eighth Air Force struck out on their first attempt on the shuttle-run on June 21st. With over 100 B-17s and 70 P-51s, they successfully bombed a synthetic oil plant at Ruhland, south of Berlin, and continued on to their safe havens near Kiev. Unknown to the American force, they had been trailed by a German He 177.

Some five hours later a German force of bombers and fighters were entering Russian territory. At a little after midnight they struck the American air force then on the ground at the Poltava air base. After dropping flares, the Luftwaffe bombed and strafed the airfield at low level, causing great destruction to the American force but getting by nearly unscathed themselves. The Russians, who demanded that they only would perform defense duty in support of the three bases, completely failed in that effort. Within a week the Americans had received Stalin's approval, or so they thought, to station an AAF night fighter squadron in the area. The first night fighter squadron that would be available from the training program was the 427th NFS which would leave its California training base on July 12th.

By early August a Canadian and American aircraft carriers, with their cargo of shiny black P-61 Black Widows and the 427th Night Fighter Squadron, docked at Casablanca, French Morocco. Louis E. Williams, who was an officer assigned to Headquarters North African Wing of ATC, observed what

Opposite:
Lts. William Humenick (pilot) and George Mueller (R/O) of the 427th NFS seated on the radome of their Widow for the camera. The quarter moon symbols along the side of the crew nacelle represent regular patrols while the quarter moon with a lightning bolt going through it represents night intruder missions. (Humenick via Thompson)

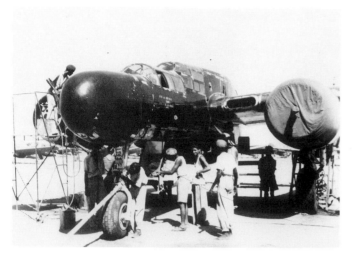

(This page and opposite) The Black Widows of the 426th Night Fighter Squadron arrived by ship at the port of Calcutta, India. From there they went to the Air Service Command's depot at Barrackpore where they were reassembled and checked out. The P-61s looked dwarfed in the huge dirigible hanger in which much of the work was accomplished out of the hot Indian sun. (Northrop via Balzer)

turned out to be quite a sight. Mr. Williams recalls:

At this time a large number of Black Widows came in by ship and were unloaded on the docks right in the city and then towed through the streets out to Gazes with little Clark line tugs. Like all North African towns, Casablanca had its share of thousands of robed Arabs in the street with nothing whatsoever to do. These vicious looking black fighters passing down the boulevards – competing with the usual street traffic of Peugeots, camels, goats, and sheep herds caused great crowds of Arab sightseers to gather. On each wing tip sat Arab civilian employees from the base lifting low hanging tree limbs which would have fouled the wings. These natives swapped obscene insults with the less fortunate unemployed friends.

Within two weeks the aircraft had been assembled, and the squadron was ready to move on to the next station – Poltava, Russia.

In Cairo the 427th Night Fighter Squadron received a change of orders. Once again the Russian leadership was not cooperating; soon FRANTIC would be dead. As for the 427th, they were now being sent to Italy to fight with the four American Beaufighter-equipped night fighter squadrons already part of the night defense of the Mediterranean. By the end of August when the 427th's aircrews joined up with their ground comrades in Pomigliano, Italy. The ground crews had arrived earlier in

August coming directly from the US For two weeks the 427th helped provide air cover in the Naples area which resulted in two night chases. The first was aborted due to an AI failure and the second due to friendly anti-aircraft making it impossible for them to continue their pursuit. In late September another change of orders was received sending them to the China-Burma-India theater. With the departure of the 427th in late September, the MTO did not see a P-61 until late December when the 414th Night Fighter Squadron would start its transitioning from their lend-lease Beaufighter aircraft to the new American night fighter.

China-Burma-India Theater of Operations

In response to Maj.Gen. Curtis E. LeMay's request for night fighters to protect his B-29 base at Chengtu, China, Gen. H.H. Arnold, Army Air Forces Commanding General, had the 426th Night Fighter Squadron allocated for that area. Due to the seemingly insurmountable supply problems that existed in the Fourteenth Air Force, Maj.Gen. Claire L. Chennault, Commanding General of the Fourteenth Air Force, felt that the night fighter squadron that was scheduled for his command would overburden his supply lines to such an extent that it would be

impossible to support them. Chennault informed General Arnold of the situation. Soon after Col. Winston W. Kratz was dispatched to China to discuss the problem with Chennault. Colonel Kratz was the commanding officer of the 481st Night Fighter Operational Training Group, and frequent emissary of Arnold's to overseas areas when night fighter operations or tactics were involved. On this mission Kratz travelled with sealed orders which were only to be opened if Chennault remained steadfast and refused to support the night fighter squadron. After much discussion, it was agreed upon that the night fighters were direly needed and somehow must be supported logistically.

Under the command of Major William C. Hellriegel, the 426th Night Fighter Squadron left Newport News, Virginia by ship in June, 1944. Upon their arrival at Bombay, India on August 8, 1944, they proceeded to their initial base that was located 40 miles from Calcutta. From here they awaited the arrival of the P-61 night fighters. The Widows came by sea transport and were assembled by Air Service Command at Barrackspore and then flown to Madhaiganj Air Base in India. Air Service Command would then make modifications (including HF radio and radio compass) at Ondal and the crews of the 426th would pick them up there. On the 5th of October the first four 61s were picked up, and with Major Hellriegel leading in the B-25H flew to Chengtu, China to begin night air defense operations for General LeMay's B 29s.

The 427th Night Fighter Squadron, with their 12 Widows and lead by a B-25C, stopped at Chengtu, China on their way to Myitkyina, Burma, where they would be under the Tenth Air Force. It was on this same day that the 426th also arrived with their first four P-61s at Chengtu. Lt.Col. James S. Michael, 427th Night Fighter Squadron's Commanding Officer, agreed to give the 426th eight of his 12 P-61s due to the 426th's need for aircraft. This was in exchange for eight of the 426th's P-61 aircraft which were in different phases of assembly in India.

The 426th Night Fighter Squadron was at full strength by month's end. The first enemy aircraft to be destroyed by the night fighters occurred on the night of October 29 when Capt. Robert R. Scott, already airborne and flying cover for Chengtu, was vectored by GCI to an incoming target. With the help of his R/O, F/O Charles W. Phillips, Scott started the intercept procedure. Following the change of heading given by the GCI controller, Captain Scott started his climb to altitude, with throttles full open. F/O Phillips got contact on his scope when they were less than three miles from their prey. As required in all night fighter intercepts, a positive visual identification had to be made. At some 11,000 feet distance this was accomplished; it was a Japanese Lily. The Widow crept to within 500 feet and Scott opened fire. The Lily, possibly alert to the fact that it was being tracked, made an abrupt diving turn to its left. The chase was on! Diving, climbing, twisting, and turning, the Widow could not be shaken. Once again within firing range, Scott let loose with another burst. Fire broke out in the Lily and crashed soon after.

Besides providing night aerial defense for the Chengtu area, the Widows assisted lost and crippled B-29s back home. Two elements were on detached service during the latter

A reassembled P-61 takes off for a test hop from Air Service Command's base at Barrackpore, India before being delivered to the 426th NFS. Once in the hands of the 426th, it will go to Ondal where field modifications would be accomplished. (Northrop via Balzer)

months of the year. Four aircraft operated out of Kunming where they provided night protection for Fourteenth Air Force's headquarters situated at that field. The 426th operated there from October 27th until late December when they were relieved of the defense of that area by a detachment of six aircraft from the 427th Night Fighter Squadron. Another element was sent to Hsian in late November, where they remained into the new year.

Scott and Phillips encountered another Lily on the night of November 21st while standing alert at Chengtu; but in this instance they were credited with a probable kill. That same night Capt. John J. Wilfong and 2nd Lt. Glenn E. Ashley (R/O) were also operating out of Chengtu. Their combat report describes the action:

> After taking off we came under control of Pony who vectored us to e/a which was flying at 6,000 ft. Due to too great an overtaking speed, I overshot target.
>
> I was then vectored on one e/a flying at 6,000 feet at a heading of 270 deg. The ground controller brought me to within four miles of the target at which time it was picked up by my R.O. While interception

was being made the enemy took mild evasive action, he climbed to 14,000 feet at which time visual contact was made. I sighted the enemy 600 ft. ahead, approximately 5 deg. above and 5 deg. to the starboard, I gave one short burst of about 40 rounds and e/a exploded. The e/a was assumed to be a Dinah or a Lily. The interception occurred at approximately 2000 hours.

Toward the end of 1944 the 427th was in Myitkyina, Burma. An advanced detachment had arrived in late November and set up a temporary camp site, and by the first of December the entire squadron had arrived and the first tent was raised at the new squadron site on the Irrawaddy River at Myitkyina North. After being assigned to four different areas at Myitkyina North by the Post Commander, the night fighters finally took up their own machetes and brush hooks in a strip of jungle off the north end of the runway. The area was exceedingly difficult to clean. By mid-December there was 1,500 feet of river front cleared, thus the 427th was established in Burma as an operational squadron.

At the ending of 1944, the 427th totaled 17 combat missions. Twelve of the "contacts" proved to be friendly aircraft without IFF, and the remaining were patrols by higher headquarters. Two enemy aircraft were detected, but neither were

Maj. William C. Hellriegel, C.O. of the 426th. (Reynolds)

Some of the 426th NFS officers: Capt. John Pemberton, Lt. Charles Schumaker, Lt. Gans, and Lt. Harry Heise. This photo was taken while they were in night fighter training at Delano, California. (Reynolds)

First four P-61s of the 426th NFS cross over the "Hump" on their sojourn from India to their airfield at Chengtu, China in October 1944. The 426th's skipper, Maj. William C. Hellriegel, is leading the flight in the squadron's B-25. Flying with Hellriegel and navigating the trip was Lt. Glen Jackson. The accompanying P-61s were flown by Maj. Robert Hamrick, Capt. John Wilfong, Capt. Robert Scott, and Capt. John Pemberton. (Wilfong via Thompson)

destroyed. The night fighters in the CBI came upon the same problems as their sister squadrons in the Pacific. Poor GCI, the trouble was untrained or poorly trained personnel. Too, the terrain in the area of the GCI Stations was quite rugged and permanent echoes appeared on their radar scopes. The men of the 427th felt that night fighters without GCI were like "kites without strings." The unit's history relates the following tale:

A peculiar incident happened during the early part of December which demonstrated fully the ability of the Japs to collect information about Allied operations. A scramble was called to the alert crew, and in the mad rush of taxiing from the revetment to the landing strip, the landing gear lock was released, and the port gear collapsed before this situation could be remedied throwing a prop and bending the port tail boom. The following day Tokyo Rose broadcasted: 'We know that the night fighters pulled the gear on their ship last night as they were taxiing to the strip. Now, they have just two operational craft on the south strip.'

January 1945 not only brought in a new year but an additional assignment for the night fighters of the 426th. They sent a detachment to Guskara, India, to set up a theater training unit. Here, where the availability of aviation gasoline was much more plentiful than in either China or Burma, they established a training unit where incoming replacement crews would be taught "how it really was" prior to going operational and the old hands of the CBI were required to take a refresher course every six months.

It would seem almost inconceivable that a single P-61 could hang around over four major enemy airfields for an hour without being challenged; but it did! Staging out of Laohokow, China, the crew of Capt. Robert R. Scott and F/O Charles W. Phillips, lifted off the runway in the early evening hours of January 19, 1945 on an intruder mission. This 426 Night Fighter Squadron crew was headed for the Hankow area to stir up some trouble.

Enroute to their target, a satellite field was passed where landing lights were observed. Capt. Scott approached the target area from the northwest at a minimum altitude from approximately 50 miles out. The crew observed that the city of Hankow was not blacked out. As their approach neared, searchlights started sweeping the sky. Scott estimated, later, that between 12

Capt. Ira C. Elrod and his R/O, Lt. Phil Orleans, along with ground crewmen of the 426th dressed appropriately for the hot oriental sun. (Reynolds)

and 15 lights were sweeping the skies for the intruder. By remaining at minimum altitude (500 feet or less) they were able to remain under and out of the lights. Phillips was able to discern large lakes, the Yangtze River, warehouses and dock areas on his radar scope; all of which aided in their navigation.

Turning from Hankow, they flew up the Yangtze River at 50 feet off the water going toward Wuchang. Near the mouth of the Han River they came abruptly upon a bridge which caused Capt. Scott to bring the nose of his craft up into a steep climb in order to avoid the obstacle. There were searchlights on each side of the river attempting to intercept the plane. The beams from these lights intercepted only each other, above the plane. The lights around the airdrome were pointed upward. During this time Scott was attempting to sight planes in the air, taking off or landing. The pilot flew to approximately 10 miles west of Hankow, going to 3,000 feet altitude and again crossed over Hankow Main Airdrome at which time he observed approximately 100 revetments. Very few airplanes, however, were visible. Leaving the Hankow Main Airdrome, the Hankow

Satellite, Wuchang Main and Wuchang Satellite were crossed at 3,000 feet.

No aircraft were distinguishable on the airfields either. Capt. Scott then went to minimum altitude and crossed Hanchow Main at which time some 25 single engine aircraft were visible in the revetments. Leaving this airdrome, he then flew over the warehouse and dock area a second time; during this pass, the searchlights were turned off. Climbing to 7,000 feet, he circled the city and field areas for fifteen minutes. No enemy aircraft were in sight during this period, and all fields were blacked out.

Because of the inactivity of the Japanese, they decided to strafe Hankow Main Airdrome. However, due to the fact that the field was blacked out, and a light error was made in calculating his position, Scott missed the field by approximately one half mile. Realizing that he had only enough gas for his return flight to Ankang, Scott decided to return to his home base. He had been over the Hankow area for one hour when he took up a heading for Laohokow and climbed to 8,500 feet enroute. A light line was observed consisting of fires and red lights pointing out a direct course to Laohokow. Some of these lights were blinking, indicating some type of code.

The GCI station at Laohokow made contact with Scott at about 50 miles from the station. Upon calling Laohokow on his HF radio, Scott was informed that he was being followed by a plane ten miles to his starboard at the same altitude. He turned off his IFF and the aircraft following him appeared to lose contact and wander about. Five minutes later the IFF was turned back on, and the enemy aircraft appeared to make contact again. It appeared that the enemy aircraft was homing on the IFF. The IFF was left off for the remainder of the flight.

Another line of lights delineated the route from Laohokow to Ankang (their home base). These lights were spaced some ten to 25 miles apart with the last light ten miles east of the field at Ankang. A successful instrument let-down was made at Ankang through an overcast 1,000 feet thick.

For the 426th's crew of Capt. Carl J. Absmeier (pilot) and 2nd Lt. James R. Smith (R/O) January was a big month. They

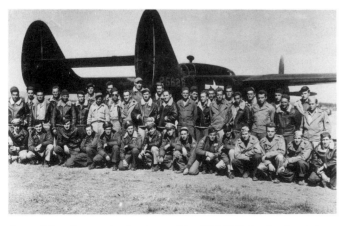

Some of the officers and enlisted men of the 426th NFS shortly after their arrival in China. The ADF football atop the crew nacelle was a unique modification accomplished on the CBI P-61s. (Absmeier via Thompson)

The 426th NFS was presented to Fourteenth Air Force's commander, Maj.Gen. Claire L. Chennault (on right, back to camera). (Hellriegel via Thompson)

After a short stay in the MTO the 427th arrived in the CBI. While the 426th NFS was under Fourteenth Air Force, the 427th operated under the Tenth Air Force and operated from Myitkyina, Burma during most of their operational existence. (Sumney)

had taken off from Laohokow at 1815 on a routine patrol. The local GCI station detected an incoming bogie 24 miles distant and some 180 deg. from the station. The controller vectored the night fighter team towards the target. Lieutenant Smith picked up the bogie on his scope at a distance of four miles. With Smith giving directions over the aircraft's intercom, Captain Absmeier closed in. At 1,500 feet Absmeier made visual contact and identified the bogie as a Lily. Closing to within 200 to 300 feet he opened fire with his 20mm cannon, sending 160 rounds of lethal lead into the enemy bomber as it was beginning its bomb run. The Lily burst into flames and dove to earth where it exploded upon impact. Smith had picked up another target on his scope but they were unable to pursue because of oil smeared on the Widow's windshield as a result of their first encounter.

Three nights later this team had a repeat performance. Taking off at 2020 they were once again vectored to a target picked up by GCI. Initially following the controller's directions, followed by Smith's during the final phase of the interception, Absmeier closed in to within 700 feet where he was able to identify yet another Lily bomber. He brought his Widow close and opened fire from 500 feet. The Japanese crew didn't know what hit them. The enemy plane started burning and exploded before it hit the ground. With this victory, Absmeier and Smith was the high scoring team within the CBI.

The 427th Night Fighter Squadron did not have such good pickings from their Burma bases. The Burma elements of the squadron, which was most of the squadron, flew patrols over Myitkyina and Bhamo as well as 12 local tactical interceptions. In all this not a single enemy aircraft was found.

On the night of January 22nd, one of those unfortunate things of war occurred. The 427th had a small detachment operating out of China. One of the detachment aircraft at Suichwan was vectored to an unidentified aircraft. The bogie was flying in a prohibited area and made no radio calls. The night fighter crew intercepted and shot down the target. It was learned later that the aircraft was a C-87.

Japanese night air activity had decreased to such a state by the beginning of 1945 that the CBI night fighters were directed to commence offensive operations much like their sister squadrons in the Pacific areas and those combating the German war machine. To give their Widows an added punch in intruder operations, Col. Michael along with the squadron's armament officer, Lt. Samuel L. Gilkey, made a trip to Kunming in mid-February. What they brought back were a three-tube bazooka type rocket launcher which would fire 4.5 inch rockets. One of these installations were attached under each wing. With their rocket carrying Widows, they initially operated against Japanese forces from Myitkyina in Burma. These night intruder

Sgt. Troy V. Golden, crew chief, stands beside this P-61 "Kentucky Colonel," at a forward base in China. Pvt. Bruce Perry, atop the aircraft, has just finished servicing the plane. This photo was taken at one of the China bases from which the 427th sent detachments on regular intervals. (Golemac via Thompson)

missions began on February 22nd with a sweep of the road net south of Lashio. A total of seven were flown in February. The following month the Kunming, China detachment would also go on the offensive.

With their new mission and capability, the morale of the 427th NFS rose markedly in February. With their cannon, bombs, and rockets they went after the enemy on his own territory. The seven intruder missions flown during those last seven days of February proved costly to the Japanese. Several convoys were hit in this period. One of the squadron's aircraft recorded seven sorties in which 2,000 pounds of demolition bombs were dropped, 26 rockets were fired, and nearly 2,000 rounds of 20mm cannon ammunition were expended.

Still in the air defense business, the 427th flew 31 tactical patrols and GCI vectored them towards 22 bogies, all of which turned out to be friendlies. On February 17th a detachment of two P-61s were sent to Chihkiang. This hot spot was about 100 miles from enemy lines and within striking distance of enemy installations.

China's 426th also went on the offensive. Night strafing and bombing missions were commenced from Ankang. Their targets were anything found in a valley just over a 10,000 foot range of mountains east of their base. Moving targets like trains and truck convoys were always fair game. Bridges and enemy encampments were also fair game. On a number of occasions the night fighters were aided by forward air controllers. Their rain of death quite often consisted of a combination of napalm bombs and parafrag clusters in anti-personnel operations. The tactic used against road convoys was to disable the lead vehicle in order to block the road and then make strafing passes. Driving at night with restricted lighting caused havoc with the Japanese convoys. A not too effective, but nerve shattering tactic that the Japanese developed against this was to fire timed fused mortar rounds straight up into the air. The pilots reported that from their point of observation it looked like the bright flash caused by firing these rounds would go back into the muzzle of the mortar.

The last enemy aircraft to be shot out of the air by the CBI night fighters occurred on the night of February 8th. First Lt. Harry W. Heise of the 426th NFS had taken off from Lachokow, China at five minutes to four in the morning. The Foxhole controller vectored Lieutenant Heise in the direction of an enemy bomber that had just dropped its load of ordnance. F/O Robert O. Brook, Heise's R/O, soon had the target on his radar screen at about 12,000 feet. For nearly twenty minutes F/O Brook directed his pilot through the darkened sky. Despite several hard turns that the bogie made, the night fighters stayed on his tail. Visual contact was made at 700 feet, Heise identified it as a Lily bomber. Closing within 350 feet, Lieutenant Heise opened fire with his cannon. The Lily exploded and fell in flames, an additional explosion occurring when it hit the ground.

The forward elements of the 427th stationed in China started flying daylight and night intruder missions in early March against rail traffic on a section of the Hankow-Canton railroad corridor. During the day intrusions P-51 Mustangs flew escort for the attacking Black Widows. The daylight flights served two purposes. First was their tactical mission of inter-

Comfort counts. Lt.Col. James S. Michael, C.O. of the 427th NFS, flying his Widow over Burma without a shirt in an attempt to keep cool in the extreme heat. (Reed via Thompson)

Two of the 426th NFS pilots, Capts. John Pemberton on the left and Ira Craig Elrod on the right. (Reynolds)

A pair of 426th P-61s drop down out of the mountains on the lookout for enemy movement. The roads and many rivers of China proved to be good pickings for the night fighters. Below is a typical example of the isolated river valleys over which the 426th NFS flew. (Greenbaum via Thompson)

Somewhat crowded conditions existed at the 427th's Myitkyina, Burma base. The fact that their Widows did not have the turret hampered the CBI night fighters very little as most of their work turned out to be against ground targets. (Holcomb via Thompson)

rupting the rail transport system and destroying rolling stock. Secondarily, it familiarized the crews with the area in preparation for night operations in the same area. Day and night offensive reconnaissance missions were also initiated against the Pangkeyhtu/Loi-Lem/Ho-Pong/Namsang road network. These operations started at mid-month. Unfortunately, these were limited due to circumstances beyond the night fighters control. In China the weather became an obstacle while in Burma smoke hindered their operations. Because of the dry season, there was much flammable material. Both Allied bombings and deliberately set fires by the Japanese to conceal their locations and movements accounted for this condition.

In April detachment missions of the 427th were halted early in the month because they ran out of fuel. During the month the squadron flew four day intruder missions from Kunming and six from Chihkiang along with one night sortie from Chihkiang. In late May, the squadron's headquarters moved to Kisselbarri near Dinjan, India. Detachments would remain active in China until the end of hostilities.

The 427th's Kunming detachment remained quite active in July 1945. Staging out of Chengkung, Chihkiang, and Naning until war's end, they claimed 155 sampans destroyed and 52 damaged along with motor and rail transport and fixed installations damaged and destroyed while flying seven day and six night intruder missions. They also flew two special missions in which they left their shiny Black Widows on the ground and took to the air in Vultee BT-13A trainers. They flew these aircraft on two occasions in which they airdropped medical supplies.

The 426th Night Fighter Squadron also finished out the war flying offensively. On one of these missions, in late July, Capt. John J. Wilfong, pilot, and 2nd Lt. Glenn E. Ashley, Wilfong's R/O, nearly didn't make it to the end of the war – just some two and a half weeks away.

They had taken off on the night of July 26th on an intruder mission. They received heavy anti-aircraft fire, most in one engine. Captain Wilfong feathered the damaged engine and

Above and below: To add a little more firepower in their ground attack missions, the 427th NFS installed an assembly of three 4.5 inch rocket tubes under each wing of their Black Widows. The night fighters found that they could wreak devastating results against sampans and like targets with these weapons. (Sumney and Holcomb via Thompson)

The 426th NFS also saw that the use of rockets would give them more firepower in their ground warfare. (Elrod via Thompson)

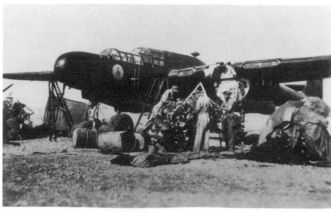

A little bit of field maintenance. Conditions were primitive and supplies were hard to get for the CBI night fighters. Here a P-61 of the 427th NFS undergoes an engine change by one of its detachments at a forward base in China. (Holcomb via Thompson)

A group of 426th NFS pilots and R/Os pose next to one of the first P-61B models to be received by the squadron. The picture was taken at Swanlu, China where the squadron had moved in March 1945. From this airfield they protected the B-29 base at nearby Hsingching. (Porter via Thompson)

Capt. John Pemberton and Lt. Fred Cliby and their P-61 "Satan 13." (Reynolds)

"Impatient Virgin" of the 426th NFS on the flight line in China. Lt. Gerald Stein, pilot, and R/O F/O James Rogers, standing next to the plane, were the crew of this Widow. (Rogers via Thompson)

they headed for friendly lines. Some 75 miles later and over friendly territory the good engine began to overheat. Their P-61, "I'll Get By," wasn't going to get much further. Both crew members bailed out, landing some distance apart. With the help of friendly Chinese, they dodged Japanese patrols and some 19 days and 150 miles later made it to an American installation where they were cleaned up, fed, and then flown back to Schwanliu just in time to linkup with the squadron and its move to Liuchow, China.

August 13 would mark the end of the war with Japan and the end of operations for the 427th NFS. All detachments were ordered to Liuchow. The aircrews flew their Widows there immediately with the ground echelons packing the squadron's belongings into trucks and went by convoy. Later on in the month they moved to Yangkai, China for processing home.

One of the last missions to be flown by the 426th NFS on August 13, 1945 might turn out to be a record of sorts. Intelligence had reported that there was large enemy troop movement in a valley just beyond a mountain range east of their base and they seemed to be moving towards the American's location. It was feared that this was "the big push" that had been expected for some time. The Chinese defenders of that area were in

disarray. The two 426th planes then located at Ankang were dispatched to the suspected area of Japanese activity that morning. Capt. Ira Craig Elrod and his R/O, 2nd Lt. Philip A. Orleans, were in the first aircraft and 1st Lt. Glen E. Jackson, pilot, and 2nd Lt. Frank Moran, R/O, were in the other P-61. With Captain Elrod in the lead plane, the duo flew over the valley and wend down on the deck. With little in the way of targets and fuel getting low, they returned to base.

That afternoon these two teams were in the air again, headed for the same general area. With the end of hostilities in sight, Glen Jackson relented to Sgt. Oakley Cassidy's (his crew

Right and below: 426th NFS nose art. "Blood N' Guts" with R/O Joe Neiner in the center. "Midnight Mistress" was photographed while at Hsian, China. Gerald Hallas was the pilot of this aircraft. Glen Jackson's "Black Jack." (Johnson, Eretzian, & Elrod-all via Thompson)

Hot and dusty conditions were present in the summer at Myitkyina, Burma. The 427th didn't find the wet winters much better for operations. Miserable was the year-round forecast. (Sumney)

"Betty Jean" of the 427th with its crew at Kunming, China, in June 1945. Standing next to the plane is R/O Lt. Richard Larson on the left, T/Sgt Donald White, crew chief, and pilot Lt. Raymond Bobles. The C-46 fuselage to the right in the background was used as the alert shack. (White via Thompson)

chief) plea to let him come along on the mission. Sitting behind Lt. Jackson on the nose wheel door they were soon in the air. Flying at 500 feet, they observed a Japanese army encampment. When they received some light ground fire, some hitting Jackson's P-61 "Black Jack", the duo dove down to skim along on the deck and decided to patrol along the road in hopes of destroying some motor transport.

Craig Elrod saw them first. A column of Japanese troops, four abreast, extending four miles or so. Elrod pulled the nose of his Widow "Harlot from Charlotte" up and banked to the left and came down the road with his 20mm cannons blazing. Jackson, who had been trailing Elrod, saw what was happening and timed his strafing run to begin when Elrod pulled up at the end of his run. The enemy troops had no place to hide in the flat country side. There were some poplar trees lined a length of the road which, as the P-61s spewed 20mm lead while fanning side to side (through rudder movement), cut down these like match sticks.

Pictured on the left are Lts. Glen Jackson, pilot, and his R/O, Frank Moran standing next to their regular aircraft, "Black Jack." While flying in "Green Eyed From Riverside" on August 13, 1945, they were severely damaged by ground fire while on an intruder mission. On the right are the remains of "Green Eyed From Riverside" lying on the edge of a small gravel landing strip. Lt. Jackson had managed to nurse the big fighter back to the strip in spite of having his hydraulics inoperative, no radio, and one engine out. They were one of the last Allied aircraft to be shot down prior to cessation of hostilities. (Moran and Eretzian via Thompson)

426th NFS aircrew. Standing, left to right: Lorne C. Reynolds, Robert R. Scott (got first 426th victory on Oct. 29, 1944), John J. Wilfong, Grace, William C. Hellriegel (C.O.). Kneeling: Herman Simon, Thomas J. Boyle, Robert A. Hamrick (Ops Officer), Charles W. Phillips. (Thompson Collection)

With ammunition expended and fuel getting low, the P-61s headed for home once again. Lt. Jackson noticed that his right fuel tank was low. Switching to the left tank, both engines could be fed through the crossfeed system in the P-61. But nothing happened. The system had been damaged by ground fire. Then, to make matters worse, he found that his radio had been knocked out also. How to communicate with Capt. Elrod? Jackson pushed the throttle for his good engine forward and sped up to Elrod where by sign language Craig Jackson communicated his predicament. As he did this, his right engine quit and the right main landing gear door fell open and a stream of black gas and oil flowed out from the wheel well – the hydraulic system was gone.

Crossing back into Allied territory they found a small gravel strip. Not being able to operate the cowl flaps, Jackson's good engine was by now so overheated that the oil and cylinder head temperatures were nearly redlined. The smart thing would have been to belly land the stricken P-61. But no, youth had its own idea, Jackson was going to land his plane. On final approach he lowered the landing flaps with what little was left in the hydraulic accumulator and pulled the emergency controls which released the gear uplock and let the gear drop. Too fast, too long.

Instead of bellying it, he applied power to the already over stressed engine with the thought of trying to go around for another try. If he continued on his current course he would be once again in enemy territory. He somehow got his wounded Widow around in a 180 degree turn. But his luck had run out. He was at low altitude and there was no chance of improving that. He barely cleared the top of a river bank when the right wing clipped a small tree. Still in control, the plane settled down and was soon going through a small corn field followed by a cemetery. The five foot high burial mounds made a bumpy ride and the left main gear soon left them. Next the nose of the plane hit a terraced area and they came to a sudden stop.

Sgt. Cassidy came flying against the back of Jackson's seat, dislodging the seat from the floor. Jackson was hitting the control column as the nose section and cockpit floor were folding up in front of him. Somewhat sandwiched, neither Jackson nor the others, miraculously were not seriously injured. They crawled out from the wreckage and obtained aid from a Navy Corpsman. It was 7 p.m. on the 13th that they were downed – they could have been the last Allied aircraft shot down in the war!

A quadruplet of 6th NFS Widows. The two light colored P-61s (actually olive drab and grey) are equipped with turrets while the black P-61s have had fixed, forward firing guns installed. (Haberman)

Chapter 13

Pacific Advance

The 6th Night Fighter Squadron, under the control of the Seventh Air Force, continued, as in the past, as a split organization. Its headquarters remained in the Territory of Hawaii at all times; though moving from John Rodgers Airport to Kipapa Strip late October 1944. Detachment A, which arrived with the invasion of Saipan in late June, remained active throughout the year. Their primary mission was the protection of the B-29s stationed at West Field on Saipan. The night fighters flew Combat Air Patrols, intercepted unknowns and hostiles, stood alert, and aided in the rescue of many crippled and lost B-29s on their return flight from long range raids.

The earlier P-61A models used by the 6th NFS were equipped with 50 caliber gun turrets. The later "A" models and early "B" models were produced without the turret. To compensate for this, a number of the Seventh Air Force P-61s had fixed, forward firing guns installed. Many times a gunner was carried on missions where the aircraft was equipped with the fixed 50 cal. guns as an extra pair of eyes. For the seven months that the 6th Night Fighter Squadron had been flying the P-61 in 1944, they had been credited with 11 confirmed enemy aircraft destroyed with only two losses of their own neither of which were due to enemy action, but accounted for by pilot error or equipment failure. The 6th had only been at Saipan for a short time when one of their aircraft, as it was coming in to land, peeled off and cut it a little too close and landed on top of another P-61 which had just touched down. Unfortunately, both crews were lost in this needless but deadly accident.

More night fighter squadrons were needed to cover the widening area that the Allied forces were capturing. In the latter part of 1944 the Seventh Air Forces' night fighter squadron strength tripled with the arrival of the 548th and 549th NFSs. Their first stop of the Pacific war was an extended stay in Hawaii where they would receive advanced tutoring by the experienced 6th NFS and assist in the defense of the Hawaiian Islands. Commanding the 548th Night Fighter Squadron was

Maj. Robert D. Curtis, who arrived in mid-September. The following month Maj. Joseph E. Pane and his 549th NFS arrived. The 548th was the first to send a detachment into the combat area. Under Capt. William H. Dames, they flew to Saipan that December where they joined 6th NFS's detachment already operating from that base.

At the end of June 1944, the Thirteenth Air Force's only night fighter squadron, the 419th, was ending its transition period from P-38/P-70 type aircraft into P-61. To further their training and gain greater experience in performing AI intercepts, the squadron was split into three detachments. Detachment A under the command of Capt. Al Lucas was sent to Nadzab, New Guinea, under Fifth Air Force control; Detachment B was sent to Los Negros in the Admiralties and the Headquarters detachment remained on Guadalcanal for nearly a month longer.

The Allies were forever pushing ahead. By the end of June 1944 heavy bombers were operating out of Hollandia on New Guinea. Soon Wakde, Biak, Owi and Woendi fell to Allied forces in rapid succession, and by June 2nd the invasion of Noemfoor Island was in progress. From the newly won airfields, operations began shortly thereafter, and the night skies of Noemfoor would have to be protected from Japanese air strikes. For this purpose, Detachment A of the 419th was transferred from Nadzab to Noemfoor in late July. By August 5th, the 419th Night Fighter Squadron had their first victory claimed. Capt. Al Lucas, commanding the detachment, made a perfect intercept on a Japanese Sally bomber and destroyed it with great ease.

In early June the Fifth Air Force's oldest night fighter squadron was operating as a night intruder rather than a night fighter. The 418th Night Fighter Squadron had finished transitioning from its P-38/P-70 aircraft mix into B-25s. Their missions were night harassment of enemy installations and anti-shipping raids.

Major Smith of the 418th NFS realized early that cooperation among other segments of the services was required:

One of the 6th NFS's big spider ships taxis into the revetment area as a couple of insect-like spotter planes line up for a landing on Saipan. The Widow is a P-61A-1 equipped with a GE turret. (USAF)

We tried this out of self-preservation of course, because our IFF gear wasn't all that good and at night people get scared. You've heard the old Maytag Charlie kind of story about the Japanese Betty or Sally or whatever that would come in on a more or less regular schedule and drop bombs and all just as a harassment to keep you awake or something. So naturally, people were skiddish at night. PT boats were awfully skiddish to start with so we made a point of trying to get acquainted with one particular batch of PT boats whose call sign was Martini, as I recall; because they seemed to like to shoot at us more than most. It was purely reflex action. They would shoot at anything that moved in the sky. We found coordination with the anti-aircraft artillery, both our own and the Australian, was to our benefit because they would sometimes shoot at us also, even though you would call in. I remember one night very vividly at Finschhafen. I came in with a flight of two; we were flying P-38s, and they proceeded to knock out one of the engines on my wing man's bird. We were in the traffic pattern with gear down, and all of a sudden they got spooked and started shooting at us.

I think probably the most flak that I ever saw was up in Manila Bay with two or three hundred friendly vessels in the harbor. We had a flight of four P-61s flying dusk cover, and we had just split into two flights of two to cover two quadrants. As soon as it got dark, we'd go into four individual flights and cover the four quadrants. When we were in the two-ship flights, all of a sudden just bingo, they started shooting at us. One moment we had been friendly, and the next moment they thought we were hostile. At the time I told them what they could do with their anti-aircraft fire, and we went home. Unfortunately, or fortunately, depending on how you look at it, I told them what I thought about their questionable ancestry over the air, and General Whitehead, who was my big boss, happened to be on board the Blue Ridge which was their

control vessel. He told me later he got sort of a chuckle out of me telling the admirals off because they were most embarrassed. In checking into the incident further, as luck would have it, some young fellow on a merchant marine vessel that had been hauling into the fray all of a sudden got scared and started shooting, and it's very contagious and everything went to pot. But that kind of thing happens from time-to-time. Another time a bakery unit, I guess kind of got bored with it all, started to shoot at us on final. So we isolated them, and put a stop to that. That sort of thing was to be expected, I guess people were frightened.

The 418th Night Fighter Squadron had worked as intruders for only about two months when they received orders that they were going to transfer into a new aircraft, the fourth aircraft for the unit, the P-61. Transitioning started in mid-August and for the next month the squadron did not see any action.

Night Hunters

The 418th Night Fighter Squadron's next move was to be to Morotai to take part in operations against Japanese in the southern Philippines. To gain further experience in their new aircraft and to aid the 421st Night Fighter Squadron, the air echelon of the 418th moved to Owi Island in mid-September. During their three week stay on Owi, the 418th continued their training patrols and alternated every other night for the island's defense with the 421st Night Fighter Squadron.

Operations from Morotai against the southern Philippines was already in progress when the ground echelon of the 418th

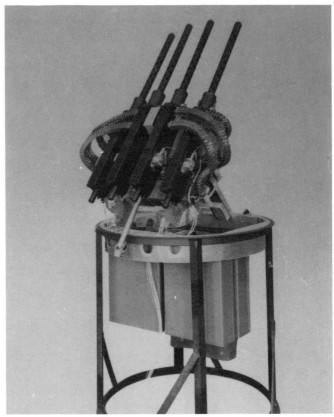

To compensate for the lack of a turret in most of the P-61s to reach the Pacific, fixed, forward firing .50 cal. guns were installed in a number of the Seventh Air Force's Widows. The photo on the left is of the turret. The massive operating mechanism can be seen. On the right is what the fixed installation looked like. (USAF & Northrop)

arrived in late September. That same month, the Fifth Air Force received a new night fighter squadron, the 547th under the command of Col. William C. Odell. The 547th spent their first month in Oro Bay, New Guinea, where they did menial tasks such as loading ammunition and working in Red Cross centers. The 547th would end the war with a relatively low number of kills, but it seemed their destiny would be as a pioneering night fighter unit. The 547th was made up of many pilots and R/Os who had night fighter and night intruder experience with the Royal Canadian Air Force, RAF and the US Eighth and Twelfth Air Forces. Many of them were well known to the commanding Generals in the area. Soon after the 547th arrived in Fifth Air Force area, Brig.Gen. Paul B. Wurtsmith, commanding general of V Fighter Command, had a meeting with Col. Odell:

Aside from operating as a night fighter unit with the ordinary missions most performed, the 547th was used to back up and reinforce many night fighter efforts in the area. This was determined by Gen. Wurtsmith at the time the 547th arrived in the theatre. His decision was based on the need for experienced and combat knowledgeable crews, and the 547th had many such crews. Whenever a lesser trained night fighter unit required assistance or were unable to perform adequately, the 547th was called upon to step in and give the extra effort needed. At a meeting at Owi Island in Gen. Wurtsmith's quarters, this was explained to me during mid-September of 1944. Gen. Earl W. Barnes,

who commanded the XIII Fighter Command, had made this proposal to Gen. Wurtsmith because of his first hand knowledge of the capabilities of the crews of the 547th. This proposal was made by Gen. Barnes with foresight since the 547th also gained the commitment of being on call by Gen. Barnes whenever the Thirteenth Air Force also needed the help of well trained crews. Thus the 547th had the opportunity to take part in operations at the most crucial times and in a great many places. It also accounts for the use of the 547th to test advanced equipment, such as the P-38s with APS-4 Radar.

When the 547th's month of menial labor was concluded at Oro Bay, they were sent to Owi Island in the Schouten Islands to relieve the 418th and to bolster the 421st. The 418th air echelon went on to Morotai to join their ground echelon and to operate in the Philippine campaign.

The air echelon of the 418th arrived at Morotai on October 5, 1944, but the following nights of inclement weather provided very little activity. On the night of October 7, 1944, they experienced their first red alert and their first victory with the P-61. Two crews of the 418th were on airborne patrol at the time of the alert. One of the crews was the commanding officer, Maj. Carroll C. Smith, and his R/O, Lt. Philip B. Porter. The incoming Japanese were closer to Smith than to the other crew; subsequently, they were vectored by GCI to an intercept course

Above is an experimental installation of four fixed .50 cal. guns accomplished by Northrop. The photo below is of a field modification accomplished on a 6th NFS P-61. As a comparison is a photo of a GE turret installed in a Black Widow. (Northrop, USAF, Northrop)

where a quick radar intercept was completed:

That Jap pilot tooling his twin-engine Dinah Mark II toward our airstrip at Morotai wasn't worried. At 8,000 feet his fighter was invisible, he thought, his 20mm cannon and 7.7mm machine guns would protect him in a clinch, and as a last resort he could climb a mile in 90 seconds or so to evade us.

He hadn't the foggiest notion that Lt. Phil Porter and I were floating in the moonlight over the field, throttled to minimum cruising speed, we were saving gas to make sure we had plenty in case a Nip came over.

He still wasn't worried when our ground control picked him up and flashed the first order: 'Darkie 1 from Nightie. Climb to 8,000 . . . cruise two zero zero . . . range about 12 miles.' Instantly, I turned my attention to my instruments. Phil shouted instructions as I swung the Black Widow into the new heading. I flipped on the water injection to pull another six inches of manifold pressure. That meant 200 to 300 more horsepower from the big Pratt & Whitney's . . . 300 feet a minute faster climb.

While ground control continued directing us toward the incoming fighter, I climbed and turned with everything jammed to the firewall. The Jap had headed for our field, bearing a load of medium bombs. A few more seconds, and we spotted each other in the brilliant moonlight, at a range of 2,000 feet. He then was within a mile of our base.

Talking about evasive action! That boy could really fly; he was worried now, for the Nips had heard about these deadly Black Widows. Ours was fairly new, but those four 20mm cannon spouting flame and shells from the belly spelled certain and swift destruction to any fighter and bomber within range.

I could see him easily as he climbed. His maneuver was no good, for the Widow was climbing even faster. I began overhauling him at 17,500 feet. Three burst failed to hit. The fourth and fifth seemed to do little damage. For the sixth I managed to pull within 150 feet of his left wing and cut loose with a full deflection shot as he roared past. Chunks exploded from the glistening Dinah. He fell, burning, a plume of smoke falling into the earth.

Col. Smith also recalls some of the problems his squadron was faced with:

Our biggest problem in the night fighter business was technological breakthrough. For example, here again Morotai is a good case in point. A Brig. Gen. who subsequently became one of the chiefs of staff at the Air Force and a very fine gentleman, called me in and read me the Riot Act one time because I commanded the night fighter squadron, and the Japs kept coming in at night and bombing and tearing us up. I had to explain to him, whether he didn't know that an Army Lt.Col. anti-aircraft artilleryman was in charge of air defense, and by decree from him, 'If we have a yellow alert on we couldn't take off nor land.' Well, we had a yellow alert on all the time, which meant that when you should be taking off you were strapped to the ground. So I told, in this particular case, Gen. White, that if he would permit me to set up an air defense of sorts that we could do a little better. So we put P-38s on searchlight co-op because we had some good searchlights, P-61s on patrol; and we still had some B-25s rigged up as night intruders. We would go to all the Jap bases within range of our B-25s and harass them. The first few days we tried it, I guess the first crack out of the box, we knocked out about eight over a three day period or so.

This was only the first of seven enemy that the 418th would destroy during their stay on Morotai.

With the invasion of Leyte in the Phillipines the 421st NFS was ordered to follow. The 547th NFS was left behind to defend Owi Island and the surrounding area. Included with the assault echelon was the ground echelon of the 421st, along with

Hovering like a giant spider, one of the 6th NFSs P-61 arrives on Saipan in the Marianas. While the squadron was protecting the combat area, an element of the squadron was always in Hawaii where it was providing night protection for the islands and assisting newly arrived night fighter squadrons from their mainland training. (USAF)

the 489th Fighter Group of day fighters. These were the first Air Force units to land on Leyte. The 421st ground personnel arrived at their new base of Tacloban on D plus 4, and were joined by their air echelon six days later. As a welcome from the Japanese, they averaged 18 raids per night, with 39 harassing raids occurring in one 24-hour period. Between the enemy action, the mud and poor facilities, the 421st was more of a liability for their first few days at Tacloban than an asset.

Phillippines Operations Begin

On their first night at Tacloban they flew two missions in which no enemy aircraft were sighted but upon returning to base an Allied anti-aircraft battery fired on them, damaging one of the planes to such an extent that it had to be salvaged. The Leyte Gulf was full of naval vessels and their commanders would not hold their antiaircraft fire long enough for the 421st night fighters to scramble or land during a raid. As a result, they made few attempts at any night interceptions.

The night fighters found the terrain around Tacloban was not suitable for night fighting. A very important element in accomplishing night intercepts is the GCI station. The one in their area was so poorly located that in most cases its sweep was only 90 degrees, which was a great handicap on the pilots being directed by the controllers. Attempts to make such interceptions were discontinued. The squadron was then put on dawn and dusk missions in which they provided convoy cover and worked with local PT boats.

Mack Ballard of the 421st found out first hand how hard it was to land at night at Tacloban:

A 419th NFS P-61 piloted by Capt. Al Lukas in the Southwest Pacific Area. A tail cone brace has been added to prevent the crew nacelle cone from imploding during high speed dives, a frequent occurrence on the early P-61s. (USAF)

One night on Leyte, early in the battle for Leyte, we had been scrambled, sent on a wild goose chase way the hell and gone. I don't know how many miles we were sent, but there was nothing there! At least we couldn't pick it up on our radar. Then they vectored us some place else. We chased there. Then we chased back in another direction. There was nothing up there in the skies that we could pick up on our radar. I flew to where they said they were supposed to be. They weren't there! We were in bad weather and nearly out of fuel. We headed back to the strip. We had learned early on to make a straight-in landing, no pattern at night. So this particular time, while we were out chasing ghosts, the Japs had come over and bombed our strip, knocking out the lights, strip lights. When the tower told me that, I said 'Well, put a jeep down at the end with the headlights on, we can pick it up.' The only thing is, they put the jeep at the wrong end of the strip. So I came in, out of fuel, coming in over the top of the jeep and set her down. It was raining like hell. A bad cross wind. Started setting her down, and I finally decided to look out. All I could see were big waves out there. So, anyway, bend the throttles, suck up the gear, bend round, get back, line up again. Mean time I do a little cussin.' 'Get the jeep up the other end!' So, as I was banking around in the turn to get back and to line up the runway, the red lights are flashing 'NO FUEL.' I line up. The cross winds are blowing at about 60 mph; which is a pretty tough cross wind. So when I set it down, I came over the top of the jeep and the strip lights, which of course were out, but I missed it far enough, that, as we slid down the runway, which was a metal mat, I could just hear these lights going 'plink,' 'plink,' 'plink,' 'plink.' I was knocking them out as we rolled down the runway. The starboard landing gear is hitting every one of them, right down the row. When we got to the end of the strip, both of the main gear tires blew out. I had been skidding all that way, it was wet but, still did enough to blow both tires.

On November 16, 1st Lt. Dorrie E. Jones was leading a flight of four P-61s on patrol south of Dulag. Somewhat to their surprise they ran into a formation of some 20 enemy aircraft. In the dog fight that followed, the night fighters were joined by some very welcomed P-38s. In the battle Lieutenant Jones destroyed a

Frank. He soon had another in his sight but as he pulled into a tight turn at some 350 mph, "he lost the entire rear gondola" (per the squadron history). He managed to complete his turn and was able to fire at three more of the planes; but they out turned the crippled P-61 and got away. By this time Jones' Widow was buffeting violently and he was starting to lose control. His crew was ready to ditch. With much force, and courage, Jones

Electronic wizard Capt. Paul H. Baldwin of the 547th developed a crude radar controlled instrument landing system using two P-61s, one airborne and the other at the touch-down end of the runway. This system aided a number of the 547th's P-61s in emergencies, saving both crew lives and hard to replace aircraft. For his work Baldwin received the Legion of Merit. (Odell)

Tony Grotzinger, Manke, and Bob Winslow of the 419th NFS plan their next mission under "Old Salty Dog II." In the background is one of the 418th's P-61s. (Grotzinger via Thompson)

Maj. Carroll C. Smith, C.O. of the 418th NFS, stands in front of squadron headquarters at Morotai, Halmaheras. (Smith)

"Bright Eyes" of the 421st NFS with a "nose protector." The plexiglass radomes on the early P-61s tended to soften in hot sunlight and sag, causing interference with the rotating radar antenna within. (Thompson)

"Sleepy Time Gal" on Saipan. Pictured, left to right, are Sgt. Leon W. Brill, crew chief, 1st Lt. John P. Acre, R/O, and Capt. Ernest R. Thomas, pilot. Thomas and Acre's P-61, "Japanese Sandman," had been destroyed in an accident back in Hawaii, and they were flown to Saipan by transport where they were assigned "Sleepy Time Gal" which was already there. (Thomas via Thompson)

regained control and was able to return to base safely. Another of the pilots, 1st Lt. Owen M. Wolf, managed to score a probable on another of the enemy; it was not confirmed as the aircraft was not seen to crash.

On November 28th, D Flight, led by Lt. Wolf was in the thick of things again. The squadron history describes the action that took place on this occasion:

The tally of the 421st was raised to 12 (later revised down to 11 as an earlier kill was disallowed) on November 28 when D Flight, on evening patrol under Lt. Wolf, bagged four planes. D Flight encountered a formation of seven enemy fighters, six Zekes and a Hamp. Closing for the attack, Lt. Wolf, with Lt. (Byron N.) Allain R/O, and S/Sgt Emil K. Weishar, gunner, destroyed one Zeke with his 20mm's. The gunner destroyed the Hamp with his turret, using a deflection shot, his burst entering the enemy's cockpit. The plane blew up and caught fire, crashing in flames.

The third enemy was destroyed by a burst from the turret of Lt. Robert C. Pew's plane, S/Sgt Ralph H. McDaniel handling the gun. R/O was 2nd Lt. John B. Cutshall. The fourth victory was scored by 1st Lt. Hoke Smith with 2nd Lt. Robert H. Bremer as Radar Observer and Sgt. James W. Pilling as gunner. The remaining Zekes, apparently mistaking the P-61s for 38s, orbited and came in on Lt. Smith's tail. Failure of the guns in one wing of the leading Jap plane probably saved the Black Widow, for the R/O saw the tracers from the one operating side firing just past his gondola. Lt. Bremer took over control of the turret from the gunner and a steady burst directly to the rear destroyed the attacking Nip. The remaining enemy aircraft turned and fled, and the 421st flight returned to base.

Daylight combat and Japanese bombing was reducing the number of flyable P-61s that the 421st had to operate. Replacement aircraft were not soon forthcoming. Spares were a rarity. The lack of spare engines had even another twist. It seems that the depots at Finschhafen and Biak did such a poor job of

properly packing the engines that they had that over 400 useless engines were created because of corrosion. The 421st felt they were having a good day if they had six flyable aircraft.

On the morning of November 10, 1944, Lt. Albert W. Lockard and his crew, Lt. Stewart A. Thornton, R/O, and S/Sgt Joseph Mazur, gunner, had completed patrols in two sections, one around the north of Leyte and the other around the south, where they had provided protection for PT boats on their outgoing and return trips. With their mission completed, they were returning to base, flying at about 7,000 feet. The sky was light enough that he could see two Tonys in the distance flying at about 100 feet. Headquarters had issued an order that P-61s were not to engage the enemy during daylight hours. Al Lockard radioed his finding and position, requesting day fighters be dispatched. He was asked to repeat his message, and Lockard did it obligingly. Being asked to repeat it a second time because his transmission was cut off by another aircraft, Lockard shouted, "Goddammit! I'll get the bastards myself!"

As the Tonys swung 100 deg. inland, Al Lockard dove his Widow at them. His turret jammed. He continued firing a burst from his 20s. The first Tony crashed into a valley below. He continued in pursuit of the second Tony. A burst from his cannons sent the second enemy crashing back to earth also.

Special Force

Soon after the 421st air echelon's arrival on Tacloban, a special detachment under the command of Capt. Paul H. Baldwin of the 547th Night Fighter Squadron arrived. Capt. Baldwin, the Chief R/O of the 547th, arrived with five modified night fighters. This special project was his conception. The two P-38s had been modified at the depot at Townsville, Australia, under the supervision of Western Electric, to carry Navy APS-4 AI radar. They remained in single-seat configuration and had been painted

Brig.Gen. Earl W. Barnes, Commander of the Thirteenth Fighter Command had his own personal, and highly modified, P-61. The turret had been removed and a long range ferry tank installed; the radar had also been removed and an aluminum nose added, 20mm guns removed and the ports covered over. An ADF antenna has been installed in the aircraft's belly. (USAF)

In the Central Pacific the Seventh Air Force's 6th NFS was kept busy. Over the period of December 25 and 26, they shot down six Japanese Bettys. The crew of Dale Haberman and Ray Mooney (on the right and left respectively) were credited with two – this brought their total of confirmed kills to four. On these latter kills Pvt. Patrick J. Farelly flew with them as gunner. (Hansen via Thompson)

gloss black. The B-25 had a similar modification. This aircraft was configured as an R/O trainer with three or four radar scopes installed along with the APS-4 radar. One of the major drawbacks of the Black Widow discovered so far in the war theatres was its lack of range and loiter time on target. The 547th obtained P-38 bomb shackles and equipped their two long range P-61s with external fuel tanks. They also had an additional APS-4 set which was used for maintenance and calibration.

Arriving on November 9th, the 547th's "special" detachment immediately went into action. The P-38 night fighter modification was in actuality part of an Air Force project. The night fighter organization back at Hammer Field in California had made a similar modification. The 547th was chosen to further test the feasibility of a P-38 as a night fighter. The crews had received some training in Australia after which they returned to the 547th NFS on Owi. Upon completion of their training, they carried out intruder missions over Japanese installations in the Dutch East Indies. Headquarters wanted them to get into the thick of the fighting so the detachment moved to Leyte. From here dawn and dusk intruder missions were flown over Japanese airdromes some 100 to 150 miles away in the areas of Sebu, Negros, and lower Luzon. The purpose of these nuisance missions was to inhibit the enemy from taking off from his fields in order to attack Allied fields at night.

The night fighters found that their mere presence in the areas of the Japanese air fields caused the enemy to go on red alert, thus preventing him from launching strikes against the Allies. The scenario of these missions was for the patrol to remain in the area until it was ascertained that daylight would meet the incoming enemy if a take-off was ordered. This would place the bombers at the mercy of Allied day fighters. Then the intruder would fly to airdromes closer to their own base and repeat the procedure. Because of the speed of the P-38, this procedure was accomplished with ease, enabling their crew to arrive over the airdrome well in time to cause a red alert before the bombers were allowed to take off. The results of these missions were felt immediately. From the time the P-38 night fighter morning or dusk patrols were initiated, Tacloban enjoyed quiet nights. During the nights that the P-38s didn't fly, the Japanese paid them visits.

Capt. William B. Sellers, operations officer of the 547th NFS, nearly lost his tail to "friendly" fire. As he was attempting to intercept an enemy aircraft, a "friendly" antiaircraft battery opened up on him, hitting the Widow. Sellers managed to keep his plane under control and make a safe landing. The squadron history states that, "the erring AA battery commander suffered only minor abrasions and cuts from an unknown assailant."

Control of and cooperation between anti-aircraft units and the night fighters seemed to be a problem throughout the Pacific theatre. The 418th Night Fighter Squadron was informed by a colonel of anti-aircraft that, "Under no circumstances will be hold the ack-ack. This is war, and a night fighter will just have to take his chances." This battery fired on the 418th's commanding officer while he was flying in the area. Major Smith took it in stride until the fifth salvo almost spelled the end for him. A confrontation ensued with the antiaircraft troops. As

Lt. Dave T. Corts' P-61 "Skippy" with the 421st NFS at their Tacloban, Leyte airfield in the Philippines. When the 421st arrived, the Japanese were firing from hills on one side of the field while ships in the harbour on the other side were firing back. Movement on the field got Japanese attention on a regular basis. (US Army)

Life for the night fighters was the exact opposite of their day fighter brothers. As the day boys, such as the P-47 Thunderbolts shown in the background, were flying during the daylight hours, night fighter ground crews were readying their aircraft for that night's missions while the aircrews rested. When the day fighters came home for the night, the night fighters were just getting started. (Campbell)

Another beautifully decorated P-61 of the 421st NFs, "Nocturnal Nuisance." Pilot Harold Burdue proudly stands by his aircraft. (Burdue via Thompson)

R/O George Arthur of the 547th NFS standing by his P-61 "Midnight Calling," a quite appropriate name, considering the time of day the night fighters worked. Lt. Arthur sports the 547th's unofficial emblem on his flight jacket. (Arthur via Thompson)

"Louisiana Lullaby" of the 6th NFS stands ready for action on Saipan. (Maita)

described in the 418th squadron's history, ". . . immediate showdown was had with the anti-aircraft people with much hair pulling and a casting of doubts upon the ancestry of various and sundry individuals of the coastal artillery." Things were a lot more peaceful for the night fighters after this.

From Morotai Maj. Smith made his third kill, second in a P-38:

The third one I shot down was a Betty in searchlight co-op. He came across at about 14,000-16,000, I guess, and was picked up by a searchlight. I was sitting in the P-38 orbiting at 25,000. I peeled off and went down after him. Then, all of a sudden, I pulled back on the wheel, and it was like it was embedded in concrete; and that's when I tried to remember what Fish Salmon had written about the P-38 in compressibility. I recalled rather vaguely that you're suppose to throttle back and run your RPM full bore. That let's the engines wind up so fast it's like you got a couple of discs out there. It worked out that way; I thought

the engines were going to come out of the airplane, but they didn't. As it worked out it made me look like I knew what I was doing, because I came out just fine. When I got control, I pulled up and low and behold there was the Betty; so I lowered the boom on him; and he burst into flame and came down like a Roman candle. Spectacular, 75% luck.

A detachment of the 419th NFS joined the 418th on Morotai in late November. In less than a month the 418th moved on to San Jose on Mindoro. But the move would prove to be disastrous as the LST which carried most of their ground service equipment was hit by Japanese kamikaze and sunk. To help out in this emergency, the 547th NFS was sent to San Jose in late December. The 547th's special operations at Tacloban were completed in mid-January 1945 and they joined the rest of the squadron at San Jose.

From their nearly three months of operations, the 547th's

Another 547th NFS member, 1st Lt. Arthur D. Bourque (pilot) and his "Swing Shift Skipper." (Farmer)

Maj. C.C. Smith and his R/O, 1st Lt. Philip B. Porter, take off in their "Time's A Wastin'." This night fighter team would be credited with five confirmed kills, plus two more Smith got while flying P-38s at night in cooperation with searchlights. (Ross)

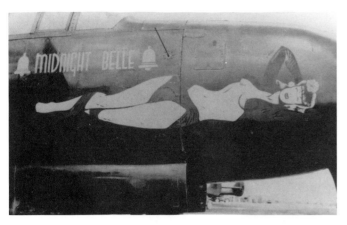

A seductive "Midnight Belle" is ready to lure an unsuspecting intruder into her electronic web where the kill will be swift and sure. (Campbell)

Quite often the night fighter squadrons obtained other "hack" or "fat cat" aircraft to use on administrative and other non-combat flights. The 418th had as one such aircraft a P-40 named "Rusty." (Ellings)

special detachment found that the added fuel of the external tanks made the Widow a very good long range night fighter. They also found that besides being a good R/O trainer, the APS-4 equipped B-25 made a very good night intruder. However, they thought very little of a P-38 as a night fighter; it was better suited for intruder operations and for dawn and dusk missions where their was a possibility of daylight fighting. They also ascertained that in order for pilots to carry out successful intruder missions, they required additional navigation training.

Reports can be deceiving. Like the 6th NFS and the 547th NFS, the 418th also tried its hand at operating P-38 night fighters. Unlike the previous examples, this one was modified to carry both pilot and R/O. Maj. Carroll Smith of the 418th Night Fighter Squadron remembers this episode with a chuckle:

We had a little radar observer named of Dubasik who wrote the report on it. He weighed 110 pounds and was about 5'2." He wrote that there's no problem of space for the radar observer, but he failed to point out his own dimensions. We put the old 540 radar, out of the P-70s, into

some P-38s. It worked moderately well, though, we didn't do too much good with them. Then later on in the States they made the 'M' model. That was sort of the same idea, but ours was just strictly a little local unit modification of putting in a little jumpseat for a radar observer to use and installing a 540 radar which came out of a P-70.

The Big Switch

History has well documented the fact that the 421st NFS swopped locations with a Marine night fighter squadron. But the reasoning behind the swop is somewhat unclear. VMF(N)-541 was stationed on Peleliu in the Palau Group while the 421st Night Fighter Squadron was at Tacloban on Leyte. The plan was for the Marine's air echelon to operate from Tacloban for a period of two weeks, being supported by the 421st ground personnel, while the 421st air echelon operated from Peleliu, being supported by the Marines.

The workhorse of the 418th NFS was the Northrop P-61 Black Widow. The distinctive squadron markings are visible on the aircraft's vertical stabilizer. Even before the Northrop factory was producing P-61s capable of carrying external fuel tanks, the troops in the field were modifying their aircraft to carry them. (Campbell)

Pilot George M. Ellings and R/O Milton Burman of the 418th NFS shortly after their destruction of a Rufe on December 30, 1944. (Ellings)

Lts. Roy Oakes and Lyle Robb of the 547th NFS. Robb, on the right, was making a name for himself, duplicating with enemy vehicles what Frank Luke did in World War I with balloons – only Robb did it while on night intruder missions. Anxious to fly every night, he would shoot up seven to 12 enemy trucks each night. The 547th had modified a P-38 by hanging Navy APS-4 radar on it. They found it was marginal in air intercept operations but Robb found it was good in hitting vehicles. Robb had destroyed nearly 200 Japanese vehicles in the three months he was in the squadron. He was quite eager and aggressive, maybe too much so. On March 5, 1945 he misjudged the distance and rammed into a Japanese motor convoy while strafing the column. He was posthumously awarded the DFC. (Odell)

Lt. William F. Sherman, R/O, and Capt. Leon O. Gunn, pilot, of the 418th NFS. Capt. Gunn was one of the squadron's most proficient pilots in attacking ground and waterborne targets. (Odell)

2nd Lt. Carl H. Bjorum, a pilot in the 421st NFS. In early September 1944 Bjorum along with his R/O, 2nd Lt. Robert C. Williams, and S/Sgt Henry E. Bobo as gunner, knocked down a Betty and Dinah in three nights time. (Odell)

Right: The crew of the 6th NFS P-61 "Virgin Widow" are, from left to right, Sgt. Leroy F. Miozzi (gunner), 2nd Lt. Charles A. Ward (R/O), and 2nd Lt. Robert L. Ferguson (pilot). They were credited with a Betty on the night of December 26, 1944. (Hansen)

As stated earlier, conditions at Tacloban were very primitive. The muddy strip was difficult for the tricycle geared P-61 to operate from. It lacked much for night operations. The runway lights were not used most of the time in fear they would attract Japanese attackers. Because of these conditions, the night fighters often had to make multiple passes in attempting to land. On the other hand, the Marines F6F-5N Hellcat night fighters with standard landing gear would encounter less difficulty in operating under such field conditions.

In Volume I of the Far East Air Force History it states:

Because of the slowness of the construction process in Leyte, the 22nd Bomb Group(H), and the 421st Night Fighter Squadron were moved to Palau to operate from facilities constructed by POA. But in

a message from Gen. MacArthur to Admiral Nimitz concerning this trade, 'Japs operating Oscars as night bombers are too fast for the P-61. In Palau the enemy is employing bombers which P-61s can effectively cope with. Would appreciate your considering a temporary swap of night fighter squadrons, the Marine squadron from Palau could operate from Leyte, and P-61s to go to Palau.' This does not seem to be realistic since the Oscar (Nakajima Ki-43) is nearly 50 MPH slower than the P-61A.

General MacArthur was dissatisfied with the dawn and dusk protection he was receiving. He had a valid complaint. Between poor GCI coverage, lack of spares, and the poor operating conditions, the 421st NFS often found itself with six or less operational P-61s! From the continuous night attacks, both

Snug in a former Japanese hanger, well ventilated by earlier action, the empennage of a P-61 frames Saipan's bustling air strip. (USAF)

from Japanese air and ground forces, that Tacloban had been receiving, the 421st had lost aircraft as well as personnel killed and wounded.

It is of interest to note that the special detachment of the 547th Night Fighter Squadron, who arrived at Tacloban shortly after the 421st had, remained there during the Marines stay. The 421st Night Fighter Squadron history states that their P-61s had been replaced by the Marines due to requirements of a longer range night fighter. The F6F does have a longer range, but the missions they flew from this Philippine strip did not require this added range most of the time.

Whatever the reasons, the Hellcats of VMF(N)-541 arrived on December 3, 1944. As it turned out, they flew out of Tacloban for five weeks instead of the two originally planned. During this time they did a commendable job, destroying 23 enemy aircraft. But once again the stated reason for the move is faulted. Most of these victories were not true night fighter kills – i.e., at night under radar direction. They were all dawn or dusk missions, a mission that the Hellcat, like the P-38 night fighter, are better suited for. The major fault of the P-61, the lack of range and loiter time, was not a factor in the Marine's operations, though external tanks were already being fitted to P-61s both in the field and at the factory. On January 11, 1945, the Marines went back to the Palau Group and the air echelon of the 421st returned to Leyte.

Aerial Victory

Destined to be the USAAF's leading night fighter pilot, Maj. Carroll C. Smith, C.O. of the 418th NFS, along with 2nd Lt. Philip B. Porter had good hunting on the night of December 29/30, 1944. Major Smith later would report on this mission:

Three of us took off shortly before dusk and flew 50 miles south to cover a convoy of 300 ships. Three minutes after the light began to fade, I sent my two wing planes back, and continued my patrol alone. It was perhaps an hour later when the fighter director messaged: 'Indications plane coming from southwest – 8,000 feet – 12 to 15 miles away.'

I set a collision course, climbing and hoping to intercept the Jap a safe distance from the convoy. I closed in fast, and first saw him tow miles away, scudding towards a cloud. Both Phil and I identified him instantly, an Irving, similar to a Nick only slightly larger. A deadly 20mm stinger in the tail, and three 12.7mm machine guns. Mustn't let him get in the first burst.

For seven minutes I chased the fellow. He turned in and out of the clouds. Gradually we descended. I hit him with a short burst as he entered one patch of cloud, and got away a second burst, the bullet striking around the wing roots, when he came out in a turn. His tail stinger was chattering, but not for long. Down he dove, burning and disappeared completely.

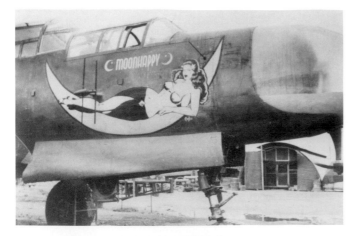

Irving before he could start his bomb run. At 800 feet, Smith let loose a short burst from his 20mm cannon. He observed hits in the canopy area while others opened up the Irving's fuel tanks. Several pieces flew off the aircraft as the plane tumbled and blazed merrily as it glided into the water.

After the destruction of the second Irving, he headed back to refuel, rearm, get a cup of coffee and possibly 40 winks before they would go on local patrol in the early morning hours. They had been on station for less than 30 minutes during their second patrol of the night when GCI picked up a contact. Vectoring Smith to the unidentified aircraft, the major was able to identify it as a Rufe, a single engine float plane of the Japanese Imperial Navy. The Rufe could fly low and slow with its maneuverings making it very difficult for the P-61 to catch. Numerous occasions during their low flying, Smith would have the Rufe in his sights only to have it disappear in its tight and low turns. Finally, by lowering his flaps half-way down and cutting his speed to 120 MPH, Smith was able to get careful aim on the aircraft. Letting loose of a short burst at about 150 feet the Rufe was destroyed with ease.

Two hours later and on station again. GCI once again had something on their scope and vectored the 418th's deadly duo to another unidentified incoming aircraft. They flew close enough and identified it as a Frank, a plane that could hit speeds of 400 mph and faster – much faster than their P-61 could go. Their only chance was to surprise the Frank pilot. Smith later reported:

I began to worry. Three kills already. How many rounds of ammunition had I used? Maybe I had a hundred left, but maybe I had

Capt. William Bradley, C.O. of the 421st NFS, had a quite distinctive art form on the side of his P-61. (Noyes)

The Irving was swallowed by the sea at 9 o'clock, straight up. We circled only long enough to confirm the kill.

After the confirmation Smith gained altitude to place them once again on station to keep a watchful eye on the convoy. It was but a few minutes later that Porter spotted another enemy aircraft coming in towards the convoy, at 11 o'clock. Both aircraft were at the same altitude; and due to the enemy's close proximity to the convoy, Smith had no time to maneuver into a more desirable attack from astern. He pushed the throttles wide open and came in on a head on attack. He dove in order to cut off the

The 548th NFS was the last night fighter squadron to get into the combat area in 1944. Capt. William H. Dames led a detachment to Saipan where they joined the 6th NFS detachment in mid-December. (Bode via Thompson)

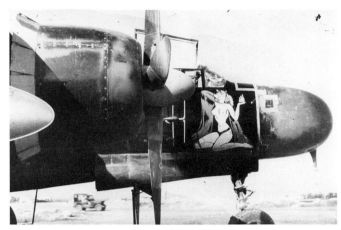

This 548th NFS P-61 shows off quite a devilish figure. (Maita)

The 548th crew of Bob Boucher, pilot, and Dean Deines, R/O, on Saipan with "Blackout Hostess" posing behind them. (Boucher via Thompson)

only two or three. I had to get him with the first burst! Phil commenced calling off the ranges. When he hit 150, he peeled out ahead. I could see the Frank looming up closer and closer. I closed to 75 feet. At that deadly range I pushed the button. Twenty, thirty, maybe forty tapered steel slugs rammed into the Frank. As he exploded I chopped the throttle, dropping back to avoid most of the debris.

They would be the only AAF night fighter team to attain four victories in a single night.

Many years later the memory of this very active night remained quite vivid in Carroll Smith's mind:

I think the one that frightened me more than anything else was the Frank, because that particular evening I shot down four with one load of ammunition. I shot down two Irvings over the fleet that was coming up. Then I landed, but I didn't re-arm because I figured I'd had about all the opportunities I'd have in that evening. Anyhow, I refueled and took off again and then fiddled around and found this little old Rufe after I'd got about 200 feet out over the water. We chased him around like trying to catch a greased pig in a barrel. We finally found him and

sort of pulled flaps down in a tight turn at 200 feet. I managed to shoot him, but it was almost daylight; you would pick up the silhouette of things real well.

The Frank was the Japs latest bird. It was quite a good airplane. Well, we sneaked up behind him – we stayed below him and behind – and I didn't know when I pulled the trigger whether I had one bullet or a hundred. I just didn't know. I thought I might have shot them all. I pulled up as close as I could behind him. It was only a real short burst, but when the four 20s hit the guy at close range, he just came completely unglued. When we landed later, they checked my remaining ammo; and I still had quite a few left. I think I'd only used something like 480 rounds, for four birds! My marksmanship improved in direct relation to how close we got to them to shoot them.

People have sometimes asked me how do I feel about knowing that you kill people. Well, I guess to say you felt good would be asinine if you don't. At the time you're not thinking in terms of people you're killing. Sure, it's a kind of contest, and you're a bit remote from the human feelings involved. If you weren't you'd drive yourself mad, I'm sure. I never saw anybody get out of an airplane I shot down. The Jap didn't have very good escape equipment in the first place, and their airplanes were rather fragile. In most cases when I shot an airplane down, it disintegrated rather thoroughly, so I'm sure nobody got out alive.

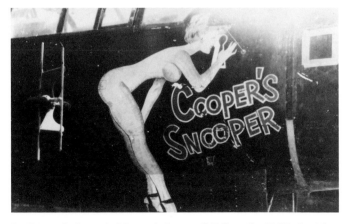

Lt. George C. Cooper's "Cooper's Snooper." Fellow pilot Mel Bode of the 548th was the artist. (Lloyd via Campbell)

La Vallon airfield in southern France with the 415th and 417th NFSs. The field was being used for emergency landings on D-day, the invasion of southern France, and was in operation by AAF units two days later. The 415th arrived in early September and the 417th joined them mid-month. (USAF)

Chapter 14

Roman Nights

For the Mediterranean air forces the war was about to intensify over the southern part of the European continent. In December 1943 all Allied air forces in the Mediterranean were merged into the Mediterranean Allied Air Forces (MAAF). This would be the final organizational form for that theater's air forces for the remainder of the war. On January 1, 1944, Lt.Gen. Ira C. Eaker took command of MAAF. Within a short time MAAF was at full strength.

The Allies initial push to free Rome was the landing of three divisions of the Fifth Army at Anzio and Nettuno on January 22. The intent of this operation was to cut the German lines of communication, turn the flank of the Gustav Line and for the troops to advance the thirty-six miles north to the "Eternal City."

All went well for the first 12 miles. The Germans had been caught off guard. But stiff resistance soon formed and the Fifth was bogged down. The Germans countered in February, threatening to push the invaders back into the sea. The support rendered by MAAF did much to prevent this disaster.

From southern France Luftwaffe night bombers attempted to interfere with the Anzio operations. These strikes were soon disrupted by the 414th NFS as it expanded its patrols over the Ligurian and Tyrrhenian sea route. The 414th NFS was stationed at Elmas, Sardinia, where it was providing air defense and air-sea rescue assistance. To intercept the incoming Germans, detachments operated out of fields on Corsica. In spite of the constant lack of sufficient Beaufighters, the squadron managed to maintain their primary missions at Sardinia and the additional work load of protecting the Anzio beachhead.

Upon the opening of the Anzio beachhead on January 22nd, the 414th NFS crews were sent nightly from their base in southern Sardinia to airfields in northern Corsica for the purpose of preventing German night attack on Anzio from airdromes in southern France. At this time the airfields in northern Corsica had just recently been taken from the Germans and had to be practically rebuilt. As the reconstruction of these fields was only partially accomplished when the 414th NFS crews took over the above assignment, they were consequently forced to operate from temporary dirt runways. Added to this hazard was the location of the fields themselves. They were bordered on one side by the sea and on the other by high mountains. Two fields were used in these operations, one at Ghisonaccia and one at Borgo, and at both of these the 414th flew the first Allied planes to operate at night.

At Ghisonaccia they faced many obstacles. No refueling service was available and crews had to perform this task for themselves. There were no tents or other shelter from the cold damp weather that time of the year. The crews stayed all night in their planes or in the back of a truck. Sleep was out of the question. Since there was no phone to the tower, a flare system had to be employed for scrambles. The dirt runway was especially unsafe. During the period of these operations, construction work was being done during the night with the employment of many heavy duty units such as tractors and steam rollers. This situation often necessitated dangerously short take-offs. Also, the muddy condition of the runway caused great difficulty as the tires of the aircraft at times sank into the surface of the runway. The only lights available for landing were flare pots lined on one side of the runway.

Conditions at Borgo were of an even worse nature. The temporary dirt runway was only 2500 feet long and so located that regardless of high velocity winds, take-offs had to be made from the mountain to the sea and landings from the sea to the mountains. The necessity to let down at night through a haze and locate so small a strip required the highest professional skill on the part of each crew. The mountain was so close to the end of the runway that it was impossible for a plane to go around and make a second approach, for it would inevitably crash into the mountain. Here crews either stayed in their ships or crowded into one small building. Again there was no phone to the tower, and flares had to be used for scrambles.

A report from a German prisoner of war who had been a M/T operator shed some light on how the Germans perceived the

Jack K. Gamble and Wallace H. Geisz of the 414th NFS inspect a flyable prize, a Junkers Ju 87, at Alghero, Sardinia. (Jenkins)

Allied night fighters in the area. According to the prisoners statement, German crews that were briefed to attack an Allied convoy between Cape Tenes and Cape Ivi on February 1, 1944 were told that two ground-controlled Night Fighter Squadrons were based on Corsica operating interception patrols. It is noted that no Allied night fighters were based on Corsica before February 1st. The only night fighters available were Beaufighters of the 414th Night Fighter Squadron that were dispatched to Corsica nightly from their base at Elmas, Sardinia.

Of the four AAF night fighter squadrons in the MTO only the 417th remained on the African continent to provide night protection for the harbors and ships on that side of the Mediterranean. On January 10 they moved from Tafaraoui, Algeria to La Senia from which their mission was the protection of the busy port of Oran. They would hit pay dirt on February 2nd as the night fighter team of 2nd Lts. Rayford W. Jeffrey and William A. Henderson were flying convoy cover. An incoming Ju 88 was intercepted and Lt. Jeffrey made several firing passes on the enemy, his fire hitting the enemy. Though wounded, the Ju 88 returned fire knocking out one of Jeffrey's engines. Another Beaufighter of the 417th, crewed by Capt. Ken K. Nelson and F/O Robert E. Perkins, assisted and also made a firing pass at the Junkers. On a single engine and flying at an extremely low altitude, Lt. Jeffrey made a final pass at this Jerry. Though wounded, the enemy was still spewing back intensive machine gun fire. Jeffrey continued the attack. The result was fatal for the Ju 88 and it crashed into the sea.

The 414th's initiation into the Anzio campaign started off with a bang. On the night of January 23rd, nine of the squadron's 12 Beaufighters participated in warding off the enemy raiders. One of the crews was 2nd Lieutenant Clyde W. George and Flight Officer Herbert C. Penn. They had taken off at 1800 hours. Obtaining a contact northeast of Ghisonaccia at five miles to their starboard, they closed to 2000 feet and made a visual; however, the fleeing aircraft was undergoing such violent evasive action that, before they could identify it, the bogey peeled off through cloud cover and the contact was lost. Presently they again obtained a fleeting echo to starboard, and turning into this F/O Penn picked up a strong contact at 11

o'clock position, three miles distance. Closing slowly at full throttle, Lieutenant George gained a visual at 4000 feet and identified the plane as a German He 177. At 800 feet he fired a five-second burst from astern setting fire to both engines. Following the hostile in a dive, Lieutenant George made two more starboard attacks and the enemy aircraft crashed to the ground in flames north of Bastia, Corsica.

In short order 1st Lt. James R. Anderson and Flight Officer John A. Armstrong obtained a fleeting echo as they dived towards Corsica approximately twenty miles west of Elba. They made a full contact five miles out of Cap Corse. As they closed towards minimum range, the hostile dropped window and started to turn to starboard. Anticipating this maneuver, Lieutenant Anderson also turned starboard and gained a fleeting visual. F/O Armstrong picked up the target again at three miles to starboard, and they closed to 100 yards where they identified the plane as a Do 217K. When a five-second burst dead astern showed no effect, Lieutenant Anderson backed off to 500 yards and fired a ten-second burst. Both engines of the enemy aircraft caught fire; it glided down to port and crashed into the sea.

Good hunting continued for the 414th NFS. A few nights later on January 26, Capt. Carroll H. Bolender and F/O Harold J. Manges, while flying patrol off the coast of Corsica, contacted a Ju 88. Immediately the enemy aircraft took vigorous evasive action in an attempt to escape interception. Pursuing the hostile plane through a hail of accurate return machine gun fire at minimum altitude over water, Capt. Bolender closed to within 600 feet and fired four bursts. Strikes were seen along the fuselage, and fire broke out in the nose as the enemy dove down toward the coast of France. Because the Mark VIII AI radar equipment in the Beaufighter was then restricted from flying over enemy territory, they were forced to break away. After flying on a vector towards Corsica for a few minutes, F/O Manges contacted an He 111. Again they closed to minimum range, and although the cannon had jammed, Capt. Bolender pressed the attack with his machine guns, setting fire to the right engine of the Heinkel. The enemy crossed the coast of France in a steep spiral at 1000 feet, and Major Bolender had to break away.

The significance of these operations may be found in the official recognition of the achievement by the French government. Each of the three pilots named above were awarded the

A Beaufighter of the 415th NFS detachment stands ready at a Piombino airfield in Italy in the summer of 1944. (Bockstege)

This was the source of most needed replacement parts. (Jenkins)

"Croix de Guerre a La Ordre de L'Aviation de Chasse" by General Bouscat. It was quite apparent that the night fighters had made themselves felt as the Germans discontinued attempting raids across the sea and started flying over the much longer and arduous land route across northern Italy.

Not far behind the Allied landings on the Italian mainland was the 416th NFS. Between January 28th and February 5th the squadron moved into their new quarters at Pomigliano D'Arco near Naples. Their primary mission was, like that of the other AAF night fighter squadrons in the area, to protect the Anzio beachhead as well as provide night air defense of the Naples area. Second Lt. James D. Urso and his R/O, F/O Daniel T. Powell, Jr., were already airborne on their patrol of the Anzio beachhead when the action commenced:

At 0500 own aircraft was coming at 260 MPH SE at 5500 feet, between S. Felice and Gaeta. Pilot thought that there was something behind. Observer could get no response on IFF. GCI said there was nothing there, but suggested that pilot do a hard port turn.

Pilot orbited and saw aircraft travelling about 200 MPH on same level at 2 o'clock position. Full moon to the west, weather good, visibility unlimited, scattered stratus. The enemy aircraft had two in-line engines, single fin and rudder, tapered, leading and trailing edges of wing. Aircraft overshot three times while orbiting. Got visuals several times. AI contacts several times. GCI helped. Enemy aircraft took course of 030 deg. GCI put aircraft on him.

Followed Me 210 inland on course of 030 deg. from about 45 miles N. of Pt. 12, to a point between Capistrello and Avezzano. Throttled back all the way and came in very slowly at 190 MPH. Aircraft sighted enemy aircraft at 1500 feet, 45 deg. above, closed in to 100 yards, identified it as hostile (Me 210) from silhouette. Also aircraft slowed down to 110 MPH and saw German markings on underside of wings. At 0529 opened fire from port side, at 100 yards range and closed in to 25 yards, enemy aircraft port engine exploded and plane broke up in two pieces. Port wing broke off in flames. No one seen to bail out. Aircraft and enemy aircraft were at 9500 feet at time of combat. 60 rounds of 20MM and 270 rounds of .303 were expended; there were no stoppages. No injuries to crew or own aircraft. At 0529 at 3000 feet, Capt. Morrison and F/O Quinn, of this squadron, on patrol 15 miles NE Pt. 11 saw blaze in two sections about 40-50 miles inland near Capistrello. At first, thought it was a flare, then identified it as a burning airplane. Saw it fall to earth in two large pieces.

The enemy aircraft did not return fire, showed no aggressiveness, but relatively slow speed of enemy aircraft indicates, perhaps, that the pilot was trying to have our aircraft overshoot. Pilot of our aircraft drew up close enough to see German Crosses on under-side of wings of enemy aircraft.

Beaufighter crew of the 415th NFS detachment at Piombino, Italy in July 1944. From left to right are: F/O Hurbert F. Moore (R/O), 2nd Lt. Henry F. Bockstege (pilot), and Sgt. Wilson (crew chief). (Bockstege)

"Dinah Mite" of the 414th NFS. Pilot Joe C. Jenkins shows that the MTO night fighters could not be out done by the ETO and Pacific night fighters when it came to "aircraft art." (Jenkins)

The 416th was busy chasing many bogies throughout the month of February, but most turned out to be A-20s and Wellingtons. The Wellingtons, as well as Allied anti-aircraft batteries, fired numerous shots at the 416th's Beaufighters, but, fortunately, no serious damage. On the ground they also had their problems with "friendlies." The February history relates one of these instances:

Those whose duties bring them to the line at night wait with fear and trembling for the inevitable challenge by the many Airbase Security troops, 'who dere?' There is a legend that a transport pilot once answered, "257 Herman Goering Panzer Squadron," and was told to 'carry on.'

On February 24, the 416th rang up their second confirmed victory. Capt. Darwin V. Brake, Jr. and F/O Alfred A. Gander were on patrol over the Anzio beachhead when Virtue directed then to incoming.

2040	10000'	Beachhead, Over to Virtue, vectored 090 around lines of beachhead. Turned north, told something 6 miles ahead; going north. Flew 10 minutes, no contact.
2050	10000'	Turned 180, flew 10 mins. and ran into edge of flak at beach. (4 flares 5 mi. north of Anzio, 1 single north of Anzio). Told to turn port 330. Virtue said bandit 4 miles to port going northeast.
2110		Vectored 330 until AI contact obtained at 3 miles. Turned stb'd to 030, pursued E/A through hard evasive action from 3 miles to 12000.' Visual obtained. E/A dived, visual lost but regained. Beau followed E/A, closed to 100.' Identified as He 111.
2125	10000'	60 Mi N.1 He 111 destroyed. Beau opened fire at Rome150 yds. Tail assemble broke in two large

pieces. Cannon strikes on port wing root. E/A seemed to fall straight down.

2140	10000'	Rome. Turned 190 and flew 15 minutes, came to Rome, then patrolled an area 3 to 5 miles over beachhead.
2155	10000'	BetweenVectored on aircraft flying S/E. Rome-BH. Obtained contact at 2&1/2 mi. E/A was dropping window.
2200		Closed in and lost 1500', cut speed to 160 and obtained visual at 300' above and at a range of 800' to stb'd. Believed to be Ju 88. Made 360 turn to port. Observed flares and 2 bomb bursts north area of harbor at Pt. A. Increased speed and got into flak. Called off by Virtue and vectored 040 around edge of flak.

Along with the 416th NFS in Italy was the 415th. Not unlike the other AAF night fighter squadrons in the MTO, they were usually in need of replacement Beaufighters (sometime down to just a handful). On the 16th of January they finally received three dearly needed replacements, though a few days later they would lose another one in a landing accident. On the 30th they made what would be the first of eight moves to take place during 1944 as they left Montecorvino for Marcainise for a two month stay.

Hunting was good here. On the night of February 7th, 1st. Lt. Charles F. Horne and his R/O, 2nd. Lt. Richard F. Urich intercepted and destroyed an He 177. More havoc on the Luftwaffe was wrought when the team of Capt. W.D. MacMonagle and F/O G.H. Wickersheim damaged an Me 210 over Anzio. Some nights later two of the 415th's Beaus had to return to base because icing conditions had caused their instruments to freeze up. Of this incident the squadron history states, "Anyone who has flown at night will tell you that it is really a sweat job under those conditions."

Part of the 415th NFS aircrews at Piombino: Chester L. Buoscio (pilot), Charles A. Fournier (pilot), Henry J. Giblin (pilot), and James W. Karkos (R/O). (Bockstege)

As the Germans were pushed north, the night fighters started flying the dual role of area defense and night intruder. Here one of the 415th NFS aircraft flies over Italy. (Bockstege)

Hawker Hurricane still in RAF markings was used by the 414th NFS as a "hack" aircraft. It was later lost in an accident. (Jenkins)

Maj. Nathaniel H. Lindsay flashes the "victory" sign soon after destroying his second enemy aircraft, a Ju 88, on March 18, 1944. Lindsay's first confirmed enemy aircraft destroyed, and the first for the 415th NFS, occurred on July 24, 1943 when he successfully intercepted a German Heinkel He 115. On both encounters Lt. Austin G. Petry was manning the radar on their Beaufighter night fighter. (USAF via Gerhart)

March turned out to be quite interesting for the 416th NFS. On the 7th, they received a memo from Headquarters 62nd Fighter Wing addressing "Operation of Mosquitoe Type Aircraft Attached to 416th Night Fighter Squadron." The memo stated that "higher headquarters" desired the squadron to service test the Mosquito "under conditions as now exist over the beachhead." A secondary purpose was to reinforce the 416th in its daily operations. They were instructed to "pay particular attention to both favorable and unfavorable operational features."

On that same day a detachment of four Mosquitos of the RAF's 256 Squadron, stationed on Malta, arrived along with eight RAF officers and 29 enlisted men. The 256 was integrated into the 416th's schedule and flew as part of the latter until they were recalled on March 19th.

March was a good month for the team of 2nd Lt. George P. Fors and F/O Arthur G. Gaudette as they got the squadrons third victory on the morning of March 17. Once again, the Beau was on patrol over Anzio when GCI vectored them onto a bandit. The Beau closed in to make a visual but soon thereafter lost contact. Another visual was made at 1,000 feet and Fors closed in to 300 feet where he identified it as a Ju 88. Fors got into position and fired at the Junkers from 500 feet dead astern. No positive results. Closing in, he fired again. Fragments flew off from the canopy area and a small white explosion erupted. Closing to about 400 feet, he fired yet a third barrage. A second explosion occurred near the cockpit area and in the starboard wing root. The Ju 88 decelerated and then gradually nosed over and went straight down into the water, exploding upon impact.

Operations expanded for the 417th NFS in March. Besides providing protection for the Oran harbor area they were now flying fighter sweeps off the east coast of Spain and in late March sent two crews to the Naples area to assist the 416th NFS. On March 28th, while on a sweep off the east coast of Spain, some 40 miles north-east of Cape Palos, two of the 417th's aircraft, crewed by Lt. R.J. Gebler with F/O E.F. Packham and Lt. William A. Larsen with F/O Joe F. Draper, encountered and engaged in combat a Ju 88. Passes were made until all ammunition was expended. The night fighters observed numerous strikes registering on the enemy aircraft. A few minutes later another Beaufighter crewed by F/O Rayford W. Jeffrey and F/O William A. Henderson, arrived on the scene. They fired one long burst and the enemy aircraft rolled on its back and crashed into the sea. F/O Jeffrey's ship was damaged by return fire from the Junkers. A successful crash landing was made at the base with no injuries to the crew.

On March 31, Jeffrey and Henderson were scrambled and after about an hours chase, and 55 miles northwest of Cape Tenes, obtained a visual on a Ju 88. Two bursts were fired from

As fast as the Luftwaffe was pushed out of an airfield, the night fighters were moved in. The high command saw the value of keeping up the pressure on the retreating Axis forces. (Cypert)

close range and many strikes were observed. The Ju 88 was east in low hanging clouds. It is believed that it did not reach its base. This belief is based on "Y" service reports.

Maj. Nathaniel H. Lindsay and F/O Austin G. Petry scored for the 415th on March 18, the second kill for the team. Their combat report makes interesting reading:

00:15 vectored onto bogey by Virtue and after 15 minutes obtained visual - fleeting - between 1000 and 1500 ft. Followed into visual range of 75 ft. and identified as a Ju 88. Dropped back to 150 yards and opened fire with 3-second burst and saw strikes on starboard engine and fuselage. E/A began to descend through clouds. Continued chase giving a further burst of 3-seconds. E/A began to descend through clouds. Continued chase giving a further burst of 3-seconds. E/A was seen to go down spiraling to left in flames. Last seen at approximately 7500 ft. Called Virtue and said, 'We've got him', then climbed back to 10,000 ft. and continued patrol. While chasing bogey and in one of the turns the target shot off a flare which gave four illuminating flashes believed to try to blind pilot. No change of appearance on AI tube at that time. Location given by GCI for final contact as being 6 miles north of Nettuno and approximately one mile out over sea. GCI personnel saw plane go down in flames. Claim one Ju 88 destroyed.

After climbing back to 10,000 ft. and continuing patrol for approximately 30 minutes told by Virtue another Bogey was in vicinity. Chased Bogey but had no contact and GCI could not help us. Vectored back to normal patrol and immediately was vectored onto another bogey. Had no contact. Had to return to base due to fuel shortage and fuel pressure warning. Partial jamming encountered during whole patrol. Moderate flak in vicinity of IAZ on Beachhead. Flak believed to be friendly.

Strangle Hold

As the Allies were attempting to put a strangle hold on the Axis forces, the Luftwaffe was striking back hard. On the night of April 10 two Beaufighters of the 416th NFS were on patrol over Anzio. Major Rulon D. Blake with 2nd Lt. Horace E. Moody were in one aircraft while Capt. Darwin V. Brake, Jr. and F/O Alfred A. Gander, Jr. were in the other. Soon about 30 German bombers seemed to be everywhere; at first the number seemed greater because of "window" being dropped. The two Beaus turned into the enemy and began the attack. Major Blake got on one of the Heinkel 177s and after a long chase scored a probable over Cape Linaro north of Anzio. A second Heinkel was soon in his sights which he managed to damage in the melee. Yet another Heinkel was engaged. Blake managed to get off several bursts of fire before the Hun disappeared into the black night. Heavy return fire was received throughout the night's combat and the Beaufighter was hit numerous times. Capt. Brake and F/O Gander were not so fortunate. Their Beaufighter was set afire during the ensuing battle and crashed into the sea with its crew. For this action, Major Blake and Lt. Moody were awarded the Distinguished Flying Cross for their extraordinary achievement.

Another mass enemy formation of 20 to 30 aircraft raided the Naples area on May 14. The 416th wasn't in the air at the time but the crews of Capt. Harris B. Cargill and F/O Freddie C. Kight along with 1st Lt. James D. Urso and F/O Daniel T. Powell, Jr. were scrambled. Capt. Cargill made contact with a Ju 88 which he destroyed five miles south of Castel Koltirno. Lt. Urso, also in pursuit of a Ju 88, destroyed his query 15 miles north of Frosinone; this was Urso's second confirmed victory.

When Lt. Emmett B. Paison returned to the States in May 1944 from his overseas tour with the 415th NFS he submitted a very interesting report on German night fighter tactics and equipment. This report reads:

1. The Germans when bombing at night usually make 4 or 5 bomb runs from different angles and evidently bomb on a time schedule. Their technique seems to be a low approach toward the target, then a climb to 8,000 feet, from which altitude the bombs are dropped, then down to the deck again and home. The exception to the rule is the Heinkel 177, which always makes a comparatively high altitude bomb run.

2. At night we found that the enemy used reconnaissance ships before a raid. They would send in a stooge aircraft or two to attract the attention of our night fighters. In this way they tried to draw the night fighters away from their bombers. These stooge aircraft engaged in violent aerobatics to protect themselves.

3. The 'window' which the Germans used (sample of which is attached) was very effective against our Mark 4 radar equipment but not so effective with our Mark 8. The enemy dropped 'window' from an altitude of 3,500 or 4,000 feet and generally saturated the area.

4. The enemy apparently has radar installed in the tails of night raiders which will detect aircraft coming up on their rear. This was indicated by the way they would go into violent action (climbing, diving, turning) which we could see in our radar screen. This tail radar apparently has an azimuth range which determines whether our approach is from the right or left and the German pilots made their evasive turns accordingly. Usually, they would first make a faint toward starboard and as our plane then had to make a violent turn to starboard to stay on their tail, they would quickly turn to port. It is because of this that I believe they know the limitations of our air-borne radar.

5. The Germans tried to jam our radar by sending out such a powerful wave that our equipment 'triggered up' and we would get only dozens of jagged lines. We could hear the hum of their jamming equipment. We tried all sorts of remedies without much success, and I am convinced that we will have to deal with radar jamming all during the war. Often they would try to jam our equipment then use 'window' from their ships.

The 417th NFS left the African continent in April and set up operations at Borgo, Corsica from which they patrolled the Corsican east coast. The 417th sent crews to assist the 416th NFS again this month. One of the crews, 1st Lt. Walter G. "Grumpy" Groom and F/O Harold L. Roth, hit the jackpot on their first mission out in the defense of the Anzio beachhead when they intercepted and destroyed a Ju 88.

During the first two weeks of April, the 415th Night Fighter Squadron was so short of aircrews that those that they did have

had to pull double duty. By mid-month they receive seven badly needed replacement crews.

May was the month that most of the 417th's activities involved chasing "Bed-Check Charlie." On the 1st, Lt. J.F. Kirwan and F/O J.M. Van Laecken caught "Bed-Check Charlie," a Ju 88, and sent him home with quite a few holes. "Charlie" acquired this name because of his nightly trips down the coast. On the 9th Capt. C.R. McCray and F/O R.D. Hamilton gave him a chase for his money and claim a damaged. The competition among the crews of the squadron was growing quite keen to see who could get him. The crews agreed to donate $5.00 to a "Kitty" each time they chased "Charlie" and fail to get him and the entire "Kitty" was to go to the crew that finally destroyed him.

On the night of May 12/13, Jerry came over the 417th area in strength for the first time. Borgo was not one of the targets but he did give the night fighters quite a scare. One string of bombs hit off the south end of the runway but did no damage. The main targets were two fields south of there. Capt. Clarence R. McCray and F/O Robert D. Hamilton were credited with one destroyed and one damaged, both of them He 177s.

"Charlie" showed up again on the night of the 13/14th. Capt. John S.M. Lee and F/O Leonard R. Potter damaged "Bed Check Charlie" again, and would probably have destroyed him had it not been for a hydraulic failure causing the chase to be broken off. Undoubtedly "Charlie" lead a charmed life.

Night Intruder

In preparation for the upcoming invasion of southern France, the 414th NFS took on a new mission – that of intruder. On June 8, 1944 they flew their first mission. Six of the squadron's Beaus participated in this operation. The area to be covered stretched from the Rhone Valley north to Avignon. They struck at shipping in Lake Berre, railroad trains, and the airdrome at Retour Des Aires. Not much could be observed from their efforts other than a number of small fires. Most of the crews were caught in the beams of searchlights during this escapade and were "quite thrilled by this experience." Some inaccurate anti-aircraft fire was experienced by a number of the crews, but this just added to the excitement. This was a small beginning, but all of the MTO night fighters would soon find themselves doing more and more of this type of work.

By June 12th they had tangible results for their intruding effort and were making plans to become even more potent in this work. On the night of June 11/12 Capt. James R. Anderson strafed a locomotive, causing it to explode. To add to the Beau's punch in this work they were planning to add aircraft rockets to their arsenal. Crews were being sent to Alghero for training in handling and firing these deadly projectiles. To check up on his MTO night fighter crews, Col. Winston W. Kratz, who headed up the night fighter training establishment in the States, dropped in on the 414th on July 18th. He was checked out in one of the squadron's Beaus and flew it for himself. The following day Col. Kratz visited the 416th NFS at Pomigliano. In his conver-

Clare Lefler of the 415th NFS was one of the many ground crew that had to put extra-human effort into maintaining the MTOs Beaufighters so the aircrews would have something to fly. (Cypert)

Borgo, Corsica, became the new home of the 414th NFS in early September. Like the other AAF night fighter squadrons, the 414th provided convoy cover, air defense over beachheads, airdromes, and troop concentrations, and was conducting night intruder missions against the retreating German forces. With a high utilization rate and few replacements, non-flyables became a major source of supply. (Jenkins)

sations with the 416th Kratz discussed the possibility of their getting Mosquito night fighters in the near future.

Like the 414th and 416th had in 1943, the 415th and 417th started having their Mark IV AI radar replaced with the Mark VIII centimetric AI radar at mid-year. This radar had increased performance and did not suffer from ground returns as did the

415th NFS "Lil Joe" in late 1944 with pilot Joe C. Jenkins. (Jenkins)

415th NFS aircrews at La Vallon, France, in September 1944. Standing are (from left to right): Henry J. Giblin (pilot), Chester L. Buoscio (pilot), Henry F. Bockstege (pilot), and Walter J. Cleary (R/O). Seated: Raymond J. Neyer (R/O), Hurbert F. Moore (R/O), Charles A. Fournier (pilot), and Hanson (R/O). (Bockstege)

Mark IV, which the Germans were well aware of. They would use this shortcoming to their advantage by diving to the deck when pursued in hopes that they would be lost amongst the clutter on the Beaufighter's radar screen.

In mid-June the 415th was on the move again. The first echelon arrived at Valtone, France on the 17th shortly after the Germans had evacuated the area. There were numerous signs of the hurried manner in which that had departed. There were still signs along the road exclaiming "ACHTUNG MINEN, ATENTIONE MINE."

Beginning in June, the 416th NFS started sending out detachments. From mid-July until early July a detachment operated out of Tre Cancello. Then in late July one was established in Tarquinia; this one would be in operation into early September. From this later field two crews supported by 22 enlisted personnel operated under the 6506th Fighter Control Area.

Lt. Hanson of the 415th celebrated the 4th of July with a real big bang. While on a test hop he saw an Allied convoy heading in a southerly direction. As he was watching he observed a periscope just west of the second ship in the convoy. Then he noticed two more periscopes between the third and fourth ships. Quick action was needed. Hanson dove his Beaufighter down and fired some 2,100 rounds from his .303 machine guns at the periscope. Soon the escorts were dropping depth charges in the vicinity. An oil slick was soon seen in the area of the attacks.

Another victory was added to the 414th's credit on the night of August 6. Crewing the Beaufighter were John E. Patterson and Roy E. Patten. Patterson's report reads:

I took off at 0055 hours, 6 August 1944, on an R/T silence convoy patrol with Backup. At 0120 hours, while I was on a course of 330, Backup started vectoring me. At that time I was at 5,000 ft., and shortly thereafter I was on a vector of 010 at 200 ft. As I was going north, Backup turned me over to Vardon, telling me the hostile was eight miles dead ahead. I was unable to contact Vardon. A fading contact

A replacement Beaufighter received by the 415th NFS at La Vallon in southern France. The RAF provided the replacement aircraft from a number of sources with one thing in common – they were well used. More than once a Beaufighter turned in by one of the AAF night fighter squadrons as unflyable and beyond repair would be given to another of the AAF night fighter squadrons by their British ally as a replacement. On this example the RAF roundel has not been replaced by the US star and bar. (Bockstege)

First to trade in their Beaufighters among the AAF night fighter squadrons in the MTO was the 416th. Much to their delight the first De Havilland Mosquito Mk 30 arrived on November 29 (above and below). (Lippincott)

showed on the eight mile ring, but not clearly enough to control interception. I checked in with Foodshop for help. They gave me vectors of 010 and 035 degrees. My R/O took over as the contact cleared at six miles. My R/O did a great job of following the hostile through a port orbit, keeping the E/A between us and the moon. Our approach was steady. I got a visual at 4,000 ft. as E/A crossed the moonpath. Closing to 300 ft. I definitely identified E/A as Ju 88. I fired two three-second bursts from astern of E/A. As I fired the second burst,

the E/A's starboard engine exploded. He then turned to port and crashed into the sea. I claim one Ju 88 destroyed.

In preparation for the invasion of southern France, Twelfth Air Force continued to send interdiction missions into northern Italy and to cut the coastal rail system between Cannes and Genoa on the Riviera. In the week before the invasion the night fighters as well as the Twelfth's medium bombers attempted to knock out all enemy airdromes in the Po Valley in northern Italy. Day and night fighters assaulted as many of the gun positions, radar stations and bivouac areas on the French and Italian Rivieras as they could.

To support the invasion effort, the 416th sent detachments to Alghero, Sicily and Borgo on Corsica the day before. On their way to Borgo, four of the 416th's Beaufighters provided cover for Britain's Prime Minister Winston Churchill. The following day, August 15th, they provided cover for the invasion. The squadron provided cover for the invasion convoy through the 23rd, at which time they returned to Pomigliano. The entire affair was fairly uneventful.

Greeting the 416th at Borgo was the 417th NFS which had been stationed there since April. Also, like the other AAF night fighter squadrons in the MTO Col. Kratz and Col. Viccellio of the War Department stayed with the 417th for awhile. They arrived on the 16th of July and Kratz, already checked out in the Beaufighter, flew a dusk patrol with the squadron. He ended up having an extremely long chase but unfortunately was not able to close in enough to obtain a visual.

On the 21st the crew of 2nd Lt. Robert W. Inglis and F/O Theodore E. Hearne hit the jackpot – though on a sad note. On their fourth operational flight they caught "Bed-Check Charlie" and shot him down. Lt. Inglis reported over his radio that he saw the enemy aircraft hit the water and that he was going down to look at the wreckage. No further transmissions were received and Inglis and Hearne failed to return. Debris and dinghy from both aircraft were found later.

The squadron flew its first intruder mission on the 28th. Lts. Theodore A. Deakyne and John F. Kirwan were airborne from Alghero, Sardinia, where they went for their briefing. The flights were over airdromes in the lower Rhone Valley.

On August 28th, the 427th Night Fighter Squadron, fresh from State-side training, arrived with their P-61 at Pomigliano and were temporarily attached to the 416th for support. The 416th NFS was moved to Rosignano on September 1st but left a detachment back at Pomigliano, where it continued bringing the 427th into operational status, which lasted until the 9th. At that time the 427th NFS took over the Naples night air defense duty from the 416th.

On September 11, Lt. Urso of the 416th NFS was honored by the British government. The squadron history for that day reads:

The Squadron basked in the reflected glory of Lt. Urso who was awarded a British D.F.C. by his Majesty the King on the recommendation of the Commander-in-Chief RAF, MEDME. Lt. Urso received a warm letter of congratulations from Air Vice Marshall Sir Hugh Lloyd, Air Officer Commanding MACAF. The A.O.C. praised Lt. Urso 'for consistently good work with the 416th Night Fighter Squadron and particularly in respect of your fine performances on the 8th of February when you got an Me 210 and on the 14th of May, when you destroyed a Ju 88.' 'It gives me all the more pleasure,' the A.O.C. wrote, 'that this fine decoration should have again been won by an American pilot in one of our U.S. Beaufighter Squadrons, and the award will do much to cement the very strong friendship which exists between yourselves and your British colleagues in the Coastal Air

The 414th NFS moved to Pontedera, Italy in late November 1944. Here one of their Mk VIII AI stands ready for the evening's missions. They were not allowed to fly over enemy territory with this new radar at first in fear that a disabled Beaufighter might fall into enemy hands. (Jenkins)

Force. Our own Beaufighter Squadrons have the greatest admiration for your performance and this award is extremely popular."

On September 12, the 417th was ordered to proceed to la Vallon airfield, in the mouth of the Rhone Valley. The squadron's history describes this less than joyous move in "glowing" terms:

Its mission was to give protection by night to the entire southern coast of France and the operational port of Marseilles which had begun receiving Allied ships within a remarkably short time after its occupation.

From almost the first day of its arrival in southern France, the squadron began experiencing a series of difficulties and obstacles which came close but never quite shattered the morale of the entire unit. Some of these difficulties should be related in detail, since, in all fairness, there should be some understanding of the tremendous mental and psychological hazard against which all personnel of the squadron labored during operations in France.

Upon arrival at la Vallon Airport, a barren, depressing field close to a range of dangerous mountains, the men erected the tent area approximately one and a half miles northeast of the runway and line. Tents were erected during a thunderous downpour. Although care was taken to place the tents behind the shelter of a long windbreak formed by closely planted fir trees, French officials and civilians warned that when the winter Mistral began, the tents would be hurled into the Mediterranean, thirty miles distant; however, there was little or no alternative to this arrangement. The nearest town capable of housing the entire personnel was 11 miles away. Transportation was seriously limited, and to establish a system of commuting between field and town would have imposed an unbearable strain.

Despite the unceasing rain, operations began within 24 hours after arrival. Patrols were immediately dispatched to intercept German reconnaissance planes which were determinedly seeking to photograph and observe the crowded harbor of Marseilles. Other Beaufighters were assigned to search for the one-man submarines which the enemy had begun to use in large numbers with varied success.

Extremely poor weather conditions were merely a harbinger of a long series of misfortunes that befell the squadron. On the night of September 26, Lieutenant J.W. Grange suffered an engine failure and was forced to ditch in the Mediterranean. Fortunately, he was picked up by a rescue craft and survived the ordeal of exposure. Three days later a message was received that the squadron was to break camp and prepare for return to an Italian base. Departmental equipment was immediately packed, tents were removed, and transportation began to move the squadron back to Marseilles. Five minutes after the last truck had departed, a small echelon which had been left behind to care for a possible enemy attack on the harbor, received a message cancelling the move. After frantic efforts a vehicle was found which ultimately intercepted the convoy at the town of Aix.

Back at the boggy, rain-swept field, the men replaced the tents, strung communications, unpacked crates and cases, prepared the planes for operations. That very night Beaufighters were sent aloft to cover the harbor of Marseilles and to guard shipping and installations against attack from the explosive-laden motorboats which the enemy had devised as another "secret weapon" of destruction.

Intrigue

The 415th found itself involved in a little intrigue in late September. The 64th Fighter Wing history recounts of this episode:

While 'Boxcar' was at Dole it assisted in one of the most dramatic interceptions ever made by the Wing. Beginning about 21 September 1944 both Control Centers daily reported an unknown track traveling from the direction of Stuttgart toward the Spanish border between 2100 and 2200 hours. A similar track, going in the opposite direction, appeared each morning between 0330 and 0430 hours. Gen. Barcus believed these tracks to be hostile and directed Maj. Julius Goldstein, Wing Senior Controller, Capt. George (W.) Schiff, Radar Officer, and Capt Harold F. Augspurger, Commanding Officer of the 415th Night Fighter Squadron, to make an interception on them. Together with their staffs they devised a method of intercept control which would not require radio transmission by the intercepting Beaufighter but would give all information necessary for making contact with the bogie. Radio silence by the aircraft was necessary so that it might escape detection by the enemy plane and by the usually efficient German 'Y' service.

The mission, originally scheduled for 26 September, was prevented by bad weather and the flight was laid on for the next night. At 2000 hours on the 27th a Beaufighter piloted by Capt. Augspurger with 2nd Lt. Austin G. Petry as observer was airborne. Jerry was not long in appearing. The Delaware GCI station picked him up at 2007 and within two minutes the track was identified as hostile. At 2010 the interception began and at 2031 with 'Eureka! It's a Jerry' the pilot announced the successful contact. The Focke-Wulf Fw 200 transport went down in a huge ball of fire, hit the ground and exploded violently. Officers of the Wing drove immediately to the scene of the crash and recovered from the wreckage documents and material of great value.

In the interception all who participated worked with a perfection rarely achieved in night fighter control. The planning by Maj. Goldstein,

Capt. Schiff and Capt. Augspurger had been so complete that the system operated flawlessly. The GCI controller, 1st Lt. Alpheus L. Withers of the 328th Fighter Control Squadron, handled his job with rare coolness and skill; the crews of the Delaware and Indiana radar stations were continually alert passing accurate information to the Control Center; and the Beaufighter was superbly handled by Capt. Augspurger and Lt. Petry. The interception was a particularly valuable and significant Allied victory because it frustrated the enemy's attempt to use in Spain one of this last remaining sources of intelligence of the outside world. After 27 September the Germans rarely attempted to send transports on the Spanish run and then only during the poorest flying weather.

Expanded Operations

The 414th and 416th Night Fighter Squadrons carried out a joint operation on the night of September 26/27 when they entered a new phase of their careers. On this night they made their first offensive sweep of the Po Valley. The 414th sent seven Beaus from the Corsican base to take part in this historic mission while the 416th supplied five. The night fighters, not being trained for this type of work, felt they had a good night. Six motor transports were destroyed and 14 damaged, a factory and power plant were damaged, and seven miscellaneous targets were damaged.

Maj. Harold F. Augspurger had held command of the 415th NFS for less than a month and he accomplished their second move in that time when they arrived at Longvic (Dijon Airdrome) on September 25th. Two nights later he along with his R/O, 2nd Lt. Austin G. Petry, were flying the units first night mission from that location. A report of the encounter gives a blow by blow account of the action:

At 20:20 hours while flying on vector of 280 at 8,500 ft. received a contact while in a turn. Contact was made at 6 miles about 10 degrees to port at 8,500 ft. Closed in to 4,000 ft. and obtained a visual on aircraft – identity unknown – then dropped into clouds and closed to 1,000 ft. and pulled out to starboard side of e/a above the clouds on same level as e/a. Enemy Aircraft identified from tail structure as either a Ju 52 or Fw 200. E/A was flying straight and level at 8,500 ft. Fired one three second burst with 20 degree deflection. Hits were seen on starboard wing and engine. E/A immediately burst into flames and crashed at 20:30 hours. Fighter rapidly overtook e/a at estimated speed at 260 mph. Positive identification was made later at the scene of the crash: Fw 200K.

Two nights later this team repeated their performance by downing an He 111.

The 414th NFS arrived on mainland Europe with their move to Pisa, Italy on October 12. From here they continued their intruder missions and patrols in support of the invasion of southern France and intruding into the Po Valley in northern Italy. More and more of their work was intruder rather than defensive. They also performed "Nickelling" missions. These were psychological warfare leaflets, called "Nickels," which were dropped in the vicinity of German troops. Their intruder work was having a devastating effect on "Jerry." Motor transport, locomotives, rail cars, railroad stations and depots, military, power, and communications installations were all feeling the effect of these efforts. Capt. Frank E. Killian flew one of these very successful missions on October 1, 1944. The squadron history describes his flight:

Night intruder sweep over the Po Valley, Italy.

Captain Killian dove to minimum altitude through a heavy barrage of anti-aircraft fire to strafe and severely damage a steam locomotive and train that was crossing a heavily defended bridge. As he maneuvered his plane into position for a second attack, shell fragments from continued ground fire damaged his aircraft, forcing him to break off combat. Then, skillfully maintaining the crippled plane airborne, Capt. Killian returned to his base and effected a safe landing.

Capt Killian had flown 260 combat hours to this point. For the above effort, which was typical for the 414th, he was awarded the Distinguished Flying Cross.

Joining the 414th at Pisa was the 416th NFS. Their abilities were somewhat taxed on this issue as stated in their squadron history:

The Squadron ended its operations at Rosignano on the night of 30 September/1 October by a maximum effort against the enemy. Eleven of our Beaufighters were airborne on night intruder missions in the Po Valley or on patrols followed by intruder sweeps in the same area. The results were excellent: Seven enemy MT destroyed, eighteen damaged; one electric train probably destroyed and two goods wagons damaged; a smelter strafed and set on fire, and four bridges strafed. Two of our Beaufighters were on patrol in the Florence area. Operations Order No. 153, 62nd Fighter Wing, 28 September 1944, stated, 'The 416th Night Fighter Squadron will cease operations at Rosignano, Italy on 1 October 1944 at 1200 hours and commence operations at 1201 hours at Pisa Airdrome. The Squadron will remain operational through the move.' It is impossible to say whether the 416th, seasoned veterans of so many moves, could have accomplished this miracle of logistics. Fortunately we were not put to the test, since our operations take place at night. At dawn we broke camp at Rosignano and began to move to the new base at Pisa/San Giusto, Italy.

By mid-November the 416th NFS knew their Mosquito night fighters were not far away. They started sending personnel of their Radio Section to attend the Radar Conversion School in Algiers at that time. On the 19th several crews flew in a B-25 to go to Foggia where Mosquito training was to be accomplished. On the 29th the first Mosquito arrived with Capt. Iribe at the controls. Those last two days of November were quite something for the 416th NFS as the unit history shows:

Capt. Iribe returned from Africa in our first Mosquito and gave the base and the villa a display of buzzing which was astonishing for its virtuosity. Headquarters was less impressed! Later in the day three more of our Mosquitos arrived. Everyone is enthusiastic about our new

aircraft. Several officers from XXII TAC arrived for an inspection of the squadron.

Three of our crews flew intruder patrols from Pontedera Airfield with the 414th Night Fighter Squadron. During the month of November the squadron flew 29 intruder missions for a total of 62:00 hours, 1 patrol for 3:45, 1 ack-ack Co-op mission for 2:10, and 2 patrol-intruder sweeps for 8:55 hours for a total of 33 missions for 76:50 operational hours. Our intruder score to date is excellent. On 44 completed intruder missions 129 M/T were destroyed, 177 M/T were damaged, 3 locomotives were destroyed, 7 were damaged, 3 railroad cars were destroyed, 17 were damaged, 3 miscellaneous targets were destroyed and 20 were damaged.

"At Last!" announces the 417th NFS history for November 29th:

At last! 1st Lt. Theodore A. Deakyne, who has 'sweated it out' for quite some time finally got a Jerry 'destroyed.' A Ju 188 no less. Lt. Deakyne has had no little service in this war, having flown Beaufighters and Mosquitos with the RAF then joining the 417 NFS and coming back to Beaufighters again. This happened when 'Jerry' was taking night photos of Marseilles and Toulon.

Elsewhere in the history it continues:

Another fortifying incident occurred on the night of November 29 when Captain Theodore Deakyne, who had fought with the British in the Battle of Britain, secured contact with a Ju 188 off the port of Marseilles. Contact was momentarily lost, but his observer (1st Lt. Robert E. Perkins) skillfully picked up another at the unusual range of six miles. After a brilliant pursuit at deck level, the enemy plane was shot down into the sea.

Major Augspurger of the 415th NFS had a rough night on November 19th. He went out on the first intruder mission of the night and was hit by flak upon arriving over the target area. His aircraft sustained considerable damage and he was losing power on one engine, causing him to turn back. As he passed over into "friendly" territory, he was hit by "friendly" fire causing greater damage to his aircraft. He managed to crash land at Ochey airport, the plane was a write-off but the crew were unharmed.

The following night Lt. Inghram and his R/O intercepted an Me 410. Lt. Inghram got close enough to get a few rounds off, causing an orange flame to stream from the enemy. The two combatants dueled for awhile until the Messerschmitt was the pursuer and the Beaufighter became the pursued. When the Beau's IFF was turned off, the German broke off the chase.

Foo-Fighter

What Lt. Edward A. Schlueter reported on November 27, 1944 has not been satisfactorily explained to date. On that night along with R/O Lt. Donald J. Meiers was the 415th NFS's intelligence

Next to trade in their Beaufighters was the 414th NFS. They received their first P-61 Black Widow on December 20. (Lippincott)

officer, Lt. Fred Ringwald. Their mission this night was as night intruder in the Rhine River area north of Strasbourg. Lt. Schlueter was flying low enough so he could detect the white steam of a blacked-out locomotive or spot the sinister bulk of an unsuspecting motor convoy along some road. He was also on the lookout for smoke stacks, barrage balloons, searchlights, flak batteries, and other dangers to him and his crew.

Ringwald spotted some lights towards some hills off in the distance and pointed them out to Schlueter. Schlueter thought they were probably stars. They discussed this theory until it dawned on Lt. Ringwald that there were no hills in that direction. There were eight or ten of these lights in a row resembling orange balls of fire moving through the air at terrific speed. He checked with GCI and was informed that there were no other aircraft in the air with him. Meiers wasn't picking anything up on his radar scope either. A few minutes later they went into a flat glide and disappeared.

A few nights later Lts. Henry Giblin and Walter Cleary were flying at about 1,000 feet when they saw a huge red light about 1,000 feet above them going at an estimated speed of 200 miles per hour. Yet again, on the night of December 22/23 another 415th crew saw two lights climbing towards them from the ground. When it reached their altitude, 10,000 feet, the lights leveled off and stayed on their tail. These large orange lights stayed with them for a couple of minutes and then peeled off and turned away. As the lights flew away they went out. The next night still another crew saw a similar phenomena. They described it as, "A glowing red object shooting straight up, which suddenly changed to a view of an aircraft doing a wing-over, going into a dive and disappearing." Within time all of the 415th crews had seen these "Foo-Fighters" as they started calling them. This name was based on the popular comic strip "Smokey Stover" in which it was frequently stated that, "Where there's foo, there's fire."

The 415th NFS wasn't the only ones to see the "Foo-Fighter." A P-47 pilot reported seeing, "a gold-colored ball, with a metallic finish, which appeared to be moving slowly through the air. As the sun was low, it was impossible to tell whether the sun reflected off it, or the light came from within."

A similar report was made by another P-47 pilot. Similar phenomena was reported by B-29 crews in the Pacific.

Such explanations as jets, rockets, weather balloons, the crews drank too much the night before, St. Elmo's fire, and such were offered by experts and bystanders alike. The 415th have considered all these explanations and have discounted them all with rational reasoning.

Good News - Bad News

All was not going well with the AAF Beaufighter squadrons and the 417th NFS's history tells quite a story after a number of engine failures and crews lost:

Such an abnormal series of mishaps and misfortunes forced a tremendous psychological burden upon every member of the squadron. Pilots faced every mission with undue tenseness and mental rigidity. They were honest enough not to conceal an ever-present feeling of anxiety and nervousness. Routine patrols were faced with more trepidation than the most dangerous intruder missions over enemy-occupied France had ever aroused. Crew chiefs and mechanics, who were responsible for the absolute proficiency of the planes became deeply depressed and labored under the mental handicap that the aircrews and personnel might believe the accidents were their fault. As a matter of fact, two reasons were immediately discernible for the serious accident rate: one, crews were using Beaufighters which should have been condemned long ago. All of the planes were at least three years old and some had been veterans of the Battle of Britain, with a record of overhauls that virtually stunned visiting American technical representatives. Several Beaufighters were received as replacements for crashed planes which the engineering section immediately recognized as ships which sister night flying squadrons had turned back for salvage! Two, several engine failures had been traced to an excessive amount of water in the fuel. Early efforts to trace the origin of this threatening factor ran into a stone wall. Fuel depot personnel asserted the gasoline had been certified as Grade 'A.' Finally, the Operations Officer, persisting in his investigation, discovered that the fuel was being loaded from pipe-lines into drums which had been left uncovered and resultantly had accumulated a considerable amount of rainwater, none of which had ever been removed. To condemn the entire amount of fuel on hand would have been unthinkable, since the supply of petrol in France at that time was dangerously low. Ground personnel were, therefore, instructed to be extremely careful in refueling planes and to halt the flow before the water line in the drums was reached. However, this was a makeshift solution, and pilots were fully aware that the planes they carried aloft were subject to the ever-present threat of defective fuel.

It must be stated, in all frankness, that other night fighter squadrons equipped with rebuilt Beaufighters, were also having serious difficulties, and as a result several aircrews requested release from flying status. In the 417th Night Fighter Squadron, *not a single aircrew made such a request*, nor sought to evade in any manner its scheduled missions.

December was a month of transition for the 416th NFS. Radar observers went to Pomigliano for training on the Mosquito's Mark X AI radar while more pilots went to Foggia for transition training. Maintenance personnel went to Algiers for their training on the Mark X radar. The aircrews attended lectures by DeHavilland and Rolls-Royce representatives. More Mosquitos were ferried in from Maison Blanche. Contrary to an earlier flight, the pilots of these latter deliveries were "well briefed" not to buzz the field. Their work culminated with two practice intercepts and patrols carried out on the night of December 17/18. Except for a couple of operational missions that some crews flew with the 414th NFS in early December, the 416th had not flown operationally since late November. Back in business again!

Santa was good to the 414th NFS. Their Christmas present was their first P-61 Black Widow. They were not overly saddened to be rid of their "Bristol Bastard." By January 20th, the squadron was transitioned and the last Beau had left their ranks. The Squadron's history tells of this event:

The 414th received its big Christmas present a little early but at any rate those big formidable looking 'Black Widows' were certainly welcomed in a big way. The scene at the base on their arrival was something like the ovation that Lindberg received when he made his flight to Paris. At the first sight of the twin booms a cry was heard, 'Hey fellas, here they are – the Widows!!' From nowhere throngs began to pour onto the field and it wasn't long before our parking strip was jammed with G.I. and English boys. Feeling quite good about the matter themselves, Major Bolender and Captain Clark decided to put on a bit of an exhibition so coming in low and fast, a beautiful 'buzz' job was given, after which a demonstration of the plane's climbing ability and maneuverability was given and upon completion of such, both 61s came in for perfect landings.

The last victory of the year for the 414th NFS, and their last in the Beaufighter, came on December 23. First Lt. Albert L. Jones was piloting the Beau with F/O John E. Rudovsky serving as his R/O. The combat report states:

Flying at 800 feet in the region just west of Mantova, F/O Rudovsky contacted a bogey, and Lieutenant Jones closed rapidly to minimum range where he obtained a visual and identified the aircraft as a German Ju 87. With extraordinary skill, Lieutenant Jones slowed his Beaufighter to such an extent as to make a target of the enemy; in view of the great differences in speed of the two aircraft, this feat could be accomplished only by the most expert maneuvering. With accurate fire Lieutenant Jones put a solid burst into the enemy and, despite steady return machine gun fire, pursued the hostile ship in a continuous attack until it crashed to earth in flames near Asola.

It would be for the crew of 1st Lt. Edward A. Schlueter and 2nd Lt. Donald J. Meiers of the 415th NFS to finish the year out in grand style. This incident is documented from the point of the ground controller in the 64th Fighter Wing's history:

In Ludres the men of Wing Headquarters and Control Center 2 were awakened several nights in succession by the coughing chatter of Jerry machine gun fire from aircraft strafing the well-traveled road which ran by Ludres to Nancy. On one occasion Wing Headquarters itself was strafed but there were no casualties. Lying on their cots in the chrysalis of the newly issued sleeping bags the men pondered the advisability of venturing into the cold outdoors to seek a foxhole or wondered if any lights were showing that might bring the strafers swooping down on the buildings and camp. While they pondered and tested the cold winter air by sticking a head from the sleeping bag the German aircraft completed their brief strafing run and were gone.

The Beaufighters of the 415th Night Fighter Squadron were active against the intruders. On 29 December Lt. Burton Robbins, GCI controller at Dakota radar station, controlled a Beaufighter onto three attackers. Two of them were shot out of the air. After the Beaufighter had shot down the first Jerry, a Heinkel 111, southeast of Nancy, he turned back toward his base at Ochey to replenish his fuel and ammunition.

Another enemy aircraft had been picked up by the Colorado SCR 270 and was shortly thereafter detected on the scope of Dakota. The GCI controller called the Beau pilot, 'Hello, Torrid 38, this is Churchman. We have another bogie. Can you go after it?'

From the Beau came, 'I haven't much ammo, but let's go.'

The chase was on. It was longer than the first one and not until the bogie had nearly reached the German lines did the Beau make contact. It was a Ju 88. Too late the quarry realized the Beau was on his tail. Almost directly over the GCI radar Washington the Beau let loose another burst which used nearly all the remaining ammunition. The hostile aircraft exploded and fell to the ground.

Chapter 15

European Engagement

In mid-September 1944 the 422nd Night Fighter Squadron was informed that they were moving north into Belgium. They were not saddened to leave the bomb torn buildings of Chateaudun with its wrecked remains of He 177s, Ju 88s, Fw 190s and such. The first half of the month wasn't very productive for these night fighters. Luck seemed to be on the side of the Luftwaffe. The one German aircraft to tread in their space got away unscathed. As a matter of fact, three of the 422nd's crews had a chance at him; two had to call off the intercept because of mechanical malfunctions. The third crew was apparently a little over anxious and overshot the target. A visual wasn't made, and when they attempted to regain contact, they only saw blank radar screens.

What the 422nd NFS found at Florennes made Chateaudun look good. All structures needed major repair. They would also soon find out how cold it could be and how muddy a field could get. But a warmer welcome they couldn't have wished for. Nearly the entire town turned out, including two German soldiers who came out of the woods to see what was going on – and surrendered. When the air echelon landed on September 17th, it was a miracle that none of the townsfolk were run over by any of the big birds.

Florennes was some 70 miles from Brussels, 65 miles from the bomb line, and 110 miles from the Rhine River. Also on the positive side, there were three GCI stations forward of the field located in such positions that they gave the night fighters coverage from Dusseldorf to Strasbourg. This field was also used by B-24s that were hauling 80 octane gasoline in from the UK for the front. One of these aircraft seemed to crash land on a regular basis. Turning ones bad fortune into another's good, Sgt. Lloyd A. Marshall of the 422nd would wait at the end of the runway on a regular basis and quite often be one of the first to reach the wreck – and syphon the gas.

There were reports that at times the 422nd would reach the wreck before the fire and rescue equipment. One of the 422nd's R/Os, Robert F. "Shorty" Graham remembers:

They would fly gasoline into our base in Germany for Patton's tank. Trucks would pick it up from planes at our base. We were short on aviation gasoline at the time and every now and then one of these B-24s would come in, and he'd run off the end of the runway. Before the fire truck could get out there, a gas truck would be there siphoning gas out of the tanks. We'd take their aviation gas, and the Army could take all the other gas they wanted. But that was the only way we could keep flying for awhile.

By the 21st the 422nd NFS was operational again. Their first victory from their new base, and the only one for the month, came on the evening of September 25th when 2nd Lts. Lewis A. Gordon and Creel H. Morrison intercepted and destroyed a Ju 188. This statistic really does not tell the entire story, for the night fighters were quite busy that month. They flew 282 sorties, had 238 GCI directed chases, 150 AI contacts made and 100 visuals accomplished (of which 97 turned out to be friendly and three enemy aircraft).

With their latest move they were given additional duties. Just prior to the night fighters' move, Brig.Gen. Ned Schramm, commander of the IX Air Defense Command, paid them a visit. At that time Gen. Schramm informed the night fighters that they would be entering the realm of intruder, in addition to their usual defensive patrols. Gen. Schramm visited them again once they were established in Belgium. He awarded the troops well deserved medals and then they talked operations. He gave them permission to strikeout on their own and to go after targets of opportunity. The 422nd's history elaborates:

Opposite:
Both diversions and a sense of humor is required in times of tension. 422nd pilots Herman Ernst, on the left, and Paul Smith, on the right, pose with a snow-pilot at Florennes. (Ernst)

Local labor was used to repair airfields just vacated by previous Luftwaffe tenants. Here the taxiways are under repair at Coulommiers. (AAF)

As a result of this new development, the need for intelligence information became acute. By reason of IX ADC's location in Versailles, and the attendant communication difficulties – again we were cut off except for carriers – it became urgently necessary to make a contact with some source for this information. Accordingly, arrangements were made with IX TAC and 67th Recon Group, as a result of which, four areas for ground strafing were laid out – each vital as a communication bottle neck to the battle lines – and GCI procedure, including R/T was worked out. 'Gangster' was the code name we adopted for the missions, while we were supposed to do intruder missions – attacking enemy airfields by night – we felt that such procedures, with the facilities at hand, was not as attractive as the free lancing for targets of opportunity, and so for the moment, that portion of our three part mission was laid aside.

This additional duty for the night fighters was a logical step in a series of events that were taking place. The Ninth Air Force had found that by using B-26 Marauders and P-47 Thunderbolts they could disrupt the enemy's rail and road networks, thus interrupting his vital supply lines. The daylight operations had been so successful that the Germans started moving their supplies by night. Secondly, any bridges that were damaged in daylight raids were being repaired at night. The next step in strangling the enemy's supply lines was to include night operations. The two night fighter squadrons of the Ninth Air Force were therefore given the assignment. To amplify their operational change from purely defensive to an offensive mission, both the 422nd and 425th Night Fighter Squadrons would be transferred from Air Defense Commands to Tactical Air Commands.

Low flying Fw 190s became the 422nd's nemesis in October. They would make hit and run raids on the front lines when the day fighters were on the ground, usually around dusk and extending a couple of hours into the night. Arrangements were worked out with higher headquarters for the night fighters to have two P-61s over the target area from about a half hour before darkness and into the night. The scheme paid off on the first mission, as the squadron history tells:

Accordingly, we flew our first twilight mission on the 21st with take-off at 1720, with (1st Lt. Theodore I.) Jones (pilot), (2nd Lt. William G., Jr.) Adams (R/O) and (1st Lt. Phillip M., Jr.) Guba (S-2) having the honor. We struck pay dirt almost immediately, when we were vectored onto four Fw 190s carrying bombs. Closing to a visual and finding one flying slightly below and to the left of the other three, T.I.(Jones), despite the unfavorable position he was in, in respect to the other three, moved in and shot him down before the other three knew what had happened. Adams and Guba had a few bad moments, as when Jones opened fire, the other three Fw 190s were some 200 feet directly overhead. Decidedly too close for comfort.

Three days later Col. O.B. Johnson and Capt. James A. Montgomery (R/O) closed in on a loose formation of three Fw 190s. With a short burst of his 20s, Johnson brought the leader down in spite of flak hits that had damaged his own aircraft. Yet again on the 28th, Col. Johnson intercepted a formation of eight bomb-laden Fw 190s. Though he could not get into a satisfactory position to fire, he did manage to break up the raid.

The moon period was right to start their intruder missions early on in the month, though the poor weather prevented them from flying more than just a few. Most of the crews got to fly this new type of mission. They started locating areas of interest along the Rhine Valley between Dusseldorf and Strasbourg. For their first month they claimed two locomotives destroyed, 26 railroad cars destroyed and an additional 140 damaged. During the time that the night fighters were flying as intruders, there was a rumor going around that there was a revolt waging in Germany. Jim Postlewaite came up with the real story:

Oh, we had one good deal on all the lights on the Ruhr in October of 1944. Everybody was saying this was small arms fire and everything else. I and Old Chet (Lt. Chester C. Hawley, Postlewaite's R/O) were always getting lost. We set all kinds of endurance records in any

422nd NFS in formation at Chateaudun for the presentation of medals. The area was beautiful but the airfield needed a good bit of work as it had suffered severely from Allied air force poundings. (Tierney)

2nd Lt. Herman E. Ernst being awarded an Air Medal. Next in line for a medal is 2nd Lt. Theodore I. Jones. (Tierney)

422nd NFS headquarters personnel: (left to right) Maj. Jack C. Pinkerton (Ex. Officer), Capt. George W. Reynolds (training and operations [S-3]), 1st Lt. Howard C. Brown (supply [S-4]), and Capt. Edward S. Page, Jr. (intelligence [S-2]). (Tierney)

airplane we ever flew for being lost. We ended up over Brussels one night and saw the same flashing; so we went down and looked. They were streetcars going by the connection, so we sort of shot that all right out of the water. I've got an article out of the *Chicago Tribune* about our suspected ground fire and revolution going on inside Germany. Bunch of streetcars going like mad was all it amounted to.

Air operations were rewarding also. They scored on three occasions, two of which were Fw 190s and one Me 410. The

Messerschmitt was the first for 1st Lt. Paul A. Smith and his R/O, Robert E. Tierney. Besides these there were a number of close chases. First Lt. Leonard F. Koehler had a real heart breaker on a beautiful moonlit night. He positioned himself behind an Bf 110 and opened fire. No strikes. He repeated this action until he was out of ammunition. Not a hit! It turned out that his sights were out of adjustment. Capt. Tadas J. Spelis got a visual on a Ju 188 but lost it when the German pilot took hard evasive action. To add insult to injury, though Spelis didn't get a shot off, the chased enemy did. Spelis had another chance on the night of October 6/7 when he caught up to a Bf 110 north of Charleroi. His shots struck home and debris from the stricken enemy damaged his radome. Cloud cover prevented him from seeing the doomed aircraft crash.

The squadron saw their first jet this month. Capt. Robert O. Elmore and 2nd Lt. Leonard F. Mapes encountered one while on patrol. In spite of the information the night fighters had been given on the jets poor turning radius, this one managed to get on their tail just as they dove into a cloud. Lt. Mapes was able to identify the craft as a Messerschmitt Me 163. On another occasion in this same month, 1st Lt. Herman E. Ernst and 2nd Lt. Edward H. Kopsel were flying combat air patrol over Acchen, Germany when they too observed a jet at night. They believed this one to be a Messerschmitt Me 262.

October was also a month of great loss for the 422nd NFS. After more than 700 missions they lost their first crew in combat. Lts. Donald J. Doyle and Norman N. Williams were flying along the Rhine River when they reported that they were going down to investigate something – this was the last message received from the ill-fated crew.

The crew of "Little Linda," a P-61A of the 422nd NFS, flew the first night mission over Germany. At right is R/O Chet Hawley and to the left is pilot Jim Postlewaite. The bright yellow nose seems quite bright during daylight hours but at night it didn't seem to give their presence away. (AAF)

"Double Trouble" flown by the 422nd NFS crew of pilot Bob Bolinder and R/O Bob Graham. As a team they would account for four German aircraft destroyed. With a head cold and unable to fly, Bolinder would be grounded while Graham would fly with another pilot and be credited with a fifth kill. (Bolinder via Thompson)

"Little Audrey" of the 422nd was one of the few late P-61B models to be received by the Ninth Air Force night fighters as replacement aircraft. (Johnson)

"Wacky Wabbit" was not appreciated by all the "higher ups," and its 422nd NFS crew had to add a second extended finger, giving Bugs Bunny a V for victory sign rather that requesting a table for one. (Tierney)

And the rains came. It rained for 28 days in November, making life miserable for the night fighters. They felt that they lived in a swamp. With such conditions encumbering them, the 422nd had a very uneventful time for more than two-thirds of the month. When they could, they got off a few intruder missions which struck against German marshalling yards. The results were of limited success as they were flying during the dark of the moon period. One of the crews that managed to get off on one of these missions was 1st Lt. Robert G. Bolinder and 2nd Lt. Robert F. Graham, R/O.

While returning from a night reconnaissance mission, they were nearly blinded by a high intensity flash that came from below their aircraft. They were also nearly deafened by the accompanying ear breaking thunder. Investigation of this phenomenon showed it to be one of the German's huge disappearing railway guns. Their find was reported when they returned to base. The next day fighter-bombers of IX Tactical Air Command pounded both ends of the tunnel in an attempt to seal the doom of the big gun.

The night of November 26/27 proved to be not only the only active night fighting night of the month, but one of the most active that the 422nd had experienced to date. It started out quiet and then Lt. Paul Smith latched on to a V-1 and shot it down before it could cause any damage. He attacked a second one and fired at it. His hits seemed to make it go faster and Smith had to give up the chase.

Then the team of 1st Lt. Robert Bolinder and 2nd Lt. Robert Graham caught up with an He 111 and shot it down in flames. They immediately picked up another target. Bolinder closed in to 200 feet under the bogie. They flew in formation for about 15 minutes but could not reconcile certain features as any enemy aircraft so they broke away. Lt. Bolinder felt he'd rather play it safe than be sorry.

Capt. Eugene Lee was next. As he closed in on the Bf 110, he opened fire. His aim was right on but his nose wheel doors partially opened and were shot away. This broke the circuit to his guns and they went silent. Luck was on the Bf 110s side this evening.

The crew of 1st Lt. Herman E. Ernst and 2nd Lt. Edward H. Kopsel got their first confirmed when they intercepted a Bf 110. To add a finale to the evening, Paul Smith found himself chasing the enemy for the third time this evening. This time it was an He 111. But the destruction was more than just the Heinkel. As the stricken aircraft plummeted to earth, it landed on the main road of a German village. As it hit, it skidded down the street, setting each building on fire as it went careening through the town.

The night fighters saw increasing numbers of V-1s and V-2s in November. One hit in the outskirts of Florennes while a number rocketed across their airfield. Bob Bolinder and "Shorty" Graham had a up-close and personal experience with one of these V weapons. Graham describes this experience:

I saw eight or ten flashes on the ground about 15 miles in front of the starboard wing. The smaller flashes were orange, the largest ones white. Directly after that I saw a glowing orange ball at 4,000 feet. It

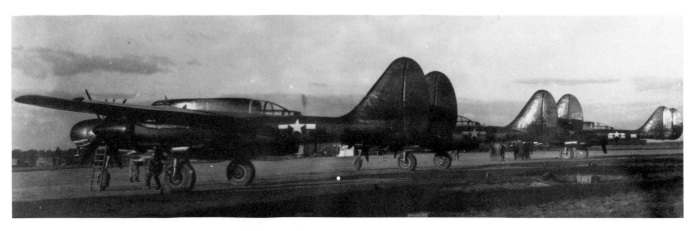

A lineup of 422nd Widows stand ready for the night's mission. (Graham)

Activity abounds at the 425th's base of operations at Coulommiers where the ground personnel readies the squadron's planes. Here a couple of P-61s are readied by armorers (the armament tent is to the right). (AAF)

As time went on, later model aircraft arrived in Europe. The Widow getting the once-over by a number of Air Force types is a P-61A-10 which was the first model to utilize water injection in its P&W R-2800s. (Smelzer via Olmsted)

shot up almost straight to over 25,000 feet in 10 or 12 seconds. At its crest it turned a brilliant white for a split second and vanished.

On November 28, the 422nd's "new" weapons of destruction arrived. Seven war weary A-20s. A vivid description of these planes is contained in the squadron's history:

When the seven wrecks did arrive, their condition gave food for some sober thought – one was a veteran of 90 missions, none were equipped with oxygen, and all were pretty well beaten up. Thus another challenge was presented to Engineering with the need for added crew chiefs beyond that called for in the T/O.

The French Line

The 425th Night Fighter Squadron arrived at their new field on September 11, 1944. Coulommiers was a short 30 miles from Paris, which was of much interest to the night fighters. It had a concrete runway and they were close to the front.

Things started to heat up by the 21st. The Luftwaffe was

pulling the same trick in the 425th's sector as was happening with the 422nd NFS. During the period of daylight when the day fighters were down and the night fighters hadn't taken to the air yet, they would slip in and strafe the Allied troops. The 425th was assigned the job to get these "bandits." To accomplish this, they had six of their P-61s take off at 6:00p.m. to cover the areas the enemy were attacking. Though they did not intercept any of the raiders, the strikes ended shortly after the 425th NFS made its presence known. Once again that old night fighter axiom stands true: "Even if you never fire your guns you've done your job."

Three of the 425th's teams had great success on their intruder missions on the night of October 2nd. Two of these pairs were Capt. Francis V. Sartanowicz and his R/O, 1st Lt. Edward M. Van Sickels and Capt. Earl W. Bierer and his R/O, 2nd Lt. James Lothrop, Jr. P-47s had hit a bridge near Bullay, France, during the daylight hours and the night fighters were to keep the pressure on that night. Around midnight, the two teams arrived in the area of the bridge and found repair work going on under the illumination of bright flood lights. They caused much panic and destruction as they made multiple firing passes until they had expended all their ammunition. It was a good night for

"Wanderin' Wench II" of the 422nd NFS. Apparently their sister squadron, the 425th, did not indulge in getting colorful nose-jobs for their aircraft. (Thompson)

"Tactless Texan" of the 422nd NFS after flying a daylight NFT (night fighter test). (Stegner via Campbell)

these night fighter teams as they had each destroyed a locomotive earlier in the evening.

Their stay at Coulommiers was short lived. By the middle of October they were again packing all of their worldly possessions. This time they went to Prosnes, which is about 12 miles east of Rheims and some 92 road miles from Coulommiers. This field had a tarpaper runway! During their first two weeks in their new home it rained so hard that operations were grossly curtailed. On the night of October 28/29 the weather cleared and a "night fighters" moon was shining. The 425th "Intruder" Squadron hit the German rail and road networks hard.

On one of these intruder missions the 425th's CO, Maj. Leon G. "Gilly" Lewis and another of the squadron's P-61s piloted by 1st Lt. Alvin E. "Bud" Anderson were out to disrupt traffic. A number of major arteries crossed some miles north of Metz. The pair approached a long line of motor transports heading for the front. They were quite low, coming in from a southerly direction. Lewis radioed that he wanted to hit the column first. Before Anderson could answer, Lewis put on full power, roaring down on the unsuspecting vehicles with his cannon firing. Anderson was lining up for his pass as a tremendous explosion occurred lighting up the area. Anderson picked his targets and pressed his attack.

With such good pickings, both pilots prepared for a second pass. As they swooped down for the second time, the Germans managed to get their antiaircraft guns activated with some accuracy. Lewis' Widow had been hit quite severely. His radio was out and the hydraulic system was not operable. Both pilots felt the prudent thing was not to press their luck on a third pass. Explosions were still occurring, and they could see wreckage strewn all over. Both major highways were temporarily blocked.

The Last Big Push

December started out with good weather and the moon period was right. The Luftwaffe wasn't showing itself to any great extent so the 422nd NFS went on the offensive. The Black

Widows struck out on the 1st to terrorize the enemy. That night they ventured between Cologne and Koblenz in the Rhine Valley. Trains, barges, factories, and warehouses all came under intensive fire from the Widow's cannon. One would wonder what could have been done if the squadron had the external fuel tanks, bombs, and rockets that they had repeatedly requested.

The 422nd's A-20 "Bomber Command" went into action. Capt. Tadas Spelis became its commander and a number of the crews were checked out in the aircraft. With the assistance of the squadron's intelligence section and the cooperation of Marmite GCI station, a system of radar bombing was established including radio procedures. The engineering, ordnance, and communications sections of the squadron put in many long, hard hours to make the Havocs airworthy. Their "baptism under fire" came on the 5th when they dropped leaflets between Julich and Lianich.

One of the "bomber pilots" was Jim Postlewaite:

Night bombing, leaflet drops, we did it all. We dropped some flares, and then were supposed to fly down underneath the flares looking for enemy troop concentrations. All of this, while we were making our flight, were locked in with the gun laying radar back at a big tent behind the lines. If you did find a target you were supposed to tell them you were over it. This would be marked on a map, and then the artillery would serenade this one spot. But I'll tell you, I flew standing up, I didn't sit down on these because it was about a million candlepower flare which was most unique. Coming from Illinois, we have a fireworks firm, National Fireworks Company or something at Galesburg, Illinois; and they made the flares. We tested some of them before we tried them on a mission over the base. The flare was an old flare, it was made in 1942, but the parachute was sort of peculiar. It had been made in Japan. These things give a monstrous light when dropped about 5,000 or 6,000 feet. Then you flew down underneath it so you could see by the light, you did. They lit a mile in diameter; and boy, on snow you could see tracks. You could see everything. Of course, they could see you, too.

"The Creep" has the words "For Sale – Cheep" added to its distinctive decor. Lts. Grady and Werner pose beside the 425th's "IITYWYBAD???" while Lts. Zollars and Davis stand next to a catchy tune, "Sleepy Time Gal." Gilly Lewis' "Wabash Cannon-Ball" with dwarf stands ready for the squadron's C.O. It looks as if "Mah Ideel" has a pilot getting ready for a flight. (Greggs, 425th collection via Anderson for the next two, Greggs, & Roberts)

Samples of the nose art sported by some of the 422nd's Widows. "No Love, NO NOTHING II!" was the second P-61 of the squadron's C.O., Lt.Col. O.B. Johnson. With "Laura Lil" are Charles Troxell and Leonard Koehler. ("Hussy" & "Judy" Johnson, other 4 Stegner via Campbell)

On the evening of December 4, Andy Anderson and J.U. Morris successfully intercepted an He 111 some 10 miles northwest of Frankfurt-Rhine. From then until mid-month things were quiet. Most activity was on the offensive side of the ledger. The weather worsened and the month went on.

On the night of the 16th, there was a sense of something just about to happen. There were more than the usual number of reports of flares, bogies which could not be closed to visuals, aircraft flying with navigation lights on, and lights on the ground were coming in. IX TAC alerted the squadron that they were expecting more that the usual amount of activity.

At midnight, 1st Lt. Robert Bolinder and 2nd Lt. Robert Graham took off for their patrol between the VII Corps lines and the Rhine River. Within an hour GCI controllers had sent them off on what turned out to be inconclusive chases. Then at about 1:00 a.m. Marmite had yet a third bogie for them. This time AI contact was established, at about two miles. Closing through window to 900 feet, a visual was made – an Fw 190. It was taking mild evasive action, so Bolinder had no trouble decreasing the distance to between 100 and 50 feet. The crosses on the fuselage were clearly visible at this range by the light of the exhaust from the engine. Bolinder pulled up and dead astern and unleashed the sting of his four 20mm cannon. He saw several hits on the enemy followed shortly by a large white explosion in the engine. The Focke-Wulf wobbled for a moment and then fell off to port. The P-61 crew could not see the craft hit the ground because of cloud cover but Marmite confirmed the kill.

With the noticeable increase in both air and ground activity, all aircrews were put on alert. Three other 422nd crews followed them up. They had a number of chases, mostly low flying stuff. Nothing tangible to report.

Then Boly and Shorty went up for their second shift of the night. Within a half hour they shot a Bf 110 out of the sky. This was followed by an He 111. The crew observed windows along the fuselage of this one, probably converted for transport duty. What a night! Three destroyed – the old hat trick. But it wasn't

Aircrew members of the 422nd NFS: 2nd Lts. William G. Adams, Jr., 2nd Lt. Robert E. Tierney, T/Sgt Richard L. Heggie, Jr., and pilot 1st Lt. John W. Anderson. Bob Tierney, along with his pilot Paul Smith, would be credited with five enemy aircraft destroyed. Sgt. Heggie, the only enlisted R/O in the 422nd, was killed on the night of December 19th along with his pilot, 1st Lt. Donald W. Allee. (Tierney)

over yet. They were vectored to yet another bogie. In night fighting, positive visual identification was mandatory to preclude the accidental damage or destruction of friendly aircraft, though this did occur in a couple of incidences. Bolinder and Graham weren't sure on this one. It looked too much like a Lockheed Loadstar. He was not able to pursue and positively identify. Reports came back later on in the war that this was an Italian aircraft taking a number of top ranking Nazis to Spain. Lt. Bolinder would receive the Silver Star and the British Distinguished Flying Cross for this night's work.

Bolinder and Graham weren't the only successful ones. Capt. Robert O. Elmore and 2nd Lt. Leonard F. Mapes also had a successful patrol as they destroyed a Ju 88. Lts. Herman Ernst

"Little Nan" and "Bunny II" of the 425th. Posed with "Nan" are pilot Garth Peterson standing to the left and his R/O, John Howe, on the right. Crew chief Marvin Clark is between the aircrew while Luke Symkowski (mechanic) and Gene Jacobs (armament) are squatting. (Greggs & 425th collection via Anderson)

and "Mouse" Kopsel got themselves a Stuka (Ju 87). But they almost fell victim to a Bf 110 night fighter themselves. At one point Ernst found himself and the Messerschmitt on a collision course. The '61 crew sweated that one out. No claims on either side in that encounter; that is, if you don't count shattered nerves.

There was much activity on the ground as well as that in the air. One of the 422nd's crews that would attack the enemy on the ground was that of 1st Lt. Donald M. Shaw, pilot, and 2nd Lt. Jesse H. Jenkins, R/O. The considerable activity perked their interest and they went down to see what was going on. Jesse Jenkins recalls that mission:

I was on patrol the night before the Germans made contact on the ground. At about 15,000 feet we could see vehicles bumper to bumper on all roads actually as far as you could see on that clear night. They had lights on . . . it looked like millions! We, of course, notified our ground control while still in the air. Our patrols watched them all night long, but higher command would not give us permission to attack the columns. They could have called out the day fighters and bombers to work at night, but they calculated that it would be better to wait until dawn. They didn't know that the Germans were rolling ahead of a giant fog which grounded everything we had by daylight.

By the time the first light of dawn appeared in the morning skies of December 17th, everyone realized something big was happening. Germany's Operation "Grief," the Ardennes Counteroffensive – the Battle of the Bulge, was beginning. This was the first large scale offensive that the Germans had attempted in three years. Its purpose was to relieve the pressure being exerted by the US First and Third Armies to the north and south. Germany's Field Marshal Karl von Rundstedt had unleashed some eight panzer grenadier divisions and ten infantry divisions, including about 500 tanks in this all-out effort. All of the Cologne Plain, from the front lines to the Rhine and from Dusseldorf to Koblenz, was a beehive of activity. Convoys were in motion everywhere, beacons were blinking, and flares were being dropped as if a celebration was going on.

The makings of "Bomber Command" arrived when seven well used A-20Gs arrived at Florennes in late November. Thanks to a handful of 422nd mechanics who had gone to the Douglas A-20 school in Santa Monica, California, these aircraft were made air worthy. Just another minor miracle performed by the night fighters. (Stegner via Campbell)

Low level strafing disease caused this. The pilot held full left rudder and trim to fly straight. He almost lost it when first hit. Only one rudder worked. (425th collection via Anderson)

"Pistolshot" Postlewaite, "Junior" Lee, Herman Ernst, and "Shorty" Graham of the 422nd NFS. (Laird)

Stan Woolley, Cletus Ormsby, and Joe Webb of the 425th take a little time off from their intensive flying schedule for a little rest and relaxation. (425th collection via Anderson)

Battle damage along with poor weather and field conditions took their toll on the 422nd's P-61s as these six pictures show. External fuel tanks would have saved both aircraft and crew lives, but higher headquarters would not back such an undertaking. (Stegner, Anderson, Stegner next 4)

That night the weather had worsened. Waves of fog were ebbing and flowing around Florennes. On a positive note, the Allies had figured out the German's system of navigational aids and by 8:00p.m. had located their IP beacon. Col. Johnson and 1st Lt. Edgar Merriman were sent to the field at St. Trond, Belgium, at the end of their shift because the weather was so bad at Florennes. To add a little thrill to this adventure, a strafing Ju 88, with an RAF Mosquito in pursuit, came between them. This action shook up the troops in the tower and, when two more of the 422nd's P-61s requested to land, they were denied permission. These two aircraft went on to Chievres where after three passes 1st Lt. Roy S. Siegle finally landed – a half mile off the runway. An hour later Siegle was extricated from the wreckage with only minor cuts and bruises. His R/O, 2nd Lt. Bernard Orzel, came out unscathed. It wasn't as fortunate for 1st Lt. Donald W. Allee and his R/O, T/Sgt Richard L. Heggie. They had orbited over Chievres until Lt. Siegle finally got down. Lt. Allee decided he wasn't going to try and radioed the tower that they were going to try another field. That was the last that was heard

from them. They crashed about four miles east of the field, both were killed.

Both the A-20s and P-61s of the 422nd were busy hitting the enemy ground troops. First Lt. Eugene Axtell would be one of the P-61 pilots that would become quite proficient in these operations. One evening, after intercepting a number of aircraft that turned out to be friendlies, he spotted a train. With a "Let's get it," he put his Widow in a 45 degree dive and prepared to attack the train from the rear. At a few hundred feet from the ground Axtell leveled off and put his cannon into action. The plane shuddered from the blasts. Bright red objects were flying up at them from the left side – flak. Then the train exploded with such force that the P-61 was bounced vertically for a 100 feet or so. It was an ammunition train.

The weather grounded the night fighters for a number of nights. Their next time in the air was a daylight armed reconnaissance to Malmedy-St. Vith. Here they observed a sizeable German column making its way towards the Meuse River, some 32 miles from Florennes. The squadron launched a number of

Like their P-61 counterparts, "Bomber Command's" A-20s also suffered battle damage and the effects of the weather. (Stegner via Campbell)

OOPS! There were also those accidents that seem to happen, like this taxiing incident. The one on the right is from the 422nd while the one on the left is from the 425th. (Stegner via Thompson & 425th collection via Anderson)

aircraft to attack the approaching enemy but only one aircraft reached the target because of the bad weather. Two P-61s got into the air that night to chase the Luftwaffe. The team of Capt. Robert O. Elmore and 2nd Lt. Leonard F. Mapes got their second confirmed victory with the destruction of a Bf 110. It was a close call, according to the squadron's history:

Moe and Lenny dropped their second, a Bf 110, though "Killer" Elmore, making certain of his kill, did not open fire until the range was closed to less than 100 feet and his Widow came off second best when they flew through the explosion.

Both this crew and that of Paul Smith and Bob Tierney were diverted to an airfield near Brussels due to weather. This was a real "hardship" as the crews were grounded there for several days, and got to see some of Brussels.

On the day of Christmas Eve the Allies got the Christmas present that they needed – the weather cleared. During the day, Allied air power pounded the German forces. That night, the night fighters got into the action again. They hit the enemy both in the air and on the ground. "J.W." Anderson and James Morgan, J.W.'s R/O, got a Ju 88. Then Smith and Tierney got their third, a Ju 88. First Lt. Thomas H. Burleson and 2nd Lt. William P. Monahan also nearly got one. Both the P-61s and "Bomber Command's" A-20s hit the ground troops hard, strafing and bombing.

No day off on Christmas Day – there was a war to fight. Weather remained good and the night fighters carried on the good fight after the day fighters came home to rest. "J.W." and Morgan had a repeat engagement and depleted the German's air force by another Ju 88. Burleson and Monahan had better hunting this evening with a Bf 110 confirmed.

The night of December 26/27 was yet another fruitful night of hunting. Smith and Tierney got a pair of Ju 188s giving them a grand total of five confirmed (besides a V-1 destroyed). Herman Ernst and Eddie Kopsel also got to claim a Ju 188 destroyed, making the third for this team. Ernst recalls this mission:

We had engaged in a number of unsuccessful chases, when on the way back to base at angels 8 we saw these navigation lights. The aircraft was at about 2,000 feet; he was pretty low, going in an easterly direction and dropping flares. Peeling off, we went down and closed behind the target at 1,500 feet. Lt. Guba, our S-2, was in the gunner's seat behind me observing with the aid of night glasses. He identified the target as a Ju 188. By this time it was on a course of zero degrees angels 2 and at about 250 mph flying straight and level. As our range closed the enemy aircraft commenced taking evasive action. At around 500 feet I gave it one burst, fired from 12 o'clock, 5 degrees, and I see strikes on the fuselage. The enemy aircraft then opened fire from the dorsal turret. Then our aircraft pulled off to starboard to avoid over-shooting. Pulling back astern and slightly below, three bursts were fired striking right and left engines, both of which exploded. The Ju 188 then fell off to port, went straight in and exploded on impact with the ground.

But the inning wasn't over, more batters were standing by. First Lt. Eugene D. Axtell flying with 2nd Lt. Bernard Orzel as his R/O also got themselves a pair this night, a Ju 88 and a Ju 188. Unfortunately, Richard "Pete" Himelright was shot down some nine miles from their airfield. William Molinari, his R/O, successfully bailed out. Robert Danielson and Joseph Fiala

Cannibalization was the major source of "spares." (Stegner via Thompson)

When the Battle of the Bulge was over Maj.Gen. Elwood Quesada of IX Tactical Air Command came to Florennes and awarded very deserved medals to the 422nd troops. Lt.Col. Johnson, squadron commander, is on the far left. On the right is night fighter ace Eugene Axtell. (Ernst)

For their assistance during the Bulge operations, XIX TAC's commander, Brig.Gen. Otto P. Weyland, awards 425th aircrews with well deserved medals. (425th collection via Anderson)

learned you had to pay the price for overshooting a Stuka. The squadron's history tells the thrilling story:

They were shot up and Fiala wounded. Thinking him unconscious, and unable to bail out, Danny turned in a beautiful performance by landing in an ammo dump just inside the lines, near Marche. He was hurt in the process and found Fiala had vamoosed. He was later picked up safely, except for a wound in his leg.

Other injuries were suffered by the 422nd when a Bf 110 strafed their area at the airfield badly wounding three. The local antiaircraft gang brought revenge on the offending Messerschmitt when he attempted to make a second pass.

The last night of operations for the 422nd in 1944 was the next evening, December 27th. Capt. Tadas Spelis and 1st Lt. Eleutherios "Lefty" Eleftherion (R/O) finally got a confirmed, having numerous "almosts" over the past months. Their unlucky victim was a Bf 110. "The Skipper" (O.B. Johnson) and James "Pop" Montgomery got the last one for the year, a Ju 188.

December and the Battle of the Bulge were quite something for the 422nd NFS. They had been flying combat operations for over five months and had received only one replacement P-61. During the Bulge operations, they were operating with as few as four P-61s. The external fuel tanks and bomb racks would do much during these hectic days. With their A-20s, the 422nd managed to drop nearly 12 tons of bombs. For their effort, Ninth Air Force awarded the 422nd NFS the Distinguished Unit Citation, the sixth and last to be awarded by the Ninth for that campaign.

The Southern Flank

Ever on the move, the 425th NFS moved again on November 8. This time it was to Etain, a town some 15 miles northeast of Verdun. At this field the runways were "mesh and hesh" type. For the remainder of November, the squadron primarily flew interdiction missions. Their total for the month was 84 intruder missions and only 32 intercept patrols.

The Battle of the Bulge started with a bang for the 425th. On the night of December 22, a lone German aircraft dropped a 500 pound bomb on their field. From then on, it was fireworks galore. The next evening the 425th would be a participant in "The Battle." The squadron history relates this experience:

The famous 'Bulge' was still expanding and on the night of 23-24 December our planes were covering that general area in an attempt to check the Luftwaffe, which was up in strength. Lt. William A. 'Andy' Andrews and James E. 'The Kid' Kleinheinz were on the prowl near Oberstein. The targets were picked up by GCI on heading 250 degrees, altitude 11,000 feet, speed 190mph. 'We made positive visual identification at 1,000 feet,' related Andrews. 'It was a Ju 188 flying straight and level and apparently unaware that we were there. We closed in and could see the Nazi markings very clearly in the moonlight. We approached from below and slightly to port.

'I fired a burst into the fuselage from a range of 300 feet. The 188 went into a steep turn to port which gave us a good opening for a deflection shot. We could see the shells exploding between the port engine and the fuselage. The Kraut went into a steep dive with engine and nacelle burning. We followed it to 5,000 feet, at which point the '188 was still in a dive with fire increasing all along the left wing. We saw a fire on the ground.'

The "Mighty Mites," 2nd Lt. Cletus T. Ormsby and his R/O, 2nd Lt. Davis M. Howerton, Jr., were on patrol the following night. They were in the vicinity of Kaiserslautern when GCI brought Ormsby to within 500 feet of an enemy aircraft at 5,000 feet altitude. They identified it as an Do 217. Ormsby closed to 300 feet at 200mph when he sent his first salvo into the starboard engine, obtaining strikes. The Dornier burst into flames on the right wing and right engine and immediately went into a spin, crashing into the ground.

Christmas Day wasn't much of a holiday for the 425th. The weather was quite cold. The crew of 1st Lt. Van A. Neiswender and 2nd Lt. David E. Parsons were on a routine patrol around Bastogne. Two hours into this mission Marmite GCI vectored them to a bogey. Soon Parsons had AI contact. Apparently the German knew he was being pursued, as he dove for the deck. Neiswender jammed his throttles forward, heading down after the fleeing foe. In this high speed chase the P-61 crew got close enough to identify their target as an Me 410. At something over 400mph the Messerschmitt was able to pull away from the Widow. Lt. Neiswender could do nothing, "It was like I was standing still!"

Once again over Kaiserslautern, the 425th decreased the Luftwaffe's inventory. Second Lts. Jack E. Slayton and Arthur B. Ferris were on patrol this evening when GCI directed them to a target. Ferris got contact on his AI radar and directed Slayton towards the bogie. At 500 feet a visual was made, a Bf 110. A 25 minute pursuit ensued as the German went through violent evasive action in an attempt to escape. Closing to 300 feet Lt. Slayton fired several bursts from dead astern. His shots were right on the money as the plane exploded and fire spread rapidly. The Bf 110 went into a vertical dive, both engines afire, and crashed about 20 miles east of Metz.

The next night the team of 1st Lt. Walter Stacey and 2nd Lt. Stephen F. Mason destroyed a Ju 188 south of Trier. That same night "Andy" and "The Kid" got their second confirmed, a Ju 88. To close out the year, the "Mighty Mites" got a Ju 88, plus another one damaged on the 30th; and for a repeat performance on the 31st, they got a Bf 110 making their total three.

One of these night kills credited to the 425th is chronicled in the history of XIX TAC's communications history from the view of the controller:

Jerry was flying in a few Ju 88s and 188s, and an occasional Me 110. He was flying out a few less. At 1740, on the afternoon of December 26th, Empire 22 was airborne on patrol. Lt. Robert Moffatt vectored him out to the patrol line, keeping a sharp look out for 'bogies.' There were a number of tracks on the screen – some C-47s in the "bulge," a squadron of fighter-bombers returning from a mission, everything identified as friendly by TCC. It was all pretty quiet until 1918 when track No.7 appeared. It started to come in from the east, and TCC said that there were no friends in that area – it must be hostile. 'Bandit – 15 miles, Empire 22,' said Moffatt on the R/T, 'Starboard 185 degrees.' 'Roger' came back 22 and the chase was on. 'Range now 12, angels 11.5.' 'Roger.' 'Range 8, bandits speed 200, on a heading of 275 degrees,' continued Moffatt, as 22 began to close in. "Range 6, Starboard 230, bandit now at angels 10.' 'Range 4, Starboard 250.' 'Roger,' then 15 seconds later, 'starboard 270 degrees, bogies course.' 'Roger – Contact.' 22 had picked up his quarry with his airborne radar and was taking over. And then followed seemingly interminable moments of silence. Empire 22 was on inter-com. Pilot and R/O were closing in for the kill, the job from the ground had been done, at least for the time being; and while two planes fought in the sky some 40 miles away, controllers, scope readers, plotters, tellers, radio men – the

scores of personnel required to keep MEW functioning, were sweating it out. And then at 1925, actually only three minutes had elapsed, 'Hello Rip 5, Empire 22. Murder!' 'Roger. Congratulations 22, what was it?' 'A Ju 88, and now how about taking me home, my gravy's getting low.'

While the 425th were experiencing good hunting in the December night skies, they were having equal success as they continued their night intruder operations. Lt. Alvin "Bud" Anderson and his R/O, Lt. John Smith, were bringing down death and destruction on the Nazi marshalling yards. On one of these missions Anderson, while at altitude looking for targets of opportunity, spotted some light. He dove his Widow at terrific speed heading for the light. As he leveled off, thundering across a railroad yard, he set his cannons aroar. Four locomotives blew up on their first pass. The train crews were so panicked that the crew of a fifth engine left its headlight on. Anderson and Smith couldn't let this present go ignored. Cranking his bomber-size fighter around, Lt. Anderson made another pass, destroying the remaining locomotive.

The intruder missions didn't always involve large targets as locomotives. One of these missions involved a German courier. The courier had been observed making nightly runs in an area east of Bastogne. Headquarters wanted to disrupt this method of communication. First Lt. Garth E. Peterson and 2nd Lt. John A. Howe were given the duty to check this out one December night. Other crews of the 425th had seen the courier, usually around midnight. So at the appointed time Peterson and Howe circled the vicinity that they expected to encounter their query. Flying at tree top level, they were on the lookout. Soon he was sighted. Lt. Peterson cranked his Widow around, coming in fast and low from the rear, and "walked" this 20mm fire up the road. It all happened too fast for the unsuspecting motorcycle rider. All of a sudden all Peterson could see was the light of the motorcycle tumbling through the air – and then nothing. Other crews checked out the area in nights to come, but the Germans were not sending couriers by that route any longer.

All jobs in night fighting are not glamorous, but can be quite necessary. One of these "unsung heroes" of the December push was 1st Lt. John R. Allen, engineering officer of the 425th NFS. He and his engineering crews had a remarkable record for keeping worn out airplanes operational, without having the proper support equipment or spares. Lt. Allen's men were cited for averaging 55 hours more per engine than any other squadron in the European Theater of Operations. This meant much initiative, resourcefulness, and many long days spent in rain, snow and mud up to somewhere.

With all the activity in the night skies, the pickings were good. Lts. Richard R. Gray and Jack W. Robinson got a Ju 188 confirmed south of Bingen. Capt. Russell Glasser and Lt. William M. Tripp got themselves a probable as well as Capt. Francis V. "Whiskey" Sartanowicz and 1st Lt. Edward M. Van Sickels who damaged another. December was quite a month for the 425th NFS. During the period of December 16 thru the 27th, they destroyed five enemy aircraft, 58 trucks, three locomotives and 16 railroad cars.

In late 1944, the Army Air Forces started looking for a successor for the P-61. The A-20/P-70 Havocs were past their prime and the A-26 was contemporary with the Widow. Jet powered aircraft would be the ultimate night fighter, but to span the gap, the long range P-82 Twin Mustang was a potential choice. The day fighter variant was on the drawing boards, and the addition of AI radar was not seen as a problem. (Bowers' Collection via Castle Graphics and North American Aviation)

Chapter 16

Advance Designs

The Havoc Trudges On

In early 1943 the Air Forces had dispatched all of the P-70s it could to the Pacific theater and to the Florida night fighter training organization. More night fighters were needed. The P-61 would not be fielded for at least a year and the British were big on promises but slow on delivery. To fill the gap, additional A-20s were modified.

It had been Douglas Aircraft's suggestion that A-20C models be made into night fighters, but they also suggested, that the standard armament be retained. Thus SCR-540 AI radar was installed. Its transmitting antenna protruded from the aircraft's nose along with the six .50 cal. machine guns that were there. Unlike the P-70, the P-70A-1 also had a crew station for a radio operator/gunner who could man the downward aimed flexible .50 cal. gun. This third man was carried quite often in the Pacific when the P-70s there flew intruder missions. These aircraft also had another flexible single .50 cal. machine gun that could be operated by the R/O. This version of the A-20/P-70 was fitted with the R-2600-23 engine. A number of these aircraft went to the 6th, 418th, 419th, and 421st Night Fighter Squadrons in the Pacific with the remainder going to the night fighter training organization in Florida.

Additional A-20s were modified that same year, these were the A-20G. These were designated P-70A-2. Engines, armament and crew size were the same as the P-70A-1. The records seen to be somewhat unclear as to who did the modifying on these two P-70 variants. Douglas Aircraft, some sources indicate, did some; AAF modification centers and local depots did others. Some of the original 59 P-70-DO aircraft were modified by Air Materiel Command's Middletown Air Depot in Pennsylvania. Here they replaced the long wave SCR-540 AI radar set with the early centimetric SCR-520.

In 1944 an A-20G was modified into the only P-70B-1 to be made. SCR-720 AI and SCR-729 IFF radar was installed. Three .50 cal. machine guns were installed in blisters on each side of the fuselage and up to 2,000 pounds of bombs could be carried on external hard points. Government documents indicate Douglas modified this one aircraft.

Additional A-20Gs and some J models were similarly configured at modification centers. Some of the A-20 modification work was accomplished at Chicago and Southern Airlines modification center in Memphis, Tennessee. These aircraft, designated P-70B-2, normally did not carry the three .50 cal. blister guns on its side. The reason seems to stem from an aerodynamic problem the single P-70B-1 was having. Flight testing of that aircraft showed that the gun blisters disturbed the air flow to the airplane's tail surfaces. These aircraft were used strictly in stateside training, most being redesignated TP-70B-2.

Super Widow

The P-61s biggest complaint from the field was the desire to increase its speed, altitude and the capability to decelerate when approaching a target. It should be noted that these characteristics were very desirable, but most pilots interviewed felt that these shortcomings did not severely hamper their operations. Due to the scarcity of enemy aircraft to intercept, most of the night air action was over by the time the Widow got into combat. So most of the American night fighter squadrons turned to intruder type work.

The AAF requested that Northrop, in conjunction with Wright Field, make a study regarding the installation of fighter brakes suggesting that they be installed on about the 201st aircraft. Northrop concluded that the earliest possible aircraft would be the 701st plane. The go-ahead was given, and P-61A, serial number 42-5485, was so modified. Northrop test pilot, Max Stanley, flew most of the test flights, including one hair raiser:

The original night fighter Havocs in the Air Corps were modified Douglas A-20-DO redesignated as P-70-DO. The major changes in this modified Havoc were the deletion of the troublesome turbo-superchargers, the installation of American produced British Mk. IV AI radar which was designated SCR-540, and four 20mm cannons in a tub attached to the belly of the aircraft. These aircraft saw service in the Pacific and, for a while, in the Panama Canal Zone. (McDonnell Douglas/Harry Gann)

Many of the P-70-DOs went to the night fighter training program in Florida. A number of these aircraft had their SCR-540 radar replaced with SCR-520 microwave AI radar. The SCR-520 was Western Electric's production version of the Radiation Lab's AI-10. (Ernst)

I had one flight where one dive brake opened when a casting broke. The asymmetrical drag brought about by this condition caused the airplane to go through some pretty wild gyrations. My first instinct was to bail out, and I made a gesture to unlatch the escape hatch. When (Eustace P.) Hetzel, the flight test engineer, saw me do this, it was his signal to get the hell out. He bailed out. Then I felt that I was pretty low, getting ready to go in; I was just east of the field. By that time I had slowed down enough so that the airplane was controllable. I landed without any problem.

In late 1943 the AAF requested studies be made concerning engine changes which would increase the altitude and speed of the P-61 night fighter and for a modification plan for a bomber escort variant. On November 11, 1943, the Air Technical Service Command was tasked with the responsibility of developing a plan to improve the P-61s performance characteristics. This request led to many study programs and long discussions with Northrop Aircraft officials, designers and engineers in an endeavor to find a most feasible manner for increasing its performance. Two major choices were considered; a type "C" engine with a two stage gear driven supercharger, or a turbo supercharger. Forces at Northrop headed by Dr. William Sears, Chief Aerodynamicist, Irving Ashkenas, and John M. Wild had preferred a turbo supercharger installation from the outset of the Air Corps design, but other powers, both at Northrop and in the Air Corps had other ideas. After all, the initial design for the English was not for high altitude, and it was this basic design that the Air Corps bought. This latest study was conducted under the direction of John Wild. His conclusions, and agreed to by Wright Field's Fighter Project Office, was that a turbo installation would give a much better performance. The initial prediction was 430 MPH (IAS) at 30,000 feet. An idea of Wild's was to incorporate a heat exchanger to cool the exhaust before the turban. This provided for a cooler exhaust and much-damped pulsations in the exhaust flow, besides providing hot air for de-icing. In early December of 1943, Northrop engineers

Next, A-20C and G models were modified into night fighters and designated P-70A-1-DO and P-70A-2-DO, respectively. These aircraft were equipped with the long-wave SCR-540 AI and were equipped with .50 cal. machine guns in the nose in lieu of the 20mm cannons in the belly tub. They also had provisions for machine guns at the R/Os station and another below him which could be fired by a radio operator/gunner. Like the P-70-DO, the P-70As saw service in the Pacific as well as being part of the night fighter training program. (Bockstege)

provided ATSC with their preliminary studies. On December 30, 1943, as a result of this report, procurement was directed to allow one P-61 with the type CH5 turbo-superchargers to be installed in a standard P-61A.

The designation of this new Widow was the XP-61C. Northrop's facilities were operating at their capacity and both Northrop and the AAF agreed that the modification work had to be accomplished elsewhere. Goodyear Aircraft in Akron, Ohio was selected; they were already manufacturing the outer wing panels and empennage for Northrop.

An Army R-2800-77 engine was to be the engine used. However, due to delays that were encountered in obtaining the production engine, which were sorely needed for front-line defensive and offensive aircraft, the Navy R-2800-14 engines were used. The difference between the -77 and the Navy -14 were minor and would have no significant effect on the per-

More A-20Gs and some A-20Js were modified as the P-70B-1 but were designated P-70B-2. Because of problems associated with the .50 cal. machine gun installation when the guns were fired, most of these aircraft were not equipped with the guns. (NASM/Smithsonian)

formance of the CH5 turbo-superchargers. In early January 1944, arrangements were made to obtain the -14W engines from the Navy, and two were delivered in late May 1944 as well as spares in July. In mid-February a P-61A-5 (serial number 42-5559) was selected for use on this project. Because of conflicts with the "C" model production effort, it was decided in April to

redesignate the experimental aircraft XP-61D. At the same time Northrop requested permission to select P-61A-10, 42-5587, to be used as a spare in case something happened to 42-5559, and thus prevent any further delays in the project.

On April 1, 1944, 42-5559 was accepted and delivered April 13, 1944; and 42-5587 was delivered on May 3, 1944. Both aircraft were flown to Goodyear in Akron, Ohio. On May 4, 1944, 42-5587 arrived at Akron, followed by 42-5559 about a month later. Proposed gross weight of these aircraft was 32,200 pounds, with a maximum speed of 430 MPH at 30,000 feet. With the installation of the CH5 turbo-supercharger, the service ceiling was raised to 41,000 feet for both aircraft, and the maximum weight fully loaded for the aircraft had risen to over 40,000 pounds. The first engine run came on November 18, 1944. Development of the XP-61D was hampered by numerous engine failures and problems with the cooling of the CH5 turbo-supercharger due to the intense heat produced by this unit which was to prove the downfall of the XP-61D project. The standard propeller blades used on the P-61 were replaced by the A.O. Smith SPA-9 paddle blades which were a much broader propeller which would hopefully absorb the increased power of the supercharged R-2800-14. Curtiss Aircraft had supplied 836 blades, which were used on the standard production models of the P-61A.

One of the XP-61D engines blew a copper gasket separating the supercharger assembly from the superheated gases of the supercharger. This resulting temperature rise annealed the wing structure of the entire aircraft causing it to become extremely

Left: The last Havoc night fighter variant was the P-70B. An A-20G was modified into the sole P-70B-1-DO. This aircraft was equipped with SCR-720 AI radar and had .50 cal. machine guns attached to the fuselage sides in blisters. (Miller via Thompson)

brittle and resulted in the scrapping of the entire aircraft. In about January 1945 the AAF took over the major portion of the testing program. After a number of engine failures the program was halted. It was felt that cooling tests should be conducted prior to further testing. Upon completion of the cooling tests, the first production P-61C was available so the decision was made to conduct all further performance tests on the production "C" model instead. The "C" included improvements derived from the earlier XP-61D tests.

The XP-61Ds were used as test beds for working out production problems in the "C" program. By the fall of 1945 they were in such a need of repair that the AAF placed them in a Ol-Z classification. Number 42-5559 was lost to reclamation on September 11, 1945 and 42-5587 in April 1946.

The P-61C was perhaps to be the ultimate of all night fighter aircraft of the P-61 line. Indeed, this aircraft was probably to be the most successful of all night fighter aircraft produced during war. Unfortunately for Northrop, the completion of the first P-61C, and its acceptance on July 14, 1945, was to prove too late to enter the World War II conflict. With the completion of the 46th P-61C, V-J Day was at hand, and immediate cutbacks in defense spending were to terminate the P-61s fighting career. The P-61C was powered by two Pratt & Whitney R-2800-73 engines with 2100 horsepower rating on each engine, and a war emergency rating of 2800 horsepower each. Each engine was to have the two-speed CH5 turbo-superchargers; and these engines, coupled with a newly designed Curtiss electric full-feathering propeller and the A.O. Smith paddle bladed props, which were both fully automatic or could be operated manually, would be the best of all engine-propeller combinations of the P-61 development program. The clean R-2800 engine line was now changed by the addition of airscoops on either side of the engine nacelle similar to the cheek scoops used on the Martin B-26. However, they were in the inverted position when compared with those of the Martin. These cheek cowlings provided the additional volumes of air for the ravenous superchargers used on the R-2800-73 engines. About 11,250

The turbo installation mockup for the XP-61C. Because of concurrent flight testing and the AAF's desire for production aircraft, the experimental aircraft were redesignated XP-61D while the production aircraft were designated P-61Cs. (Northrop)

The new Pratt & Whitney's have been installed, but the changeover to the wide-chord propellers has not taken place yet. (From the Collection of Pratt & Whitney Aircraft)

The speed brakes can be clearly seen in the extended position. They are not normally extended on one wing only. This occurred during a flight test in which test pilot Max Stanley was able to safely land the aircraft. Note the housing in the background. On a number of occasions these residents found that it was not the safest place to live. In one incident, they were doused with a purple dye solution in a chemical dispersing test with an airborne P-61 over the airfield. On another occasion, the .50 cal. machine guns on a Widow's turret accidentally went off, hitting a number of the houses. (Northrop)

cubic feet per minute of air was sucked into these huge engines at the high blower stage. Over heating problems and super-charger/engine fires caused the loss of a number of these aircraft.

Another novel innovation of the P-61C design was the fighter brake which had been previously requested by the P-61 pilots who had flown the aircraft in combat and had the unfortunate experience of overshooting a pursued aircraft. The fighter brakes were similar to a picket fence on both upper and lower surfaces of the wings of the P-61C. These fighter brakes were perforated structures which were hinged antagonistically such that the raising of the top brake assisted in the lowering of the bottom fighter brake. This system was used to minimize forces actuating the brakes. Since the speed of the P-61C had risen appreciably from the P-61A and B to approximately 430 MPH, these fighter brakes were thought to be a necessity to avoid overshooting pursued targets and provide a more accurate stable gun platform. The counter forces exerted upon the

aircraft fighter brakes at high speed were equal approximately to 1G.

The test pilot who first flew the P-61C with fighter brakes was Max Stanley. Stanley while performing a maximum per-formance dive near Hawthorne, California, activated the fighter brakes and the huge aircraft seemed to stop in mid-air. This is still very vivid in Stanley's memory:

I think that one of the most interesting phases of the test work was the P-61C, the one with the dive brakes. We had to demonstrate the use of dive brakes at maximum indicated air speed, at the critical Mach number and at maximum load factor. When all three points came together, you have a real problem. I pulled the airplane apart with the dive brakes. As a result of my experience it was determined that at high Mach numbers for that airplane there was a shift in the span-wise lift distribution, and also a change in the airflow over the wings.

The change in the airflow over the wing pretty much blanked out the elevator so that when the dive brake opened you almost have to zero

Because Northrop's facilities were at capacity, the modification effort on the two P-61As that were to become XP-61Ds was contracted out to Goodyear in Akron, Ohio. Here P-61A-10, s/n 42-5587, arrived over Akron with an escort of three Goodyear Corsairs. (Goodyear Aerospace Corp. via Daniels)

the stick force, and that is just what happened in my case. When you dive against 4.67Gs I guess, and considering all factors, the stick just came back in my lap; and I saw the accelerometer peg at 8G's, a couple of times. The wings broke loss, then both booms came off.

My guardian angel was looking out after me. When the first failure occurred, I think it was the wings that occurred first, the airplane pitched down. It was so violent that it threw me forward and tore the seat right out of the structure. I hit my face on the windscreen. I reached back to undo the canopy, but it was already gone; it must have left when we first pitched. As I undid my safety belts the plane tucked, and I was catapulted out.

Observers on the ground say that Stanley could not have been more than a few hundred feet off the ground when he managed to bail out of the doomed aircraft.

Only 41 P-61Cs were produced. The remainder of airframes that were on the assembly line were either cut up, scrapped or used in the production of the F-15A photo recon Reporter. If the jet aircraft had not been developed so rapidly during the World War II period and subsequent thereto, the P-

61C would have remained in the US Air Force arsenal for a great number of years, since the aircraft was truly ahead of its time in both design and development. Only a few of the 41 Cs produced were integrated with P-61Bs in post war night fighter/all weather fighter squadrons.

A study had been undertaken in mid-1944 on a turbo-supercharged night fighter, designated the XP-61F. The XP-61F was quite similar to the XP-61E bomber escort fighter except for the turbo installation and some equipment changes. P-61C, serial number 43-8338, had been selected for modification into this configuration; but when the project was cancelled on October 24, 1945, it was completed as a standard "C."

Radar Directed Gunfire

Further advancement in weaponry was the modification of P-61Bs into the -25 configuration. These aircraft were to be equipped with a computer and gun aiming radar. Though initial quantities of ten were ordered only seven were actually modified, and these aircraft never proceeded beyond the prototype stages due to fire control problems that plagued these aircraft during the evaluation at Hammer Field in California and for a number of years afterwards at Eglin Field in Florida.

Below: The finished product. The two XP-61Ds would be scrapped shortly after the war's end, which also marked the climax and end of the piston-engined fighter as a primary weapon of war. (Northrop via Balzer)

Close-ups of the turbo-supercharged R-2800 engine installation. (From the Collection of Pratt & Whitney Aircraft and Northrop via Balzer)

Night Lightning

Along with Douglas and Northrop Aircraft, Lockheed entered the night fighter field with the modification of the P-38. The AAF realized that the P-70 was falling short of their expecta-

tions. In the summer of 1943, a P-38J-5 (serial no. 42-67104) was assigned to Wright Field, Ohio, where it was to be used as a test bed for a set of Navy AN/APS-4 AI radar. The first location tried for the radar "bomb" (the container for the radar antenna and black boxes) was under the fuselage to the rear of

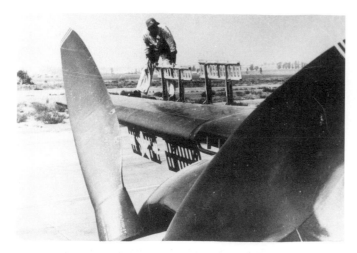

Closeup of the P-61Cs fighter brakes in the extended position. The upper fighter brakes were linked to the lower set in such a manner that air coming over the top of the wing would push the upper set back. They were mechanically linked to the lower set and pushed the lower ones forward into the airstream. (Northrop via Balzer)

the nose wheel area. In this location, ejected cartridge cases from the plane's guns struck the plastic nose of the "bomb" and caused it to crack or shatter.

To eliminate the dome damage, the "bomb" was next installed under the wing, outboard of the right engine. At about this time, in early 1944, the testing was turned over to the AAF Tactical Center at Orlando, Florida. Here the actual flight testing was carried out by Squadron F of the 904th AAF Base Unit at Kissimmee Field.

The flight tests showed that the right engine of the plane blanked out 25 deg. on the left side of the radar coverage, and that the remaining coverage was 50 deg. left to 70 deg. right of the airplane's heading. Difficulty was encountered when operating the APS-4 (also known as ASH) equipment at or near the same levels as towering cumulus or cumulo-nimbus clouds, though this was not unusual for other types of airborne radar at

that time. The indicator showed considerable return from clouds or layers of cloud within the sweep of the radar. Distant cloud indications could be distinguished from true target indications, but cloud returns from huge cumulus could cover the indicator to such an extent as to render the equipment useless.

These tests seemed to be more of an evaluation of the handling of the aircraft with the radar modification that of it as a night fighter. The flight tests were flown by four day fighter pilots who were familiar with the Lightning and had limited knowledge of radar operations, and by one pilot "acquainted" with radar operation but had limited knowledge of the P-38.

They found that the flight characteristics of the P-38 with the radar attached were not materially affected. It was felt that special training was needed for night fighter pilots before operating a single seat P-38 with AI under combat conditions. At the end of the Night Lightning evaluation, it was recommended

E.P. Hetzel, Hugo R. Pink, and Max R. Stanley in early "high altitude" flight suits. Max Stanley would have a number of hair-raising experiences in the P-61 flight test program. (Northrop via Pink)

AAF test pilots on the P-61C program included Lt. H.H. Johnson on the left and Capt. Warren E. Foss on the right. (Northrop)

The production P-61C did not make it in time to see service during the war and in peace time only a few were integrated in Air Defense Command's P-61B equipped squadrons. Most of the P-61Cs duties were with Air Materiel Command and other test organizations. (Northrop via Balzer)

When the P-61C contract was cancelled, this aircraft and others would be scrapped. Only 41 of the "C" models would be delivered to the Air Force. (Northrop via Balzer)

that the radar pod be placed under the fuselage in front of the nose wheel and that a Radar Observer's position be added.

While the P-38 evaluation was taking place in Florida during 1944, the AAF night fighter training establishment at Hammer Field in California was carrying out their own P-38 night fighter program. There were three different installations of the APS-4 radar equipment tried on P-38 aircraft at Hammer Field in an attempt to determine the best possible position for this equipment. In two of these installations no provisions were made for a radar observer. The third installation was a modification of a P-38J into a piggyback configuration allowing room for a radar observer. The positioning of the APS-4 equipment during the Hammer Field tests was found unsatisfactory. In two of the installations the equipment was installed under the fuselage, aft of the nose wheel well, thus restricting upward scanning of the radar. In the other installation, the equipment was mounted on the right outer wing panel thus restricting scanning to the left because of interference with the right engine nacelle.

From Hammer Field P-38J-20, S/N 44-23336, was sent to the Pacific in early 1944 for flight test evaluation. This aircraft was one of the single seat radar equipped P-38s. The pilots

evaluation of this aircraft was almost identical with the conclusion that the 547th had made with their single seat radar equipped P-38Js. The pilot's evaluation states:

During moonlight periods this airplane should be as capable as, or more capable than, the P-61. During these periods the airplane can be flown with reference to the ground and horizon; more time may be spent observing the indicator; the airplane can be maneuvered more rapidly; and the night blinding effect of the indicator is negligible. During darkness periods or inclement weather this plane is unsatisfactory. Tracking during any evasive action by the target is impossible. The night blinding effect of the indicator is slight. Due to the scarcity of enemy aircraft in this theater, and the fact that raids usually consist of one or two airplanes, it would not be worth a chance to try to intercept with this airplane when the P-61 is so far more dependable.

Around mid-year a two-place P-38J piggyback was also sent to the Philippines for evaluation. The major problem found with this aircraft was the cramped position from which the radar operator had to work, and on the whole did not find favor with the crews that had to operate it.

Above: The P-38J-5 Lightning after its second modification at Wright Field is ready for trials as a night fighter. Below: -The AN/APS-4 radar is now carried in a pod under the starboard wing (the initial installation under the fuselage to the rear of the nose wheel bay had been found unsatisfactory). (AAF via Greenhalgh)

Drawing experience from the P-38 night fighter tests both at Hammer Field and in the Pacific, Lockheed's Dallas Modification Center undertook to redesign a P-38L-5 into a true night fighter configuration. The chief engineer on this project was Robert C. Pote who, with Harry Shuhart as the project engineer, was backed up by A.M. McConnell on the structures section of Lockheed's Burbank plant. A completely modified aft compartment was designed for the radar operator with the radar "bomb" being mounted under the nose of the aircraft forward of the nose wheel well.

A P-38L-5, serial number 44-25237, was selected as the night fighter guinea pig. It arrived at the Lockheed-Dallas Modification Center at Love Field on October 26, 1944. During its various stages of modification in January of 1945 numerous flight tests were undertaken by Lockheed to determine the effects on the aircraft's flying ability due to the modifications.

On February 5, 1945, modification work was completed, and an Air Force team composing of personnel from Wright and Hammer Fields were present at Dallas to observe and participate in the flight tests in this new night fighter. The first flight took place on that same date during which all handling characteristics seemed to be comparable to the standard P-38L-5 with the exception that war Emergency Power could not be obtained at critical altitudes.

The sixth flight a few nights later was being made to check the operation of the AN/APN-1 radio altimeter and to obtain an approximate indication of the speed difference brought about by operating and closing the intercooler doors. During take-off, just as the wheels broke ground, the left engine failed completely. The pilot was able to right the plane and place it back on the ground; but due to the combat loading of the airplane and the shortness of the field, he was unable to bring the airplane to a stop before reaching the field's boundary, and the airplane was demolished in the resulting collision.

It was felt by all observers that this prototype night fighter had attained satisfactory results, and it was determined that the Lockheed Dallas Modification Center should proceed with the production model, the P-38M-5 Night Lightning. The purpose of the P-38M was to supplement the P-61B until such time as an improved P-61 could be produced, presumably the P-61C. The Dallas Modification Center received orders almost immediately to convert 75 P-38L-5 day fighters into P-38M-5 night fighters.

By early March 1945 the Air Forces had a schedule established for the first dozen or so of the black Lightnings. The first two would be used in flight test operations at the Lockheed-Dallas Modification Center. Aircraft number three was slated for the Proving Ground Command at Eglin Field, Florida. The following eight M's were allocated to Far East Air Forces where they would undergo combat suitability testing. Subsequent craft were to be assigned to the 319th Wing at Hammer Field, California, to participate in the night fighter training there.

Ship three was scheduled to be used in the Operational Suitability Test, initial plans calling for it to arrive at Eglin Field, Florida on May 15, 1945. It wasn't until June 30th that the P-38M finally arrived. For the next two months the P-38M-5

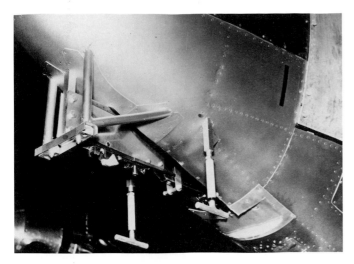

Lockheed's modification to the P-38L-5 at Dallas, Texas, for the installation of the ASH type AI radar. To the right, the radar "bomb" is installed. (Lockheed)

Somewhat cramped quarters for the pilot (above) and R/O (right). The one R/O that had written that the R/Os area was comfortable stood under 5'5". (Lockheed)

was flown against a standard P-38L-5 and a somewhat "test weary" P-61B.

The P-38M was found operationally suitable as a night fighter as far as airplane performance and characteristics were concerned. But, before Air Proving Ground Command would give its seal of approval, three of its 12 recommendations to improve general suitability had to be carried out: (1) the interphone system had to be improved; (2) only men of small stature (maximum of 5 feet 6 inches height and 150 pounds weight) could be assigned as radar operators; and (3) the single fluorescent light be removed from the control column and be replaced by two, one on each side of the cockpit.

Compared to the P-38L-5, the Ms handling qualities and flying characteristics had not been materially affected, though its top speed was about 15 miles per hour lower. Its combat radius of action with two 165-gallon external fuel tanks was found to be approximately 700 miles – not any better than the P-61B; range was one of the major complaints against the P-61.

In the Florida tests, the P-38M was found superior to the P-61B in speed at altitudes, rate of climb, operational ceiling, and ease of flying at high speeds. War Emergency power was not always obtainable on either of the aircraft which prevented a complete evaluation.

The first conversion of a P-38L-5 by the Lockheed-Dallas Modification Center into the night fighter configuration. This particular aircraft was destroyed at the end of its sixth flight, but the loss did not alter plans for the modification of a batch of aircraft to similar configuration as P-38M-5s. (Lockheed)

The P-38M cockpit as modified for a crew of two. The crew areas of the P-61 and P-38M were like comparing a luxury sedan to a sports car. Comfort of the P-38 crew depended a lot on the height and weight of the crew member. (Lockheed)

The P-38M was, like its day fighter P-38L counterpart, capable of carrying HVARs on "trees." The 547th NFS in the Pacific found that their night fighter modified P-38s were well suited for the ground attack role. (Lockheed)

The ultimate end for most of the "Ms" was the scrap yard. A great majority of the Lightnings modified into night fighters never saw service even in the night fighter training organization. (Bowers' Collection via Castle Graphics)

The test report concluded:

The equipment carried by the P-61B gives it a certain advantage over the P-38M. Its armament, three-man crew and turret give it flexibility in the manner of approach to the enemy airplane, and ability to cope with evasive tactics without resorting to extreme maneuvers. The greater variety of specialized radar and radio equipment increases its effectiveness. The gunner is in an excellent position for visual search, and he can maintain a higher degree of dark adaptation than the pilot. This would result in a higher percentage of visual contacts.

The P-38M, because of its fixed armament, can make only one effective approach to an enemy airplane at night – a level stern approach. If the enemy airplane attempts evasive action, the P-38 airplane must maneuver just as violently or else repeat the chase from the beginning. The pilot has no help in visual search, and his own dark adaptation will be impaired by instrument illumination, and the necessity of changing the focus of his eyes.

Photographed shortly after the end of the war, these five P-38Ms were assigned to Hammer Field, California, for training use; the radar pods are not installed. Shortly after this photograph was taken, the aircraft were flown to a scrap yard. (Fraser)

Another long range escort fighter was also considered for the next generation night fighter-the jet powered Bell XP-83. The first flight of the XP-83 took place on February 25, 1945. It had a range of 1,580 miles with internal fuel only; this could be extended to 2,200 miles with external tanks. Its service ceiling was 45,000 feet and it had a max speed of 468 mph (some sources show a maximum speed of 522 mph at 15,600 feet). (Bell)

In all-around effectiveness the P-38M would probably be superior to the P-61B because its performance would enable it to intercept enemy airplanes which the P-61B is incapable of intercepting. Against enemy types which both airplanes are capable of intercepting, the P-61B would probably prove more effective because of its superior equipment and armament arrangement.

The training of crews to fly the Night Lightning started in earnest in early 1945. About six pilots and a like number of R/Os, most having already been in combat, were gathered together at Hammer Field. Their aircraft were the Piggy-Back P-38Js. The two-place Piggy-Backs, designated TP-38J (official Air Forces sanction of this designation is in question) had been modified with the APS-4 AI radar. There was only a makeshift seat for the R/O – in fact, it wasn't really a seat, he sat on a portion of the wing. The R/Os feet hung over the main spar, down along each side of the pilot.

By early summer the organization had changed somewhat. A group consisting of a mix of four combat experienced crews and four crews fresh from the regular AAF night fighter training program was established. Somewhat later another group was formed; the exact number and mix (of veterans and neophytes) is not known. The plan was for this elite group to be trained in the Night Lightning, then to go overseas to train and lead others in this aircraft.

The five P-38Ms assigned to the night fighter training program finally arrived in July 1945. Now the pressure was on – gunnery, airborne intercept training, and night operations were all the order of the day. Gunnery training took place around Van Nuys in southern California. During these missions, it was not uncommon to run into other fighter types, such as P-51s from Oxnard and Navy F6F Hellcats and F7F Tigercats. Being the sportsmen that fighter pilots are, a mock dog fight was not unusual.

Above and two below: The Air Force awarded a contract to Curtiss-Wright on December 26, 1945 for the XP-87 Blackhawk. Hindsight would tell us that the Air Force would probably have been better off with the P-83. The XP-87 made its first flight on February 15, 1948. A comparison of the P-82F, XP-83, and XP-87 is interesting (all AF Museum):

Aircraft:	XP-82	XP-83	XP-87
First Flight:	6/12/45	2/25/45	2/15/48
Max Speed:	468 mph	468 mph	452 mph
Range (int. fuel):	1,390 miles	1,580 miles	1,000 miles
Service Ceiling:	41,600 ft.	45,000 ft.	41,000 ft.

Above: Northrop's entry into the new all-weather fighter market was the F-89 Scorpion. Under military characteristics developed in the spring of 1945, the AAF requested proposals from the aircraft industry in late August 1945. Northrop entered four designs; one of which was selected and became the P-89. The mockup is shown above as it appeared in January 1947. (Northrop via Balzer)

Partially due to the problems that the F-87 program was having, not to mention the inner turmoil within the Curtiss-Wright organization, the Air Force scheduled a "fly-off" to be held on October 6 and 7, 1948. It was to be between the Air Force's XF-87 and XF-89 as well as the US Navy's Douglas-built XF3D-1. Experienced night fighter pilots, R/Os, and mechanics performed the evaluation. These men gave their results to an 11 man Committee on Evaluation. The pilots were fairly split in their opinions of the aircrafts' performance. The pilots and R/Os preferred the side-by-side seating of the XF-87 and XF3D-1. The three maintenance noncoms preferred the Douglas craft by far the best, followed by the Blackhawk and then the Scorpion. In spite of the favorable comments for the XF-87 and the XF3D-1, none of the committee voted for these aircraft. Instead seven members voted to procure the F-89 and the remaining four voted against procurement. (McDonnell Douglas/Harry Gann)

Apparently the Lockheed lobby had been at work. The 11 member committee also voted unanimously to procure a modified TF-80C (later designated F-94) as an interim all-weather fighter to take up the lag time until the F-89 could be put into the field. (USAF)

Besides practice intercept missions, the black Lightnings were scrambled, or diverted from other missions, to chase Japanese balloons, while under GCI control. The R/Os became quite proficient in guiding their pilots. A favorite game of the crews was to get in the traffic pattern at nearby Merced and follow training planes right down to their final approach.

Overall, the pilots preferred the P-38 to the P-61; it was faster, had a higher rate of climb, and a higher operational ceiling. For the R/O, it was another story. It was cramped and the P-38 had an inferior AI radar. Operationally, overspeeding of the turbo seemed to be a problem. The pilots made it routine procedure to manually lock in the turbo for takeoff. As a safety item, it became a "religious" practice to check that the fuel caps were secured. It seems that on a number of occasions the inboard fuel caps were not secured tightly and the fuel tended to syphon and catch fire when it swept past the hot turbo. This was a spectacular sight at night!

With their training completed, the first group of eight crews were sent to the Port of Embarkation at Salinas, California. While stationed there, the war ended. After nearly a month had been spent at Salinas, the Night Lightning crews were sent back to Hammer Field for disposition.

Once again at Hammer, the Salinas returnees, along with the second group of P-38M crews that had entered the training program, were split up. Some were discharged, some reassigned, and others waited for further orders. A couple of weeks later four of the crews were sent to the Chico, California, POE for shipment to the Pacific. The four P-38Ms that they were to fly left the west coast on October 4, 1945. The Night Lightning would have only a brief post war life. Another generation of aircraft called all-weather fighters were on their way.

Chapter 17

The Waning War

The new year started out with a bang. In the early morning hours Lts. Herman Ernst and Edward Kopsel were in pursuit of another Stuka when, once again for Ernst, the nose gear doors partially opened, cutting off the firing circuit to his 20mm cannon. Then at about 3:00a.m. "Ax" (Lt. Eugene Axtell) and "J.U." (Lt. John U. Morris, Jr.) got on the trail of a Ju 88 and sent it down in flames.

With such a start, the 422nd crews thought it was going to be another good month for hunting. But it wasn't. That was it for the month! The weather was quite foul (not until the winter of 1980/1981 would this one be matched). On the nights they could have flown, IX TAC had them stand down "to save their strength." For what (their squadron history asks)?

For their efforts during the "Battle of the Bulge," the 422nd NFS received a commendation from the Commanding General of the 101st Airborne Division at Bastogne which read:

For the excellent quality of air protection afforded to his command . . . (the 422nd) Night Fighters on several occasions broke up and drove off German Night Fighter attacks on his positions . . . the high degree of efficiency and proficiency of employment of the night air weapon as demonstrated by the 422nd Night Fighter Squadron, reflects great credit both to the personnel thereof and to the Ninth Air Force.

A good bit of "Bomber Command" rotated back to the good 'ol USA. The baton was passed to "Pistolshot" Postlewaite to carry on this work:

The first mission was flown after the Bulge. There wasn't much activity on that front. I flew standing up in the cockpit so if they shot at you there would be less to hit. It's hard to hit your feet, but your seat is a little bit bigger. We didn't like those missions; they were lousy. Our A-20s were mostly for this type of work. The guy with this gun laying radar had a Nordon bomb site which moved on a large scale map. We

were flying at 8,000 feet altitude, 220 air speed, and he'd give us the countdown to drop the bombs on major intersections. Usually we would try to get on each target maybe three times a night. We had a beautiful bomb load. There were only four 500 pounders because the runway wasn't any longer, and we couldn't get off. It sometimes wasn't long enough. Our bomb load usually consisted of one instantaneous, one with a one-hour delay fuse, one with a two-hour delay fuse, and one with a four-hour.

I've been over the same targets four hours later and saw that one go. What it was, was a harassing element to the Germans; plus we understood that the results were real good. The bombs were hitting the old crossroads and putting a hole in them, which is what we wanted to do. We'd drop the last bombs about six in the morning, and they went off at 10:00 a.m. Maybe the first one was dropped at 8:00 at night; well, this is a lot of harassment, especially if the crossroads is in a small village or something like that. The people didn't get too much sleep because by that time the day fighters were over there beating them up. This was what it was, just an harassing type of mission.

The scope of "Bomber Command's" mission was going to increase. To be added to their repertoire was leaflet sorties, flare dropping, and artillery adjustment missions. And yet another twist, cloak and dagger work. The squadron history tells of this mystery:

The curtain went up on the melodrama when amid very hush-hush circumstances, a colonel from Ninth Army arrived to discuss the possibilities of accurately dropping one of his agents behind the enemy lines on a very high priority mission. After a study of his needs, we decided the mission could be laid on and accordingly the "Pigeon" arrived in town closely guarded by a couple of sergeants who appeared thoroughly competent to handle any situation. The M.P.s promptly smelled a rat and though serious consequences were averted, they were far from satisfied at our guarantees. After sweating out several false alarms due to bad weather and once when the engines wouldn't start, the 'Pigeon' flew away on the 16th. He was a Luxenbourger, formerly engaged in running 'things' across the border, but when dressed in the opera bouffe costume of a German railway worker and equipped down to the last detail with German bread, cheese, cigarettes, clothing, etc., he surely looked the part. His orders were to kill anyone who accosted him other than fellow railroad workers – with a long wrench! To add to his troubles, of briefing on the mission, it was his first 'aeroplane' ride and consequently the first time he had ever seen, much less used a parachute. However, he disappeared into the snow and darkness through the hatch with a nonchalant 'Bon soir – a bientot.'

There were a number of these agent dropping missions that the 422nd's "Bomber Command" would be involved with. As Jim Postlewaite remembers some of this activity:

There was an Army Intelligence sergeant dumping them out the back. I dropped one behind the lines and another one shot himself in the airplane before we dropped him and had to bring him back. I think intelligence shot him before sunrise anyway. They took him off base; we didn't know where. The medics came back about an hour later and said they didn't know where he had been taken. They didn't know anything about it and hadn't seen anybody in fact. And then, there was an American Army Intelligence Officer along; and he said, 'If he did that on purpose he would never see the sun rise. I'll personally shoot him.' But I don't know what happened. We unloaded him right out of the plane, off the end of the runway.

I'm sort of glad we didn't drop him because he would have headed toward this island in the middle of the Rhine River. We were radar controlled up until about the last 50 miles and believe it or not, at night I could see that island because there was so much German anti-aircraft fire going on that you could see it. It was lit up. I didn't have to have anybody tell me where the island was because I could see it 50 miles away. At night you can see 10 times as much as you can in the daytime, it's terrific. I'm glad we didn't have to make it because we were going to have to go in low and slow and drop him out with two other equipment chutes.

I don't think that the first agent we dropped pulled his rip cord. He was given the last rites of the Church for ten nights before we took him. He was all dressed up in a German railroad worker's uniform and had a tool bag with him and a long wrench. Like all rails the German rails were put together with bolts to hold them together. At each rail joint there's a plate on each side, and it's bolted. He was suppose to go in, and sabotage some of the rail system and had this big wrench sewn in his parachute. I think if he opened it the wrench went on through and might have peeled him out of it. The sergeant with him never saw a parachute open. So after that we put a chock cord on all of them to make sure when they dropped out that the chute would open. Gene Lee dropped two outside of Frankfurt on an island. I believe in the Rhine, and we never saw them again. We flew by and flew by and were suppose to give them some check the next night, and they never answered so we figured the Germans had picked them.

The Widow drivers were also in on the ground action when they could fly. Axtell and Morris found a long line of German motor transport in the vicinity of Stadtkyll. There were about 200 or so trying to retreat east but the front part of the column was having considerable difficulty navigating the icy hill leading out of town. It was an inviting target. Axtell and Morris wanted to give them a good sendoff. "Ax" would strafe those negotiating the hill, thus causing a complete stoppage. Then he circled around and clobbered the vehicles on the flat, causing a massive road block at the other end. He became so "enthusiastic" over the matter that he made eight passes – and lived to tell about it!

January was also a month for "visitors." On January 14, eight Beaufighters and crews of the 417th came up from the southern war. This was totally unexpected by the 422nd. As a matter of fact, the rumor mill had it for some time prior to the 417th's detachment arrived that the 422nd would be receiving eight Beaufighters that they would have to fly. To say the least, they were quite displeased with the prospects of flying the "death traps." With the air action in a lull and no plans made or coordinated as to what the 417th crews were to do, they just

While the MTOs 415th and 417th NFSs moved up into France, the 414th and 416th remained in Italy. Here, 414th Widows are being prepared to continue the pounding at night that the day boys were giving the retreating German forces during the daylight hours. (NASM/Smithsonian)

"hung around" for six days and then went back to their home base in southern France.

Next came a detachment from yet another of the Twelfth Air Force's night fighter squadrons, the 414th. They arrived with their Widows on the 29th. This squadron had just finished transitioning from the Beaufighter to the P-61. What awed the 422nd crews was that the 414th's Black Widows had bomb racks.

The 425th NFS was having a similar month. A detachment from the Mosquito equipped 416th NFS joined the 425 at Etain on January 6th. As in the case with the 422nd and the arrival of the 417th, the 425th had no idea that the 416th's detachment was coming, much less what to do with them.

As attacking ground targets were becoming their major effort in the war, the 425th NFS thought up ways of causing greater destruction. To this end, the first P-61 was modified to carry eight high velocity aircraft rockets, commonly called HVARs. Capt. Russell Glasser flew the first flight with their new weapons on January 14th, hitting the marshalling yards at Homburg and Neunkirchen. He found that at night the rocket exhaust blinded him. So he worked out a system in which he would, "sight, close eyes, fire, count five, and open eyes."

January and February were months of low activity and the 425th's aircrews were feeling jumpy. They wanted to fly. The weather just wouldn't let up. TAC headquarters stated, "per missions flown, the night fighters have done as good, if not a better job than the day fighters."

The 425th had a change in command in February. Their "Skipper," Lt.Col. Leon "Gilly" Lewis was going home. Replacing Col. Lewis was the squadron's operations officer, Capt. Russell Glasser. Like Lewis, Glasser had flown bombers in the southwest Pacific prior to becoming a night fighter.

In aerial victories the 422nd also had no luck in February. But the 414th detachment flying with them had a little better hunting. On February 4th the 414th's team of 2nd Lts. Orin K.

On January 4th, a detachment from the 416th arrived at Etain, France, where they would fly in support of the 425th NFS with their Mosquitos until about February 20th. (Greggs)

Goodrich and Raymond J. Lane got a Ju 87 under quite adverse conditions under which the enemy was taking hard evasive maneuvers at low altitudes:

P-61A 39378, took off at 2322 hrs, 3 Feb 45, on a defensive patrol of the First Army area and the bomb line at Angels 10. Four chases and six free-lance contacts were made, which resulted in 2 visuals. One unidentified A/C peeled-off and was lost. Contact was made from 12,000 ft, and closed to 1,200 ft for a visual identification of a Ju 88 from 500 ft. Two short bursts were fired on the enemy while he was taking evasive action and a fire was seen on the left engine, then a long burst was fired and the enemy A/C spun off the right, hit the ground and burned brightly. No parachutes were seen to open. The fight was over at 0120 hrs, 4 Feb 45. There were thin patches at Angels 12 with unlimited visibility. A/C landed at 0205 hrs, 4 Feb 45.

This was a bright spot in the 414th detachment's day. Earlier in the day they had lost their second P-61 in an accident, and they hadn't flown operational yet. At the time of the second accident the squadron's history states that Major J.E. Patterson, the detachment's commander, "doesn't look happy today."

To provide more "punch" in their offensive operations, the 425th modified their P-61s to carry napalm in drop tanks and high-velocity aircraft rockets (HVARs). (425th collection via Anderson)

In early January 1945 the rumor mill had it that the 422nd NFS was to receive and fly eight Beaufighters as replacement aircraft. This touched off much consternation among the troops. The truth was arrived at with the arrival of eight Beaufighters, and crews, from the 417th NFS which was stationed in southern France. (Reed)

The 417th's stay with the 422nd was short lived, and they returned south before month's end. Their departure was about as mysterious to the 422nd as their arrival. They never really understood why the detachment was sent. Another headquarters SNAFU? (Reed)

Both the 422nd's P-61s and A-20s were busy with their "ground work." Axtell and Morris were in the thick of this work as usual. On the 27th they were patrolling between Bonn and Koblenz. On one of their passes over the Bonn area they were hit hard by flak. The right inboard fuel tank was set afire and the radio was knocked out. Johnny Morris had been wounded. When the fire got too hot back in the R/Os compartment, and with no communications with his pilot, he bailed out somewhere northwest of Bonn. In the meantime, Axtell, thinking Morris was wounded and incapable of bailing out, courageously flew the burning airplane back to friendly lines. Enroute he passed over other hostile antiaircraft batteries who added even more damage to his stricken craft. He belly landed the plane back home at Florennes. Upon inspecting the R/Os compartment they found one shoe. The extent of his wounds were unknown.

Another 422nd team flying intruder missions was Pappy More and Jim Haas. On their mission they found a busy railroad

No sooner had the 417th Beaufighters left than a detachment from the 414th NFS arrived from Italy. This detachment consisted of 26 officers, 40 enlisted men, and (as the 422nd squadron history states), ". . . wonder of wonders, a P-61 equipped with bomb racks." Their mission was to assist the 422nd with the drives from the west. With this detachment was Capt. Albert F. Jones and his R/O, 2nd Lt. John E. Rudovsky (right and left respectively). This night fighter team would be credited with two of the five kills the 414th would score while operating with the 422nd. (Thompson)

track on which to practice their lethal profession. With their mission completed, they headed for home. As they crossed the Rhine River in a westerly course, an unidentified aircraft fired on them, knocking out their port engine. After getting back to their airfield safely, an inspection showed they had also suffered a cracked spar in the port wing, punctured oil tank and two-thirds of their port rudder and horizontal stabilizer looked like swiss cheese. They also found the remains of British type 20mm semi-armor piercing and incendiary projectiles. As the squadron history puts it, "Looked as if there were a species of mosquito flitting around Germany."

This wasn't the first time a 422nd P-61 had been fired on by an RAF Mosquito. The night fighters felt that there wasn't any excuse for that – with the Black Widow's distinctive features. They wanted to get some measure of revenge (but not shoot one down, of course!). First Lieutenant Herman E. Ernst had the honors:

We were mad at these Mosquito boys and we were determined to shake them up a little bit. One evening I intercepted one of these Mosquitos. Of course, we knew a Mosquito wasn't going to shoot back at us from the back, so I pulled in on him right close. All at once the Mosquito's pilot turned around – imagine what he felt seeing this big black thing sitting right there. He really started to squirm. We were determined that he wasn't going to get away that evening so we just stayed right with him. He shot the colors of the day with a flare gun and everything else he could think of in trying to get us off his back. We just stayed right with him. Finally he pulled a German stunt and just peeled off and hit the deck and we went right with him. We followed this old Mosquito boy all the way to the ground, right down to the tree tops. Finally, we just let him go. We just wanted to shake them up a little bit.

Aerial hunting would be much better in March, especially for the 422nd's team of Ernst and Kopsel. "Herman and The Mouse" got two Ju 87s and damaged a Bf 110 on the 2nd. Some years later Herman Ernst recalled this quite active night:

This was one of the last stands of any size, where there was much air activity that the Germans put on. I don't think Eddy and I were supposed to fly that night. We had flown the night before. But Bolinder, who was working in operations, said he would let us know if anything was going on. So he called us out in the early morning, about 3:50. We went out and called Nuthouse, a ground station that we were to work with. It was an Eighth Air Force radar station. There was a lot of activity in its area. On calling the controller, he told me that we would have to stand by a few minutes because he had too many targets on his scope. Nuthouse asked us to stand by and man, our ack-ack, they locked lights on us and started shooting. We were receiving some damage from this so we went over on the German side where we were a little safer. We checked everything over and the damage we got wouldn't prevent us from operating. The radar was still operating so Eddy was still on the ball.

It was just a matter of a few minutes that we were there (on the German side), that things started to happen. We had a heyday out there. In just a few minutes we had two confirmed and a third one damaged.

With these two confirmed enemy aircraft destroyed, Ernst and Kopsel became the 422nd's second "ace" team.

It wasn't much of a surprise to the 425th NFS when TAC ordered straight intruder missions and a cessation of patrols.

With this emphasis on aerial operations placed on crippling what remained of the German transportation system, the 425th making frequent flights with their P-61s loaded with rockets, bombs, and napalm. Almost half of the missions flown out of Etain, France, were of this type in which they attacked rail and road traffic, and other installations.

Russ Glasser, as the new commander of the 425th, had to do a lot of coordination with higher headquarters in order to accomplish their new task:

Each month we had a staff meeting at General Weyland's office (Brig.Gen. Otto P. Weyland, Commander XIX TAC), mainly to discuss new locations, problems, and to award medals. After my first meeting, I was asked to stop in to see General Patton. The General asked me a number of questions; mainly our mission, what we could do to help him. Then he said, 'Captain, I want to give you four years at West Point in four words: analyze, organize, deputize and supervise.' Then he said, 'Dismissed, MAJOR.' I popped a salute to him and walked out. There was an aide sitting at the desk. He said, 'Con-

General Patton held regular staff meetings. The 425th NFS was protecting his tank force from enemy night attacks as well as flying offensively against the German ground forces. Maj. Russ Glass was a regular attendee at those meetings as the 425th's representative. (Glasser)

gratulations, Major. I guess you said the right thing to the old man. Here are your informal promotion orders. Take them to XIX TAC, and they will cut your formal orders today.' I said something like 'I'll be damned,' and asked what would have happened if I had said the wrong thing? 'He would have dismissed you as a captain, and we would have asked for a replacement for you. That's the way the old man operates,' was the aide's reply.

The history of the 425th was a sad one on a night in late March. "The Mighty Mites," Lts. Ormsby and Howerton, failed to return from a mission. They were struck by friendly flak near Darmstadt. Howerton, with two broken legs and other injuries, parachuted to safety and was picked up by Allied troops. Of this experience Howerton would later write:

> We were in the process of shooting down an old Stuka (our sixth kill), and just as he exploded and started down, we were hit by all the flak in West Germany. Unfortunately, Tommy had bought it right then (from my personal observation), but my injuries were confined to fractures of both femurs and other leg injuries. I managed to get the hatch off and pull up and out. The Wehrmacht picked me up and I went from a German aid station to a hospital where the Jerrys proceeded to save my life! A crazy war.

Lt. Howerton had a bird's eye view of what was going on, as the 425th had moved their R/Os from the back of the crew nacelle to the gunners position just behind and a little above the pilot. Though the Air Force records show Lts. Cletus T. Ormsby and Davis M. Howerton, Jr. having only three confirmed kills, Howerton and many of the other 425th Squadron members do not understand what happened to the other kills that had been acknowledged at the time as "confirmed."

Also scoring for the 425th in March were Capt. Francis V. Sartanowicz and 1st Lt. Edward Van Sickels. On March 24th they caught up to a Ju 87 that was circling at 3,000 feet. Flying at about 150mph Captain Sartanowicz had to ensure that he didn't just fly past his target. Lt. Van Sickels made AI contact and guided his pilot to within 2,000 feet from which a visual ID was made. Closing in, Sartanowicz fired at 400 feet astern of the Stuka. Stricken, the enemy rolled over on its back and crashed.

Aerial combat had picked up in March for the 422nd. Besides the encounters that Lts. Ernst and Kopsel were having, other 422nd teams were also experiencing activity at last. "Sack" Gordon and "Gentleman" Joe Crew were busy trying in vain to catch some fast flying Me 163 rocket planes. Two nights in a row they met up with this speedy craft at the same time slot just northeast of Koblenz. After these chases, the Me 163 didn't appear in that area again.

There were also more kills to add to the scoreboard. On the night of March 21 a pair of Do 217s were knocked out of the air by two 422nd crews. For Capt. Leonard F. Koehler and 1st Lt. Louis L. Best this was a real morale booster as they hadn't scored since August. The other Do 217 was intercepted by a crew of Capt. Raymond A. Anderson and 2nd Lt. Robert F. Graham. "Shorty" Graham's regular pilot, Robert Bolinder,

"Tabitha" of the 425th NFS. (Greggs)

One of the 425th's A-20s came decorated with the name of "Twin Titty Kitty from Okie City." (Hinkson)

When Capt. Russ Glasser took over the 425th on February 10th, they were very active flying offensive missions. Glasser pressed the point that they needed more firepower and was promised six Douglas A-26 Invaders. Soon after he received his attack aircraft, they were well-worn A-20 Havocs. (425th collection via Anderson)

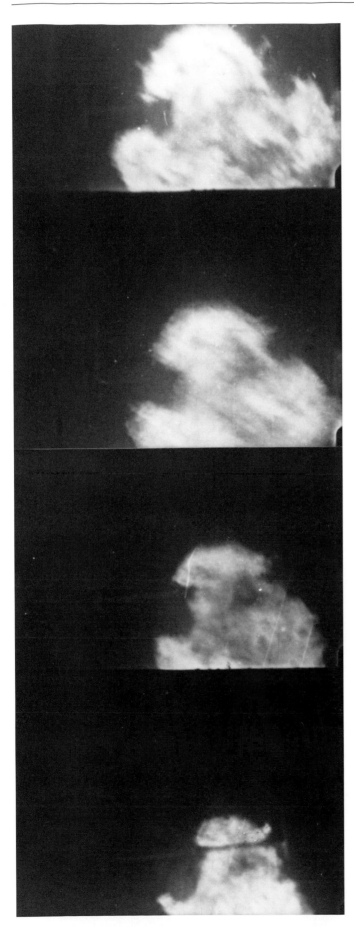

Left: Gun cameras were not standard equipment on the P-61. But on the night of March 21, 1945, the P-61 piloted by Capt. Raymond A. Anderson with 2nd Lt. Robert F. Graham, flying as R/O, was so equipped. The above series of photos show the destruction of a Dornier Do 217-K2; the fifth kill for Graham. (Graham)

had been grounded because of illness. The encounter report states:

Their patrol period was more or less uneventful and the few chases given by Marmite control were lost due to a faulty weapon. At 0015 hours, while returning to base, Marmite informed them a bogey was approaching from the SE (Koblenz area) at 8,500 feet. After several vectors from ground control, the airborne radar picked up the target at one and a half miles, taking violent evasive action in the form of 180 deg. turns, dives and climbs. AI contact was lost several times and regained with the help of Marmite. Finally after three unsuccessful runs, AI contact was again obtained at one and a half miles, the bogey still jinking violently. This time range was closed to 1,200 feet where pilot obtained a visual on twin exhausts and tails, target travelling generally 270, altitude by now, 3,500 feet, IAS 140-150. Finding it difficult to stay in position behind the target, pilot opened his cowl flaps to slow himself down. At 300 foot range, target 30 degrees above, the bogey was identified as a Do 217-K2 by twin tails, tapered wings and pencil shaped fuselage. For some reason the bandit abandoned evasive action and was flying straight and level. The pilot then dropped back dead astern and climbed slightly above the enemy aircraft. At 400 foot range, fire was opened with one long burst and the target immediately exploded and burst into flame, debris and fire trailing off. Turning and diving to port to avoid collision, the pilot saw the German crosses, saw one wing fall off and a parachute open. The target crashed into the ground and burned fiercely.

This made the fifth confirmed that Graham had participated in, four being with Lt. Bolinder. Graham would be the only AAF night fighter R/O to be credited with five while flying with different pilots. The 422nd had another "ace."

With the war coming to a close, a number of the 422nd crews were making the magic 70 mission mark. One of these was Lt. James F. Postlewaite, III:

I finished good, on my birthday. Man, did Chet and I get drunk for two days. It was the most memorable day I can remember. Of course, I can remember the date at the time, at 3:00 in the morning on March 24, 1945; that was also the big jump-off to cross the Rhine River. We were just coming back from out last mission; it was an intruder mission. We just flew it low, fast and kept our eyes closed the whole time. When we came out we gained some altitude and were coming over the front lines at 3:00 o'clock in the morning. Suddenly absolutely everything blew up. The artillery started to go so the Allies could start to make their advance. It was without a doubt one of the most dramatic displays of artillery fire I've ever witnessed.

When we got back and were debriefed, I asked Doc Page what in the world happened at 3:00 this morning. That front just literally blew up. He said it was the jump-off to cross the Rhine, and they made it. That was the day the First Army started to move, and that was the only

March saw the "Mighty Mites" of the 425th shot down, by Allied anti-aircraft fire. Pilot Cletus Ormsby was killed and R/O Davis Howerton was seriously wounded and taken prisoner. (425th collection via Anderson)

thing we had to report on our mission, because we didn't look for a thing the whole time. We volunteered for it, too. I forget, somebody didn't feel too good so Chet and I thought; well, let's go. I said let's make it because it's going to be my birthday, and we'll have a big celebration, so we ran it and went.

By early 1945 the 422nd had managed to get bomb racks on only a few of their P-61s. In March they got what they had wanted for quite a long time, two P-61Bs complete with turrets and bomb racks. No interceptor were these "B" models going to be, for plans were being laid for ground attack missions. Their A-20 force had started using napalm, incendiaries, and frags in their war of destruction sometime earlier. Like the 425th, the 422nd was doing more and more ground work. Barracks, factories, warehouses and ammo dumps all were hit. In their spare time, they were still dropping agents for the OSS.

The 414th with its new P-61s were becoming quite proficient with this aircraft under the guiding hands of the 422nd. A typical intruder mission flown by the 414th in late March is chronicled in their unit's history:

P-61A No 30378, took off at 2052 hrs, on an intruder patrol of the area E of the First Army Area. Strafed a train E of Holzmunden, saw strikes on cars and locomotive. Strafed train near Rotenburg, destroyed engine. Strafed two single MT on road N of Gottinken, the other NW of Kassel and damaged both. Intense accurate light flak S of Hoxter area, light - meager - inaccurate flak in Hersfeld area, A/C slightly damaged by former. In Hersfeld area saw many lights around buildings which went out when our A/C orbited S of the position. A/C landed at 0032 hrs, 31 Mar 45.

Unknown to the 422nd, the month before the end of the war in Europe would be one of their busiest in aerial combat. On April 6, 1945 they moved from Florennes, Belgium to what would be

a short 18 day stay at Strassfeldt, Germany where the 422nd, along with the detachment of the 414th that was flying with them, would account for 14 enemy aircraft destroyed!

It started out with the 414th detachment getting one a night between April 7th and 10th. Capt. Albert L. Jones and 2nd Lt. John E. Rudovsky were credited for the first two. The 414th's history recalls these encounters:

Capt. A.L. Jones came through with two fine victories last night: an Me 410, which he shot down in the landing pattern at Halle A/D, and a Ju 88. Lt. (Robert P.) Lutz had the first take-off last night, so he was the first American night fighter to fly operationally from a German base. It also follows naturally that the two victories were the first for American night fighters from a German Base. The weather is still good. April 9, 1945, 1st Lt. Robert P. Lutz (pilot) and 2nd Lt. Wallace A. Morrissette (R/O). Lt. Lutz added another to our victory list by shooting down a Ju 188 last night. Every one's morale is rising perceptibly. Incredibly, the weather is still good. On April 10, 1945 1st Lt. Thomas J. Greenfield (pilot) and 2nd Lt. Joseph E. Swartz (R/O). Last night Lt. Greenfield made it three nights in a row by getting a Ju 52. Now we have the first four victories for American night fighters operating out of Germany.

Like the 414th, the 416th traded in their Beaufighters in late 1944 also but for the Mosquito. The 416th fell in love with the "Mossie" at first sight. (Atwell)

In the couple of months the 415th and 417th NFSs had the P-61 prior to the cessation of hostilities, they made the transition to their new aircraft effortlessly and became quite proficient in attacking road and rail targets as well as fixed installations and troop concentrations. The aircraft pictured is from the 415th. (Cypert)

The MTO's 414th NFS, the first night fighter squadron to get P-61s in that theater, had just become operational as the new year opened (the first Widow arrived just that past December 20th). Here Capts. Joe C. Jenkins (pilot), on the left, and David L. McAbee (communications officer) give "Black Magic" a once-over. (USAF)

Punched in the nose? Apparently a pressure imbalance caused this implosion of the radome. (425th collection via Anderson)

Jim Postlewaite recalls that many interesting people were in the 422nd Night Fighter Squadron; one was Lt. Alfred F. Dorner:

Al Dorner's dad was a full colonel in the German Army before WW II, and he got busted or broke or something and came over to the U.S. Army as a captain. According to what I remember, Dorner's uncle (Dr.Ing. Claude Dornier of Dornier-Werke G.m.b.II.) built the Dornier 217. The last ten missions I lived with Gene Lee and Dorner and Chet in the same tent. Well, the last ten missions Dorner got dressed every night to the teeth, complete with swagger stick, chamois gloves, shined his shoes, flew in a uniform, no flight suit. He said, 'If I get shot down, and I give my name when I get to the Duloftlup Luftstalag I'm in for a tough time; so I plan to go in style.' And he did, he sweat the last ten;

it was like bullets. When he left, boy, oh, the sweat was running down his face.

After the 414th's detachment had a run at the Luftwaffe between April 7th and 10th, the 422nd had its turn at them between the 11th and 13th. In started on the night of April 10/ 11 when the Germans made a last ditch attempt at running supplies into the "Rose Pocket" and on the trip out, trying to evacuate VIPs. First to participate in what could be called a decimation of the transports was the crew of Lt. Eugene Axtell flying with Lt. Creel H. Morrison as his R/O. They intercepted a low flying Ju 52 with much help from the Marmite controller. Creel Morrison was having trouble with his AI radar set in that

Officers of the 414th NFS at Pontedera, Italy, in the spring of 1945. Only eight of these men were original members of the squadron when it was organized in March 1943. Col. Carroll H. Bolender, C.O., is ninth from the left, standing. On the far right of those standing is the operations officer, Maj. Francis B. Clark. (Dawson via Thompson)

he couldn't get a range reading. Marmite was able to get them within eye sight of the target where Axtell was able to get a visual and was able to record another destroyed enemy.

This was followed by "Sack" Gordon and Joe Crew who bagged two, a Ju 88 and another Ju 52. This was soon followed by another Ju 52 destroyed by Robert "Moe" Elmore and Leonard "Lenny" Mapes. Marmite informed that these, ". . . kills represented, to the Germans, a loss of 50% of their effort as shown by the plots on their scopes."

The following night the action continued. First Capt. Tadas Spellis and Lt. "Lefty" Eleftherion got a Ju 88. Next "Ax" and Creel got a Ju 52 for the second night in a row. This brought Axtell's score to five confirmed (he flew with four different R/Os). Then three more Ju 52s went down in rapid succession to the gun-slinging 422nd. These were accredited to the crews 1st Lt. Edgar E. Merriman and 2nd Lt. Delbert W. Dow, then 1st Lt. Fred E. Benett and his R/O, F/O Clifford E. Brandt got theirs, and the night closed with Capt. Robert Elmore and 2nd Lt. Leonard F. Mapes getting the last one. This made Elmore and Mapes "semi-aces" with a total of four confirmed aircraft destroyed and one V-1 downed. The squadron's history has an interesting comment on how this night ended:

. . . everyone was sweating out another victory; three times now we had gotten five and we sure wanted to break this record. But about this time, it began to dawn on the square heads that there was very little future in that particular milk run, so instead of vectoring us to another area, they called off flying for the night.

This was quite an evening for the night fighters. Marmite later reported that they had a total of six plots that evening, of which the 422nd destroyed five. The sixth one, probably seeing what happened to the other aircraft, thought better of trying to complete his mission and went back home.

The weather worsened. With 10/10 cloud cover at 5,000 feet and terrain that went from 800 to 4,500 feet and visibility of less than a mile in rain, the night fighters were just about out of business. Even so, when duty called, they were there. On the night of April 12/13 two crews were sent on intercepts. The one aircraft, after an extended chase, couldn't get a visual contact on two occasions. The other crew, 1st Lts. Theodore I. Jones and William G. Adams, Jr., were much more fortunate. They spotted the exhaust of their target through the raid and closed in on it. Finally Jones could see part of the plane; it was the landing gear of a Ju 52. He backed off to shoot from a preferred position but lost sight of everything but the exhaust. The weather was bad! With flaps down and wallowing at 100mph (almost stalling speed for the P-61) he fired a long burst towards where he thought the target was. Scratch another Ju 52. And this was the last kill for the 422nd.

For the 414th's detachment the month ended on a down note. On the evening the 422nd got its last victory, the 414th crew of 2nd Lt. W.C. Donald and 1st Lt. O.S. Anderson were in pursuit of another Ju 52. When coming in from below to get into firing position, they hit a hill about 100 feet from its crest. The weather had taken a victim.

Maj. Francis B. Clark, operations officer of the 414th NFS, sitting in his P-61 "Black Magic." (Dawson via Thompson)

For the few weeks left in the European war the 422nd concentrated all its efforts on intruder missions. They were covering an area bounded by the First and Third US Armies in the south, in the west by Maulde, north to Berlin, and going east to the Russian lines.

Captain Russell Glasser, C.O. of the 425th NFS, was a regular attendee of staff meetings at General George Patton's headquarters:

Towards the end of the war, we knew the war would end pretty soon. I was up at a staff meeting. General Patton came in to give us our briefing. I believe it was just after the Yalta meeting. He said, 'Gentlemen, here is the bomb line. This is as far as we are going.' The tears came out of his eyes. 'Gentlemen, we have the men, the material and the momentum to go all the way to Moscow, but we are stopping here.' Indicating on the large map beside him. 'In 20 years from now your sons will be fighting the war that we could win in a breeze.'

Movement again. This time the 422nd went to Langensalza, from which they would operate for the approximate two weeks left in the war. This had been a German night fighter base, modification center, and experimental center. There was a number of German night fighter aircraft and radar around the field. The 422nd troops spent a good bit of time investigating, and in some cases, rebuilding the equipment to see how it worked.

The rest of the flying operations for the 422nd were against what remained of Germany's communications and transportation systems. Lt.Col. C.K. Wilcox, Staff Weather Officer for the 422nd NFS, recalls:

My other strong recollection of life in Langensalza had to do with V-E Day. Early in the morning of 6 May 1945 I was startled to hear a loud explosion down the hall of a large barracks. I stuck my head out of the door of my room to see what was going on, and nearly had it shot off. One of the pilots was firing his .45 automatic in all directions with one hand, while in the other he was brandishing a bottle of some kind and yelling, 'Whoopee', or words to that effect. I was finally able to ascertain that we had won the war – in Europe at any rate.

He further commented that the intruder work that the night fighters had undertaken caused them to curtail their training efforts, disrupted their supply and communications line, and had knocked out a GCI station. And, much to the night fighters amazement, he claimed that the German night fighters had not knocked down a single Black Widow.

Movement was ordered for the 425th NFS also. On April 12, they too moved into Germany. Their base was at Frankfurt-am Main. Here the night fighters found many souvenirs, as this had been the home of the Graf Zeppelin. There were also other items of interest, particularly the latest jet aircraft.

From this base the 425th downed its last enemy on the night of April 24/25. First Lieutenants Jack E. Slayton and his R/O, Jack W. Robinson, were on patrol that evening when contact was made. The combat report states:

AI contact was picked up at about three miles with GCI still no help as they lost track of bogey. Followed AI contact in with bogey taking evasive action and climbing to 12,000 feet from 8,000 – speed 230, no particular heading. Chased 10 minutes before obtaining visual at 3,000 feet, closed into 300 feet for positive identification, recognized Ju 188. Pulled up and fired down from dead astern, obtaining strikes in starboard engine which burst into flames. Enemy aircraft went into gentle spiral to right, losing altitude and three chutes were seen to open. Aircraft spun straight into ground where it exploded.

In a report entitled "Tactical Air Operations in Europe," prepared by XIX Tactical Air Command, some of the 425th history of intruder is given:

The note behind the above picture is somewhat comical: "This guy flew a Fw 190 in and landed. He got out of his plane with his hands up hollerin' 'comrade.' Everyone ran out to get his P-38 (pistol) and look at his airplane; and ignored the poor guy after they took his gun." (425th collection via Anderson)

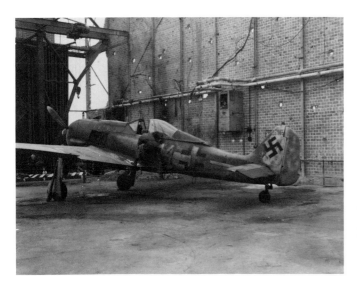

The last few days of the war had a couple of interesting points for the 422nd. The crew of 2nd Lts. Matthew Gray and Cecil R. Allbee latched on to a Fw 189. As Gray was about ready to fire, they threw a prop blade. With a great deal of effort they barely made it back to base, but the plane was a washout.

The second incident was when Lt. Leonard Koehler was sent to England to interrogate a German prisoner. It turned out that he was the operational officer in control of all the German night fighters from the Ruhr to Koblenz. When the officer was questioned as to the affectivity of the American night fighters, his reply was that the German night fighters were ordered to avoid the P-61 because of their superior fire power and speed.

Like the previous photo, this one has quite a story as told by the 415th. "April Fool's night a weird thing happened. Sgts. (John H.) Eichhorn and (George A.) Linck were on night duty when the tower called that a Beaufighter was circling. The night crew rubbed the sleep out of their four eyes, jumped into a jeep and tore out to the end of the runway to guide the pilot in. As he circled they noticed that his engines sounded very rough. He landed and skidded into a ground loop as one tire blew out. As Eichhorn and Linck drove up they saw a swastika on the tail and then they made out the outline of a Ju 88. Not daunted, the alert night crew handled their flashlights as if they were service .45s and calmly received the surrender of the two war-weary supermen. The Jerry crew said that they had quit voluntarily because they knew the jig was up and that we could expect more to do the same thing." (Cypert)

The guests have arrived. A month before V-E Day, both Ninth Air Force night fighter squadrons advanced into Germany. The unwelcome intruders who had spent the final months of the war dropping delayed action bombs, saboteurs, and huge flares, while harassing the last vestiges of Nazi Germany's air defense, were now parked on the aprons of German fighter bases, overlooked by shattered control towers which had once vectored enemy interceptors to seek out and destroy them. (USAF)

An artful nose wheel cover on one of the 422nd's Widows. (Stegner via Campbell)

Except during the Luftwaffe's brief resurgence in connection with the Ardennes Counter-Offensive, German night operations in the XIX TAC area did not justify much effort in defensive patrols. Offensive intruder missions proved a far more profitable employment of out night fighter squadron (the 425th). Several of the P-61s were equipped to carry HVAR as well as high-explosive bombs, incendiaries, and napalm.

It went on to say the mode of operation was to bomb the target first with 165 gallon tanks filled with napalm. Then, using the fire set by the napalm as an aiming point, fire the HVARs. A majority of this work was armed recon along roads and the rail network with marshalling yards and factories being secondary. The report continued:

Night intruder operations form an important and necessary complement to daylight fighter-bomber activity, giving the enemy no rest.

The 425th thought it was here to stay for the remainder of the war. But headquarters had a different point of view. With but

days left in the war, they arrived at Furth, near Nurnberg, on May 2nd. The facilities here were the best that they ever had. They settled down fast in the cool, concrete barracks where they had "real" beds, hot showers, and "semi-automatic" latrines.

At 1:41a.m. on May 7, 1945 the war in Europe was over.

A piece of night fighter humor that the AAF night fighters have passed on, though its origin in uncertain:

A retired Swedish night fighter of WWII was invited to address the local DAR chapter to relate some of his war experiences. He was well into his story telling the girls, 'Well, there we were flying along on patrol over the Rhine when all of a sudden two Fokkers came at us out of nowhere-our GCI crew must have been out on a coffee break . . .' The embarrassed MC broke in with,' . . . Now ladies, the Col. is referring to a German Aircraft named Fokker . . .' 'The hell you say,' broke in the Swede, 'those damn Fokkers were Messerschmitt Bf 109s . . .'

The War Ends in the Mediterranean

The Beaufigher equipped 415th NFS had just arrived at their new airfield at Ochey, France, on December 30, 1944 and were in the process of settling in when they were called upon in the early morning hours of January 1, 1945. The crew of 1st Lt. Edward A. Schlueter and 2nd Lt. Donald J. Meiers were on patrol that night when an incoming target was picked up:

At 03:15 hours was told there was a bogey at 15,000' coming from S.W. and going N.E. Vectored 180 degrees and contacted Churchman at 03:20. Told bogey was at 12,000. Lowered angles and picked up contact at 6 miles. Bogey above at 12,500 at 03:40. Closed in gradually, climbing flat out on general N.E. heading. After AI contact bogey used violent evasive action – hard turns and steep dives and climbs. Weak AI contact showed bogey hard above. Beau at 16,000 with very weak AI contact hard above, 6 miles. Called Ignite and was told bogey was at 12,500' below. Bogey climbing and we were following at 6 mi. range. Closed to 4 1/2 where very violent evasive action was encountered which continued all the way up to 4,000' range. Beau flat out and could not close further for a period of 5 min. Slowly closed in to 1,900' where pilot made visual. Interrogated bogey for full minute – no results. Closed to 500'. Identified as Ju 88 15 degrees above, dead ahead. Fired one long burst observing strikes on left engine and fuselage and trailing edge of right wing. Gave a second burst. Right engine caught fire. Plane fell off into spin to the right – debris falling off. Spiraled down to 10,000' and broke in to with 2 large balls of fire striking ground. Lost angels to 10,000 and decided to continue patrol but due to extreme cold and frostbite returned to base. No parachutes were seen. Used 'Tiptoe' procedure during chase.

Tragedy would also strike the 415th on January 1st. While on patrol, Capt. Varillus O. Jones and Lt. Sussman were fired on by a B-17. The fire was quite accurate as it shot out one engine and tail surfaces. Lt. Sussman, the R/O, was wounded. Capt. Jones elected to try to bring his damaged Beaufighter back to an Allied field because Sussman was not able to bail out. The last words the controller received before the stricken plane spun in was, "I guess we've had it."

The 416th NFS were just getting comfortable in their new Mosquito night fighters when headquarters directed them to send a detachment to the Ninth Air Force. Under the command of Capt. Paul Iribe, 16 officers and 28 enlisted men along with five of the squadron's Mosquitos and went to Etain, France, where they would work in conjunction with the 425th NFS. Some of the Mosquitos landed in Paris, "to get their VHF changed to match (Etain's) frequency."

By January 15th the 416th's detachment at Etain was having support difficulties. The evening's patrols had been called off because the detachment didn't have sufficient oxygen, hydraulic fluid, and spare parts. The squadron history comments that, "Someone made the remark that operating Mosquitos here is about the same as 'Jerry' trying to operate Ju 88s in England." A number of the 416th's R/Os flew with 425th pilots in their P-61s. The R/Os felt that the '61 was a good plane. Capt. Iribe flew the first patrol on the 16th. It was quite uneventful.

On November 28, 1944 the 414th NFS moved from Pisa to Pontedera Airfield, Italy. For a Christmas present they received their first P-61 "Black Widow," though they continued operating the Beaufighter while undergoing transitioning into the P-

A view from within the control tower at Langensalza (R-21), Germany. The 422nd arrived here on April 24th; this would be their last wartime station. (Laird, Stegner, Stegner)

61. By January 20, 1945 the last had left the squadron. On January 27, 26 officers and 52 enlisted men, along with six of their new fighter, left the squadron for Florennes, Belgium. Here they were to work with the 422nd NFS in the Campaign of western Germany.

By early February the 414th NFS crews were anxious to get into intruder work with their Widows. By the 8th they had received reports from their detachment in Belgium with the 422nd NFS on how they were doing in the ground attack

ENGLAND   FRANCE   BELGIUM   GERMANY

422nd
NIGHT FIGHTER SQDN.

15 Jul. '44	Ernst - Kopsel	V-1
17 Jul. '44	Elmore - Mapes	V-1
18 Jul. '44	Anderson - Mogan	V-1
20 Jul. '44	Spelis - Eleftherion	V-1
27 Jul. '44	Smith - Tierney	V-1
7 Aug. '44	Anderson - Morris ★	Ju-88
9 Aug. '44	Romeus - Morin	Ju-88
19 Aug. '44	Koehler - Bost	Do-217
25 Sept. '44	Gordon - Morrison	Ju188
4 Oct. '44	Smith - Tierney	Me-410
21 Oct. '44	Jones - Adams	Fw-190
24 Oct. '44	Johnson - Montgomery	Fw190
26 Nov. '44	Bolinder - Graham	He-111
27 Nov. '44	Smith - Tierney	He-111
27 Nov. '44	Ernst - Kopsel	Me-110
4 Dec. '44	Anderson - Morris ★	He-111
17 Dec. '44	Bolinder - Graham	Fw-190
17 Dec. '44	Bolinder - Graham	Me-110
17 Dec. '44	Bolinder - Graham	He-111
17 Dec. '44	Ernst - Kopsel	Ju-87
17 Dec. '44	Elmore - Mapes	Ju-88
22 Dec. '44	Elmore - Mapes	Me-110
24 Dec. '44	Anderson - Mogan	Ju-88
25 Dec. '44	Smith - Tierney	Ju-88
25 Dec. '44	Anderson - Mogan	Ju-188
26 Dec. '44	Burleson - Monahan	Me-110
26 Dec. '44	Smith - Tierney	Ju-188
26 Dec. '44	Smith - Tierney	Ju-188
27 Dec. '44	Axtell - Orzel	Ju-88

27 Dec. '44	Axtell - Orzel	Ju-188
27 Dec. '44	Ernst - Kopsel	Ju-188
27 Dec. '44	Johnson - Montgomery	Ju-188
27 Dec. '44	Spelis - Eleftherion	Me-110
1 Jan. '45	Axtell - Morris ★	Ju-188
2 Mar. '45	Ernst - Kopsel	Ju-87
2 Mar. '45	Ernst - Kopsel	Ju-87
21 Mar. '45	Anderson - Graham	Do-217
21 Mar. '45	Koehler - Bost	Do-217
11 Apr. '45	Axtell - Morrison	Ju-52
11 Apr. '45	Axtell - Morrison	Ju-52
11 Apr. '45	Elmore - Mapes	Ju-52
11 Apr. '45	Gordon - Crew	Ju-52
11 Apr. '45	Gordon - Crew	Ju-88
11 Apr. '45	Spelis - Eleftherion	Ju-88
11 Apr. '45	Merriman - Dow	Ju-52
12 Apr. '45	Burnette - Brandt	Ju-52
12 Apr. '45	Elmore - Mapes	Ju-52
13 Apr. '45	Jones - Adams	Ju-52
? 6 Aug. '44	Axtell - Crew	Do-217
? 6 Aug. '44	Gordon - Morrison	Ju-188
? 7 Aug. '44	Smith - Tierney	Me-110
? 25 Aug. '44	Axtell - Crew	Ju-188
? 7 Oct. '44	Spelis - Eleftherion	Me-110
* 14 Aug. '44	Gordon - Morrison	He-117
* 26 Nov. '44	Lee - Dorner	Me-110
* 27 Dec. '44	Ernst - Kopsel	Ju-88
* 14 Dec. '44	Allee ★ - Heggie ★	Ju-88
* 2 Mar. '44	Ernst - Kopsel	Me-110

TOTAL SORTIES FLOWN 1,576   AIRCRAFT

TOTAL BOMBS DROPPED   3-5-5

MOTOR TRANSPORTS 14 - 435   I

LOCOMOTIVES   -35   RAILWAY CARS 41 - 435

FACTORIES -20   BO   -4 - 0

PRISONERS 10

missions. But the main body of the squadron in Italy had not dropped a bomb in the Po Valley, their main hunting ground, yet. Matter of fact, by this date they had dropped only six practice bombs. They would start soon.

On February 16, Lt. Gravel and F/O Moore were on a mission near Pisa when they spotted something. Their report of this incident states:

At 0130 hours, while patrolling at 15,000 ft, near Pisa Air Base, fighter observed a flare and upon circling flare asked Ackbridge for a fix. Fix placed fighter and scene of flare approximately ten miles north of Pontedera. At 0140 hours, fighter observed a second flare which appeared to have fallen between Pontedera and Pisa. At 0145 hours, fighter observed a third flare, which seemed to spiral, in the vicinity of Pisa. Blue Sector control reported that this third flare dropped at Marina D' Pisa. The flares were observed to burn at 6,000 feet, then disappear below overcast. At 0150 hours, fighter saw a spurt of flame, which went out immediately just west of Viareggio. This spurt of flame appeared to be between 10,000 and 13,000 ft. Fighter gave chase immediately. During chase two more spurts of flame were observed with the last spurt of flame continuing until it was lost in clouds below 6,000 ft. This believed to be jet propelled aircraft made two 290 degree turns then continued on a straight course and losing altitude during chase. Fighter chased the jet propelled aircraft for fifty miles out to sea west of Pisa, on a 240 and 270 deg. heading where aircraft was lost in clouds. Due to a shortage of gas, fighter broke off chase at 0215 hours and returned to base. During chase, on a straight and level course, fighter was indicating an air speed of 290 M.P.H. (ground speed of approximately 350-360 M.P.H.) and as fighter dove to 6,000 feet, he indicated an air speed of 400 M.P.H. Fighter was unable to obtain A.I. contact.

As with a number of the other AAF night fighter squadrons, the 416th NFS was encountering Foo-Fighters. In mid-February a number of the crews reported such sightings. Both the GCI controllers and Intelligence were mystified. At first some voiced the opinion that it was a "post-cognac manifestation." But even the "teatotalers" observed these apparitions.

Capt. Lawrence E. Englert and 2nd Lt. Earl R. Dickey of the 416th were scrambled from Pontedera Airfield in Italy to intercept a hostile aircraft that GCI had picked up on its scopes. What would transpire in this all-but-usual intercept would include the first aerial victory for the 416th's Mosquito and a Silver Star for Capt. Englert. The enthralling combat reports gives the story:

At 2154 hours our Mk. XXX Mosquito, No. MM746 was scrambled from Pontedera Airfield for a hostile aircraft which was reported by Blue Sector to have dropped flares over Naples. Our aircraft, altitude 8000 feet, 180 MPH, went from Bacon to Cooler GCI, and was vectored 090 deg. to Florence. The radar observer then picked

Opposite:
The 422nd Night Fighter Squadron's scoreboard. (Tierney)

As part of the celebration of the Allies' victory over the Axis forces, a P-61 was placed on display at the Champs de Mars in Paris. (USAF Museum)

up contacts on window. There were multiple targets to port and starboard of aircraft. These targets appeared on the scope and then faded very rapidly, and no permanent contact could be established. Cooler vectored our aircraft 360 deg. to a point 20 miles north of Florence and handed us over to Canine GCI which gave us a vector of 270 deg. to Montecatini. We were still making altitude at 180 MPH. Canine reported the enemy aircraft 20 miles Southeast of Florence at 23000 feet, 260 MPH. Our aircraft orbited and made angels 17 at 180 MPH, although the supercharger was not working. We were then vectored 360 deg. for ten minutes, and then given a vector of 050 deg. In order to gain speed, the wing tanks were now jettisoned.

At 2247 hours, 4 miles northwest of Pavullo (L 4535), the radar observer obtained an AI contact, head on, 20 deg. above at 7 mile range. Our aircraft was at altitude 22500 feet, 180 MPH; enemy aircraft at 23500 feet. We made a starboard turn and maintained contact, closing to 5 miles range at which time the starboard engine cut out. We continued our chase on single engine. We informed GCI that we had an AI contact; thereafter we had no further contact with GCI. The enemy aircraft, flying due north, was taking gentle to moderate evasive action, but we maintained contact and followed at 5 miles range. 10 miles southwest of Modena the enemy aircraft dove to 17000 feet, and our aircraft followed in the dive at 210 MPH and closed in to 3 miles range, dead ahead. We maintained contact, flying on a vector of 360 deg over Mantova.

At 2305 hours, altitude 17000 feet, speed 210 MPH, 8 miles northwest of Villafranca di Verona, our aircraft closed to 1500 feet and obtained a visual on an enemy aircraft, type Ju 188, 30 deg. to port and 5 deg. below. The moon was behind and to the starboard of our aircraft, and it was bright enough so that identification was readily made. The hostile was recognized as a Ju 188 by the very wide wing span, square-tipped tail plane, high fin and rudder. Our aircraft then pulled up behind, and observed distinctive wide-spanned wings with pointed tips. At 2307 hours, our aircraft closed to 400 feet, enemy aircraft dead ahead, and gave the enemy a two second burst. The tail of the enemy aircraft was seen to shake very violently as strikes were made. The enemy aircraft went nose down in a shallow dive towards the ground, and again the distinctive long pointed wings were observed. Our aircraft followed the hostile and gave a second burst of two seconds

As the Allies took-over Luftwaffe airfields, many German aircraft were seen up close for the first time. Here a number of Messerschmitt Bf 110Gs are seen with USAAF P-47 Thunderbolts in the background. (Ernst)

American night fighter ace Herman E. Ernst gets up-close and personal with a Bf 110G. He was credited with one Bf 110 destroyed and another damaged. (Ernst)

duration. The shells exploded about ten feet forward of the tail of the enemy aircraft. A third burst of two seconds duration again shook the aircraft and resulted in strikes on the fuselage. At a final burst of two seconds duration large portions of the enemy aircraft were blown off. Flames enveloped the aircraft from the engines and there was a large explosion. Our aircraft flew through debris and brown smoke. The enemy aircraft spun down in flames and hit the ground. A large fire and a smaller fire were then observed on the ground and an explosion also was observed. We opened fire at 400 feet range and closed to 50 feet. No return fire was experienced by our aircraft during this combat. No one was seen to bail out of the enemy aircraft.

At approximately 2309 hours our aircraft vectored 180 deg. for base. The starboard engine caught fire and we feathered the propeller. The starboard wheel came down and we were unable to raise it. At the same time the flight instruments went out, but we continued towards the base, although we were losing altitude steadily and it was necessary to cross the mountains through a pass at 8000 feet. At 2321 hours Novel GCI picked us up 35-40 miles south of Parma. At 2345 hours our aircraft at 6000 feet, 180 MPH, was over base at Pontedera. The tower reported 9/10 to 10/10 overcast at 800 to 1000 feet over base. We attempted to get through the overcast, but the starboard engine was windmilling and we had no instruments. We did not have sufficient rudder control to make controlled turns with the aircraft. From the time when the starboard wheel came down it was necessary for the pilot to hold full left rudder, and he required the aid of the observer who pulled back on the right rudder pedal with his hand. Realizing that it was impossible to land the aircraft, we climbed to our maximum possible altitude of 4000 feet and bailed out at 2359 hours. The observer came down four miles east of base, the pilot one mile east of base. The aircraft then crashed in an open area one mile south of base. The pilot and observer suffered minor sprains and abrasions.

On March 3, 1945 the 415th NFSs crew of 1st Lt. Henry J. Giblin and 2nd Lt. Walter J. Cleary were flying patrol in their Beaufighter when a GCI controller picked up a target:

Churchman took over and vectored Travel 33 North East and lower to angels 7. Bogey showed at 5 o'clock and below at 2 miles. He throttled back and let down to angels 3 1/2 through and into broken overcast and then closed in to 500' and slightly below and off to starboard. Identified a/c as Fw 200. Dropped back to 1,000' and approximately 10 degrees off to port side. Both bandit and Travel 33 opened fire. Bandit using single gun and firing from rear. Tracer crossed Beau's starboard wing. Beau's cannon and machine guns hit 2 starboard engines which caught fire immediately and debris began flying back. Beau broke away to below and starboard then pulled up to port again. Both a/c went into overcast off to port on top of cloud at angels 3. Bandit traveling 090. Fired again but observed no hits. Saw bandit hit ground at 06:20.

Officials from XII TAC and 64th Fighter Wing identified wreckage as a B-17, Jerry flown. There is a good more to this story, as told in the history of the 82nd Fighter Control Squadron. The incident is described in that history by the controller, 1st Lt. Harold Lapidus:

On March 3, 1945, about 0530, I was advised by Control Center 2, that a hostile aircraft was coming into out territory and that a night fighter which we had sent on an intruder mission was being recalled and that I was to take over control as soon as I picked him up. I contacted the night fighter, Travel 33, which whom, incidentally, I had obtained my first kill and at 0550 picked up the aircraft, identified as hostile. The chase began and at 0600 a contact was obtained. At 0610 Travel 33 called requesting return to base and announced that he had identified the aircraft as an Fw 200, a four engine bomber, and had shot it down. Investigation of the wreck (it was shot down in friendly territory) proved it to be a B-17 but, nevertheless, hostile, as six Germans were removed from the wreckage, five of them alive. Interrogation by First TAF revealed that fact that this aircraft was one of two the Germans had and had used it to drop agents on the Russian front and had just transferred to our front for the same purpose. This was the maiden flight for them on our front. They admitted that they

A captured Junkers Ju 88 and Fw 190. (Conway via Campbell)

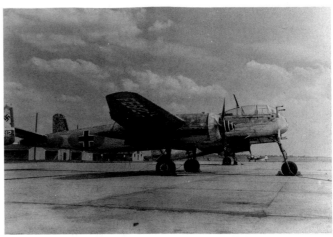

A Heinkel He 219 "UHU" (Owl) with most of its antenna array removed. (Davis via Campbell)

had dropped six agents and their equipment before they were shot down, two of whom, I later learned, were captured in the Nance area.

Paul Evans, a pilot who had just joined the 414th NFS in December 1944, met up with a cable stretched across the Arno River in Italy:

They had big dikes on each side of the river. Every once in a while they would stretch a cable across. The cable was probably 30 to 40 feet in the air. I never saw the cable. I saw a boat down in the river, I was off to one side. I had just started to pull up when I hit that cable – square, center on the Widow's nose. The fiberglass nose cracked. My left propeller cut the cable and one end of the cable came lose and came flying back like a rubber band. It whipped back around the nose and caught the other propeller and wrapped around it. I was pulling it like an anchor. The cable had come lose from the other bank and I was dragging about 150 yards of cable. One engine lost – the propeller was windmilling, I couldn't feather it. So I just had to let the engine run and try to get a little power from the other one. I had just enough left in that engine to get back to the field and land.

The night fighters always seemed to be on the move. On March 18th the 415th NFS moved to St. Dizier, France. The next day 1st Lt. Henry F. Bockstege and his R/O, 2nd Lt. Hurbert F. Moore were forced to bail out after their Beaufigher was shot up over Germany. A couple days later Moore was listed as killed and Bockstege was MIA. On April 26th Lt. Bockstege would return to the 415th after quite an ordeal in which he was captured by the Germans and held prisoner for 35 days. During that time he attempted escape on a number of occasions, but was recaptured each time. He was finally freed when an American armored unit overtook the area in which he was held.

The Twelfth Air Force's night fighter squadrons seem to change aircraft in pairs. As the 414th and 417th turned in their Beaufighters for P-61s and Mosquitos, respectively, in December 1944, so the 417th and 415th will follow suit in March 1945.

The 417th received their first P-61 on the 14th while the 415th took delivery on their first two on the 20th. The 415th would not completely replace their Beaufighters prior to the end of hostilities. The 417th would have 11 Widows by April 1st.

Joe Jenkins of the 414th NFS had a "fun" but exasperating time with a Fieseler Storch on one occasion:

We got after a Fieseler Storch up there one night; that's great fun. He would sit there and make turns inside of you. You could get your gear down and try to slow down, and he would make this tight turn while you were staggering and stumbling around. He would be back going the other way before you could get turned around. Of course, you're only doing about 90 miles an hour. He would turn around and look at you while making another turn and you still weren't going in the right direction to get him. I ran into one north of Marseilles, towards Lyon and Dijon. I couldn't get near him. It was frustrating. If he knew you were back there, you were done with because he could turn, cut power, pretty near stop in the air – and you would overrun him.

As March was coming to a close the 416th, not to be out done by the other night fighter squadrons, was on the move. For them it was to Pontedera, Italy. Three days after their arrival they found themselves engaged in an immensive all-out air offensive that was aimed at completely destroying German air power in Italy along with disruption of all lines of communication. The squadron flew night cover for the Allied troops as well as intruder missions into German territory. On April 22, they were pressed into daylight intruder operations, while maintaining their commitments for night missions.

The suddenness at which the 416th was directed to commence these missions did not give them time to properly brief their crews. The urgent need for the night fighters in this effort was due to the day fighters being grounded by a heavy overcast. With a lack of sleep from the missions flown the night before, the stalwart crews went back into the air at 10:00 a.m. on the

22nd. They were to fly armed reconnaissance missions into the Po Valley. The purpose was simple, to prevent the enemy forces from getting men and material across the Po River, and becoming a possible future threat.

April 1st was quite a night for the 415th, one quite fitting for that day. The squadron history recounts the events of that evening:

> April Fool's night a weird thing happened. Sgts. Eichhorn and Linck were on night duty when the tower called that a Beaufighter was circling. The night crew rubbed the sleep out of their four eyes, jumped into a jeep and tore out to the end of the runway to guide the pilot in. As he circled they noticed that his engines sounded very rough. He landed and skidded into a ground loop as one tire blew out. As Eichhorn and Linck drove up they saw a swastika on the tail and then they made out the outline of a Ju 88. Nothing daunted, the alert night crew handled their flashlights as if they were service .45's and calmly received the surrender of the two war-weary supermen. The Jerry crew said that they had quit voluntarily because they knew the jig was up and that we could expect more to do the same thing.

Paul Evans of the 414th NFS was busy busting trains, as was most of the 414th, in the last few months of the war in Italy:

> When we were flying in the Po Valley that winter of 1944/45, I was basically trying to chase trains. With the snow on the ground they would paint those cars white, they were kind of hard to find. So I figured out one night how to find one. I figured out that they had been going along there on those tracks long enough where the track was just a dark streak. When that dark streak stopped, where it was white, I figured that was where the train was. I flew around there for 15 or 20 minutes until I found one. He had just stopped. He shut his locomotive down and everything. I figured where the black streak stopped is where the train was. So I went back about a mile and came down that track. When I saw the white, where the dark streak quit, I strafed, the whole length of it. Then turned around and came back the other way and I hit that locomotive, that thing just . . . Oh boy, that thing just opened that up. I saw a picture of it the next day or two after the day boys got up there and took a picture of it. It just showed that thing was just opened like a flower.

April seemed to be the month for the European night fighters to move around the continent. The two Ninth Air Force squadrons moved that month as well as two of the Twelfth Air Force's squadrons. The 415th NFS moved to Gross-Gerau on the 19th while the 417th made two moves during the month. First they moved from La Vallon to St. Dizier where they joined the 415th on the 5th. Then movement orders again and they were on their way to Germany, arriving at Giebelstadt on the 24th.

From their new German airfield the 417th went operational immediately. Their primary mission was nightly patrols against enemy reconnaissance and intruder aircraft. It was at this time that they flew their first operational missions with the Widow. The 417th were also given the responsibility of protecting the bridgeheads of Ulm, Dillingen and Donauworth. These were part of the major supply arteries for the Allied forces. Though

Above and below: This collection of German Dornier Do 217 aircraft was discovered in a bombed out hanger on an abandoned German airfield. (Ernst)

no enemy aircraft were destroyed, a number of them were driven off before they could inflict any damage on the bridgeheads. The 417 NFS lost one crew when their aircraft was shot down by friendly antiaircraft fire, a common danger in night fighter operations.

Messerschmitt Me 410 "Hornisse" (Hornet) heavy fighter and fighter/bomber. (Kratz)

April was a most outstanding month for the 414th NFS. Although only three months had elapsed since they received their first P-61, aircraft serviceability for the month of April was 91%. During this period the aircrews flew 293 missions, 256 of which were sorties, for an amazing total of 719 operational hours. With great accuracy they dropped a record total of 181,500 pounds of general purpose demolition and fragmentation bombs.

The biggest single night in the history of the squadron was in April. At 8:30p.m., on Sunday, April 22, without any previous warning, the squadron was called upon to put up a maximum effort on armed reconnaissance missions in the Po Valley. The squadron had neither flown day operations nor night bombing in the P-61. They would soon show that they could do both, and with accuracy.

At the time the message came down, all their aircraft were undergoing either routine daily, 50-hour, or 100-hour inspections; and no bombs were loaded. Nevertheless, by 6:00a.m. every aircraft was in operational commission. By 1:00p.m. every P-61 assigned to the organization was in the air carrying 500 or 1,000 pound bombs – most of which had been loaded by hand. Not experienced in daylight operations, the squadron completed 21 day and 11 night sorties. Throughout the afternoon every man that could be spared from the motor pool, headquarters, mess, and supply was on the flight line – even a cook who had never touched a bomb before was out there helping to lift 1000-pounders six feet in the air to its shackle. Every pilot in the outfit, excepting those on Detached Service in Germany, flew two sorties. Every aircraft flew three sorties except the one that was lost on its second mission. Two ships flew four sorties.

With the war winding down, there was no lack of heroism in the 416th NFS. Maj. James D. Urso, squadron operations officer, would be awarded the Distinguished Service Cross, for his actions while flying one of the squadron's many intruder missions into the Po Valley. On April 22, a total of 21 sorties were flown in which three of the Mosquitos were shot down and two others were so badly damaged that it was only by the skill and bravery of the pilots that they made it back to their airfields. For Maj. Urso's part in this mission, the citation reads:

MAJOR URSO, as leader of a formation of Mosquitos, was assigned a dangerous daytime, low-level strafing attack on an important Po River crossing, over which the enemy was retreating in force. While engaged in strafing the crossing, his aircraft sustained many hits from intense and accurate anti-aircraft fire. One engine was knocked out and the plane, of wooden construction, started burning fiercely. He immediately ordered his navigator (1st Lt. Talmadge F. Simpson) to abandon the aircraft. MAJOR URSO released his harness and went to the assistance of the navigator who was trapped in the escape hatch, finding it necessary to push and twist the navigator and finally to kick him from the plane, since he was not only caught in the hatch, but blinded by flames, eyebrows and lashes being singed. Heroically and courageously, with no thought of his own safety up to this time, MAJOR URSO had ignored altogether his chance of escape through the pilot's escape hatch. The plane was now flying too low for him to abandon the aircraft; he immediately crash-landed the flaming plane. Thrown from his seat, the engine controls fell on him, and he was so seriously wounded that amputation of his left foot was necessary. MAJOR URSO'S heroism and readiness to sacrifice his own life for the safety of his crew are exemplar of the manner in which he has performed his numerous assignments, and reflect great credit upon himself and the Armed Forces of the United States of America.

Urso and Simpson had bailed out over enemy territory and were captured. For Major Urso, it was a short ordeal. When the Germans picked him up, he was immediately treated by a doctor and then they abandoned him that same day – they were in a hasty retreat. By April 6th Lt. Simpson was in Florence and safe.

On May 7, the 416th sent two pilots to Naples to get the squadrons first two P-61s. To say that they came too late to see any action with this unit would be an understatement as that afternoon word reached them that the war in Europe was over. The next day, V-E Day, was also "Hangover Day." Also, the two pilots sent to Naples came back empty handed. The Widows were to be sent to where they could still contribute to the war effort.

Paul Evans of the 414th had quite a day when the war ended for the MTO:

It was the last day of the war over there. I had a load of bombs, 4 or 500 pounds of bombs, and I was supposed to go up to this airfield in northern Italy to drop these bombs on it and then set up in a pattern just south of it. I got up there and saw all these lights, all the lights in the place were on. I thought 'Something's wrong here!' So we got a little closer and I got shot at on the first pass. So I decided I had to get a better look. I got a little closer and I saw something running around the field. So I got even closer and what I saw were big white stars on these tanks, US tanks, American tanks with the big stars. Ah, shoot. It's all over. So I radioed back and said, 'There's American tanks on this field.' They said 'Well, back off.' So I backed off and sat there for 15 or 20 minutes or so until they did a little investigating. Then they came back and said 'Why, it's all over.' So I had to go out over the ocean and dump my bombs and then land. That was the end of the war.

Chapter 18

Intrude, Interdict, Intercept

In their drive towards the Philippines, US Army forces invaded Morotai Island on September 15, 1944 in an effort to control the northern area of the Molucca Sea. The ground echelon of the 418th NFS arrived twelve days after the invasion and had traveled some 900 miles by LST. To keep on schedule for the October Leyte invasion, airfields on Morotai had to be made operational. The abandoned Japanese airfield was in very poor condition, but an alternate site at Wama seemed promising. The engineers had four thousand feet of steel mat down by October 4th. Maj. Carroll Smith arrived the following day with the air echelon of the 418th NFS.

After the fall of Morotai, American forces landed at Ormoc Bay on Leyte in the Philippines that October. About two weeks later, the 421st NFS arrived at Tacloban airfield, where artillery duels had shells criss-crossing the field. Pushing hard, the Allies next landed on Mindoro on December 15th. Once again the AAF's night fighters were not far behind. The 418th NFS moved up from its Morotai base on the 26th; a detachment of the 419th NFS, which had arrived on Morotai in late November, took over the 418th's responsibilities there.

As 1945 opened, the night fighters were still moving in shortly after the Allied ground forces took another island. Following in the tradition of the older night fighter squadrons in the Southwest Pacific Area, newcomer 547th NFS (they arrived on New Guinea in September 1944) were amongst the first aircraft to arrive at Lingayen on Luzon Island. The duties of all of these night fighter squadrons were to protect their home airfields, the nearby naval convoys and beachheads, and to strike at the Japanese installations within their reach.

From their new station at San Jose on Mindoro, the 418th NFS started off the year adding two more victories to their score, and learned the rewards could be quite pleasurable. On the night of January 4, 1945, 1st Lt. Albert R. Sorbo and 2nd Lt.

George N. Kerstetter intercepted and destroyed two Jake reconnaissance seaplanes over the local PT boat base. Bright and early the next morning, the PT base commander presented the night fighters with two cases of cold beer. He also stated he would continue supplying a case for every enemy aircraft destroyed over his base. The night fighters considered, for a moment at least, allowing all incoming Japanese to get over the PT base before knocking them down. The next evening Sorbo and Kerstetter got their third kill, a Val this time – though not over the PT base.

On January 18th, the 418th team of 2nd Lts. James R. McQueen, Jr. and Hugh L. Gordon, while on convoy cover, came across four Japanese bombers with their lights on! Not looking a gift horse in the mouth, they quickly dispatched two of them while the remaining two jettisoned their bombs and fled for their lives.

Other squadrons would score in the air in January. This would turn out to be one of the better months during 1945 in which the night fighters would participate in any amount of air combat. First. Lt. Ralph R. LeVitt, 2nd Lt. Frederic J. Kahn, and S/Sgt John O. Graham of the 419th NFS got a Betty on January 9th. The 421st's team of 1st Lts. Owen M. Wolf and Byron N. Allain, with S/Sgt Donald H. Trabing as gunner, on this January 24th mission, scored their fourth victory. They were flying patrol over Leyte when they were vectored by GCI to a target. R/O Allain made contact with his AI radar and guided Wolf to within 1,000 feet of the Zeke 32. With Lt. Wolf firing the 20mm cannon and Sgt. Trabing firing the .50 cal. turret guns, they closed in on the enemy aircraft. The enemy craft burst into flames and crashed a short distance from General Frederic Smith's V Fighter Command.

The 547th's special flight of three P-61s and a P-38 night fighter was in the air on January 9th. Piloting one of the Widows

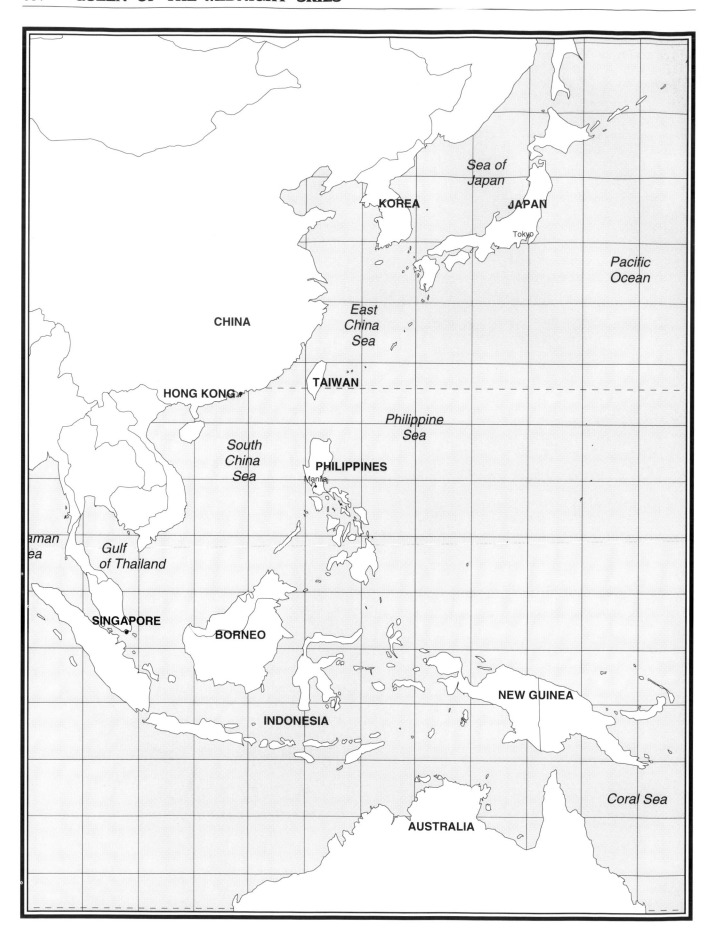

was Capt. Edwin C. Annis with his R/O, 2nd Lt. Nicholas Detz. The combat report for this mission tells the story:

I (Capt. Annis) came in over Lingayen Gulf just about 20 miles to the east and contacted Broomstick. We were a flight of four ships; the flight consisted of three P-61s and one P-38 night fighter aircraft. After a short time of patrolling at 8,000 feet, Broomstick sent us north to cover a convoy. We started out for the convoy, but my ship and the P-38 were called back to south of the bridge-head on the beach. A smoke screen was moving in on the shore. Just south of Lingayen the P-38 saw a Jap aircraft, a Hamp, at about 1900/I/9. A pass at the Jap plane was made by the P-38 (flown by 1st Lt. Roy E. Oakes) and shortly thereafter the P-61 fired 150 rounds of HE ammunition into the Jap's tail at short range, 700 to 900 feet. Three bursts were fired and the Jap went into the clouds or smoke screen. A half minute later, after my ship peeled off to the right, we saw the Jap plane hit the ground in the area between Umanday and Aguillar and spread over the ground in flames. There was a beautiful smoke screen and Able was really throwing up the stuff. My R/O saw the Jap fighter first and also saw him hit the deck in flames.

The night fighters of the SWPA were finding that their talents, as strictly a defensive organization were not being fully used. As with the German aircraft in Europe, Japanese aircraft were not plentiful at the time. But, once again, as in the European theater, night offensive operations would greatly help. The 547th NFS started attaching bomb shackles to the bottom of their P-61s crew nacelle, which was capable of carrying a 1,000 pound bomb, plus one under each wing. To give their P-61s extended range so they could strike enemy installations further away, they removed their turrets to lighten the aircraft and added a fuel tank in the cavity thus provided. For this effort, the squadron's engineering officer, Capt. Dale Strausser, was awarded the Bronze Star.

This squadron seemed to be full of bright ideas. Another one was their own homemade napalm bomb and detonation device. They also came up with their own delayed fusing device.

The 418th's C.O., Major Carroll C. Smith, was sent back to the US for a well deserved rest in February. Taking over command of the squadron was Capt. William B. Sellers, who had transferred in from the 547th NFS. By mid-March, Capt. Sellers was flying the 418th's first intruder mission in a Widow. Loaded with a 250 pound demolition bomb, he attacked the Japanese held town of Logaspi where he dropped his bomb and made numerous strafing passes.

Many replacements were joining the night fighter squadrons as many of the "old hands" were going back Stateside. One of the 421st NFS's new crews, with less than a month with the squadron, showed that they had the right stuff. On the night of March 11th, one of these new crews was on patrol. Second Lt. Carl R. Remington, F/O William E. Boze, and gunner T/Sgt Brady W. Sweeney were vectored by GCI to an enemy aircraft southwest of Lingayen. R/O Boze soon had the target on his scope. Despite the heavy use of window, Boze managed to keep contact and guided Lt. Remington into range. Closing in, Sgt.

The 418th NFS was just settling in at their new airfield at San Jose on Mindoro in the Philippines as the new year opened. They would be operating from this field for six months before being moved to Okinawa in preparation for the invasion of the Japanese Islands. (AAHS)

Thirteenth Air Force's 419th NFS was still operating from Middelburg Island in the NEI as the new year commenced. Like the 418th, it was quite busy flying intruder missions. Detachment A was flying out of Morotai, Halmaheras during most of this period also. (Lukas)

Still muddled in the politics of command, the 421st's air echelon was flying out of Peleliu in the Palau Group. They would return from their banishment on January 11th and resume air operations from Tacloban on Leyte, PI. (Hernandez collection)

Sweeney fired the turret guns at the Betty. The stricken bomber burst into flames and dove into the ocean.

With this victory the squadron total did not change! First Lt. David T. Corts had engaged a number of enemy bombers on September 9, 1944. In the pursuing aerial battle, as one enemy bomber was attempting to shoot at Lt. Corts' P-61, it actually shot down one of the other Japanese planes. Far East Air Forces had given Corts credit for this victory on October 10th, but on December 30th Fifth Air Force rescinded the credit.

The saving of lost or damaged aircraft in poor weather and at night was another capability of the P-61. In the CBI, the 426th Night Fighter Squadron aided damaged B-29s in the return to their base at Chengtu, China. The 6th, 548th and 549th Night Fighter Squadrons performed similar missions in the Saipan, Iwo Jima and the Okinawa areas. The 547th NFS personnel in the Southwest Pacific Area went a little further and worked out

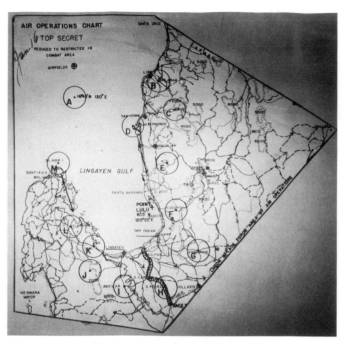

Air operations chart for January 16, 1945. (Ellings)

Below: The 547th NFS moved from Owi Island, just off northeast New Guinea, to Lingayen on Luzon, PI, on January 16th. This was not their first presence in the Philippines as their special detachment of P-61s, P-38s and a B-25 had been operating from Tacloban on Leyte since November 9th. (Jones via Thompson)

a GCA system – P-61 style. The 547th reports:

The idea that poor weather landings can be accomplished with the use of airborne radar was largely accidental. During a period in which ground forces had released smoke to conceal the airstrip at Lingayen, one of the 547th's P-61s was returning from an intruder mission to Formosa. Upon approaching the field, the pilot was unable to locate the strip since it was partially obscured by smoke. The R/O, Lt. John Cross, however, noticed a bright return on his scope during a nose down turn made by his pilot, Capt. Kenneth Schrieber. The echo corresponded to the pierced steel plank (PSP) strip of the airfield hard stands. At the time of the incident, Capt. Baldwin, serving as R/O for Col. Odell (Squadron CO), was viewing his observer's scope while the aircraft was taxiing to take-off position for a mission. Capt. Baldwin picked up the airborne P-61 in the distance at the time he heard Lt. Cross broadcast that he had the PSP strip on his scope. This resulted in a two-way fix on the runway – from the airborne craft and from the P-61 on the landing end of the field. The aircraft on the ground was pointed in the direction of the incoming plane. By multiple guidance, with Lt. Cross vectoring Capt. Schrieber to lineup squarely with the runway, and with Capt. Baldwin calling out elevations of the airborne P-61

above the landing point, Capt. Schrieber was able to descend in line with the PSP strip while safely clearing the terrain till he passed over the ground guiding P-61 at an altitude he estimated at less than 100 feet.

Following this unusual experiment in low visibility landing, additional landings were made during daylight, initially, and later at night. The project was called Rough Pancake because of some unusual attitudes of the aircraft using the system, and was later given the name RADPAN (Radar Pancake).

During seven weeks of experimentation, the 547th made one hundred and sixteen landings under varying conditions utilizing this technique. Of course, a good instrument pilot with confidence in his R/O and equipment was a major requirement in such operations, and the SCR-720 AI radar had to be properly tuned.

Scores against the airborne enemy continued for the 547th in February and March. On February 19th, the crew of 1st Lt. Arthur D. Borque and 2nd Lt. Bonnie B. Rucks was credited with two Bettys. Almost ten days later, 1st Lt. Kenneth R. Schrieber, with 2nd Lt. Bonnie B. Rucks flying as R/O again,

"Old Salty Dog II" of the 419th shows that the white squadron aircraft numbers have moved from the nose of the aircraft to the tail and that two red diagonal stripes have been added to the booms. (Vincent)

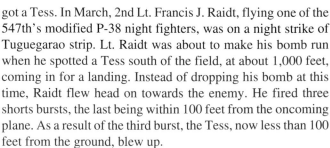

Lts. Arthur B. Bourque, pilot, and Bonnie B. Rucks, R/O, of the 547th NFS take off from Lingayen airstrip, Luzon for a dusk patrol in "Swing Shift Skipper." The 547th worked closely with Navy PT boat crews during dusk and night operations. (USAF)

Lts. Albert R. Sorbo, pilot, and George N. Kerstetter, R/O, of the 418th NFS. Team work was very important in a night fighter crew. Lt. Sorbo reported: "First of all, the pilot and radar observer should have a complete understanding of each other's methods, which should be consistent. For example, the pilot should establish a fairly definite rate of turn for gentle and hard turns; otherwise, the radar observer may be confused at times whether to use a hard turn or gentle, and jinking might be the result, which is very undesirable at close range. They should also agree on the phraseology to be used during interception. It should be brief and easy to understand." (Odell)

got a Tess. In March, 2nd Lt. Francis J. Raidt, flying one of the 547th's modified P-38 night fighters, was on a night strike of Tuguegarao strip. Lt. Raidt was about to make his bomb run when he spotted a Tess south of the field, at about 1,000 feet, coming in for a landing. Instead of dropping his bomb at this time, Raidt flew head on towards the enemy. He fired three shorts bursts, the last being within 100 feet from the oncoming plane. As a result of the third burst, the Tess, now less than 100 feet from the ground, blew up.

In May, the 418th NFS started flying intruder missions to Formosa from their Mindoro base. These missions consisted of dropping a 1,000 pound bomb and strafing. The 550th NFS was also experimenting with ways to make their intruder missions a little more deadly. To enable them to extend their intruding work they modified their P-61s to take 310 gallon external fuel tanks instead of the standard 165 gallon tanks. The 419th was glad to get some P-61s that could carry the 165 gallon tanks. They found that the external drop tanks extended their flight time from four to six and a half hours. Eventually, the 419th also got the 310 gallon tanks and found that with them they could fly at economy cruise for 11 hours.

Capt. John H. Streibel was a relative newcomer to the 550th. He had much experience as a night fighter. Before the US entered the war, he was flying with the Royal Air Force in Europe. After America's entry, he joined the AAF's night fighter program in the States. No AAF aircraft in the Thirteenth Air Force were equipped to carry rockets, but the Navy did. Under the guiding eyes of Capt. Streibel, the assistance of Northrop technical representative Scott Johnson, and by obtaining the required items by ways and means best left unknown, they had a P-61 modified by mid-April. Results from flight tests were so encouraging that all the squadron's P-61s were so modified by early June.

The 419th's C.O., Lt.Col. Norman M. Jacob, hit upon a like idea. Rocket launchers and associated equipment were salvaged from a wrecked USN Ventura. To give the pilot an estimated target range an AN/APN-1 radar altimeter was installed. They found that the rockets were unsuitable for aerial combat because they dispersed when fired; however, they were effective against enemy ground targets. Not many of the 419th's aircraft were so modified because of the lack of launching equipment.

As the Allies constantly moved in a northerly direction in late 1944 and early 1945, it was advantageous to bypass certain areas controlled by the Japanese. One of these was the Japanese forces on Borneo in the Netherlands East Indies. Constant pressure by Allied aircraft had inhibited Japanese forces in this area from interfering with their push towards the Japanese home islands. But in the planning of the invasion of Japan itself, it could be seen that this bypassed area could inhibit operations in the South China Sea.

The invasion of Borneo included joint air operations by Fifth and Thirteenth Air Forces along with Royal Australian Air Force units. It was also unique in that a number of AAF night fighter squadrons would be engaged in joint operations. To provide night cover for the Allies, as well as intruder mission against Japanese targets, detachments of the 418th, 419th, and 550th NFS operated from Sanga Sanga in the Sulu Archipelago. The invasion at Balikpapan on the east coast of Borneo was set for July 1st. Air bombardment began earlier and included night operations by the night fighters, the 550th was the first to take part when they arrived on June 1st. The 418th and 419th detachments arrived in the latter part of the month to give added strength in protection of the invasion fleet and post invasion protection for the Allies on Borneo.

Part of the 550th's contingent was P-61 pilot Donald D. Coski, who remembers those southwest Pacific operations:

Part of the 550th flew down to Zamboanga on Mindanao and flew top cover for convoys moving in that area. We stayed here only a short time, then moved on south to the small island of Sanga Sanga, the southern most island in the Philippines. Here, we flew convoy top cover and cover for the invasion of Balikpapan, Borneo. Generally, these were long missions of about six to eight hours. That is a long time to sit on that CO_2 bottle in the life raft package which we sat on. We carried four 165 gallon droppable fuel tanks.

We were covering some mine sweepers that were clearing the waters for the landing at Balikpapan. It took us about two hours to go down there. We patrolled for two hours and then two hours back. We didn't maintain any strict radio silence, and the Japs must have had our radios monitored. Because more than once, a flight would abort and have to return to base and the pilot would have to radio back for a replacement. This would leave up to a two hour gap with no cover over the mine sweepers. The Japs would have a flight of Betty's in there in no time blasting those mine sweepers. Those boys on the mine sweepers would sure plead for cover, but there was nothing we could do. The Japs would be gone by the time replacement P-61s could get down there.

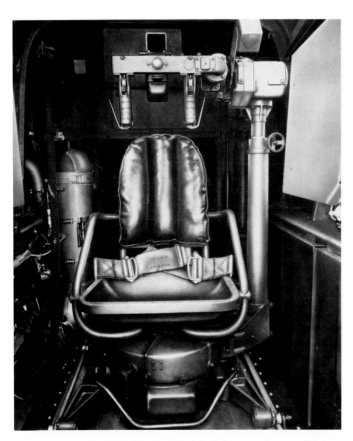

Gunner's station in a P-61. The Pacific night fighter squadrons used their gunners on a number of missions. The 421st was quite happy to have their turret equipped Widows and gunners aboard when a flight of their aircraft mixed it up with Japanese fighters on a number of occasions. (Northrop via Balzer)

In mid-February, leading AAF night fighter ace and C.O. of the 418th NFS was transferred back to the US for a well deserved rest and reassignment. Taking over the helm was Capt. William B. Sellers who had just transferred in from the 547th NFS. Lt. Hap Halliday is on the left and Capt. Bill Sellers is on the right in this photo. (Odell)

Above: Club Philippines? This was the living and operating quarters of the 547th NFS at Lingayen. The 547th never had a chance to "dig in" until the last six months of the war. Before that time, they were "island hopping" and constantly moving forward to be in the first line of defense in the theater. These photos show what an outfit with a lot of "esprit de corps" can do along with Yankee ingenuity. (Odell)

One of the pilots in our squadron said, 'I know what I'll do; I'll radio in I'm returning to base; and I'll drop down low; and when the Betty's come in, I'll get me some victories.' Another pilot spoke up and said, 'What do you think those boys on the mine sweepers would think of your idea?' That ended that. I guess Northrop had done a good job publishing the ability of those P-61s because the Japs sure never came around when one was in the air.

Bronc (R.J. Foreman, Coski's R/O) and I were scrambled into the air one night and vectored onto a bogey by Sector Control. They said that the bogey was out about 75 miles. We pursued for a few minutes. The bogey cut out; then they turned us back and had us patrol over the airfield until morning. That was, as far as I know, the closest anyone in our outfit got to an enemy plane in the air.

There were three night fighter squadrons operating out of Sanga Sanga on the Borneo campaign; our squadron, and the 419th Night Fighter Squadron, both of the Thirteenth Air Force, and a flight from the 418th NFS of the Fifth Air Force. The Black Widows were having engine trouble on take-off and the ships would wind up in the ocean off the end of the runway. Our squadron lost one ship, and I believe there were two other losses. Twice an engine coughed with Bronc and myself; however, I cut the power both times and got the plane stopped by the end of the runway. One night on our way to Balikpapan, the floor felt slick under the rudder pedals. I turned on the light and saw an hydraulic leak, and we had to return to base. They had notified my squadron that I was making an emergency landing; and when the landing was uneventful, my buddies all went back to bed grumbling about us getting them out of bed in the middle of the night and then no crash!

The P-38 boys were flying top cover in the daytime, and the P-61s were covering at night. When the weather got bad, and the 38s couldn't get through to the patrol area, they started sending us out in the P-61s. I'm not sure of this, but I always figured it was then that they first conceived the idea to change the night fighters to the 'All Weather Fighters.'

The campaign was finished so we took down our tents, loaded everything aboard our planes, and took off for our home base at Leyte. We had agreed to pass over and buzz the airstrip as we left. As they buzzed the strip, each plane got progressively lower. I was one of the last planes, and the plane ahead of me had his propellers ticking the coral, so I pulled up and over into a barrel roll as we passed over the strip. Bronc, and the mechanic aboard, moaned a little at the time but were all grins later. Also, I received a slight reprimand from my flight leader.

The 547th NFS, like the 418th, enlarged their scope of operations by flying extended missions to Formosa and the Chinese mainland. On some occasions these missions were flying protective cover for Army B-24 and Navy PB4Y Privateer aircraft, and on other occasions flying harassment missions armed with 1,000 pound bombs. This caused little destruction but great confusion to the enemy ground installations on Formosa. These wide ranging missions are graphically illustrated in a report from the 547th Night Fighter Squadron:

A number of highly successful missions employing the 'shadow tactics' devised by Capt. Paul H. Baldwin have been completed. Crews

On March 6th the 419th moved up to Puerto Princesa on Palaway, PI. One of their P-61s buzzes the strip upon arrival. (USAF)

The 419th is soon operational and providing cover for the advancing Allied forces and striking out at enemy airfields to prevent them from getting off night flights. (Vincent)

Late April saw the 421st on the move again. This time they were stationed at Clark Field north of the Philippine capitol of Manila. (USAF)

The 308th Bomb Wing had operational control over the 547th NFS. Col. Robert L. Johnston, Wing operations officer, was a product of day fighters and had no faith in the night fighters. He was invited by the 547th to go on patrol with them. On the night of February 28th he flew in the gunner's seat with the crew of 1st Lt. Kenneth R. Schrieber (pilot) and 2nd Lt. Bonnie B. Rucks (R/O). Airborne some 35 minutes, they found a target. With only 16 rounds of 20mm ammunition expended, the Japanese Tess transport exploded. They had closed so fast on the Tess that the exploding enemy showered the P-61 with fragments. The following day the victorious crew posed beside their aircraft with a freshly applied Japanese flag just below the pilot's cockpit. From left to right are: Col. Johnston, Lt. Schrieber, Lt. Rucks, and crew chief T/Sgt. J.J. Crough. Lt.Col. William C. Odell, the 547th's C.O., immediately recommended a decoration for Col. Johnston (as a crew member) with credit for one enemy aircraft destroyed. He got it, and from that time forward was a staunch supporter of the 547th and the night fighter effort in general. (Odell)

of Navy Privateers have high praise for the protection given by our crews throughout the South China Sea patrols. The main disadvantage of this type of night fighter escort mission is a difference in range and endurance between the P-61 and the Privateer. Although, it is most effective during that part of the mission when the P-61 can tail the Navy patrol aircraft. In the past 22 days, 14 such missions were flown during which there were six enemy encounters. All of which were driven off prior to attack upon the Navy aircraft. No kills were made, although two probably damaged aircraft were reported.

Upon completion of the field modifications to P-61 aircraft proposed by Lt. Gillespie in which the central turret will be removed and B-24 fuselage ferry tanks installed in the cavity, greater range and endurance will result and permit night fighter escort 'on-station' time to be extended. Navy pilots are requesting the P-61 night trailers directly to the squadron, and it is regrettable that other commitments prevent full cooperation. They have overcome their concern that the trailing night fighter will mistake the Privateer for an enemy aircraft. This was brought out by a daylight demonstration in which two P-61s and our B-25 Fat-Cat craft were used. Lt. Commander J.B. Wilson participated in the demonstration. He was an observer in the trailing aircraft in which six mock attacks were made upon the second P-61 acting as an attacking enemy. The trail P-61 maintained a six to eight mile interval between itself and the B-25. The attacking P-61 injected itself between the trailer and target at ranges from three to five miles behind the B-25. Upon incident of the intermediate echo between the

trailer and the blip representing the B-25, the trailer closed to within firing range before the attacking P-61 could close. This type of tactic, in which the escorting night fighter shadows the aircraft to be protected, is valid as long as the range of the airborne radar and the shadowing aircraft is greater than that possessed by the enemy. It is interesting to note that night attacks upon Navy Privateers have reduced since the shadow tactics have been employed. The conclusion is that the Japanese air defense is reluctant to dispatch fighters against a patrol aircraft that has a shadow aircraft in trail. In two recent missions, the tail warning device on the trail P-61 has been triggered, indicating that Japanese night fighters are being vectored against the escort aircraft rather than the patrol bomber. No encounters resulted from these incidents.

Central Pacific

As 1945 opened, the battle waged around the Marianas. The Seventh Air Force's three night fighter squadrons were all on

R/O Milton Burman of the 418th NFS poses with his P-61. In the background is one of the P-70s still being used in intruder work and a Navy Privateer. The night fighters flew cooperative missions with the big PB4Ys. (Ellings)

421st NFS crew go over the ops orders for an upcoming mission. A parachute is draped over the plexiglass nose of a P-61. These early radomes tended to soften and droop inward in high heat. The later fiberglass radomes solved this problem. (Hernandez collection)

It was the exception when the night fighters didn't work solo and to have multiple squadrons working together was quire rare. In the summer of 1945, detachments of the 418th, 419th, and 550th NFSs operated detachments from Sanga Sanga Island in the Sulu Archipelago in support of the Borneo campaign. The 419th P-61 is quite recognizable with its distinctive diagonal striping on its booms and squadron aircraft number on the vertical stabilizer. The P-61 of the 550th on the left has been modified to carry 5" HVARs – a quite lethal weapon in hitting ground targets. (Lortz via Thompson)

Seventh Air Force's 6th NFS was still on Saipan in the Marianas when the year opened, and would have a presence there until late April. The 548th NFS, which was under the wing of the 6th's Hawaii based element, would join them on Saipan on January 26th. (Maita)

The nose art of "Anonymous" is quite distinctive, to say the least. "Anonymous" was added to the light rectangular area below the pilot's compartment after this photo of the 548th's aircraft was taken on Saipan. (Maita)

418th NFS family portrait. (Ellings)

A P-61 of the 548th NFS taxies to the parking area at No.1 Airfield on Iwo Jima, Bonin Islands, in early March 1945. This is the first night fighter to land at this field. (USAF)

Crew of the first P-61 to land on Iwo pose beside their aircraft. From left to right are: Maj. Robert D. Curtis (pilot and C.O. of the 548th NFS), Capt. Philip K. Horrigan (R/O), and S/Sgt George M. Duncan (crew chief).

Maj. Dave Curtis, C.O. of the 548th NFS, on the right, welcomes Maj. Joseph E. Payne, C.O. of the 549th, as the latter arrived on Iwo on March 6, 1945. "Little Joe" was Maj. Payne's aircraft. (USAF)

Saipan providing night protection. When Saipan based B-29s started hitting the Japanese home islands, the Japanese struck back at Saipan. The 6th NFS, which had had a presence on Saipan since June 1944, started the year out with three kills.

On January 1st the crew of 2nd Lts. Donald T. Evans and Nicholas R. DeVita, pilot and R/O, and Cpl. Raymond L. Golden, gunner, was airborne on a combat air patrol (CAP) when GCI vectored them on a bogie. Lt. Evans closed to within 500 feet and identified the plane as a Betty. At this point he fired and hits were observed in the engine nacelle. The engine started to smoke and the aircraft went in. The following evening they repeated their feat.

That same evening another 6th crew, F/Os John J. Szpila and Alfred H. Borges, Jr. was scrambled during the first flash

red. GCI vectored them to the target, taking them to 15,000 feet. F/O Borges could not make AI contact and the chase was called off. When the second alert was called, they were vectored to the north and made contact. During the chase, radar contact was lost twice because of radar malfunction. A third contact was established at six miles. Visual was made at 1,500 feet and the target was identified as a Frances. Still closing in, F/O Szpila opened fire at 1,000 feet. Hits were observed on both engines. Soon after, the Frances exploded close to the water and went in.

With the slackening of Japanese attacks on Saipan in February, things slowed down for the night fighters. Also at this time, the Allies were invading Iwo Jima in the Volcano Islands which put them much closer to Japan. From Iwo Jima fighters would escort the B-29s to Japan. The 6th NFS, 548th NFS and

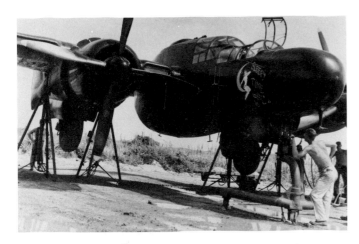

"Sleepy Time Gal II" of the 6th NFS having its landing gear cycled during a maintenance check. (Irwin via Thompson)

"Saddle Happy" of the 548th NFS. R/O of this ship was Ployer Hill. His father was namesake for Hill Air Force Base in the state of Utah in the US. (Bode via Thompson)

549th NFS arrived soon after the invasion to provide night protection. The Japanese felt the night fighters' presence on March 25th when two of the 6th's crews dispatched a couple of Betty bombers.

By the end of April, Okinawa in the Ryukyus had been secured. By mid-June, the 548th moved to the tiny island of Ie Shima which was some seven miles from Okinawa. They were soon followed by the 421st and 547th NFSs from the SWPA. In late July, the 418th NFS arrived on Okinawa.

One of the stranger tasks to be performed by a night fighter crew occurred on June 9, 1945. The 548th Night Fighter Squadron was on an Air-Sea Rescue mission. A VII Fighter Command report cited the action as follows:

Thousands of men on Iwo watched the Black Widow go after the Superfort. Had the big bomber eluded the fighter and crashed on Iwo,

some of these men would surely have lost their lives, a Headquarters spokesman said.

Over Osaka, the B-29 took a direct flack hit just as it was ready to release it bombs. The shell tore a three-foot hole through the pilot's compartment, killing the plane commander. The bomb-bay doors were jammed shut and could not be opened again. A stunned and bleeding co-pilot faced the terrific job of flying a hopelessly crippled plane back to a friendly base.

Left far behind by other planes in the formation and with all radio equipment useless, the Superfort staggered along toward Iwo.

It was still miles from its goal when the Black Widow, on a routine patrol flight, sighted the bomber and saw that it was in trouble. In the fighter plane Lt. Arthur C. Shepherd of Seattle and Lt. Arvid Shulenberger of Washington, D.C., quickly sent a radio warning to other aircraft to beware of the damaged Superfort, and then undertook to lead the sky giant to Iwo.

549th NFS's flight line on the east side of Southern airstrip on Iwo Jima in the Bonin Islands. (Tigner)

The toothy character belongs to the 550th NFS – the last night fighter squadron activated in the AAF. R/O George Irby is standing under the right wing, not in photo is Capt. Edward A. Grossheider, pilot. (Stevick via Thompson)

In June 1945, the 418th, 419th, and 550th NFSs sent detachments to Sanga Sanga Island in the Sulu Archipelago which was the Air Force staging area for the Borneo invasion. Pictured above is a crew from the 550th NFS. "OHLAMI" was not the name of some South Pacific beauty that the crew of this craft knew. It was an acronym made from the abbreviation of the crew's home states: (OH) Ohio, (LA) Louisiana, and (MI) Michigan. Beside the aircraft are Newell P. Witte (pilot), H.C. O'Brien (R/O), and a couple of ground crewmen (one is crew chief S/Sgt. T.C. Cope). (Witte via Thompson)

"Gruesome Twosome" of the 550th on Morotai in the Halmaheras. (Stevick via Thompson)

Flying close to the B-29, the Black Widow crew could see that the big ship was too badly damaged to attempt a landing and that the crew was preparing to bail out.

Finally, over Iwo the co-pilot ordered the crew to 'hit the silk.' Eight crewmen leaped on the first run over the island. Then the co-pilot swung back, set the automatic pilot, and he and the remaining crewmen jumped to safety.

Empty except for its death-dealing bomb load, and the body of its commander, the big plane started its wild 'Ghost Ride' pursued by the Black Widow intent on shooting it down over the water.

'As soon as we cleared the island, we started shooting with all eight guns,' said Shepherd. 'Our first burst went into the left outside engine which began to smoke and then flame. The bomber continued to fly. The loss of one engine swung it in another orbit back toward Iwo. We held our fire until it had swung clear of the island again. Then we gave it everything we had.'

The Black Widow poured 564 rounds of .50 caliber machine-gun fire and 320 rounds of 20mm cannon shells into the staggering Superfort.

'We could see the bullets stitching the left wing from tip to fuselage.' Shepherd added, 'Then fire raced back to the tail. The .50s made neat small holes, and the 20s tore chunks out of the plane as they

went through. We were flying close enough to see where practically every round was hitting and wondered how long the big bomber could keep taking it. Finally, just as it began to seem as if the plane would keep flying forever, it headed downward and plunged into the sea.'

In June, the night fighters got their last flurry of enemy aircraft. From Ie Shima the 548th claimed a Tojo, Rufe and a Betty while the 549th still on Iwo Jima destroyed a Betty also. The airmen in the SWPA added a couple to their score when the 419th based at Puerto Princesa on Palawan in the Philippines got a Nick.

Mack Ballard of the 421st got a rude awakening one morning when he found whose convoy he had been protecting:

I was vectored out to cover a navy convoy. It was about 300 miles away (from Ie Shima). We went out, right on the nose of where they had vectored us. There was cloud cover between 5,000 and 7,000 feet. We were flying at about 10,000 feet. Everything was fine. No enemy aircraft, no bogeys any place. When daylight arrived, we spotted the flight of four P-38s coming out to relieve us. I did the usual thing by going down through the cloud cover and buzzing the ships in the convoy, waggling the wings, and taking off for home. One problem was, when I got down and looked across – they were Japanese ships!

Here we were – no bombs, we did have our machine guns and cannon, but I was out of fuel. The P-38s were still on their way to relieve us. So I radioed them and told them what had happened. They in turn said they would cover the convoy until the bombers got out there. Then the P-38s and B-25s that came out worked over that convoy of Jap ships.

When Ballard went down and waggled his wings at the convoy, there was no indication that they knew he was the enemy:

Completely caught them by surprise. And here I had been up there buzzing around all night. I guess they thought it was one of their planes protecting them. And of course they didn't have the radar that we had.

The last Pacific kill credited to the night fighters was accomplished by the 548th NFS team of 1st Lt. Thomas W. Schultz, 2nd Lt. Ployer P. Hill, and S/Sgt Benjamin J. Boscardin, when they shot down a Betty on August 5, 1944. But to another 548th crew went the claim of the last enemy aircraft destroyed in the war. On the night of August 14th the crew of 2nd Lts. Robert W. Clyde and Bruce K. Leford who, in the course of chasing an Oscar at wave-height, caused the enemy to crash into the ocean.

The three night fighter squadrons stationed on Ie Shima even got in on the post-war show as that tiny island was the stopover point where the surrender party from Japan stopped to transfer to a USAAF transport prior to going on to the Philippines to discuss the Japanese capitulation. On their return trip and subsequent transfer back to their white Bettys, the 421st NFS participated in escorting them back to Japan. From the beginning (the 6th in Hawaii on December 7, 1941) to the last (the 548th last enemy destroyed and the 421st's escorting the surrender party), the night fighters saw it all!

A Widow of the 547th stands ready on pierced steel plank apron at Lingayen airstrip on Luzon. (Schrieber)

"327" of the 419th NFS takes off from its Philippine airstrip. (Vincent)

The 419th NFS is surrounded by a tropical paradise, or so the travel brochure says. (Vincent)

Due to very limited night action, the 550th turned to intruder work, as did most of the night fighter squadrons. Field modifications were made to enable their P-61s to carry 5" rockets. (USAF Archives)

The story goes that a high-speed dive followed by a sharp pull-up over-stressed even this rugged Widow, which prompted this dramatic reconfiguration upon landing. (Thompson)

A fearsome Widow. (Gaudette via Ivie)

548th NFS on Iwo Jima. Most of the squadron's aircraft carried the squadron insignia below the pilot's compartment. The distinctively decorated "Spook" can be seen in the background. (USAF)

Posing beside the 549th's "Sleepy Time Gal" are (from left to right): Larry Garland, Louis Alford, and Joe Hendrickson. (Alford via Thompson)

Maj. Louis Alford in the cockpit of "Sleepy Time Gal." Note the photo of his daughter Emily in the center of the control column. (Alford via Thompson)

"Miss Jeannette" of the 549th NFS. (Charlesworth via Thompson)

Walt Wernsing standing by "Midnite Madness." (Bode and Wernsing)

The pylons for four external fuel tanks and eight rocket rails for HVARs on this 549th P-61 are an indication of the changed role of the P-61. Designed to be a night defender of cities and airfields, the changing requirements of war made it into an offensive weapon – which it proved itself quite capable of doing. (Tigner)

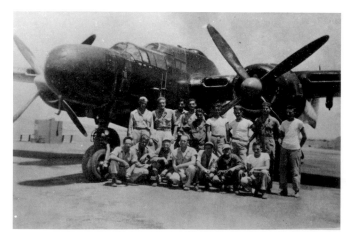

Radar maintenance section of the 549th NFS on Iwo Jima. (Wheeler via Thompson)

Capt. William H. Dames (pilot, on the right) and 2nd Lt. Eugene P. D'Andrea (R/O), the crew of the 548th's "Bat Outa Hell." (Hansen)

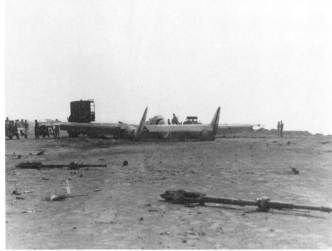

On the morning of April 20th a flight of four 548th P-61s were heading back to their home base on Iwo Jima as the sun came up. But atmospheric conditions were not in their favor. A very thick fog also came in and covered the island. It was so thick that Army troops searching for snipers in the nearby hills had to call off the hunt as they couldn't see where they were walking. The aircraft were returning from a three hour mission and were instructed by the tower to orbit – which they did, for an hour. With low fuel, the tower talked "Midnite Madness" piloted by Capt. James Bradford down. This was really flying blind. Somehow Bradford landed safely, suffering only a blown tire. Next "The Spook" flown by Melvin Bode was coached down by the tower. As he was about 25 feet off the ground, Bode saw he was too far to the right and attempted to slip his craft to the left. His wing tip dug into the ground and they went whirling down the runway. They hit "Midnite Madness" and bounced some 25 feet into the air before they continued their frightening trip along the ground. The first photo shows "The Spook" in its final resting place with "Midnite Madness" in the background. As "Spook" skidded along the ground the 20mm cannons started firing and didn't cease until they ripped themselves from the belly of the aircraft. Their final resting place is shown in the second picture. Photo three shows the damage to the front portion of "Spook's" crew nacelle. Capt. Bradford, his gunner, M/Sgt. Reno H. Sukow, and R/O 1st Lt. Lawrence Lunt were unhurt in the incident. Bode's crew of S/Sgt. John Hope, gunner, and 1st Lt. Avery Miller, R/O, got away with just minor scratches. The final photo shows the damage to "Midnite Madness." The crew of the third 548th P-61 elected to bailout as fuel was nearly gone. Capt. William Dames was able to stay aloft until the fog cleared enough for him to bring his Widow down for a safe landing. (USAF)

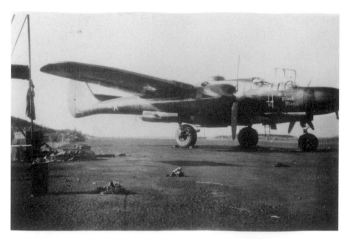

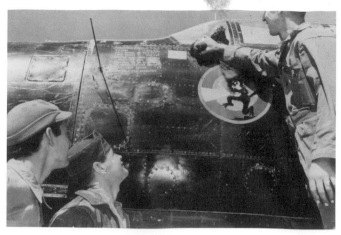

"Old Black Magic" of the 549th was photographed on Iwo Jima in mid-1945. The long range fuel tank (note the dome structure on top of the crew nacelle) was retained after reaching their forward base and used for long range strikes on the Japanese homeland. (Charlesworth via Thompson)

A detachment from the 6th NFS worked with the 548th on Iwo Jima. Here the 6th's Dan Hinz (R/O) on the far left and pilot Myrle McCumber next to him watch a "Kill" flag being applied to a 548th P-61 they flew when they shot down a Betty bomber. (Hansen via Thompson)

"Trigger Happy" and her 549th crew. From left to right: Lts. Fred O. Paige III (R/O), Earl M. Tigner (pilot), and T/Sgt. Abraham Lincoln Stein. (Tigner)

Some of the 548th gang. Standing, from left to right: John Scheerer, Charles Rouse, Larry Lunt, and two unidentified. Seated: Sol Solomon, Fred Kuykendall, James Bradford, and Herb Jones. (Bradford)

"Hop'n Ditty" of the 549th was piloted by William R. Charlesworth (he became squadron C.O. in September 1945). In the second photo "Esquire's" Petty Girl has been added. (Charlesworth via Thompson and Rust)

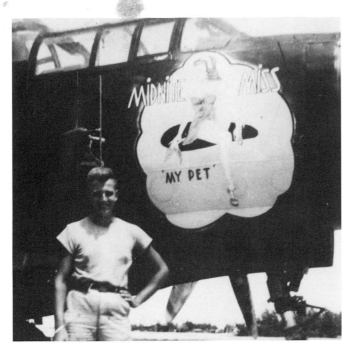

Art work decorated the P-61s in the combat theaters as profusely as any other combat aircraft. These five beauties are from the 548th NFS. (Wernsing, Hernandez, Bode, Weisman, & Boucher)

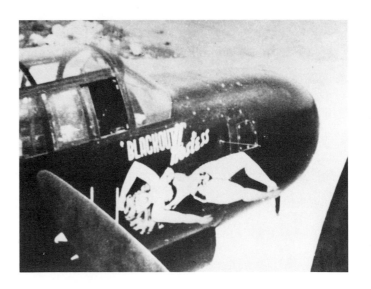

Above: What it looks like coming in to Ie Shima. (Bode)

418th NFS P-61 being refueled on Kadena Strip B on Okinawa. The 165 gallon wing tanks enabled the plane to go on long patrols, averaging approximately 7 1/2 to 8 hours flying time with four of these tanks. (USAF)

418th Officers Club on Okinawa. (Thompson)

With engines running, Lt. Ernest Thomas of the 6th NFS test fires the remote controlled top turret of his P-61, "Midnight Mickey," into a bunker on Saipan. No evidence of the firing other than the smoke can be seen of the four .50 cal. machine guns because all powder flashes are dampened and no tracer ammunition is used. (USAF)

6th NFS crews get ready for an upcoming mission. In the above photo are James Ketchum (R/O) and Francis Eaton (pilot). On the right are (left to right): Pvt. Peter Dutkanicz (gunner), Myrle McCumber (pilot), and Daniel Hinz (R/O). (Hansen)

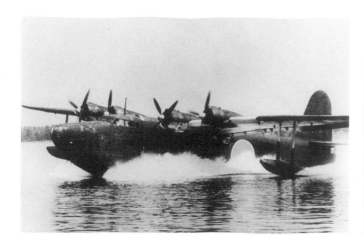

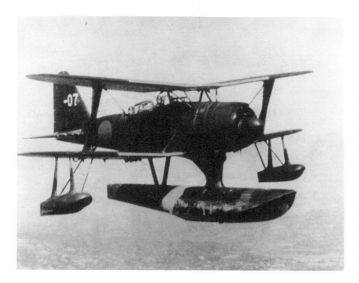

Some of the enemy aircraft the night fighters encountered. In order, they are: Kawanishi Emily, Aichi D3A Val, Mitsubishi Pete, Aichi Val, Nakajima B5N Kate, Mitsubishi Zero. (Campbell)

The sun goes down on Japan. (Charlesworth via Thompson)

Above: Though the war was supposedly over, GCI was still directing the night fighters in chasing "enemy" aircraft, and on the night of August 16th, the "Lady in the Dark's" crew of Capt. Solie Solomon (pilot, on the left [now Lee Kendall]) and Lt. John Scheerer (R/O, on the right) chased a Tojo until it too crashed into the Pacific. In ceremonies held at March AFB near Riverside, California, in late November 1990 Lee Kendall was finally awarded an Air Medal for this action. (Boucher via Thompson)

Right: The last kill of the war, and without a shot being fired, came on the night of August 14/15 when Lts. Robert W. Clyde, pilot (on the right), and Bruce K. Leford, R/O (on the left), of the 548th NFS chased an Oscar into the Pacific off Ie Shima, while flying "Lady in the Dark." (Kendall via Thompson)

The new Tactical Air Command received the 414th and 415th Night Fighter Squadrons, but this was short-lived. The 414th NFS was soon sent to Panama where it was to protect the night skies over the Panama Canal Zone. Like the other night fighter squadrons, it too was redesignated; becoming the 317th Fighter Squadron. This photo is a view from the control tower of the 319th at Rio Hato. (DiLabbio via Thompson)

Chapter 19

Post War Operations

V-E Day, May 8, 1945, saw an immediate shift in priorities. Decisions had to be made as to which units would remain in a theater as occupational forces and which would be sent to the Pacific to fight the war against Japan. On an individual basis, those troops with high enough points would be sent back to the States for rest and reassignment, and new or lower point troops in the theater would have to be shuffled around to take their places. With the war in Europe over by June 1945, the 414th and 416th Night Fighter Squadrons were the last American night fighters in Italy, both non-operational at this time. The 414th was informed to cease all flying operations with their P-61s and to turn them over to the 416th, who had been ordered earlier to cease operations with their Mosquitos, which in about a month's time were returned to Great Britain. The 416th seemed to be destined for occupational duty in Europe, but the 414th troops spent most of their time playing baseball and wondering if they would be sent directly to the Pacific or the CBI. They managed to put in their required monthly flying time in a conglomeration of aircraft consisting of two B-25s, two A-36s, one P-38, one P-51 and a lonely but faithful L-5. In Germany the 422nd had become nonoperational and was waiting to be shipped back to the US prior to being reassigned to the Pacific theater. The 425th, though operational, also expected to receive movement orders for other parts of the world.

Soon V-J Day came, and World War II had come to an end. Now was the time when everyone wanted to forget about killing; demobilization and drastic reductions in the armed forces were the order of the day.

Post War Night Lightning

The end of the war also marked the end of the Lockheed P-38M Night Lightning as an operational aircraft. Four squadrons, designated Squadron A, B, C and D, were in their final phase of training under the 450th AAFBU at Hammer Field, California,

when hostilities ceased. As a result of the cessation, the four squadrons were disbanded and the personnel were either transferred to other units or were discharged from the service.

None of the P-38Ms saw action during the war, though four were sent to the Philippines after the end of hostilities. After reassembly, the 418th Night Fighter Squadron at Atsugi, Japan, was assigned the four aircraft in the third week of January 1946. This special unit of the P-61 equipped 418th was placed under the command of Capt. Gerald B. Bliss. During January and February, the Black Lightnings flew surveillance patrols and training flights.

While on a surveillance mission on January 31, 1946, one of the Lightnings experienced a mechanical failure and was forced to ditch in the ocean near the Japanese village of Nechi-Hazu. It was officially listed as a mechanical failure, cause unknown. Unofficially, the cause was believed to be that the pilot flew too close to the water with the prop tips dipping into the ocean. The crew managed to escape without serious injury.

In February, the P-38M project was assigned to the 421st NFS at Fukuoka, Japan. This was only short-lived as Headquarters ordered the project rescinded before month's end. The three remaining P-38Ms were flown to the 45th Service Group at Clark Field in the Philippines on March 8th, where they were ultimately turned into scrap.

The squadrons did not find them to be an asset in any manner. The R/Os were cramped and uncomfortable, even on minimal missions; plus the APS-4 radar had a lesser range than the SCR-720 in the Widow. The pilots felt that the P-61 was an overall better aircraft.

Reorganization

As part of the occupational forces, the 418th and 547th Night Fighter Squadrons arrived at Atsugi Air Base, Japan, during the first week of October. Close on their heels in the latter part of November, was the 421st Night Fighter Squadron at Itazuke.

"My good fortune, immediately after the German war, to be set down with a study team with the title 'The Tactical Deployment of the Luftwaffe.' I went over to handle the night fighter portion of it. I had the opportunity to interrogate General (Josef) Kammhuber for two weeks. He was at Berchtesgaden. The Luftwaffe had moved its entire organization out of Berlin to Berchtesgaden where in mountain redoubt they could at least give orders without being decimated; as all the other headquarters had been in Berlin. To make a very long story short, Kammhuber was absolute head of all the night fighter forces of the Reich. He was an extremely good officer. I asked him, 'What are you going to do after the war?' He said, 'Well, I was a ski instructor. I may go back doing that. I really don't see much future for German generals at this time.' At that time there was none! He did tell me about their aircraft. They had more night fighter versions of the Ju 88 than any other aircraft for night fighting. Imagine my astonishment in going to Las Vegas with the Congress of Flight about seven or eight years ago to meet Kammhuber, he is now chief of the West German Air Force." The following insight was part of a talk given by Brig.Gen. Winston "Winkie" Kratz, USAF Res. (Ret) (right), at the 1978 Night Fighter Reunion in Dayton, Ohio. In the photo above is "Winkie" Kratz (on the left) with Ed Walsh in Europe as part of the study team. In the photo on the right is General Josef Kammhuber. (Kratz)

The 421st found conditions not as favorable as their predecessors, since the airstrip was in poor repair. The aircraft of the 421st under the command of Capt. Lawrence W. Lackey had to be sent to Ashiya. By the end of December, the American night fighter program had drastically changed.

The 422nd, 426th, 427th, 548th and 550th had been deactivated and would soon be followed by the 547th in late February 1946. The duties for night protection in the Pacific fell upon the 419th at Puerto Princesa on Palawan Island in the Philippines, the 549th on Iwo Jima, as well as the 418th and 421st in Japan. Many miles away, the 6th Night Fighter Squadron was operating from Wheeler Field in the Hawaiian Islands. The 414th and 425th were located back in the US at Camp Pinedale, California, both of these units non-operational. On August 7, 1945, the U.S. Air Forces in Europe was organized with their night fighter arm consisting of the 415th Night Fighter Squadron at Nordholz and the 417th at Kessel/Rothwestern, Germany and the 416th at Horsching, Austria.

As 1946 began, the strength of the US Army Air Forces was down to about a third from its peak with only half the amount of aircraft and still decreasing. A reorganization of the AAF came on March 21, 1946 when three major operational commands were established: Strategic Air Command, Tactical Air Command and Air Defense Command. The latter two commands would initially gain night fighter units.

Commanding Tactical Air Command was Lt.Gen. Elwood R. "Pete" Quesada. As a Brig.Gen., Quesada had commanded the IX Fighter Command of the European theater's Ninth Air Force during World War II and knew well the value of night fighters. During the war, Ninth Air Force had two night fighter squadrons. Now within TAC were the two C.O.'s of those squadrons, Lt.Col. O.B. Johnson of the 422nd and Lt.Col. Leon G. "Gilly" Lewis of the 425th. Quesada visited these units in the field on a number of occasions. Both of these men would have a role in developing the air defense program within the new Air Force. Both Johnson and Quesada saw the need for a continued and updated night fighter program. From TAC headquarters at Langley Field, Virginia, General Quesada sent Col. Johnson to Washington, D.C. to work on night fighter development for the new Air Force. Their conversation went something like this according to O.B. Johnson:

After World War II was over, I was working for Gen. Pete Quesada, who was commander TAC at that time, down at Langley Field. General Quesada came home from Washington one day and he said, 'I was up there talking to Gen. Pat Partridge and he said the Air

Force has made a decision that we're going to expand the air defense force of the United States of America. I have recommended that you go up there. Wouldn't you like to volunteer?' I said, 'No sir. I never volunteer for anything.' He said, 'Well, you go home and talk it over with Susie and come and see me in the morning.' And I did. And he said, 'I have cut your orders yesterday and you are going to Washington on the first of July and you are going to work with Pat Partridge in air defense requirements in the Pentagon.' It was there that we really gave birth to the Johnny-come-lately's, if you will, in the air defense/night fighter/all-weather business. First thing we had to do was to look at what was available at that point in time. All we had was the P-61.

Apparently Col. Johnson did his work well. The 415th NFS, which was originally allocated to the newly created Strategic Air Command, was assigned to TAC on July 13, 1946. Likewise, the 414th NFS, which was originally assigned to Air Defense Command, came under TAC on July 31st.

At Shaw Field, South Carolina, the 414th and 415th NFSs were reestablished and re-equipped with P-61 Black Widows. By early 1947, the 414th was transferred to Rio Hato in the Panama Canal Zone to provide night cover for that area under the Caribbean Air Command. The 415th was transferred a couple of months later in the opposite direction to Adak, Alaska, placed under the Alaskan Air Command to provide aerial night cover at the top of the world.

Both Johnson and Lewis wanted to command the squadron going to Panama. Johnson tells of a trick he pulled on his good friend:

Gilly Lewis and I have been very good friends and kind of competitors over the years. Right after the war they were activating two night fighter squadrons at Shaw Field. Gilly wanted one of them. One of them was going to Panama and one of them was going to Alaska. And I wanted one of them. I was the headquarters type, so he came to a friend and asked, 'Which one is going to Panama?' I told Gilly which one was going to Panama, but I got the numbers mixed up! I gave him the number that was going to Alaska because I wanted to go to Panama. He ended up in Alaska right after the war in a P-61 outfit.

It worked. Col. Lewis went to Alaska with the P-61 equipped 415th NFS. But Johnson stayed on at TAC and in August 1947 was reassigned to Headquarters US Air Force in Washington where he was on the staff of the Deputy Chief of Staff for Operations. Col. Julius Alford who had served with the 6th NFS in the Pacific, and was its C.O. later on, became C.O. of the 414th in Panama.

Air Defense Command had the responsibility for the air defense of the continental United States. Commanding ADC was Lt.Gen. George Stratemeyer who had served in AAF headquarters and later in the Pacific theater during the war. Two units were initially assigned to ADC – the 414th and 425th Night Fighter Squadrons, each based at March Field, California, and non-operational at the time. By late July, ADC had lost the 414th NFS to TAC. On September 1st of that year, the 425th Night Fighter Squadron was transferred to McChord Field, Washington, where it was reactivated and assigned Fourth Air

In post war Europe only three of the six night fighter squadrons that had operated under the Ninth and Twelfth Air Forces were left. The 415th NFS remained active only into February 1947 when they were transferred on paper back to the US. Pictured at their Darmstadt, Germany home above, they had a mix of Black Widows and Beaufighters for awhile. (McPartland)

Force, a component of ADC. At this time the P-61 equipped 425th Night Fighter Squadron was one of two squadrons that was under ADC, and the only one equipped with night fighters. The other one was a P-47 equipped squadron at Mitchel Field in New York. This unit would soon be removed from ADC's jurisdiction.

Besides providing night defense in the Pacific, the F-61 squadrons (the "P" for pursuit having been changed to "F" for fighter) also aided in the photographing of Japan and Korea. With the reorganization and turmoil of the late 1940s, the 347th

The 417th, seen above at their Kassel, Germany, home, was redesignated 2nd Fighter Squadron on November 9, 1946 and became part of the 52nd Fighter Group. In June 1947 they, for all intents, were disbanded as they were transferred, less personnel and aircraft, back to the US. (Dowd via Thompson)

Only four Lockheed P-38M Night Lightnings made it into the Pacific theater, and these arrived after cessation of hostilities. After being reassembled in the Philippines, they were first assigned to the 418th NFS then stationed at Atsugi, Japan. They were operated by the 418th during the latter part of January and early February 1946. The project, aircraft and crews were then assigned to the 421st NFS at Fukuoka, Japan. By early March the project, as well as the aircraft, had been scrapped. (Hopwood)

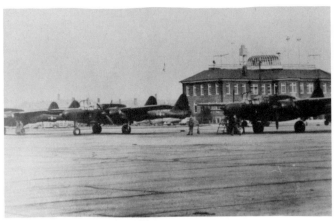

In the US their is a reorganization in the military and the US Army Air Forces is organized into three major commands: Strategic Air Command, Tactical Air Command, and Air Defense Command; the latter two would initially receive night fighter squadrons assigned in the continental US. ADC started out with two squadrons: the P-61 425th NFS at McChord Field, Washington, and a P-47 squadron at Mitchel Field in New York state. Soon the P-47 squadron was relieved from ADC duties and the 52 FG with its 2nd and 5th Fighter Squadrons were restaffed and reequipped with Black Widows at Mitchel Field, as shown above. (USAF via Greenhalgh)

Fighter Group was activated at Nagoya, Japan. Assigned to the 347th Fighter Group were the 6th, 418th, and 421st Night Fighter Squadrons; but their designations were changed to the 339th, 4th, and 68th Fighter Squadrons, respectively. These changes were in designation only, and the new squadrons consisted of the same personnel. On the same date, the 419th Night Fighter Squadron which had been stationed at Floridablanca, Luzon, in the Philippines for nearly a year was inactivated, and the 419th Night Fighter Squadron which was a non-operational unit on the island of Guam was also inactivated. Some three months earlier the 52nd Fighter Group was activated at Schweinfurt, Germany, which also caused a reidentification. At this same base was the 416th and 417th Night Fighter Squadrons, who under the new 52nd Fighter Group, became the 2nd and 5th Fighter Squadrons, respectively.

Air Defense Command strength increased in 1947. On May 21st, the 325th Fighter Group with its 318th Fighter Squadron equipped with P-61s, was activated at Mitchel Field, New York, bringing ADCs 61 strength up to two squadrons. Within a month, the 52nd Fighter Group along with its 2nd and 5th Fighter Squadrons were transferred, without personnel and aircraft, to Mitchel Field where they were reorganized and re-equipped with Widows thus doubling ADCs interceptor strength.

Another Aircraft, Another War

In 1948 the North American F-82F, G and H Twin Mustang interceptors were entering the Air Force's inventory. One of the earliest units to convert from the Widow to the Twin Mustang was the 319th Fighter Squadron in the Canal Zone in early 1948, prior to their return to the US and reassignment to the 325th Fighter Group under ADC. The 415th Night Fighter Squadron, which was redesignated the 449th Fighter Squadron, was operating from Adak, Elmendorf, Davis and Ladd Air Fields in Alaska, when they converted to the F-82H. The "H" was a modified F-82F and G model which had additional radio equipment for their Arctic duties. The last units to be equipped with the newer F-82 were those of the 347th Fighter Group in the Pacific, who were still in the process of transitioning in early 1950. The new night fighters in the Pacific hadn't been completely transitioned for very long when the Korean War broke out on June 25, 1950. At this time, the F-82s were the only fighters in the Fifth Air Force with sufficient range to reach the battle area. On 27 June 1950, on a combined fighter sweep of the 4th (which had left its Okinawa Base and joined the 68th and 339th Squadrons at Itazuke, Japan, for the Korean operations), the first aerial kill of the war was made by the 68th Squadron. This was followed by their second confirmed and one by the 339th within minutes. These were the only kills that the 82s would claim during their two years of operations in the war.

The Black Widows were gone and the Twin Mustangs were on borrowed time. The jet age was already here. The limited role of the night fighter defender had evolved into the all-weather fighter. But men like Capt. Philip B. Porter, who as Col. Carroll C. Smith's R/O with the 418th Night Fighter Squadron in the Pacific during World War II, were now flying in another war and using much of the experience they gained in the night fighters of World War II.

Appendix A
Operational Night Fighter Squadron Statistics

Detachment 'A' Night Fighter Squadron

Activated: Redesignated Detachment 'A' Night Fighter Squadron
September 14, 1943 (was 6th Night Fighter Squadron [Det])

Disbanded: December 15, 1943

Wartime Commanding Officers:
Sept. 14 - Dec. 15, 1943: Capt. Robert W. McLeod

Operational Stations:
Kila (3 Mile), New Guinea
Detachments: Jackson (7 Mile), New Guinea
Dobodura, New Guinea

Operational Aircraft:
P-70, P-38G (2 with AI radar)

Enemy Aircraft:
None as Detachment 'A' - See 6th NFS for credits prior to
redesignation.

Detachment 'B' Night Fighter Squadron

Activated: Redesignated Detachment 'B' Night Fighter Squadron
September 16, 1943 (was 6th Night Fighter Squadron [Det])

Disbanded: December 15, 1943

Wartime Commanding Officers:
Sept. 14 - 26, 1943:   Capt. Ralph F. Jones
Sept. 26 - Oct 9, 1943: Capt Emerson Y. Barker
Oct. 9 - Nov. 21, 1943: Ralph F. Jones
Nov. 21 - 28, 1943:   Emerson Y. Barker
Nov. 28 - Dec. 15, 1943: Earl C. Bennett

Operational Stations:
Henderson Field, Guadalcanal, Solomons
Detachments: Russell Islands, Solomons
New Georgia Island, Solomons

Operational Aircraft:
P-70, P-38G

Enemy Aircraft:
P-38: 3/0/0
P-70: None
See 6th NFS for credits prior to redesignation

Confirmed Aircrew Victories:

2nd Lt. Henry Meigs II	P-38	Sept 21, 43	Betty
2nd Lt. Henry Meigs II	P-38	Sept 21, 43	Betty
1st Lt. Charles E. Van Bibber	P-38	Nov 6, 43	Hap

1st PURSUIT SQUADRON (NIGHT FIGHTER)

Activated: Redesignated 1st PS (NF) March 26, 1942 (was 15th Bomb
Squadron (L)

Inactivated: Redesignated 15th Bombardment Squadron (Light) May 31,
1942

Wartime Commanding Officers:
March 26 - May 31, 1942: Maj. John W. Griffith

Stations:
March 26 - April 19, 1942: Lawson Field, Georgia
May 14 - 31, 1942: Grafton Underwood Airdrome, England

Operational Aircraft:
None - This squadron was scheduled to be trained in Turbinlite modified RAF
DB-7's. Due to political pressures for the USAAF to go operational in Europe,
this squadron reverted back to a light bombardment squadron prior to any real
night fighter training. As the 15th BS(L), it had the distinction of inaugurating
AAF bombardment operations in the ETO on July 4, 1942.

Enemy Aircraft:
None

6th Night Fighter Squadron

Activated: Redesignated 6th Fighter Squadron May 22, 1942 (was 6th
Pursuit Squadron (Interceptor)
Redesignated 6th Night Fighter Squadron January 18, 1943

Inactivated: February 20, 1947 (became 339th Fighter Squadron)

Wartime Commanding Officers:
Sept. 27, 1941 - Sept. 14, 1942: Lt. James R. Watt
Sept. 14, 1942 - Feb. 18, 1943: Capt Sidney F. Wharton
Feb. 18 - Apr. 11, 1943: Capt. Victor M. Mahr
Apr. 12 - May 1, 1943: Capt. Julius E. Alford (Acting)
May. 1 - Jun. 15, 1943: Capt. Victor M. Mahr
Jun 16 - Jul 7, 1943: Capt. Julius E. Alford (Acting)
Jul 8, 1943 - Apr. 1, 1944: Maj. Victor M. Mahr
Apr. 1 - 15, 1944: Maj. Julius E. Alford
Apr. 15 - May 15, 1944: Maj. Victor M. Mahr
May 15 - Oct. 1944: Maj. Julius E. Alford
Oct. - Dec. 18, 1944: Capt. Mark E. Martin
Dec. 18, 1944 - Jan. 11, 1945: 1st Lt. Robert T. Merrill III
Jan. 11 - Mar. 7, 1945: Capt. Mark E. Martin
Mar. 7, 1945 - Oct. 1946: Capt. George W. Mulholland

Operational Stations:
Jan. 11, 1927: Wheeler Field, Oahu, TH
Dec. 19, 1941: Hickam Field, Oahu, TH
Jan. 3, 1942: Stanley Field, Oahu, TH
Aug. 30, 1942: Kahuka, Oahu, TH
Nov. 17, 1942: Kipapa Gulch, Oahu, TH
Feb. 18 - Sept. 16, 1943 Guadalcanal, Solomons, Detachment
(Redesignated Detachment 'B' Night Fighter
Squadron)
Mar. 19 - Sept. 14, 1943 New Guinea Detachment
(Redesignated Detachment 'A' Night Fighter
Squadron)
Apr. 10, 1943 (short stay) Canton Island, Phoenix Islands
Detachment.

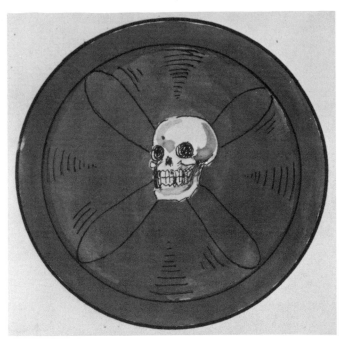

Official 6th Night Fighter Squadron emblem

Above and below: Two versions of unofficial 6th NFS emblem used in 1942 and 1943.

May 24, 1943 John Rogers NAS, Oahu, TH (detachments there
 on irregular intervals)
Jun. 11, 1944: Mokuleia Airfield, Oahu, TH
Jun. 21, 1944: John Rogers Airport, NAS, Oahu, TH
Jun. 21 - Dec. 11, 1944 Saipan, Marianas, Detachment
Oct. 28, 1944: Kipapa Airfield, Oahu, TH
c. Oct. 1944 Wheeler Field, Oahu, TH Detachment
Dec. 11, 1944: Saipan, Marianas
Dec 11, 1944 - Apr. 29, 1945 Kipapa Airfield, TH Det.
Mar. 6 - Apr. 5, 1945 Iwo Jima, Volcano Is. Detachment
Apr. 29, 1945: Kipapa Airfield, Oahu, TH
Oct. 1, 1945: Wheeler Airfield, Oahu, TH

Operational Aircraft:
 1941-1942 P-36A
 1941-1943 P-40B
 1942-1943 P-39
 1942-1944 P-47D
 1942-1944 P-70 & P-70A
 1944-1945 P-61A & B

Enemy Aircraft:
 P-38: 5/0/1
 P-70: 2/0/0
 P-61: 16/2/1
 Squadron Total: 23/2/2 (See Detachment 'B' Night Fighter
  Squadron also.)

Confirmed Aircrew Victories:

Capt. Earl C. Bennett(P)   P-70   Apr 19, 43   Sally
 Cpl. Edwin E. Tomlinson(R/O)
2nd Lt. Burnell W. Adams(P)   P-70   May 15, 43   Sally
 F/O Paul DiLabbio(R/O)
1st Lt. Charles E. Van Bibber   P-38   Jun 16, 43   Hap
1st Lt. Ralph F. Tuttle   P-38   Jul 12, 43   Betty
1st Lt. James A. Harrell III   P-38   Jul 17, 43   Betty
1st Lt. James A. Harrell III   P-38   Aug 14, 43   Betty
2nd Lt. Henry Meigs II   P-38   Aug 15, 43   Betty
2nd Lt. Dale F. Haberman(P)   P-61   Jun 30, 44   Betty
 F/O Raymond P. Mooney(R/O)
1st Lt. Francis C. Eaton(P)   P-61   Jul 6, 44   Betty
 2nd Lt. James E. Ketchum(R/O)
 S/Sgt. William S. Anderson III(G)
2nd Lt. Jerome M. Hansen(P)   P-61   Jul 7, 44   Betty

 2nd Lt. William K. Wallace(R/O)
1st Lt. Dale F. Haberman(P)   P-61   Jul 14, 44   Betty
 F/O Raymond P. Mooney(R/O)
1st Lt. Francis C. Eaton(P)   P-61   Nov 3, 44   Betty
 2nd Lt. James E. Ketchum(R/O)
1st Lt. Dale F. Haberman(P)   P-61   Dec 25, 44   Betty
 2nd Lt. Raymond P. Mooney(R/O)
 Pvt. Patrick J. Farelly(G)
1st Lt. Dale F. Haberman(P)   P-61   Dec 25, 44   Betty

2nd Lt. Raymond P. Mooney(R/O)				
Pvt. Patrick J. Farelly(G)				
1st Lt. Ernest R. Thomas(P)	P-61	Dec 25, 44	Betty	
1st Lt. John P. Acre(R/O)				
1st Lt. James C. Crumley(P)	P-61	Dec 26, 44	Betty	
2nd Lt. Jean B. Desclos(R/O)				
Pvt. Otis H. O'Hair(G)				
2nd Lt. Myrle W. McCumber(P)	P-61	Dec 26, 44	Betty	
F/O Daniel L. Hinz(R/O)				
Pvt. Peter Dutkanicz(G)				
2nd Lt. Robert L. Ferguson(P)	P-61	Dec 26, 44	Betty	
2nd Lt. Charles A. Ward(R/O)				
Sgt. Leroy F. Miozzi(G)				
2nd Lt. Donald T. Evans(P)	P-61	Jan 1, 45	Betty	
2nd Lt. Nicholas R. DeVita(R/O)				
Cpl. Raymond L. Golden(G)				
2nd Lt. Donald T. Evans(P)	P-61	Jan 2, 45	Betty	
2nd Lt. Nicholas R. DeVita(R/O)				
Cpl. Raymond L. Golden(G)				
F/O John J. Szpila(P)	P-61	Jan 2, 45	Frances	
F/O Alfred H. Borges, Jr.(R/O)				
Capt. Ernest R. Thomas(P)	P-61	Mar 25, 45	Betty	
1st Lt. John P. Acre(R/O)				
Cpl. Jesse V. Tew (G-548th NFS)				
2nd Lt. Myrle W. McCumber(P)	P-61	Mar 25, 45	Betty	
F/O Daniel L. Hinz(R/O)				
S/Sgt. Benjamin J. Boscardin (G-548th NFS)				

Unofficial 414th NFS (no official established) emblem.

414th Night Fighter Squadron

Activated: January 26, 1943

Inactivated: August 31, 1947 (became 319th Fighter Squadron)

Wartime Commanding Officers:
  Jan. 26 - Sept. 16, 1943:   Maj. Arden W. Cowgill
  Sept. 16, 1943 - Jun. 1, 1944: Maj. Earl T. Smith
  Jun. 1, 1944 - Jan. 21, 1943: Maj. Carroll H. Bolender

Operational Stations:
  May. 10, 1943: La Senia, Algeria
  Jun. 11, 1943: Reghaia, Algeria (Advance air echelon arrived
        at Reghaia from training in England on July 8, 1943)
  Jul. 23 - 29, 1943 Protville, Tunisia Detachment
  Nov. 12, 1943: Elmas, Sardinia
  Jan. 9 - Feb. 4, 1944 Ghisonaccia, Corsica Detachment
  Mar. 20 Jul. 15, 1944 Ghisonaccia, Corsica Detachment
  Feb. 5 - Jul. 15, 1944 Borgo, Corsica Detachment
  May 11 - Jun. 22, 1944 Alghero, Sardinia Detachment
  Jun. 22, 1944: Alghero, Sardinia
  Sept. 5, 1944: Borgo, Corsica
  Oct. 13, 1944: Pisa, Italy
  Nov. 25, 1944: Pontedera, Italy
  Jan. 27 - Apr. 3, 1945 Florennes (A-78), Belgium Det.
  Apr. 3 - 23, 1945 Strossfeld (Y-78), Germany (operated with the
        422nd Night Fighter Squadron at the above two
        locations)
  Jul. 15, 1945: Bagnoli, Italy

Operational Aircraft:
  1943   Beaufighter Mk VI (Mk IV AI)
  1943-1945 Beaufighter Mk VI (Mk VIII AI)
  1944-1945 P-61A & B

Enemy Aircraft:
  Beaufighter: 8/1/1
  P-61:   5/0/0
  Squadron Total: 13/1/1

Confirmed Aircrew Victories:

Capt. Charnley K. Atwater(P)	Beaufighter Jul 27, 43	SM 82	
F/O David L. McAbee(R/O)			
1st Lt. George J. Holbig(P)	Beaufighter Jul 29, 43	SM 82	
F/O Irving Wohl(R/O)			
Capt. Earl T. Smith(P)	Beaufighter Aug 18, 43	Ju 88	

2nd Lt. Francis B. Clark(P)	Beaufighter Nov 26, 43	He 177	
1st Lt. James R. Anderson(P)	Beaufighter Jan 23, 44	Do 217K	
F/O John A. Armstrong(R/O)			
2nd Lt. Clyde W. George(P)	Beaufighter Jan 23, 44	He 177	
F/O Herbert C. Penn(R/O)			
2nd Lt. Roy E. Patten(P)	Beaufighter Aug 6, 44	Ju 88	
Capt. John E. Patterson(R/O)			
1st Lt. Albert L. Jones(P)	Beaufighter Dec 23, 44	Ju 87	
F/O John E. Rudovsky(R/O)			
2nd Lt. Orin K. Goodrich(P)	P-61	Feb 4, 45	Ju 88
2nd Lt. Raymond J. Lane(R/O)			
Capt. Albert L. Jones(P)	P-61	Apr 7, 45	Me 410
2nd Lt. John E. Rudovsky(R/O)			
Capt. Albert L. Jones(P)	P-61	Apr 8, 45	Ju 88
2nd Lt. John E. Rudovsky(R/O)			
1st Lt. Robert P. Lutz(P)	P-61	Apr 9, 45	Ju 188
2nd Lt. Wallace A. Morrissette(R/O)			
1st Lt. Thomas J. Greenfield(P)	P-61	Apr 10, 45	Ju 52
2nd Lt. Joseph E. Swartz(R/O)			

415th Night Fighter Squadron

Activated: February 10, 1943

Inactivated: September 1, 1947 (became 449th Fighter Squadron)

Wartime Commanding Officers:
  Feb. 10, 1943 - Aug. 31, 1944: Capt. Gordon D. Timmons
  Aug. 31, 1944 - Feb. 15, 1946: Maj. Harold F. Augspurger

Operational Stations:
  May. 12, 1943: La Senia, Algeria
  Jun. 22, 1943: La Sebala II, Tunisia
  Jun. 25, 1943: Monastir, Tunisia (Air echelon arrived at Monastir
        from training in England on July 3, 1943)
  Jul. 23 - 29, 1943 Protville, Tunisia Detachment
  Jul. 29, 1943: La Sebala II, Tunisia
  Sept. 3, 1943: Cassibile, Sicily
  Nov. 5, 1943: Cantania, Sicily
  Nov. 29 - Dec. 26, 1943 Montecorvino, Italy Detachment
  Dec. 6, 1943 - Jan. 30, 1944 Gaudo, Italy Detachment
  Dec. 26, 1943: Montecorvino, Italy
  Jan. 30, 1944: Marcainise, Italy
  Mar. 25, 1944: Pomigliano, Italy
  Jun. 11, 1944: La Blanca, Italy
  Jun. 17, 1944: Valtone, Italy
  Jul. 9, 1944: Solonzara, Corsica

Jul. 23 - Aug. 5, 1944 Piombino, Italy Detachment
Sept. 1, 1944: La Vellon, France
Sept. 25, 1944: Longvic, France
Dec. 30, 1944: Ochey, France
Mar. 18, 1945: St. Dizier (A-64), France
Apr. 19, 1945: Gross-Gerau (Y-72), Germany

Operational Aircraft:
  1943-1944 Beaufighter Mk VI (Mk IV AI)
  1944-1945 Beaufighter Mk VI (Mk VIII AI)
  1945   P-61A & B

Enemy Aircraft:
  Beaufighter: 11/5/1
  P-61: 0/0/0
  Squadron Total: 11/5/1

Confirmed Aircrew Victories:

Capt. Nathaniel H. Lindsay(P)	Beaufighter	Jul 24, 43	He 115
F/O Austin G. Petry(R/O)			
1st Lt. Robert E. Walber(P)	Beaufighter	Aug 16, 43	Cant 1007
F/O Emmett B. Faison, Jr.(R/O)			
1st Lt. Charles F. Horne (P)	Beaufighter	Feb 7, 44	He 177
2nd Lt. Richard F. Urich(R/O)			
Maj. Nathaniel H. Lindsay(P)	Beaufighter	Mar 18, 44	Ju 88
F/O Austin G. Petry(R/O)			
Capt. Harold F. Augspurger(P)	Beaufighter	Sept 27, 44	Fw 200K
2nd Lt. Austin G. Petry(R/O)			
Capt. Harold F. Augspurger(P)	Beaufighter	Sept 29, 44	He 111
2nd Lt. Austin G. Petry(R/O)			
1st Lt. Henry J. Giblin(P)	Beaufighter	Dec 12, 44	Ju 88
2nd Lt. Walter J. Cleary(R/O)			
1st Lt. Edward A. Schlueter(P)	Beaufighter	Dec 29, 44	He 111
2nd Lt. Donald J. Meiers(R/O)			
1st Lt. Edward A. Schlueter(P)	Beaufighter	Dec 29, 44	Ju 88
2nd Lt. Donald J. Meiers(R/O)			
1st Lt. Edward A. Schlueter(P)	Beaufighter	Jan 1, 45	Ju 88
2nd Lt. Donald J. Meiers(R/O)			
1st Lt. Henry J. Giblin(P)	Beaufighter	Mar 3, 45	B-17 (GAF)
2nd Lt. Walter J. Cleary(R/O)			

Official 416th NFS emblem.

416th Night Fighter Squadron

Activated: February 20, 1943

Inactivated: November 9, 1946 (became 2nd Fighter Squadron)

Wartime Commanding Officers:
  Mar. 6 - Jun. 25, 1943: Capt. Jack C. Davis
  Jun. 25, 1943 - Apr. 29, 1944: Capt. Amberse M. Banks
  Apr. 29 - Jul. 19, 1944: Maj. Rulon D. Blake
  Jul. 19 - Sept. 19, 1944: Lt. Col. Amberse M. Banks
  Sept. 19, 1944 - Dec. 2, 1945: Capt. Carl S. Morrison, Jr.

Operational Stations:
  Aug. 8, 1943: Algiers, Algeria
  Aug. 17, 1943: Bone, Algeria
  Sept. 15, 1943: Bizerta, Tunisia
  Sept. 21, 1943: Catania, Sicily
  Sept. 27, 1943: Lecce, Italy
  Sept. 30, 1943: Grottagile, Italy
  Dec. 27, 1943 - Jan. 25, 1944 Reghaia, Algeria Det.
  Jan. 28, 1944: Pomigliano, Italy
  Jun. 14 - Jul. 8, 1944 Tre Cancello, Italy Detachment
  Jul. 27 - Sept. 4, 1944 Tarquinia, Italy Detachment
  Aug. 14 - 22, 1944 Alghero, Sicily Detachment
  Aug. 14 - 23, 1944 Borgo, Corsica Detachment
  Sept. 1, 1944: Rosignano, Italy
  Sept. 1 - 9, 1944 Pomigliano, Italy Detachment
  Oct. 1, 1944: Pisa, Italy
  Jan. 4 - Feb. 20, 1945 Etain (A-82), France Detachment
      (Operated with the 425th Night Fighter Squadron)
  Mar. 27, 1945: Pontedera, Italy
  Aug. 13, 1945: Horsching, Austria

Operational Aircraft:
  1943-1944 Beaufighter Mk VI (Mk IV AI)
  1943-1944 Beaufighter Mk VIII (Mk VIII AI)
  1944-1945 Mosquito NF Mk 30 (Mk X AI)

Enemy Aircraft:
  Beaufighter: 4/2/1
  Mosquito: 1/0/0
  Squadron Total: 5/2/1

Confirmed Aircrew Victories:

2nd Lt. James D. Urso(P)	Beaufighter	Feb 8, 44	Me 210
F/O Daniel T. Powell(R/O)			

Official 415th NFS emblem

Capt. Darwin V. Brake, Jr.(P)   Beaufighter Feb 24, 44   He 111
    F/O Alfred A. Gander(R/O)
2nd Lt. George P. Fors(P)   Beaufigher Mar 17, 44   Ju 88
    F/O Arthur G. Gaudette(R/O)
2nd Lt. James D. Urso(P)   Beaufighter May 14, 44   Ju 88
    F/O Daniel T. Powell(R/O)
Capt. Lawrence E. Englert(P)   Mosquito Feb 28, 45   Ju 188
    2nd Lt. Earl R. Dickey(R/O)

417th Night Fighter Squadron

Activated: February 20, 1943

Inactivated: November 9, 1946 (became 5th Fighter Squadron)

Wartime Commanding Officers:
    Mar. 6, 1943 - Jun. 16, 1944: Capt. Joseph T. Ehlinger
    Jun. 25, 1944 - Apr. 19, 1945: Capt. William A. Larsen
    Apr. 19 - Sept. 30, 1945: Maj. Clarence R. McCray

Operational Stations:
    Aug. 8, 1943: Tafaraoui, Algeria
    Jan. 7 - Apr. 25, 1944 Ghisonaccia, Corsica
        (Ground echelon only)
    Jan. 10, 1944: La Senia, Algeria
    Apr. 25, 1944: Borgo, Corsica
    Sept. 12, 1944: La Vallon, France
    Jan. 6 - 22, 1945 Florennes (A-78), Belgium Detachment
        (Operated with the 422nd Night Fighter Squadron)
    Apr. 5, 1945: St. Dizier (A-64), France
    Apr. 24, 1945: Giebelstadt (Y-90), Germany
    May 22, 1945: Biblis (Y-78), Germany
    Jun. 26, 1945: Braunschardt, Germany

Operational Aircraft:
    1943-1944 Beaufighter Mk VI (Mk IV AI)
    1944-1945 Beaufighter Mk VIII (Mk VIII AI)
    1945   P-61A & B

Enemy Aircraft:
    Beaufighter: 9/2/15
    P-61:   0/0/0
    Squadron Total: 9/2/15

Confirmed Aircrew Victories:

1st Lt. Clarence R. McCray(P)   Beaufighter Nov 11, 43   Do 217
    F/O Robert D. Hamilton(R/O)
2nd Lt. Rayford W. Jeffrey(P)   Beaufighter Feb 2, 44   Ju 88
    2nd Lt. William A. Henderson(R/O)
2nd Lt. Rayford W. Jeffrey(P)   Beaufighter Mar 28, 44   Ju 88
    2nd Lt. William A. Henderson(R/O)
1st Lt. Walter G. Groom(P)   Beaufighter Apr 16, 44   Ju 88
    F/O Harold L. Roth(R/O)
Capt. Clarence R. McCray(P)   Beaufighter May 13, 44   He 177
    F/O Robert D. Hamilton(R/O)
2nd Lt. Robert W. Inglis(P)   Beaufighter Jul 20, 44   UNK
    F/O Theodore E. Hearne(R/O)
1st Lt. William R. Williamson(P)Beaufighter Aug 3, 44   Ju 188
    2nd Lt. Dan B. Cordell(R/O)
1st Lt. Theodore A. Deakyne(P) Beaufighter Nov 28, 44   Ju 188
    1st Lt. Robert E. Perkins(R/O)
1st Lt. Malcolm D. Campbell(P)Beaufighter Dec 28, 44   Ju 290
    2nd Lt. Robert J. McCullen(R/O)

418th Night Fighter Squadron

Activated: April 1, 1943

Inactivated: February 20, 1947 (became 4th Fighter Squadron)

Wartime Commanding Officers:
    Apr. 1, 1943 - Feb. 15, 1945: Maj. Carroll C. Smith
    Feb. 15, 1944 - Nov. 5, 1945: Capt. William B. Sellers
    Apr. 19 - Sept. 30, 1945: Maj. Clarence R. McCray

Official 418th NFS emblem

Unofficial 418th NFS emblem

Operational Stations:
    Nov. 2, 1943: Milne Bay, New Guinea
    Nov. 22, 1943: Dobodura, New Guinea
    Mar. 28, 1944: Finschhafen, New Guinea
    May 12, 1944: Hollandia, New Guinea
    Jun. 8 - Aug. 18, 1944 Insoemoar (Wakde) Island, Wakde
        Islands Detachment
    Sept. 16 - Oct. 5, 1944 Owi Island, Padaido Is. Detachment
    Sept. 28, 1944: Morotai, Halmaheras
    Nov. 14 - 30, 1944 Dulag, Leyte, PI Detachment
        (Ground echelon only)
    Dec. 15 - 26, 1944 San Jose, Mindoro, PI Detachment
        (Ground echelon only)
    Dec. 26, 1944: San Jose, Mindoro, PI

418th NFS ace team of 1st Lt. Philip B. Porter (R/O) on the left and Maj. Carroll C. Smith (Pilot) on the right, with their aircraft at top and bottom right.

Jun. - Jul. 1945 Sanga Sanga Is., Sulu Arch.
Jul. 26, 1945: Okinawa, Ryukyus

Operational Aircraft:
1943-1944 P-70 & P-70A
1943-1944 P-38F, G, & J
1944   B-25H
1944-1945 P-61A & B

Enemy Aircraft:
P-70: 0/0/0
P-38: 2/2/0
P-61: 18/1/0
Squadron Total: 20/3/0

Confirmed Aircrew Victories:

Maj. Carroll C. Smith(P)	P-38	Jan 13, 44	Val	
Maj. Carroll C. Smith(P)	P-61	Oct 7, 44	Dinah Mk II	
1st Lt. Philip B. Porter(R/O)				
1st Lt. William F. Ross(P)	P-61	Nov 6, 44	Betty	
2nd Lt. Raymond L. Duethman(R/O)				
1st Lt. Harold B. Whittern(P)	P-61	Nov 13, 44	TE bomber	
2nd Lt. Bunyan A. Crain, Jr.(R/O)				
Maj. Carroll C. Smith(P)	P-38	Nov 28, 44	Betty	
2nd Lt. Bertram C. Tompkins(P)	P-61	Dec 9, 44	Floatplane	
F/O Vincent Wertin(R/O)				
1st Lt. Malcolm L. Ritchie(P)	P-61	Dec 27, 44	Tony	
F/O Vincent Wertin(R/O)				
2nd Lt. Bertram C. Tompkins(P)	P-61	Dec 28, 44	Tony	
F/O Vincent Wertin(R/O)				
2nd Lt. Bertram C. Tompkins(P)	P-61	Dec 28, 44	Tony	
F/O Vincent Wertin(R/O)				
Maj. Carroll C. Smith(P)	P-61	Dec 29, 44	Irving	

1st Lt. Philip B. Porter(R/O)			
Maj. Carroll C. Smith(P)	P-61	Dec 29, 44	Irving
1st Lt. Philip B. Porter(R/O)			
2nd Lt. George M. Ellings(P)	P-61	Dec 30, 44	Rufe
F/O Milton Burman (R/O)			
Maj. Carroll C. Smith(P)	P-61	Dec 30, 44	Rufe
1st Lt. Philip B. Porter(R/O)			
Maj. Carroll C. Smith(P)	P-61	Dec 30, 44	Frank
1st Lt. Philip B. Porter(R/O)			
1st Lt. Albert R. Sorbo(P)	P-61	Jan 4, 45	Jake
2nd Lt. George N. Kerstetter(R/O)			
1st Lt. Albert R. Sorbo(P)	P-61	Jan 4, 45	Jake
2nd Lt. George N. Kerstetter(R/O)			
1st Lt. Albert R. Sorbo(P)	P-61	Jan 5, 45	Val
2nd Lt. George N. Kerstetter(R/O)			
2nd Lt. James R. McQueen,Jr.(P)	P-61	Jan 18, 45	TE bomber
2nd Lt. Hugh L. Gordon(R/O)			
2nd Lt. James R. McQueen,Jr.(P)	P-61	Jan 18, 45	TE bomber
2nd Lt. Hugh L. Gordon(R/O)			
2nd Lt. Curtis R. Griffitts,Jr.(P)	P-61	Aug 7, 45	Betty
2nd Lt. Myron G. Bigler(R/O)			

419th Night Fighter Squadron

Activated: April 1, 1943

Inactivated: February 20, 1947

Wartime Commanding Officers:
Apr. 1 - Nov. 22, 1943: Capt. John J. McCloskey
Nov. 23 - Dec. 22, 1943: Maj. Ralph F. Jones

Unofficial 419th NFS (no official established) emblem

Dec. 22, 1943 - Jan. 16, 1944: Capt. Emerson Y. Barker
Jan. 17 - Feb. 20, 1944: Maj. Ralph F. Jones
Feb. 20 - Apr. 8, 1944: Capt. Emerson Y. Barker
Apr. 8 - 12, 1944: Capt. Howard G. Daniel
Apr. 12 - Jun. 12, 1944: Maj. Emerson Y. Barker
Jun. 13 - 15, 1944: Capt. Alphonse Lukas
Jun. 16 - 30, 1944: Maj. Andrew J. Bing
Jul. 1, 1944 - Jan. 30, 1945: Maj. Joseph A. Shulmistras
Feb. 1 - Apr. 1945: Capt. Richard O. Stewart
Apr. - Nov. 1945: Lt. Col. Norman M. Jacob

Operational Stations:
　　Nov. 15, 1943: Guadalcanal, Solomons
　　Jan. 25 - Mar. 27, 1944 Bougainville, Solomons Det. A
　　Jun. 27 - Jul. 25, 1944 Nadzab, New Guinea Det. A
　　Jun. 28 - Aug. 18, 1944 Los Negros, Admiraltys Det. B
　　Jun. 25 - Nov. 27, 1944 Noemfoor Is., Schouten Islands,
　　　　Detachment A
　　Aug. 18, 1944: Middelburg Island, Halmaheras
　　Nov. 27, 1944 - Mar. 16, 1945 Morotai, Halmaheras Det A
　　Mar. 6, 1945: Puerto Princesa, Palawan, PI
　　Mar. 16 - Jul. 20, 1945 Zamboanga, Mindanao, PI Det. A
　　Jun. 20 - Jul. 27, 1945 Sanga Sanga, Sulu Arch. Det. B
　　Jul. 27, 1945: Puerto Princesa, Palawan, PI

Operational Aircraft:
　　1943-1944 P-70 & P-70A
　　1943-1944 P-38G & J
　　1944-1945 P-61A & B

Enemy Aircraft:
　　P-70: 0/0/0
　　P-38: 1/0/0
　　P-61: 5/1/0
　　Squadron Total: 6/1/0

Confirmed Aircrew Victories:

Capt. Alphonse Lukas(P)　　　　P-61　　　Aug 5, 44　　　　Sally
　　2nd Lt. John S. Blankenship, Jr.(R/O)
　　S/Sgt. Glen O. DeForrest(G)
2nd Lt. James F. Schroth(P)　　　P-61　　　Sept 1, 44　　　Dinah
　　F/O Fred R. James(R/O)
　　S/Sgt. Glen O. Deforrest(G)

1st Lt. Donald M. Dessert(P)　　　P-61　　Oct 2, 44　　　　Dinah
　　2nd Lt. Lane K. Thompson(R/O)
　　S/Sgt. Frank A. McCormack(G)
Capt. Richard O. Stewart(P)　　　P-38　　Dec 30, 44　　　Betty
1st Lt. Ralph R. LeVitt(P)　　　　P-61　　Jan 9, 45　　　　Betty
　　2nd Lt. Frederic J. Kahn(R/O)
　　S/Sgt. John O. Graham(G)
1st Lt. Harold E. Michels(P)　　　P-61　　Jun 13, 45　　　Nick
　　F/O Verna J. Morgan(R/O)
　　Sgt. Joseph C. Snyder(G)

421st Night Fighter Squadron

Activated: May 1, 1943

Inactivated: February 20, 1947 (became 68th Fighter Squadron)

Wartime Commanding Officers:
　　May 1, 1943 - May 13, 1944: Maj. Walter S. Pharr
　　May 15, 1944 - Jan. 2, 1945: Capt. William T. Bradley
　　Jan. 2 - 15, 1945: Capt. Paul R. Zimmer
　　Jan. 15 - 20, 1945: 1st Lt. Dorrie E. Jones
　　Jan. 20 - Dec. 15, 1945: Capt. Richard D. Kiick

Operational Stations:
　　Jan. 4, 1944: Milne Bay, New Guinea
　　Jan. 27, 1944: Nadzab, New Guinea
　　April 1944 Finschhaven, New Guinea Detachment
　　Apr. 5 - 25, 1944 Saidor, New Guinea Detachment
　　May 2 - 13, 1944 Saidor, New Guinea Detachment
　　May 16 - 18, 1944 Hollandia, New Guinea Detachment
　　May 28 - Sept. 21, 1944 Insoemoar (Wakde) Island, Wakde
　　　　Islands Detachment
　　Jun. 28, 1944: Owi Island, Padaido Islands
　　Aug. 1 - 3, 1944 Noemfoor Is., Schouten Islands Detachment
　　Oct. 25, 1944: Tacloban, Leyte, PI
　　Dec. 3, 1944 - Jan. 11, 1945 Peleliu, Palau Group (Air echelon
　　　　only)
　　Feb. 8, 1945: San Marcelino, Luzon, PI
　　Feb. 9 - Mar. 23, 1945 Tacloban, Leyte, PI Detachment
　　Apr. 26, 1945: Clark Field, Luzon, PI
　　Aug. 8, 1945: Ie Shima, Ryukyus

Official 421st NFS emblem

Operational Aircraft:
    1944   P-70 & P-70A
    1944   P-38F, G, & H
    1944-1945 P-61A & B

Enemy Aircraft:
    P-70: 0/0/0
    P-38: 0/0/0
    P-61: 13/1/3
    Squadron Total: 13/1/3

Confirmed Aircrew Victories:

1st Lt. Owen M. Wolf(P)	P-61	Jul 7, 44	Sally or
2nd Lt. Byron N. Allain(R/O)			Dinah
S/Sgt. Emil K. Weishar(G)			
2nd Lt. David J. Pahlka(P)	P-61	Aug 12, 44	Helen
2nd Lt. Ralph V. Hulsey(R/O)			
T/Sgt. Harold L. Cobb(G)			
2nd Lt. Carl H. Bjorum(P)	P-61	Sept 7, 44	Betty
2nd Lt. Robert C. Williams(R/O)			
S/Sgt. Henry E. Bobo(G)			
2nd Lt. Carl H. Bjorum(P)	P-61	Sept 9, 44	Dinah
2nd Lt. Robert C. Williams(R/O)			
S/Sgt. Henry E. Bobo(G)			
1st Lt. Albert W. Lockard(P)	P-61	Nov 10, 44	Tony
2nd Lt. Stuart A. Thornton(R/O)			
S/Sgt. Joseph Mazur(G)			
1st Lt. Albert W. Lockard(P)	P-61	Nov 10, 44	Tony
2nd Lt. Stuart A. Thornton(R/O)			
S/Sgt. Joseph Mazur(G)			
1st Lt. Dorrie E. Jones(P)	P-61	Nov 16, 44	Frank
1st Lt. Alton C. Woodring(R/O)			
S/Sgt. Lacy Potter(G)			
1st Lt. Hoke Smith(P)	P-61	Nov 28, 44	Zeke
2nd Lt. Robert H. Bremer(R/O)			
Sgt. James W. Pilling(G)			
1st Lt. Owen M. Wolf(P)	P-61	Nov 28, 44	Zeke
2nd Lt. Byron N. Allain(R/O)			
S/Sgt. Emil K. Weishar(G)			
1st Lt. Owen M. Wolf(P)	P-61	Nov 28, 44	Zeke32
2nd Lt. Byron N. Allain(R/O)			
S/Sgt. Emil K. Weishar(G)			
2nd Lt. Robert C. Pew(P)	P-61	Nov 28, 44	Zeke
2nd Lt. John B. Cutshall(R/O)			
S/Sgt. Ralph H. McDaniel(G)			
1st Lt. Owen M. Wolf(P)	P-61	Jan 24, 45	Zeke32
1st Lt. Byron N. Allain(R/O)			
S/Sgt. Donald H. Trabing(G)			
2nd Lt. Carl R. Remington(P)	P-61	Mar 11, 45	Betty
F/O William E. Boze(R/O)			
T/Sgt. Brady W. Swinney(G)			

422nd Night Fighter Squadron

Activated: August 1, 1943

Inactivated: September 30, 1945

Wartime Commanding Officers:
    Aug. 1, 1943 - Sept. 30, 1945: Maj. Oris B. Johnson

Operational Stations:
    Mar. 7, 1944: Charmy Down, England
    May. 6, 1944: Scorton, England
    Jun. 28 - Jul. 11, 1944 Hurn Airdrome, England Detachment
    Jul. 16 - 26, 1944 Ford Airdrome, England Detachment
    Jul. 25, 1944: Maupertus (A-15), France
    Aug. 27, 1944: Chateaudun (A-39), France
    Sept. 16, 1944: Florennes (A-78), Belgium
    Apr. 6, 1945: Strassfeldt (Y-59), Germany
    Apr. 24, 1945: Langensalza (R-2), Germany
    May 26, 1945: Kassel (R-12), Germany

Operational Aircraft:
    1944-1945 P-61A & B
    1944-1945 A-20J

Official 422nd NFS emblem

422nd NFS ace team of 1st Lt. Herman E. Ernst (pilot) on the left and 2nd Lt. Edward H. Kopsel (R/O) on the right.

422nd NFS ace team of 1st Lt. Paul A Smith (pilot) and 2nd Lt. Robert E. Tierney (R/O)

422nd NFS R/O ace 2nd Lt. Robert F. Graham (on the right). His regular pilot, 1st Lt. Robert G. Bolinder on the left, participated on four of the kills.

Enemy Aircraft:
       P-61: 43/5/5 plus 5 V-1's
       Squadron Total: 48/5/5

Confirmed Aircrew Victories:

2nd Lt. Herman E. Ernst(P)	P-61	Jul 15, 44	V-1
F/O Edward H. Kopsel (R/O)			
1st Lt Robert O. Elmore(P)	P-61	Jul 17, 44	V-1
F/O Leonard F. Mapes(R/O)			
1st Lt. John W. Anderson(P)	P-61	Jul 18, 44	V-1
F/O James W. Mogan(R/O)			
Capt. Tadas J. Spelis(P)	P-61	Jul 20, 44	V-1
F/O Eleutherios Eleftherion(R/O)			
1st Lt. Raymond A. Anderson(P)	P-61	Aug 7, 44	Ju 88
2nd Lt. John U. Morris, Jr.(R/O)			
2nd Lt. Raymond L. Romens(P)	P-61	Aug 9, 44	Ju 88
2nd Lt. Joseph R. Morin(R/O)			
1st Lt. Leonard F. Koehler(P)	P-61	Aug 19, 44	Do 217
2nd Lt. Louis L. Bost(R/O)			
2nd Lt. Lewis A. Gordon(P)	P-61	Sept 25, 44	Ju 188
2nd Lt. Creel H. Morrison(R/O)			
1st Lt. Paul A. Smith (P)	P-61	Oct 4, 44	Me 410
2nd Lt. Robert E. Tierney(R/O)			
1st Lt. Theodore I. Jones(P)	P-61	Oct 21, 44	Fw 190
2nd Lt. William G. Adams, Jr.(R/O)			
Lt. Col. Oris B. Johnson(P)	P-61	Oct 24, 44	Fw 190
Capt. James A. Montgomery(R/O)			
1st Lt. Robert G. Bolinder(P)	P-61	Nov 26, 44	He 111
2nd Lt. Robert F. Graham(R/O)			
1st Lt. Paul A. Smith (P)	P-61	Nov 27, 44	V-1
2nd Lt. Robert E. Tierney(R/O)			
1st Lt. Herman E. Ernst(P)	P-61	Nov 27, 44	Bf 110
2nd Lt. Edward H. Kopsel (R/O)			
1st Lt. Paul A. Smith (P)	P-61	Nov 27, 44	He 111
2nd Lt. Robert E. Tierney(R/O)			
Capt. Raymond A. Anderson(P)	P-61	Dec 4, 44	He 111
2nd Lt. John U. Morris, Jr.(R/O)			
1st Lt. Robert G. Bolinder(P)	P-61	Dec 16, 44	Fw 190
2nd Lt. Robert F. Graham(R/O)			
1st Lt. Robert G. Bolinder(P)	P-61	Dec 17, 44	Bf 110
2nd Lt. Robert F. Graham(R/O)			
1st Lt. Robert G. Bolinder(P)	P-61	Dec 17, 44	He 111
2nd Lt. Robert F. Graham(R/O)			
1st Lt. Herman E. Ernst(P)	P-61	Dec 17, 44	Ju 87
2nd Lt. Edward H. Kopsel (R/O)			
Capt. Robert O. Elmore(P)	P-61	Dec 17, 44	Ju 88
2nd Lt. Leonard F. Mapes(R/O)			
Capt. Robert O. Elmore(P)	P-61	Dec 22, 44	Bf 110
2nd Lt. Leonard F. Mapes(R/O)			
1st Lt. John W. Anderson(P)	P-61	Dec 24, 44	Ju 88
2nd Lt. James W. Mogan(R/O)			

422nd NFS pilot ace 1st Lt. Eugene D. Axtell.

422nd NFS team of 2nd Lt. Leonard F. Mapes (R/O) on the left and 1st Lt. Robert O. Elmore (pilot) were credited with four aircraft and one V-1 destroyed.

Capt. Tadas J. Spelis(P)	P-61	Apr 11, 45	Ju 88
1st Lt. Eleutherios Eleftherion(R/O)			
1st Lt. Fred E. Burnett(P)	P-61	Apr 12, 45	Ju 52
F/O Clifford E. Brandt(R/O)			
Capt. Robert O. Elmore(P)	P-61	Apr 12, 45	Ju 52
2nd Lt. Leonard F. Mapes(R/O)			
1st Lt. Theodore I. Jones(P)	P-61	Apr 13, 45	Ju 52
1st Lt. William G. Adams, Jr.(R/O)			

1st Lt. Thomas H. Burleson(P)	P-61	Dec 25, 44	Bf 110
2nd Lt. William P. Monahan(R/O)			
1st Lt. John W. Anderson(P)	P-61	Dec 25, 44	Ju 88
2nd Lt. James W. Mogan(R/O)			
1st Lt. Paul A. Smith (P)	P-61	Dec 25, 44	Ju 88
1st Lt. Robert E. Tierney(R/O)			
1st Lt. Herman E. Ernst(P)	P-61	Dec 26, 44	Ju 188
2nd Lt. Edward H. Kopsel (R/O)			
1st Lt. Paul A. Smith (P)	P-61	Dec 26, 44	Ju 188
1st Lt. Robert E. Tierney(R/O)			
1st Lt. Robert A. Smith(P)	P-61	Dec 26, 44	Ju 188
1st Lt. Robert E. Tierney(R/O)			
1st Lt. Eugene D. Axtell(P)	P-61	Dec 26, 44	Ju 88
2nd Lt. Bernard Orzel(R/O)			
1st Lt. Eugene D. Axtell(P)	P-61	Dec 26, 44	Ju 188
2nd Lt. Bernard Orzel(R/O)			
Lt. Col. Oris B. Johnson(P)	P-61	Dec 27, 44	Ju 188
Capt. James A. Montgomery(R/O)			
Capt. Tadas J. Spelis(P)	P-61	Dec 27, 44	Bf 110
1st Lt. Eleutherios Eleftherion(R/O)			
1st Lt. Eugene D. Axtell(P)	P-61	Jan 1, 45	Ju 188
2nd Lt. John U. Morris, Jr.(R/O)			
1st Lt. Herman E. Ernst(P)	P-61	Mar 2, 45	Ju 87
1st Lt. Edward H. Kopsel (R/O)			
1st Lt. Herman E. Ernst(P)	P-61	Mar 2, 45	Ju 87
1st Lt. Edward H. Kopsel (R/O)			
Capt. Leonard F. Koehler(P)	P-61	Mar 21, 45	Do 217
1st Lt. Louis L. Bost(R/O)			
Capt. Raymond A. Anderson(P)	P-61	Mar 21, 45	Do 217
2nd Lt. Robert F. Graham(R/O)			
1st Lt. Eugene D. Axtell(P)	P-61	Apr 11, 45	Ju 52
1st Lt. Creel H. Morrison(R/O)			
1st Lt. Eugene D. Axtell(P)	P-61	Apr 11, 45	Ju 52
1st Lt. Creel H. Morrison(R/O)			
1st Lt. Lewis A. Gordon(P)	P-61	Apr 11, 45	Ju 52
F/O Joseph F. Crew(R/O)			
1st Lt. Lewis A. Gordon(P)	P-61	Apr 11, 45	Ju 88
F/O Joseph F. Crew(R/O)			
Capt. Robert O. Elmore(P)	P-61	Apr 11, 45	Ju 52
2nd Lt. Leonard F. Mapes(R/O)			
1st Lt. Edgar E. Merriman(P)	P-61	Apr 11, 45	Ju 52
2nd Lt. Delbert W. Dow(R/O)			

423rd Night Fighter Squadron

Activated: September 1, 1943

Redesignated: 155th Photographic Reconnaissance Squadron
June 22, 1944

Wartime Commanding Officers:
Sept. 1, 1943: Maj. Joe G. Gillespie

Official 423rd NFS emblem

Operational Stations:
>Apr. 17, 1944: Charmy Down, England
>May. 20, 1944: Chalgrove, England

Operational Aircraft:
>1944-1945 A-20J (never assigned operational night fighter aircraft)

Enemy Aircraft:
>None

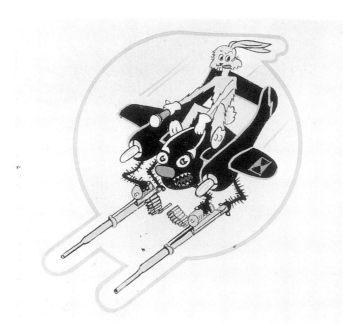

Official 425th NFS emblem

425th NFS crew of Lts. Cletus T. Ormsby (pilot) and Davis M. Howerton, Jr. (R/O) are officially credited with three kills but a number of squadron mates attest to the fact that paperwork had gone in on two other kills besides the Ju 87 they shot down just prior to their being shot down, and Ormsby killed instantly, by "Friendly" flak.

425th Night Fighter Squadron

Activated: December 1, 1943

Inactivated: August 25, 1947 (became 317th Fighter Squadron)

Wartime Commanding Officers:
>Dec. 10, 1943: Capt. Leon G. Lewis
>Feb. 10, 1945: Maj. Russell Glasser
>May 7, 1945: Capt. Morris T. McDonald
>May , 1945: Lt. Col. Leon G. Lewis

Operational Stations:
>May 26, 1944: Charmy Down, England
>Jun. 12, 1944: Scorton, England
>Jun. 28 - Jul. 11, 1944 Hurn Airdrome, England Detachment
>Jul. 16 - 26, 1944 Ford Airdrome, England Detachment
>Aug. 18, 1944: Vannes, France (A-33N)
>Sept. 11, 1944: Coulommiers (A-58), France
>Oct. 13, 1944: Prosnes (A-79), France
>Nov 9, 1944: Etain (A-82), France
>Apr. 12, 1945: Frankfurt-am Main (Y-73), Germany
>May 2, 1945: Furth (R-30), Germany

Operational Aircraft:
>1944-1945 P-61A & B
>1945   A-20

Enemy Aircraft:
>P-61: 10/1/0 plus 4 V-1's
>Squadron Total: 14/1/0

Confirmed Aircrew Victories:

1st Lt. Garth E. Peterson(P)	P-61	Aug 5, 44	V-1
2nd Lt. John A. Howe(R/O)			
1st Lt. Garth E. Peterson(P)	P-61	Aug 6, 44	V-1
2nd Lt. John A. Howe(R/O)			
Capt. Francis V. Sartanowicz(P)	P-61	Aug 7, 44	V-1
1st Lt. Edward M. Van Sickels(R/O)			
1st Lt. James L. Thompson(P)	P-61	Aug 8, 44	V-1
F/O Joseph E. Downey(R/O)			
1st Lt. William A. Andrews(P)	P-61	Dec 24, 44	Ju 188
2nd Lt. James E. Kleinheinz(R/O)			
2nd Lt. Jack E. Slayton(P)	P-61	Dec 25, 44	Bf 110
2nd Lt. Arthur B. Ferris(R/O)			
2nd Lt. Cletus T. Ormsby(P)	P-61	Dec 25, 44	Do 217
2nd Lt. Davis M. Howerton, Jr.(R/O)			
1st Lt. Walter Stacey(P)	P-61	Dec 26, 44	Ju 188
2nd Lt. Stephen F. Mason(R/O)			
1st Lt. William A. Andrews(P)	P-61	Dec 27, 44	Ju 88
2nd Lt. James E. Kleinheinz(R/O)			
1st Lt. Richard R. Gray(P)	P-61	Dec 29, 44	Ju 188
1st Lt. Jack W. Robinson(R/O)			
2nd Lt. Cletus T. Ormsby(P)	P-61	Dec 30, 44	Ju 188
2nd Lt. Davis M. Howerton, Jr.(R/O)			
2nd Lt. Cletus T. Ormsby(P)	P-61	Dec 31, 44	Bf 110
2nd Lt. Davis M. Howerton, Jr.(R/O)			
Capt. Francis V. Sartanowicz(P)	P-61	Mar 24, 45	Ju 87
1st Lt. Edward M. Van Sickels(R/O)			
1st Lt. Jack E. Slayton(P)	P-61	Apr 24, 45	Ju 188
1st Lt. Jack W. Robinson(R/O)			

426th Night Fighter Squadron

Activated: January 1, 1944

Inactivated: November 5, 1945

Wartime Commanding Officers:
>Jan. 1, 1944 - Nov. 5, 1945: Maj. William C. Hellriegel

Operational Stations:
>Aug. 9, 1944: Madhaiganj, India
>Oct. 5, 1944: Chengtu, China
>Oct. 27 - Dec. 25, 1944 Kunming, China Detachment
>Nov. 27, 1944 - Aug. 17, 1945 Hsian, China Detachment
>Jan. - Aug. 1945 Guskhara, India Detachment
>Mar. 1945: Shwangliu, China
>Apr. - Aug. 19, 1945 Liangshan, China Detachment
>Apr. - Aug. 21, 1945 Ankang, China Detachment

Official 426th NFS emblem

Official 427th NFS emblem

Operational Aircraft:
    1944-1945 P-61A & B

Enemy Aircraft:
    P-61: 5/1/0
    Squadron Total: 5/1/0

Confirmed Aircrew Victories:

Capt. Robert R. Scott(P)   P-61   Oct 29, 44   Lily
    F/O Charles W. Phillips(R/O)
Capt. John J. Wilfong(P)   P-61   Nov 21, 44   Dinah or
    2nd Lt. Glenn E. Ashley(R/O)   Lily
Capt. Carl J. Absmeier(P)   P-61   Jan 27, 45   Lily
    2nd Lt. James R. Smith(R/O)
Capt. Carl J. Absmeier(P)   P-61   Jan 30, 45   Lily
    2nd Lt. James R. Smith(R/O)
1st Lt. Harry W. Heise(P)   P-61   Feb 8, 45   Lily
    F/O Robert C. Brock(R/O)

427th Night Fighter Squadron

Activated: February 1, 1944

Inactivated: October 29, 1945

Wartime Commanding Officers:
    Feb. 1, 1944 - May 20, 1945: Maj. James S. Michael
    May 21, 1945 - Jun. 1945: Maj. Thomas N. Wilson
    Jun. - Oct. 29, 1945: Maj. Edwin J. Witzenburger

Operational Stations:
    Sept. 3 - 22, 1944: Pomigliano, Italy
    Oct. 4, 1944: Barrackpore, India (Air echelon)
    Oct. 31, 1944: Pandaveswar, India
    Nov. 13 - Dec. 23, 1944 Myitkyina, Burma Detachment
    Dec. 19, 1944 - Aug 16, 1945 Kunming, China Detachment
        Kunming Detachment staged out of the following
        areas at various times during the period Jan. to Aug.
        1945: Chengkung, China
               Chihkiang, China
               Nanning, China

Dec. 23, 1944: Myitkyina, Burma
May 25, 1945: Kisselbarri, India
Aug. 13, 1945: Liuchow, China

Operational Aircraft:
    1944-1945 P-61A & B

Enemy Aircraft:
    None

547th Night Fighter Squadron

Activated: March 1, 1944

Inactivated: February 20, 1946

Wartime Commanding Officers:
    Mar. 1, 1944 - Jul. 21, 1945: Lt. Col. William C. Odell
    Jul. 21 - Nov. 11, 1945: Capt. William C. Behnke

Operational Stations:
    Sept. 5, 1944: Oro Bay, New Guinea
    Oct. 6, 1944: Owi Island, Padaido Islands
    Nov. 9, 1944 - Jan. 11, 1945 Tacloban, Leyte, PI Det.
    Dec. 1944 - Jan. 16, 1945 San Jose, Mindoro, PI Det.
    Jan. 16, 1945: Lingayen, Luzon, PI
    Aug. 13, 1945: Ie Shima, Ryukyus

Operational Aircraft:
    1944-1945 P-61A & B
    1945   2 P-38J's with ASH-4 AI radar

Enemy Aircraft:
    P-61: 6/0/0
    P-38: 1/0/0 (Squadron records show assist with P-61 crew on one
        kill)
    Squadron Total: 7/0/0

Confirmed Aircrew Victories:

Capt. Robert C. Blackman(P)   P-61   Dec 25, 44 TE aircraft
    1st Lt. Jean B. Harper(R/O)

Two unofficial 547th NFS (no official established) emblems

Official 548th NFS emblem

Operational Stations:
Sept. 16, 1944: Hickam Field, Oahu, TH
Oct. 17, 1944: Kipapa Gulch, Oahu, TH
Dec. 15, 1944 - Jan. 26, 1945 Saipan, Marianas Det.
Jan. 26, 1945: Saipan, Marianas
Feb. 28 - Mar. 5, 1945 Iwo Jima, Volcano Is. Det

(Ground echelon only)
Mar. 5, 1945: Iwo Jima, Volcano Islands
Jun. 12, 1945: Ie Shima, Ryukyus

Operational Aircraft:
1944-1945 P-61A & B

Enemy Aircraft:
P-61: 5/1/0
Squadron Total: 5/1/0

Confirmed Aircrew Victories:

1st Lt. Arthur C. Shepherd(P)	P-61	Jun 22, 45	Tojo
1st Lt. Arvid L. Shulenberger(R/O)			
M/Sgt. Donald E. Meech(G)			
Capt. William H. Dames(P)	P-61	Jun 22, 45	Rufe
2nd Lt. Eugene P. D'Andrea(R/O)			
Sgt. Raymond C. Ryder(G)			
Capt. James W. Bradford(P)	P-61	Jun 24, 45	Betty
1st Lt. Lawrence K. Lunt, Jr.(R/O)			
M/Sgt. Reno H. Sukow(G)			
1st Lt. Robert O. Bertram(P)	P-61	Jul 29, 45	Betty
2nd Lt. George W. Fairweather(R/O)			
Cpl. Jesse V. Tew(G)			
1st Lt. Thomas W. Schultz(P)	P-61	Aug 5, 45	Betty
F/O Ployer P. Hill(R/O)			
S/Sgt. Benjamin J. Boscardin(G)			

549th Night Fighter Squadron

Activated: May 1, 1944

Inactivated: February 5, 1946

Capt. Edwin C. Annis(P)*	P-61	Jan 9, 45	Hamp
2nd Lt. Nicholas Detz(R/O)			
1st Lt. Arthur D. Bourque(P)	P-61	Feb 19, 45	Betty
2nd Lt. Bonnie B. Rucks(R/O)			
1st Lt. Arthur D. Bourque(P)	P-61	Feb 19, 45	Betty
2nd Lt. Bonnie B. Rucks(R/O)			
1st Lt. Kenneth R. Schrieber(P)	P-61	Feb 28, 45	Tess
2nd Lt. Bonnie B. Rucks(R/O)			
2nd Lt. Francis J. Raidt(P)	P-38	Mar 9, 45	Tess
1st Lt. Roy E. Oakes(P)	P-61	Jun 18, 45	Tess
1st Lt. Ralph N. Jacqmin(R/O)			
S/Sgt. Ralph M. Knight(G)			

548th Night Fighter Squadron

Activated: April 10, 1944

Inactivated: December 19, 1945

Wartime Commanding Officers:
Apr. 10, 1944 - Dec. 19, 1945: Maj. Robert D. Curtis

Official 549th NFS emblem

Wartime Commanding Officers:
        May 1, 1944 - Sept. 25, 1945: Maj. Joseph E. Payne
        Sept. 25, 1945 - Jan. 16, 1946: Capt. William R. Charlesworth

Operational Stations:
        Oct. 20, 1944: Kipapa Gulch, Oahu, TH
        Feb. 20, 1945: Saipan, Marianas
        Mar. 14 - 20, 1945 Iwo Jima, Volcano Islands Det. (Ground
                echelon only)
        Mar. 20, 1945: Iwo Jima, Volcano Islands

Operational Aircraft:
        1944-1945 P-61A & B

Enemy Aircraft:
        P-61: 1/0/0
        Squadron Total: 1/0/0

Confirmed Aircrew Victories:

F/O Donald U. Gendreau(P)   P-61   Jun 23, 45   Betty
        F/O Elia A. Chiappinelli(R/O)
        S/Sgt. William S. Dare(G)

550th Night Fighter Squadron

Activated: June 1, 1944

Inactivated: January 1, 1946

Wartime Commanding Officers:
        Jun. 1, 1944 - Jan. 4, 1946: Maj. Robert A. Tyler

Operational Stations:
        Dec. 14, 1944: Hollandia, New Guinea
        Dec. 31, 1944 - Feb. 19, 1945 Middelburg Island, Halmaheras
                Detachment
        Feb. 14, 1945: Morotai, Halmaheras
        Mar. 1 - Apr. 7, 1945 Tacloban, Leyte, PI Det.
        Apr. 7, 1945: Tacloban, Leyte, PI
        Apr. 27 - Jun. 17, 1945 Zamboanga, Mindanao, PI Det.
        Jun. 1 - Aug. 1945 Sanga Sanga, Sulu Arch. Det.
        Jun. 9 - 19, 1945 Puerto Princesa, Palawan, PI Det.

Operational Aircraft:
        1944-1945 P-61A & B

Enemy Aircraft:
        None

Unofficial 550th NFS (no official established) emblem

Bibliography

Archival Material

HQ USAF Historical Research Center, Research Division, Maxwell AFB, Alabama. Unit histories, war diaries, combat reports, and like items on the following units:

Army Air Forces School of Applied Tactics
Detachment 'A' Night Fighter Squadron
Detachment 'B' Night Fighter Squadron
Interceptor (later Fighter) Command School
1st Pursuit Squadron (Night Fighter)
6th Fighter/Night Fighter Squadron
24th Fighter Squadron
50th Fighter Group
81st Fighter Squadron
319th Wing
348th Night Fighter Squadron
349th Night Fighter Squadron
414th Night Fighter Squadron
415th Night Fighter Squadron
416th Night Fighter Squadron
417th Night Fighter Squadron
418th Night Fighter Squadron
419th Night Fighter Squadron
420th Night Fighter Squadron
421st Night Fighter Squadron
422nd Night Fighter Squadron
423rd Night Fighter Squadron
424th Night Fighter Squadron
425th Night Fighter Squadron
426th Night Fighter Squadron
427th Night Fighter Squadron
441st Army Air Forces Base Unit
450th Army Air Forces Base Unit
451st Army Air Forces Base Unit
481st Night Fighter Operational Training Group
547th Night Fighter Squadron
548th Night Fighter Squadron
549th Night Fighter Squadron
550th Night Fighter Squadron

National Archives, Washington, D.C.
US Army Air Corps/Air Forces correspondence and reports. This includes correspondence within the service, reports, plans, and correspondence with various aircraft manufacturers, the British, and some incoming correspondence. This includes aircraft design, modification, production, purchase of foreign aircraft, radar development, and operations. 130 such documents were used in the preparation of this book.

Air Force Museum, Wright-Patterson AFB, Ohio
The museum's archives contains photographs of personnel, aircraft, and installations. Copies of aircraft drawings, pilots manuals, and maintenance instructions. Some information on radar. Personal and official documents.

Smithsonian Institution, National Air And Space Museum, Washington, D.C. and Suitland, MD

Photographs and USAAF Individual Aircraft Record Cards

Government Studies

Historical Study No.1-2, *Organization and Functions of the Fourth Air Force, 1942-1945*, Fourth Air Force

Historical Study No.3, *Case History of A-26 Airplane*, Historical Division, Intelligence, T-2, Air Technical Service Command, Wright Field; October 1945

Historical Study No.34, *Case History of The F-82E, F and G Airplanes and Related Engines (V-1710-143 and V-1710-145)*, Martin J. Miller, Jr. and Margaret C. Bagwell, Historical Office, Executive Secretariat, Air Materiel Command, Wright-Patterson Air Force Base; January 1951

Historical Study No.79, *Case History of AGL-2*, Historical Office, Air Technical Service Command, Wright Field; October 1944

Historical Study No.81, *Case History of Radar Gunsights*, Historical Division, Intelligence, T-2, Air Materiel Command, Wright Field; February 1946

Historical Study No.82, *Case History of Radar Range Finders*, Historical Division, Intelligence, T-2, Air Materiel Command, Wright Field; April 1946

Historical Study No.186, *Case History of IFF Radar Equipment*, Historical Division, Intelligence, T-2, Air Materiel Command, Wright Field; March 1946

Military Publications

Airplane Characteristics and Performance (Monthly & Quarterly charts), Air Materiel Command, Engineering Division, Technical Data Laboratory (P-61 series and P-70 series aircraft)

Armament and Bomb Installations (Monthly & Quarterly charts), Air Materiel Command, Engineering Division, Technical Data Laboratory (P-61 series and P-70 series aircraft)

Individual Aircraft Record Card (P-38M, P-61 series, P-70, and XA-26A)

Pilot Training Manual For The Black Widow

Report of Serial Numbers Assigned to Aircraft on Active Air Force Contracts (AFPI Form 41)

Standard Aircraft Characteristics, P-61C Black Widow

Tactical Planning Characteristics & Performance Chart (P-61)

TO 00-20A-2-P-61, U.S. Army Air Forces Aircraft Inspection and Maintenance Guide for P-61 Series Aircraft, 1 January 1945

TO 01-15FB-1, Pilot's Flight Operating Instructions For Army Model P-61A Airplane, 20 July 1944

AN 01-15FB-1, Pilot's Flight Operating Instructions For Army Models

P-61A and P-61B Airplanes, 8 November 1945

TO 01-15FB-2, P-61A Service Instructions, November 1943

AN 01-15FB-4, Parts Catalog For P-61A and P-61B Airplanes, 15 October 1944

AN 01-15FC-1, Handbook - Flight Operating Instructions, USAF Series F-61C Aircraft, 14 October 1949

AN 01-15FC-2, Erection and Maintenance Instructions For Model P-61C Airplanes, 4 March 1946

AN 01-15FC-4, Parts Catalog For F-61C Airplanes

TO 01-40AJ-1, Pilot's Handbook of Flight Operating Instructions for the Model XA-26A Airplane Powered with Tow Model R-2800-27 Engines

TO 01-40FA-1, Pilot's Flight Operating Instructions - P-70 Airplane, February 15, 1943

TO 01-40FA-2, Service Instructions for the Model P-70 Fighter Airplane

AN 11-70A-26, Operating and Service Instructions For Remote Control Turret Systems Models 2CFR12C2 and 2CFR12C3, 23 November 1945

AN 16-40SCR720-3, SCR-720 Handbook, 24 June 1946

AP 2653K-PPN, Provisional Pilot's Notes, Mosquito N.F. Mk.30, August 1944

Military Reports

Accelerated Service Test of P-61C Type Aircraft Nos. 43-8325, 43-8322 and 43-8337, Memorandum Report TSFTE-2068, 14 April 1947, Prepared by Albert L. Jackson, Jr.

Acceptance Performance Tests - XP-61 Airplane, Army Air Forces Serial Number 41-19509, Memorandum Report ENG-19-1605-A

Aircraft Model Designation, Report No.TSEST-A7, 1 June 1946

Cold Weather Test of P-61A Type Aircraft, Army Air Forces Board Project (M-1)16b, 20 June 1944, Prepared by Capt. F.E. Graizer, A.C.

Final Report of the Development, Procurement, Performance, and Acceptance of the XP-61D Airplane, AFTR 5693, 27 April 1948

Final Report of the Procurement, Inspection, Testing and Acceptance of Northrop Airplane Model XP-61, Army Air Forces Technical Report No.5070, 15 December 1943, Prepared by Capt. W.G. Logan, A.C.

Final Report on the Test of YP-61 Airplanes, Army Air Forces Proving Ground Command Project (M-5)17, 9 June 1944, Prepared by 2nd Lt. John L. Decker, A.C.

Inspection and Flight Tests of Prototype P-38 Aircraft for Night Fighter Purposes, Army Air Forces Air Technical Service Command, Engineering Division Memorandum Report TSSSE-2C-1144, 15 February 1945, Prepared by Maj. J.F. Aldridge, A.C.

Operational Suitability of the YP-61 Airplane, Army Air Forces Board Project (M-1)16, 20 June 1944, Prepared by Maj. B.R. Muldoon, A.C.

Operational Suitability Test of the Two-Place P-38 Night Fighter Airplane Equipped with ASH (AN/APS-4), Army Air Forces Board Project No.4578C452.1, 25 October 1945, Prepared by Capt. F.W. Bruner, AC

Performance Flight Tests of the Northrop Black Widow P-61A Airplane, AAF No.42-5488, Memorandum Report ENG-47-1796-A, 28 August 1944, Prepared by Willard A. Burrell and Capt. Jack D. Onerem, A.C.

Stability Check on P-38L, 44-25237 with Radar Bomb and Observers Cockpit Installations, Air Technical Service Command, TSCEP5E-1834, 8 February 1945, Prepared by 1st Lt. Henry A. Johnson, A.C.

Supplementary Test of Operational Suitability of P-38 with ASH (AN/APS-4) As A Night Fighter, Army Air Forces Board Project No.3836B452.1, 9 January 1945, Prepared by Maj. R.D. Blake, AC, and Capt. N.A. Bollum, AC

Aircraft Manufacturer's Documents

1. Douglas Aircraft Company

Memorandum, Subject: Model A-26 Publicity, dated April 15, 1943, To: A.M. Rochlen, From: E.H. Heinemann

History of Light Bomber Series Airplanes, Report No.1 SM10908, December 4, 1944, Prepared by T.R. Smith

2. Northrop Aircraft, Inc.

Basic Dimension Report, Model and Description, Night Interceptor Pursuit XP-61, YP-61, P-61A, B, Report No.D-2

Zap Wing Conversion of OS2U-1, Report No.NS-6

Model Specification, Night Interceptor Pursuit, Air Corps Model XP-61, Report No.NS-8A

Model Specification, Night Interceptor Pursuit, Air Corps Model P-61, Report No.NS-8C

Model Specification, Night Interceptor Pursuit, Army Air Force Model P-61B, Report No.NS-8D

Model Specification, Night Interceptor Pursuit, Army Air Force Model P-61C, Report No.NS-8E

Model Specification, Night Interceptor Pursuit, Army Air Force Model XP-61D, Report No.NS-8F

Drawing No.502948, General Arrangement (Three View), Project VNT

Drawing No.504944, General Arrangement (Three View), Model XP-61

Drawing No.505100, General Arrangement (Three View), Models XP-61, YP-61, P-61A-1, P-61B-1

NEWS releases:

History of the Black Widow, c. late 1945

The Northrop Retractable Aileron System, May 1946

Newest Black Widow Is Nation's First Peacetime Warplane, September 3, 1945

Operation of the "Retractable Aileron" System of the Black Widow P-61 Night Fighter, Moye Stephens, Chief Production Test Pilot, NAI, September 15, 1944

Miscellaneous Documents

Beavers, William W., *The Northrop P-61 "Black Widow" - America's First Night Fighter*, Fresno State College, History 199, January 12, 1965

Danford, Edward C., Lt.Col., ed. *History of the 64th Fighter Wing, 1942-1945*, c.1945

Greenberg, Eugene M., Capt. *Signals, The Story of Communications in the XIX Tactical Air Command up to V-E Day*, c.1945

Hall, L.R., Capt. *Notes on Night Fighting, Army Air Forces School of Applied Tactics*, c.1943

Lapidus, Harold, 1st Lt., "Nighty Interception Over France," *History of the 82nd Fighter Control Squadron, 1942-1945*, c.1945

Radio Transcript, *Top of the Evening*, with Ted Malone, December 19 and 20, 1944

Periodicals

"All in a Night's Work," *Air Force*, December 1944

"How to Fly a P-61," *Air News with Air Tech*, September 1945

Boesen, Victor, "The Legal Eagle," *Skyways*, October 1946

Buchanan, R.E., Lt., "P-61s on the Prowl." *Flying Age*, July 1945

Harald, Eric, "P-61 Black Widow," *Skyways*, September 1944

Gellhorn, Martha, "Night Life in the Sky," *Collier's*, March 1945

Creekmore, Raymond, Capt., "All in a Night's Work," *Air Force*, December 1944

Kratz, Winston W., Lt.Col., "Night Fighters - Commandos of the Air," *Air Force*, January 1944

Leford, Dale, Major, "The Last Kill," *Air Classics*, May - June 1965 (Note: error by magazine, author's first name is Bruce)

Littrell, Gaith, "The 'Black Widow' Boys," *Flying*, June 1945

Munson, Donn H., "Nipponese Nightmare," *Yank*, c.1944

Myers, John, "Scourge of the Night Skies," *Flying Aces*, March 1945

Pames, George, "The Great Cabanatuan Raid," *Air Classics*, September and October 1984

"Radar in Air Combat," compiled by Flying's editors, *Flying*, October 1945

Skolnik, Merrill I., "Fifty Years of Radar," *Proceedings of the IEE*, February 1985

Smith, Carroll C., "My Sweetheart Is A Black Widow," *Popular Science*, July 1945

Thompson, Warren, "Night Hunter," *Wings*, June 1986

–. "Northrop's Mean Lady," *Aeroplane Monthly*, November 1980

–. "The Nocturnal Nighthawk," *AIR Enthusiast*, March-June 1985

–. "Terror in the Dark," *Wings*, October 1984

Vieweger, Arthur L., "Radar in the Signal Corps," *IRE Transactions on Military Electronics*, October 1960

Winters, M.M., "Evolution   Widow." *Skyways*, September 1945

Books

Anderson, Fred, *Northrop: An Aeronautical History*, Century City: Northrop, 1976

Belote, James H. and William M. Belote, *Typhoon of Steel: The Battle for Okinawa*, New York: Harper & Row, 1970

Birdsall, Steve, *Flying Buccaneers*, Garden City: Doubleday, 1977

Brown, K.S. et al, comp., *United States Army and Air Force Fighters 1916-1961*, Ed. Bruce Robertson. Letchworth: Harleyford, 1961

Burns, Russell, ed., *Radar Development to 1945*, London: Peter Peregrinus, 1988

Coleman, Ted, *Jack Northrop and the Flying Wing*, New York: Paragon, 1988

Copp, DeWitt S., *Forged in Fire*, Garden City: Doubleday, 1982

Craven, Wesley Frank and James Lea Cate, eds., *The Army Air Forces In World War II*, 7 vols. Chicago: U. of Chicago P, 1948

Gunston, Bill, *NIGHT FIGHTERS, A Development & Combat History*, New York: Charles Scribner's Sons, 1976

Gurney, Gene, Captain, USAF, *Five Down and Glory*, Ed. Mark P. Friedlander, Jr. New York: Putnam, 1958

Heinemann, Edward H. and Rosario Rausa, *Ed Heinemann, Combat Aircraft Designer*, Annapolis: Naval Institute Press, 1980

Hess, William N., *Pacific Sweep*, Garden City: Doubleday, 1974

–. *The American Aces of World War II and Korea*, New York: Arco, 1968

Holley, Irving Brinton, Jr., *United States Army in World War II, Special Studies*, "Buying Aircraft: Materiel Procurement for the Army Air Forces," Washington D.C.: U.S. Government Printing Office, 1964

Maurer, Maurer, ed., *Air Force Combat Units of World War II*, New York: Franklin Watts, 1963

–. *Combat Squadrons of the Air Force*, Washington: U.S. Government Printing Office, 1969

McEwen, Charles, Jr., *422nd Night Fighter Squadron*, 422nd Night Fighter Squadron Association, 1983

Olynyk, Frank J., *Victory List No.3, USAAF* (Pacific Theater) "Credits for the Destruction of Enemy Aircraft in Air-to-Air Combat, World War 2," Aurora, Frank J. Olynyk, 1985

Olynyk, Frank J., *Victory List No.4, AVG & USAAF* (China-Burma-India Theater) "Credits for the Destruction of Enemy Aircraft in Air-to-Air Combat, World War 2," Aurora, Frank J. Olynyk, October 1986

Olynyk, Frank J., *Victory List No.5, USAAF* (European Theater) "Credits for the Destruction of Enemy Aircraft in Air-to-Air Combat, World War 2," Aurora, Frank J. Olynyk, 1987

Olynyk, Frank J., *Victory List No.6, USAAF* (Mediterranean Theater) "Credits for the Destruction of Enemy Aircraft in Air-to-Air Combat, World War II," Aurora, Frank J. Olynyk, June 1987

Reintjes, J. Francis and Godfrey T. Coate, eds., *Principles of Radar*, By

Members of the Staff of the Radar School, Massachusetts Institute of Technolo ... New York: McGraw-Hill, 1952

Ridenour, Louis N., Ed.-in-Chief., *Massachusetts Institute of Technology Radiation Laboratory Series*, 28 vols. New York: McGraw-Hill, 1947-1953

Rust, Kenn C., *Fifteenth Air Force Story*, Temple City: Historical Aviation Album, 1976

–. *Fifth Air Force Story*, Temple City: Historical Aviation Album, 1973

–. *Fourteenth Air Force Story*, Temple City: Historical Aviation Album, 1977

–. *Seventh Air Force Story*, Temple City: Historical Aviation Album, 1979

–. *The 9th Air Force in World War II*, Fallbrook: Aero, 1967

–. *Twelfth Air Force Story*, Temple City: Historical Aviation Album, 1975

Sargent, Frederic O., Comp., *Night Fighters: An Unofficial History of the 415th Night Fighter Squadron*, Madison: Sargent, 1946

Skolnik, Merrill I., *Introduction to Radar Systems*, New York: McGraw-Hill, 1962

Swords, S.S., *Technical History of the Beginnings of RADAR*, London: Peter Peregrinus, 1986

Terrett, Dulaney, *United States Army in World War II, The Technical Services*, "The Signal Corps: The Emergency (To December 1941)," Washington, D.C.: U.S. Government Printing Office, 1956

Thompson, George Raynor, et al., *United States Army in World War II, The Technical Services*, "The Signal Corps: The Test (December 1941 to July 1943)," Washington, D.C.: U.S. Government Printing Office, 1957

Thompson, George Raynor and Dixie R. Harris, *United States Army in World War II, The Technical Services*, "The Signal Corps: The Outcome (Mid-1943 through 1945)," Washington, D.C.: U.S. Government Printing Office, 1966

Index